ちょびっツ

Chobits

CLAMP

Satsuki Igarashi
Nanase Ohkawa
Mick Nekoi
Mokona Apapa

ALSO AVAILABLE FROM 🐱TOKYOPOP®

MANGA

@LARGE (August 2003)
ANGELIC LAYER*
BABY BIRTH* (September 2003)
BATTLE ROYALE*
BRAIN POWERED*
BRIGADOON* (August 2003)
CARDCAPTOR SAKURA
CARDCAPTOR SAKURA: MASTER OF THE CLOW*
CHOBITS*
CHRONICLES OF THE CURSED SWORD
CLAMP SCHOOL DETECTIVES*
CLOVER
CONFIDENTIAL CONFESSIONS* (July 2003)
CORRECTOR YUI
COWBOY BEBOP*
COWBOY BEBOP: SHOOTING STAR*
DEMON DIARY
DIGIMON*
DRAGON HUNTER
DRAGON KNIGHTS*
DUKLYON: CLAMP SCHOOL DEFENDERS*
ERICA SAKURAZAWA*
ESCAFLOWNE* (July 2003)
FAKE*
FLCL* (September 2003)
FORBIDDEN DANCE* (August 2003)
GATE KEEPERS*
G GUNDAM*
GRAVITATION*
GTO*
GUNDAM WING
GUNDAM WING: BATTLEFIELD OF PACIFISTS
GUNDAM WING: ENDLESS WALTZ*
GUNDAM WING: THE LAST OUTPOST*
HAPPY MANIA*
HARLEM BEAT
I.N.V.U.
INITIAL D*
ISLAND
JING: KING OF BANDITS*
JULINE
KARE KANO*
KINDAICHI CASE FILES, THE*
KING OF HELL
KODOCHA: SANA'S STAGE*
LOVE HINA*
LUPIN III*
MAGIC KNIGHT RAYEARTH* (August 2003)

MAGIC KNIGHT RAYEARTH II* (COMING SOON)
MAN OF MANY FACES*
MARMALADE BOY*
MARS*
MIRACLE GIRLS
MIYUKI-CHAN IN WONDERLAND* (October 2003)
MONSTERS, INC.
NIEA_7* (August 2003)
PARADISE KISS*
PARASYTE
PEACH GIRL
PEACH GIRL: CHANGE OF HEART*
PET SHOP OF HORRORS*
PLANET LADDER*
PLANETES* (October 2003)
PRIEST
RAGNAROK
RAVE MASTER*
REALITY CHECK
REBIRTH
REBOUND*
RISING STARS OF MANGA
SABER MARIONETTE J* (July 2003)
SAILOR MOON
SAINT TAIL
SAMURAI DEEPER KYO* (August 2003)
SAMURAI GIRL: REAL BOUT HIGH SCHOOL*
SCRYED*
SHAOLIN SISTERS*
SHIRAHIME-SYO: SNOW GODDESS TALES* (Dec. 2003)
SHUTTERBOX (November 2003)
SORCERER HUNTERS
THE SKULL MAN*
TOKYO MEW MEW*
UNDER THE GLASS MOON
VAMPIRE GAME
WILD ACT* (July 2003)
WISH*
WORLD OF HARTZ (August 2003)
X-DAY* (August 2003)
ZODIAC P.I. * (July 2003)

*INDICATES 100% AUTHENTIC MANGA (RIGHT-TO-LEFT FORMAT)

CINE-MANGA™

CARDCAPTORS
JACKIE CHAN ADVENTURES (COMING SOON)
JIMMY NEUTRON (September 2003)
KIM POSSIBLE
LIZZIE MCGUIRE
POWER RANGERS: NINJA STORM (August 2003)
SPONGEBOB SQUAREPANTS (September 2003)
SPY KIDS 2

NOVELS

KARMA CLUB (July 2003)
SAILOR MOON

TOKYOPOP KIDS

STRAY SHEEP (September 2003)

ART BOOKS

CARDCAPTOR SAKURA*
MAGIC KNIGHT RAYEARTH*

ANIME GUIDES

COWBOY BEBOP ANIME GUIDES
GUNDAM TECHNICAL MANUALS
SAILOR MOON SCOUT GUIDES

Volume 6 of 8

Story and Art By
CLAMP

TOKYOPOP®
Los Angeles • Tokyo • London

Translator – Shirley Kubo
Editor – Jake Forbes
Retouch & Lettering – Christine Holmes
Copy Editor – Paul Morrissey

Managing Editor - Jill Freshney
Production Coordinator - Antonio DePietro
Production Manager - Jennifer Miller
Art Director - Matt Alford
Editorial Director - Jeremy Ross
VP of Production & Manufacturing - Ron Klamert
President & C.O.O. - John Parker
Publisher & C.E.O. - Stuart Levy

Email: editor@TOKYOPOP.com
Come visit us online at www.TOKYOPOP.com

A  Manga
TOKYOPOP® is an imprint of Mixx Entertainment, Inc.
5900 Wilshire Blvd. Suite 2000, Los Angeles, CA 90036

ISBN: 1-59182-257-2

First TOKYOPOP® printing: June 2003

10 9 8 7 6 5 4 3 2 1

Printed in the USA

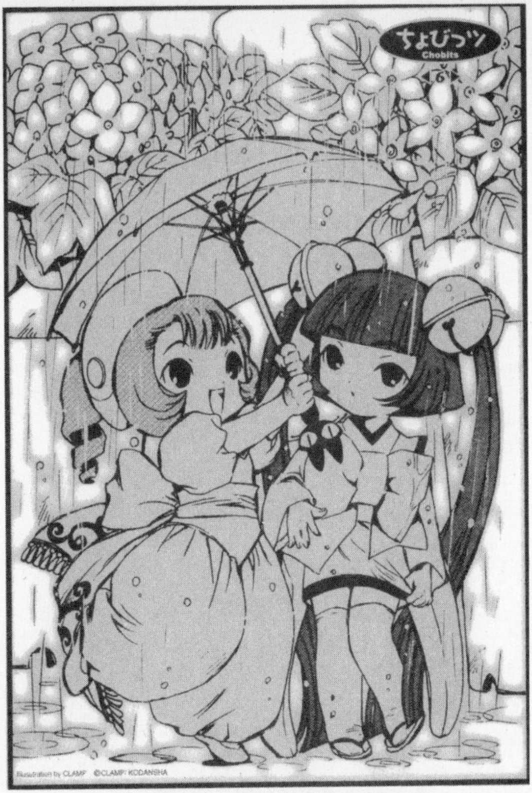
ちょびっツ
Chobits
Illustration by CLAMP ©CLAMP· KODANSHA

www.Contents.com

MUST SEE Persoconns

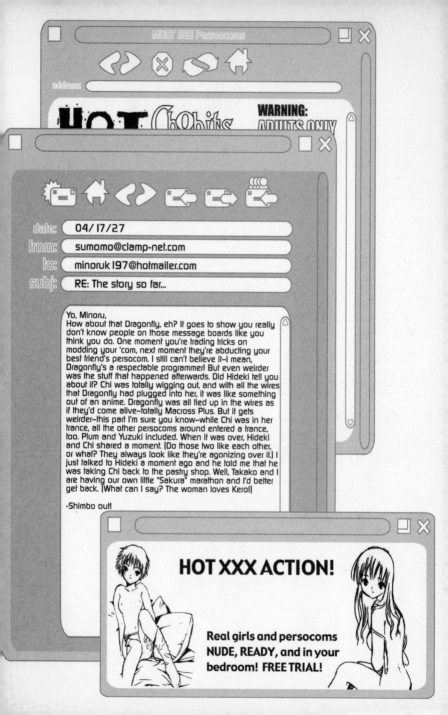

address:

HOT Chobits WARNING: ADULTS ONLY

date: 04/17/27

from: sumomo@clamp-net.com

to: minoruk197@hotmailer.com

subj: RE: The story so far...

Yo, Minoru,

How about that Dragonfly, eh? It goes to show you really don't know people on those message boards like you think you do. One moment you're trading tricks on modding your 'com, next moment they're abducting your best friend's persocom. I still can't believe it–I mean, Dragonfly's a respectable programmer! But even weirder was the stuff that happened afterwards. Did Hideki tell you about it? Chi was totally wigging out, and with all the wires that Dragonfly had plugged into her, it was like something out of an anime. Dragonfly was all tied up in the wires as if they'd come alive–totally Macross Plus. But it gets weirder–this part I'm sure you know–while Chi was in her trance, all the other persocoms around entered a trance, too. Plum and Yuzuki included. When it was over, Hideki and Chi shared a moment. (Do those two like each other, or what? They always look like they're agonizing over it.) I just talked to Hideki a moment ago and he told me that he was taking Chi back to the pastry shop. Well, Takako and I are having our own little "Sakura" marathon and I'd better get back. (What can I say? The woman loves Kero!)

-Shimbo out!

HOT XXX ACTION!
Real girls and persocoms NUDE, READY, and in your bedroom! FREE TRIAL!

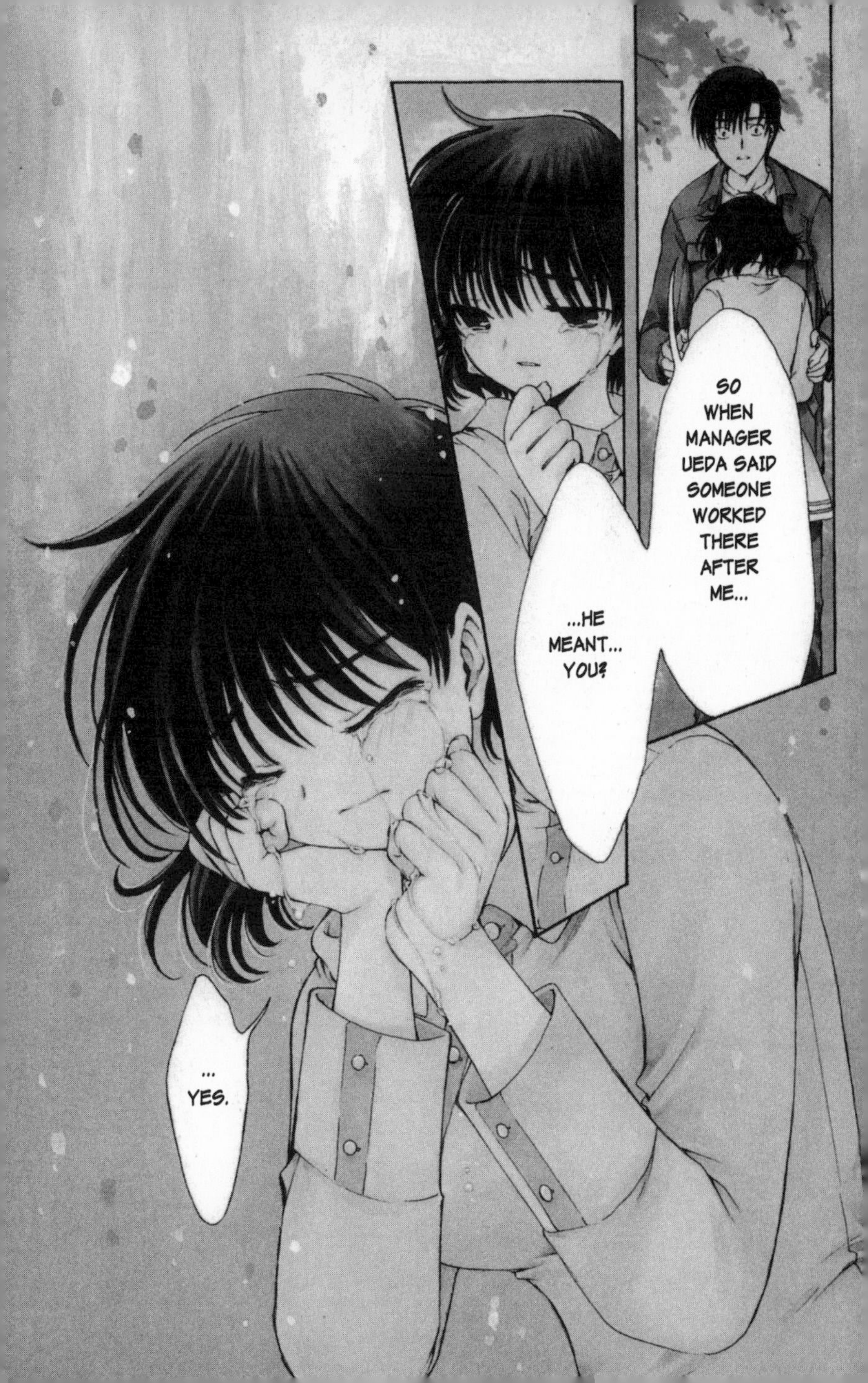
SO WHEN MANAGER UEDA SAID SOMEONE WORKED THERE AFTER ME...
...HE MEANT... YOU?
... YES.

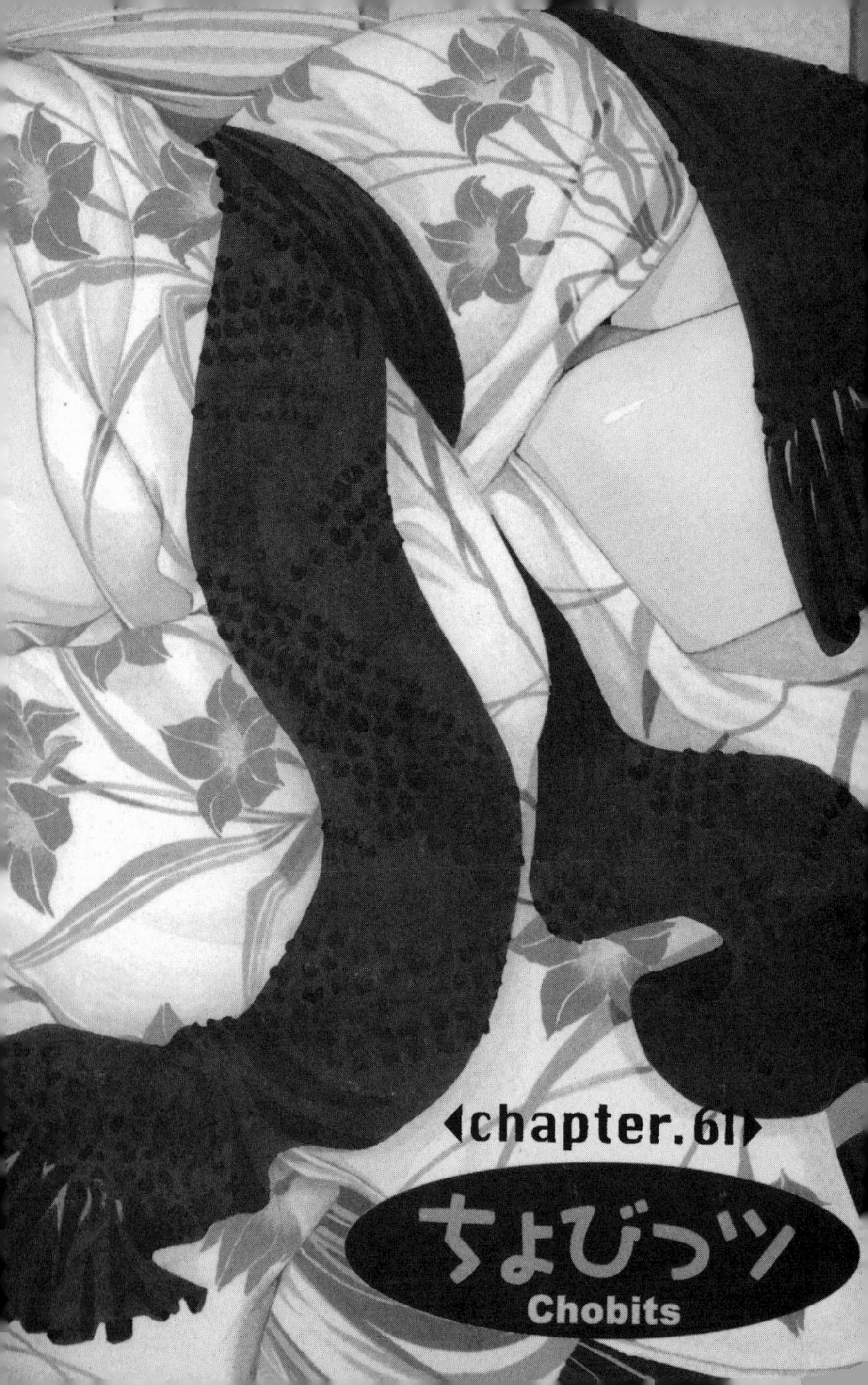
chapter.61
ちょびっツ
Chobits

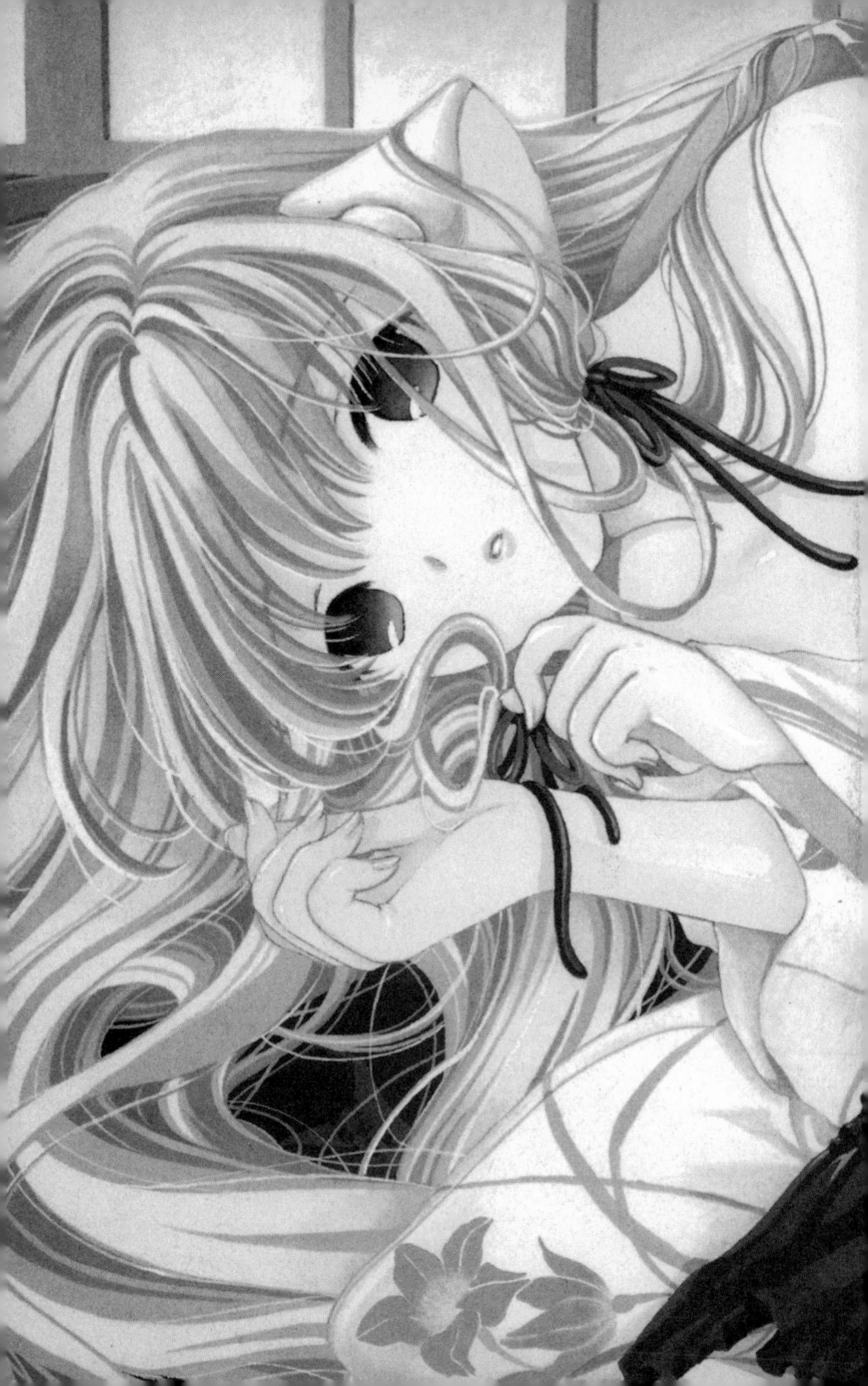

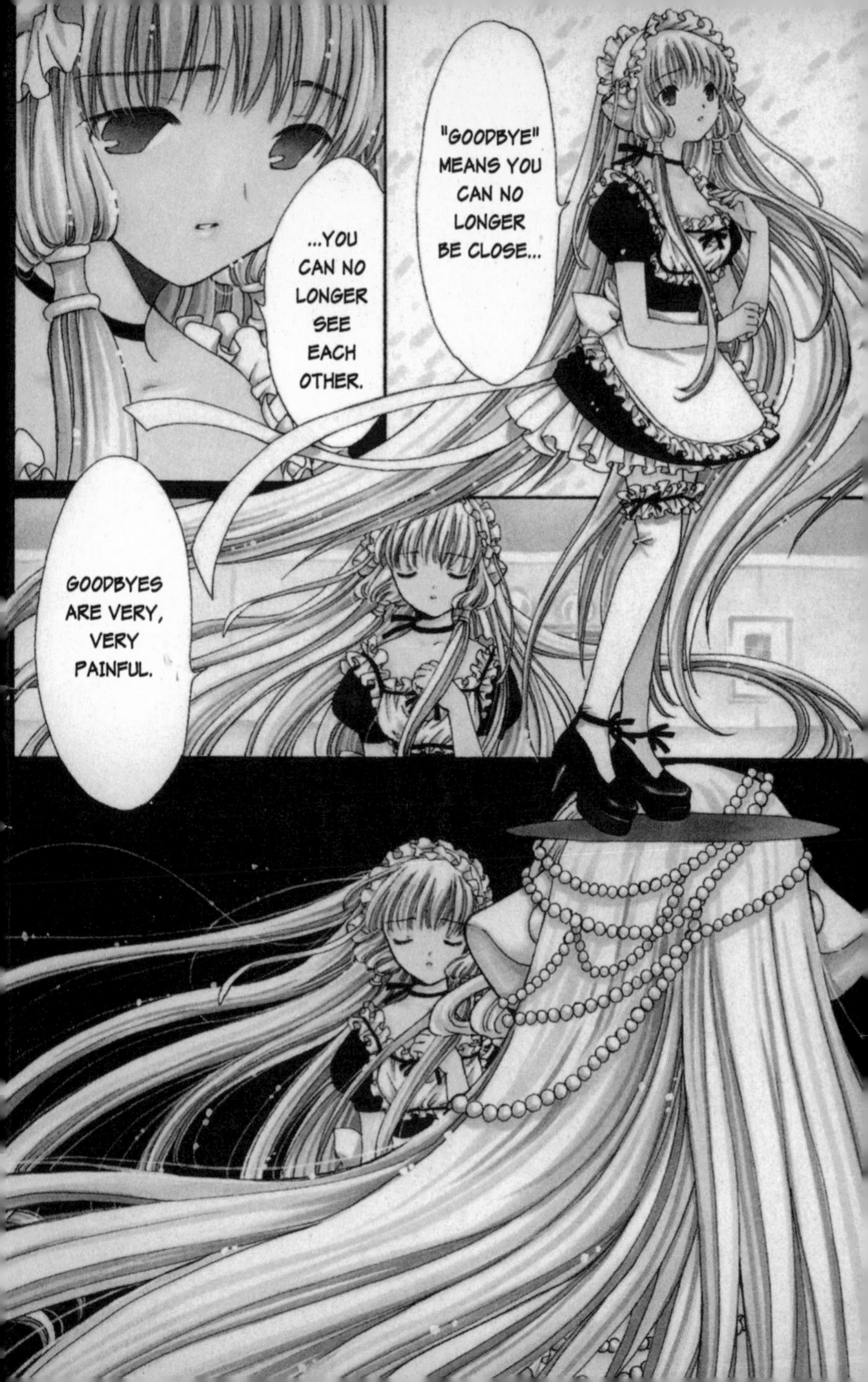
"GOODBYE" MEANS YOU CAN NO LONGER BE CLOSE...
...YOU CAN NO LONGER SEE EACH OTHER.
GOODBYES ARE VERY, VERY PAINFUL.

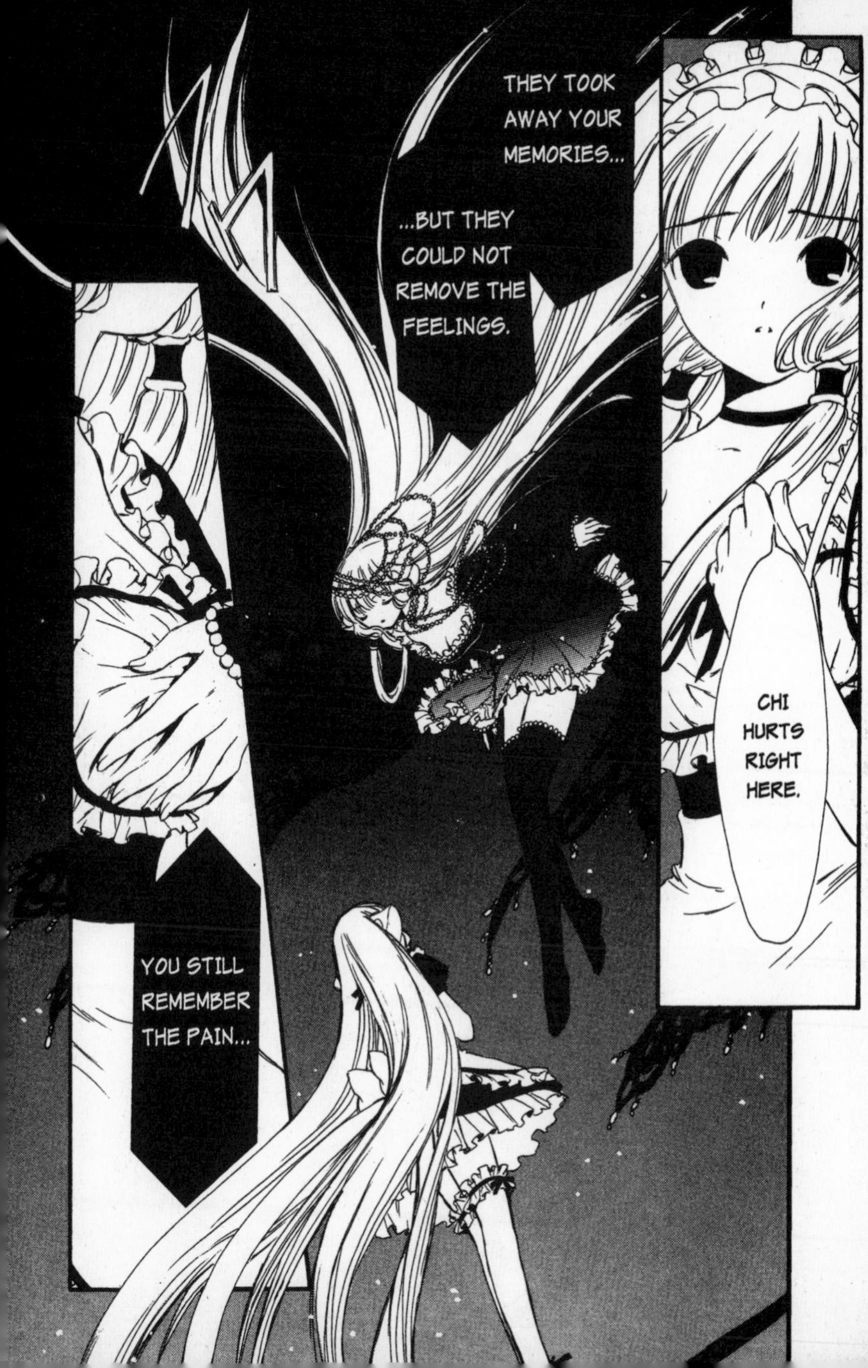
THEY TOOK AWAY YOUR MEMORIES...
...BUT THEY COULD NOT REMOVE THE FEELINGS.
CHI HURTS RIGHT HERE.
YOU STILL REMEMBER THE PAIN...

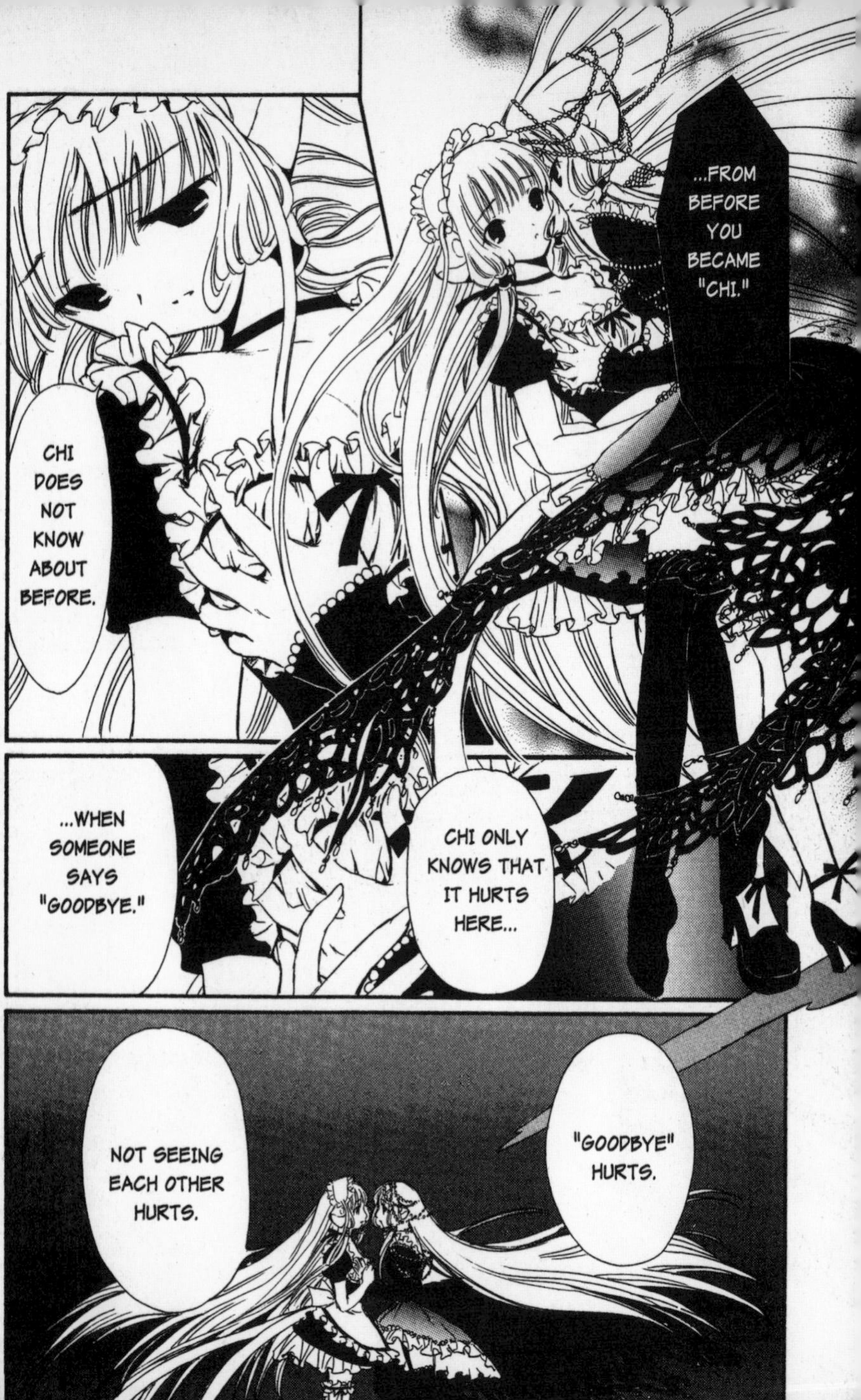
...FROM BEFORE YOU BECAME "CHI."
CHI DOES NOT KNOW ABOUT BEFORE.
CHI ONLY KNOWS THAT IT HURTS HERE...
...WHEN SOMEONE SAYS "GOODBYE."
"GOODBYE" HURTS.
NOT SEEING EACH OTHER HURTS.

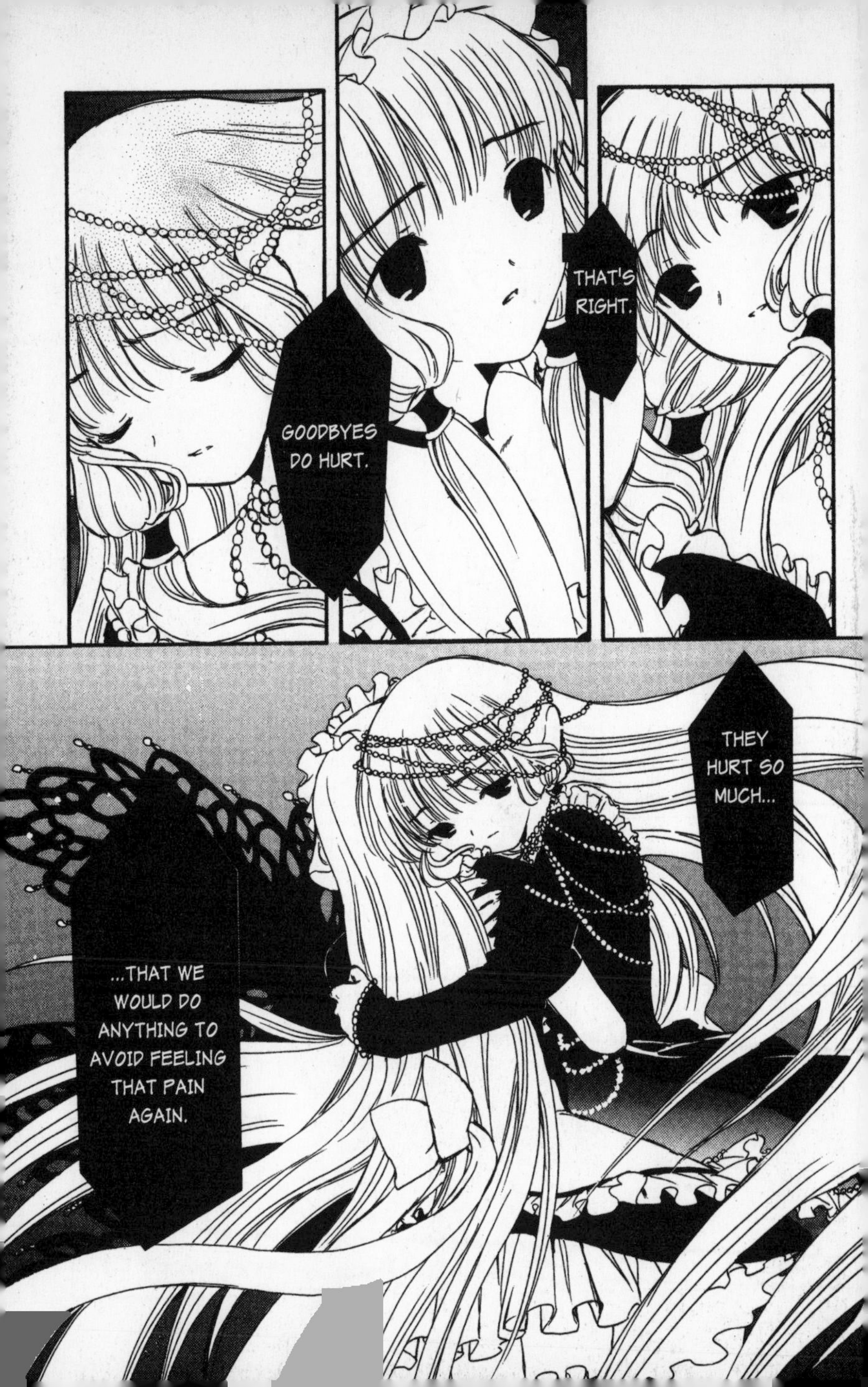
THAT'S RIGHT.
GOODBYES DO HURT.
THEY HURT SO MUCH...
...THAT WE WOULD DO ANYTHING TO AVOID FEELING THAT PAIN AGAIN.

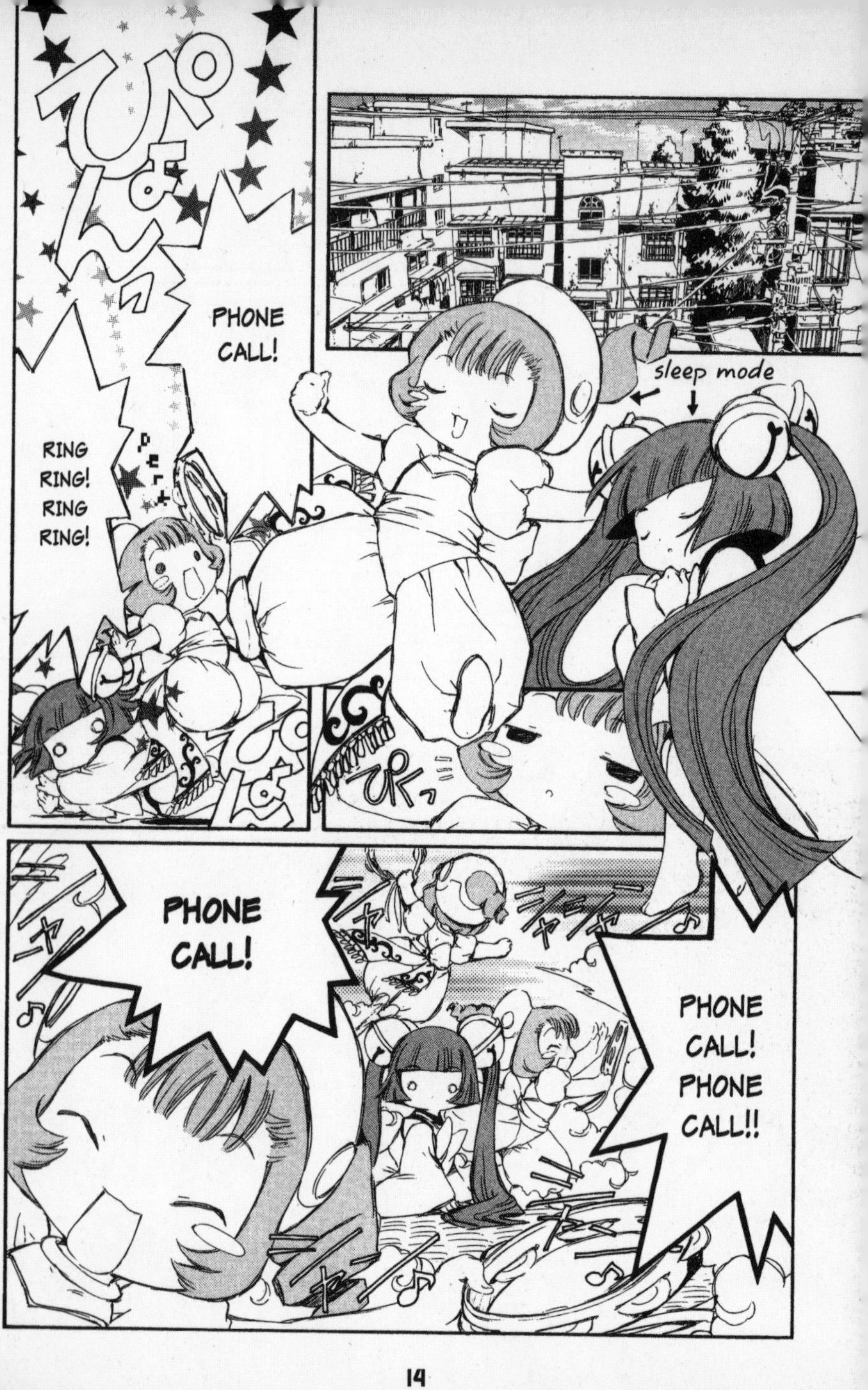
sleep mode
PHONE CALL!
RING RING! RING RING!
PHONE CALL! PHONE CALL!!
PHONE CALL!

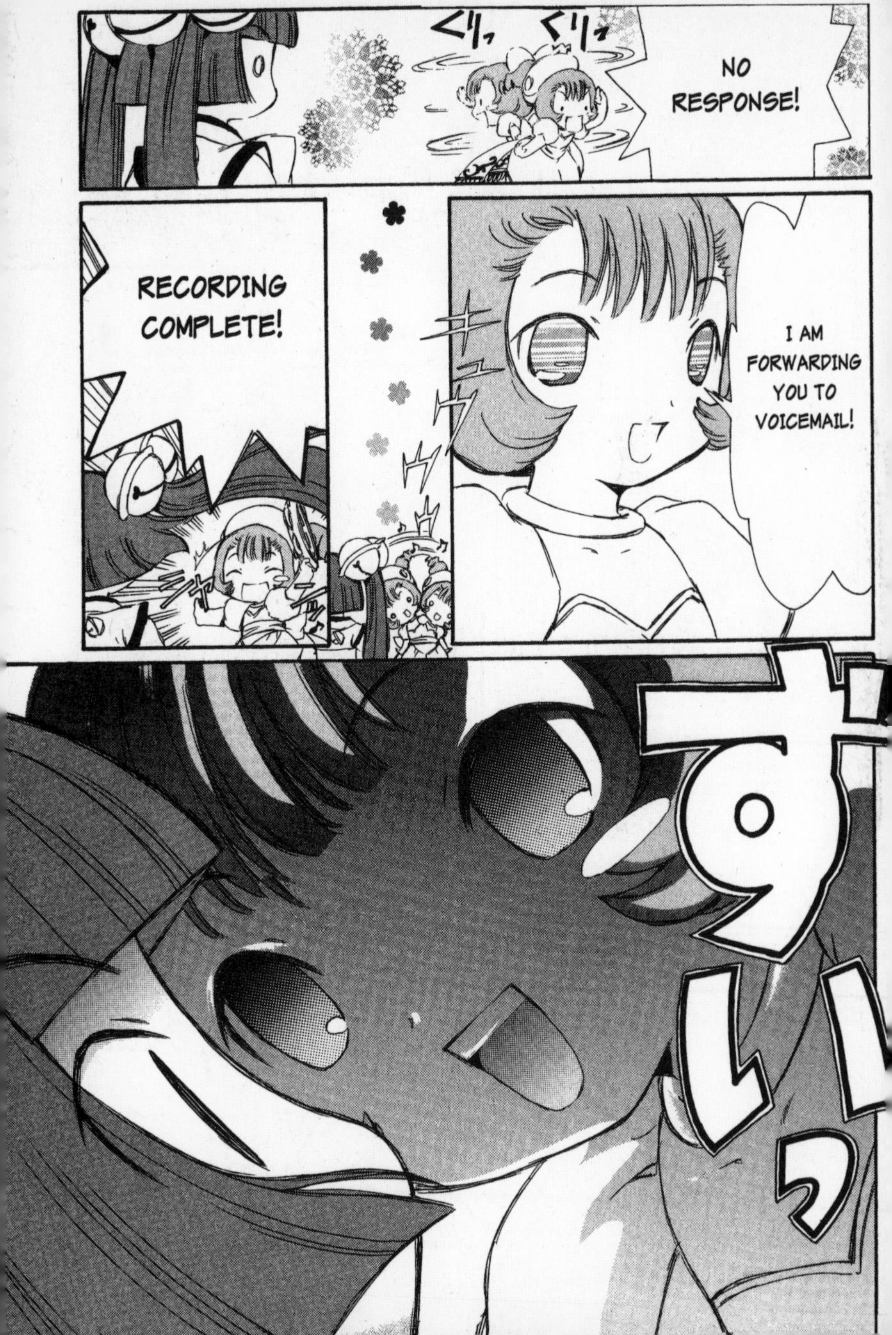
NO RESPONSE!
I AM FORWARDING YOU TO VOICEMAIL!
RECORDING COMPLETE!
すいっ

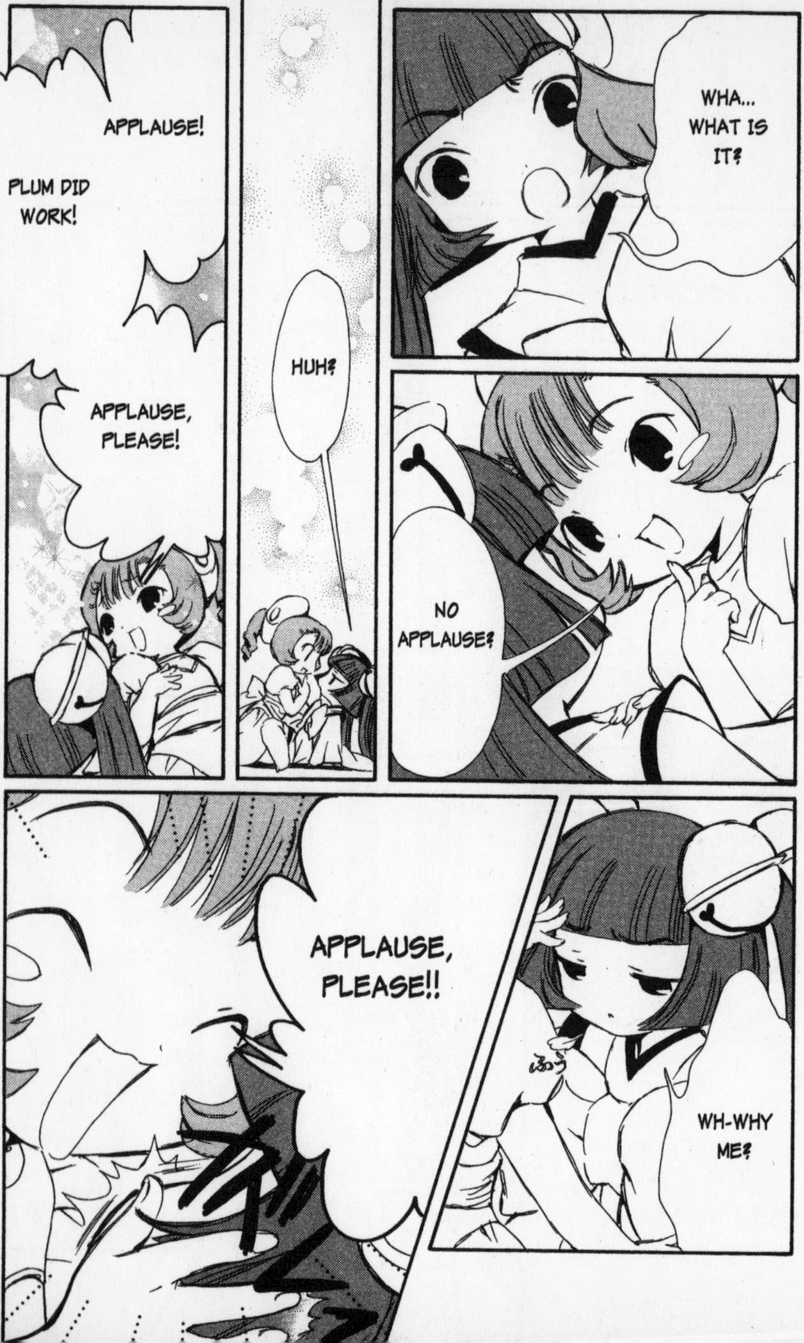
WHA... WHAT IS IT?
NO APPLAUSE?
HUH?
APPLAUSE!
PLUM DID WORK!
APPLAUSE, PLEASE!
WH-WHY ME?
APPLAUSE, PLEASE!!

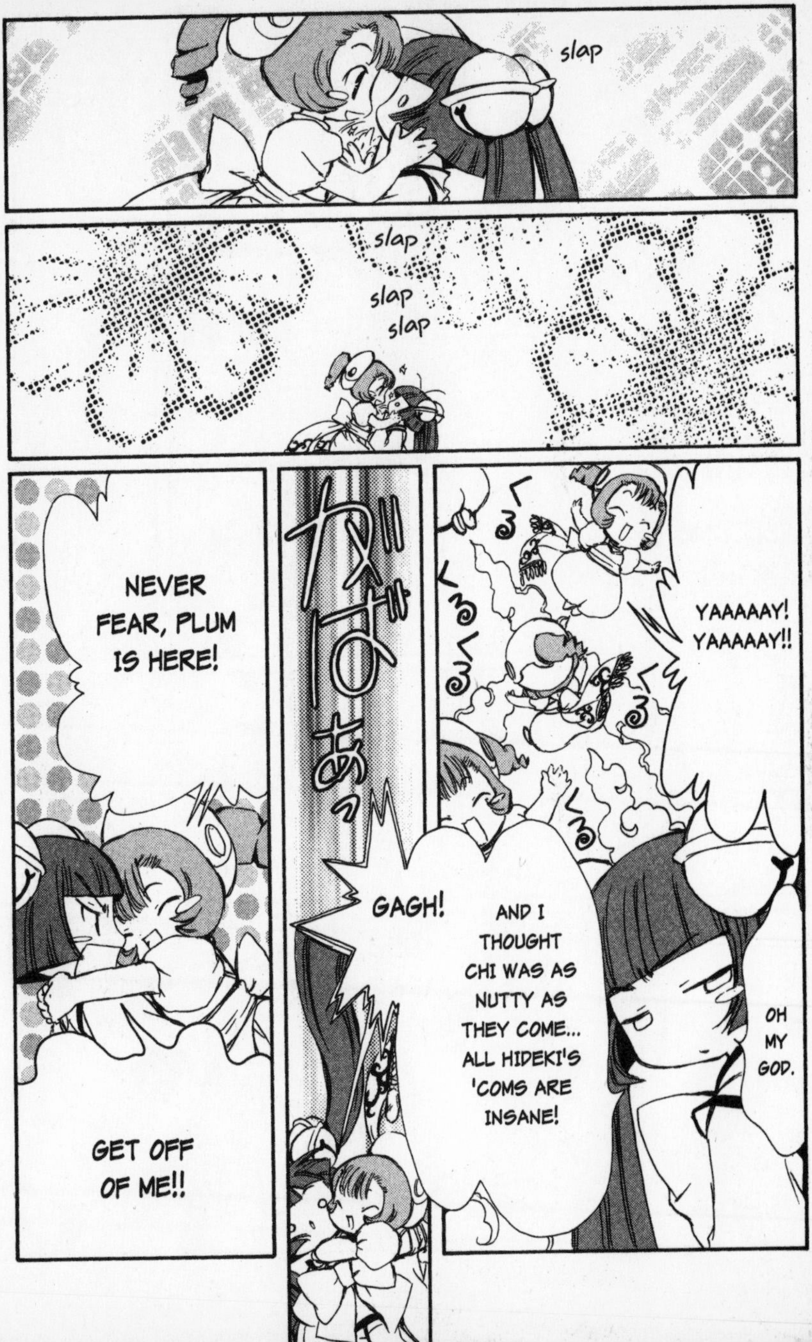

slap
slap
slap
slap
くる
くるくる
くる
YAAAAAY! YAAAAAY!!
くる
OH MY GOD.
AND I THOUGHT CHI WAS AS NUTTY AS THEY COME... ALL HIDEKI'S 'COMS ARE INSANE!
がばあっ
GAGH!
NEVER FEAR, PLUM IS HERE!
GET OFF OF ME!!

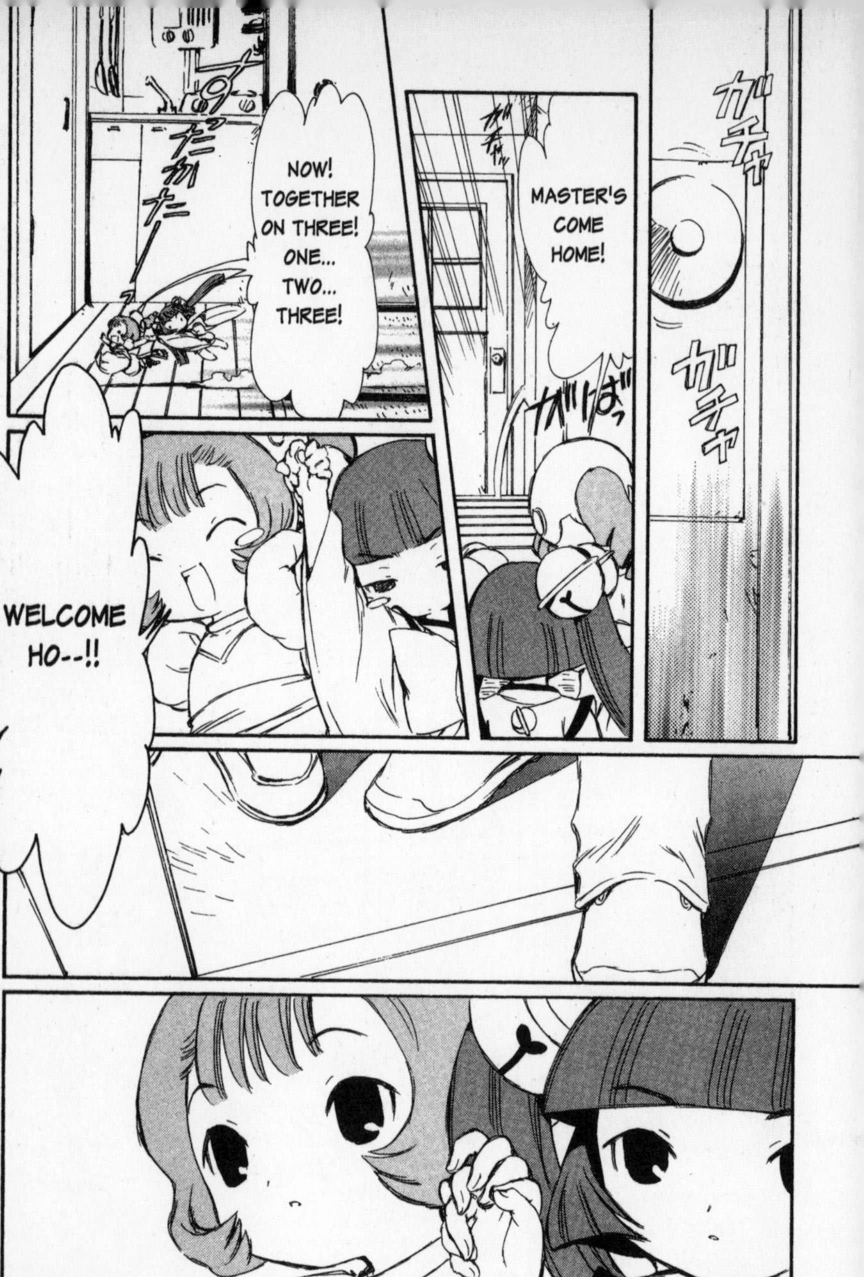
ガチャ
ガチャ
MASTER'S COME HOME!
ガばっ
NOW! TOGETHER ON THREE! ONE... TWO... THREE!
WELCOME HO--!!

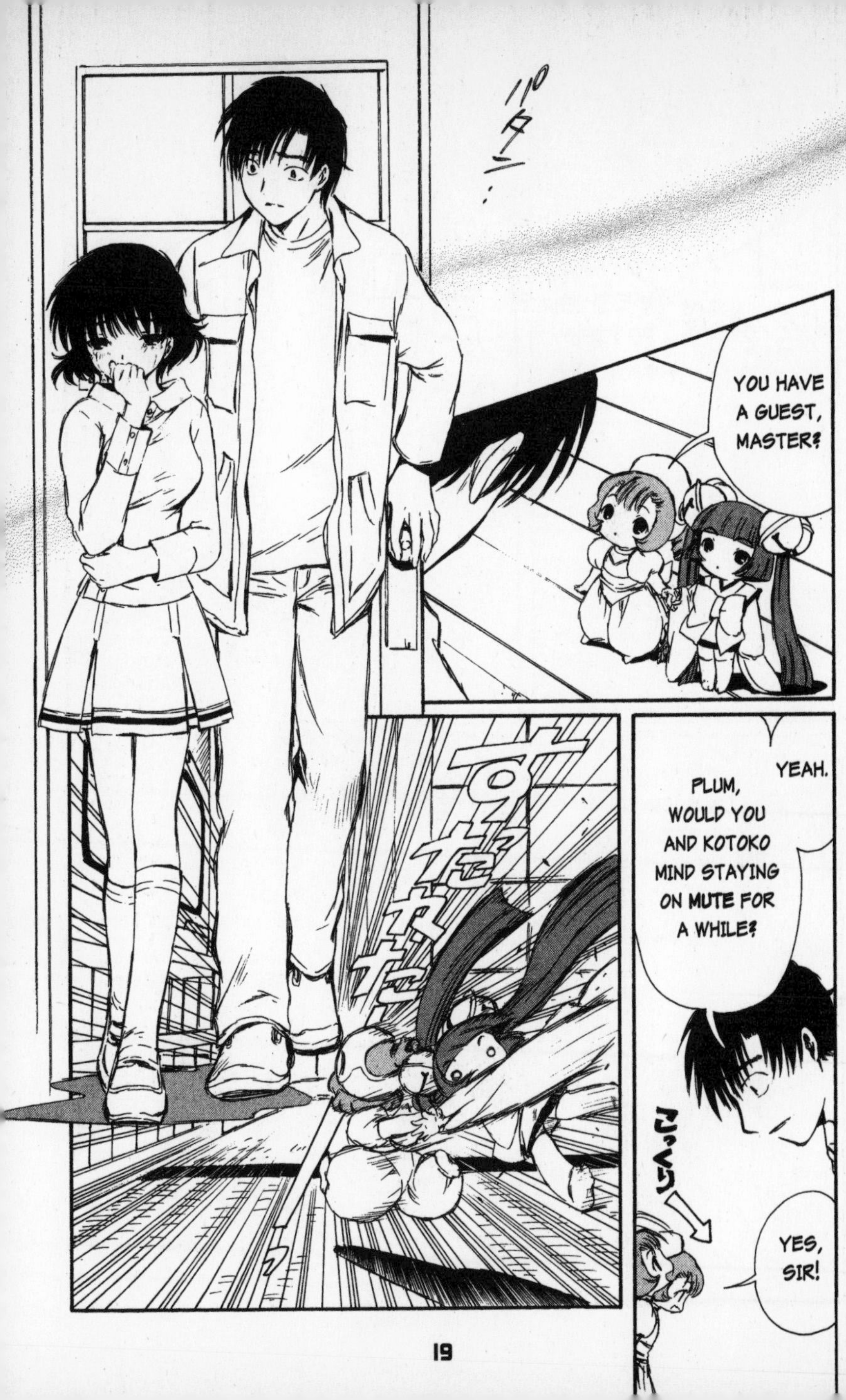

パタン…
YOU HAVE A GUEST, MASTER?
YEAH.
PLUM, WOULD YOU AND KOTOKO MIND STAYING ON MUTE FOR A WHILE?
YES, SIR!

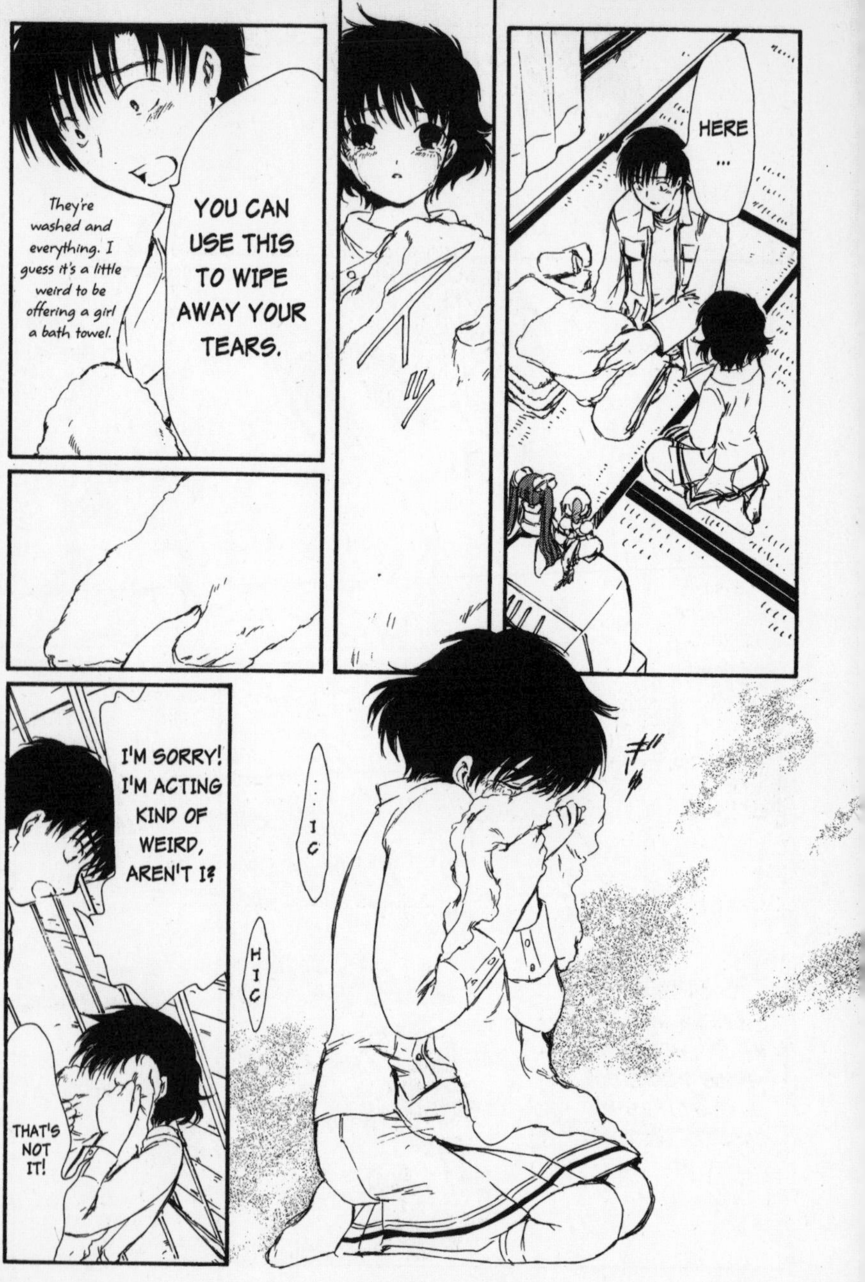
HERE ...
YOU CAN USE THIS TO WIPE AWAY YOUR TEARS.
They're washed and everything. I guess it's a little weird to be offering a girl a bath towel.
... IC
HIC
I'M SORRY! I'M ACTING KIND OF WEIRD, AREN'T I?
THAT'S NOT IT!

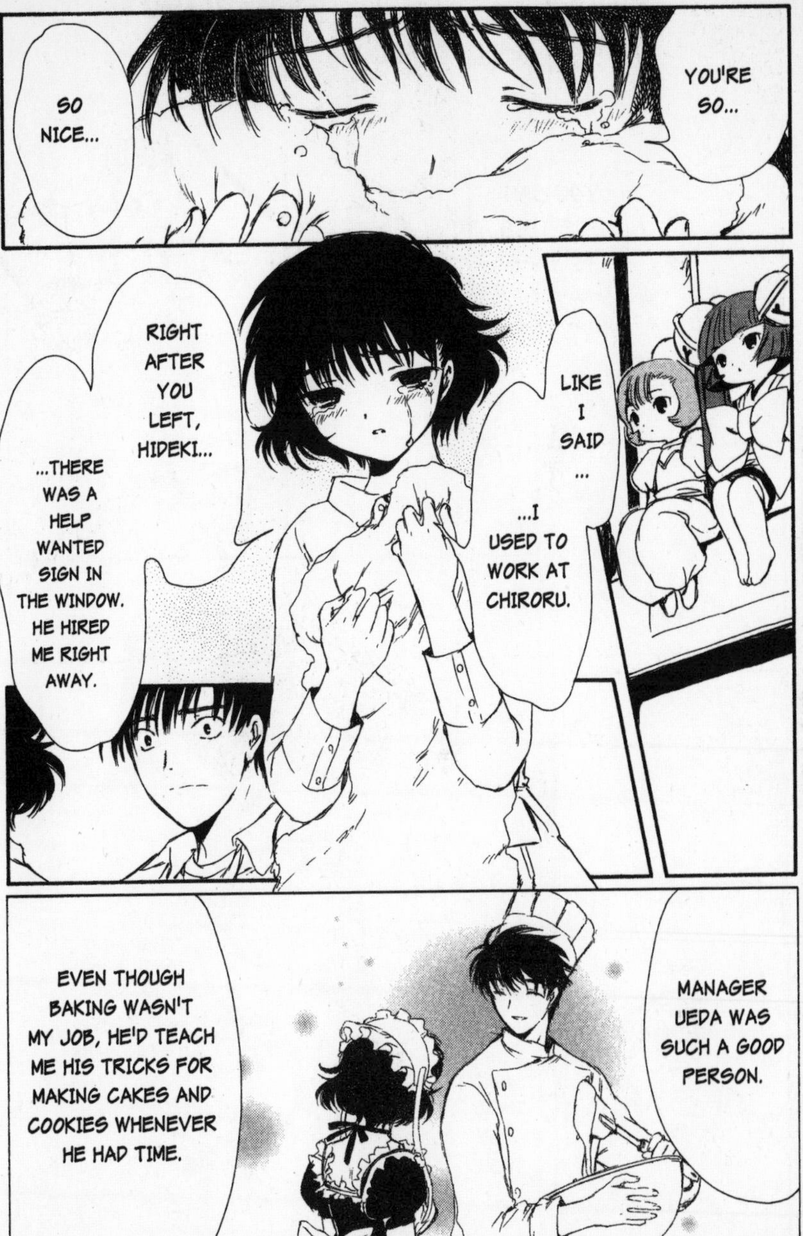
YOU'RE SO...
SO NICE...
LIKE I SAID ...
...I USED TO WORK AT CHIRORU.
RIGHT AFTER YOU LEFT, HIDEKI...
...THERE WAS A HELP WANTED SIGN IN THE WINDOW. HE HIRED ME RIGHT AWAY.
MANAGER UEDA WAS SUCH A GOOD PERSON.
EVEN THOUGH BAKING WASN'T MY JOB, HE'D TEACH ME HIS TRICKS FOR MAKING CAKES AND COOKIES WHENEVER HE HAD TIME.

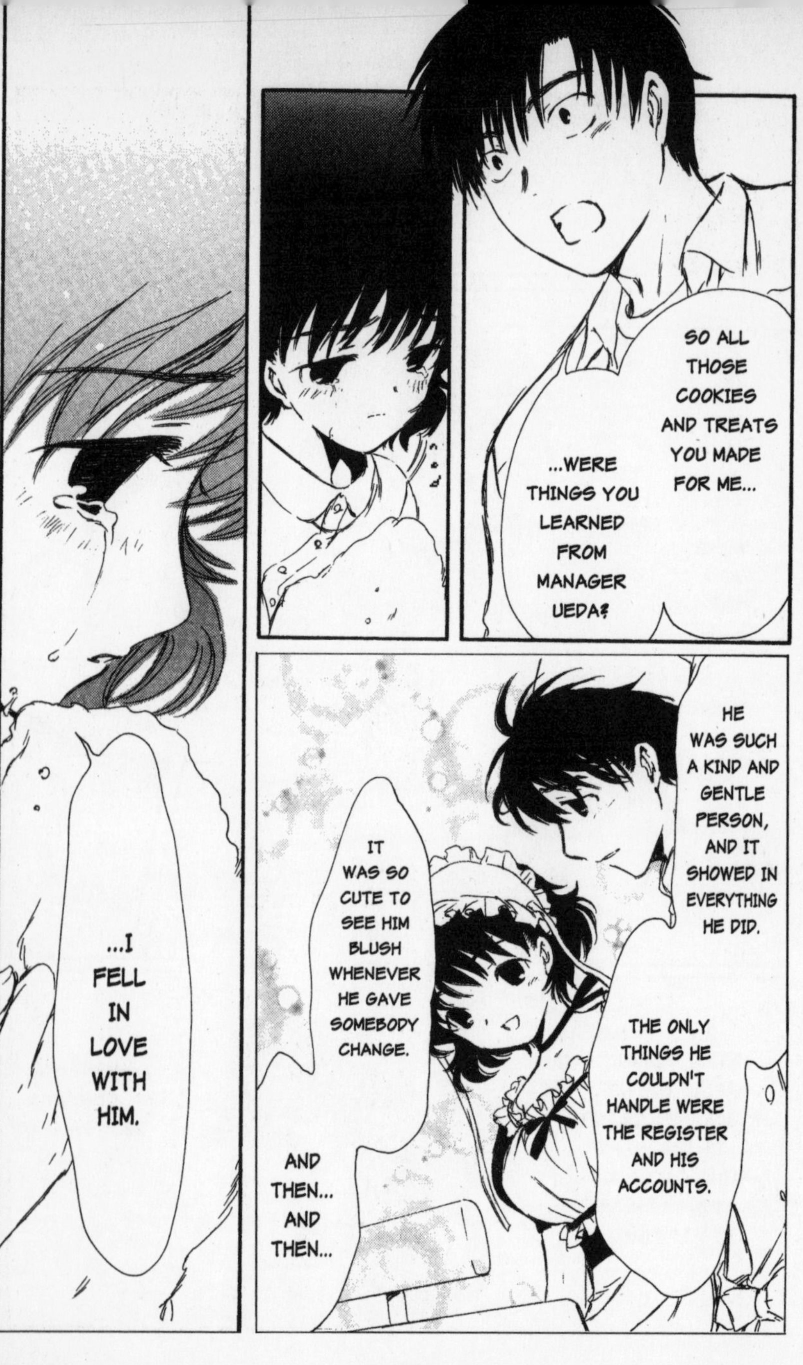
SO ALL THOSE COOKIES AND TREATS YOU MADE FOR ME...
...WERE THINGS YOU LEARNED FROM MANAGER UEDA?
HE WAS SUCH A KIND AND GENTLE PERSON, AND IT SHOWED IN EVERYTHING HE DID.
THE ONLY THINGS HE COULDN'T HANDLE WERE THE REGISTER AND HIS ACCOUNTS.
IT WAS SO CUTE TO SEE HIM BLUSH WHENEVER HE GAVE SOMEBODY CHANGE.
AND THEN... AND THEN...
...I FELL IN LOVE WITH HIM.

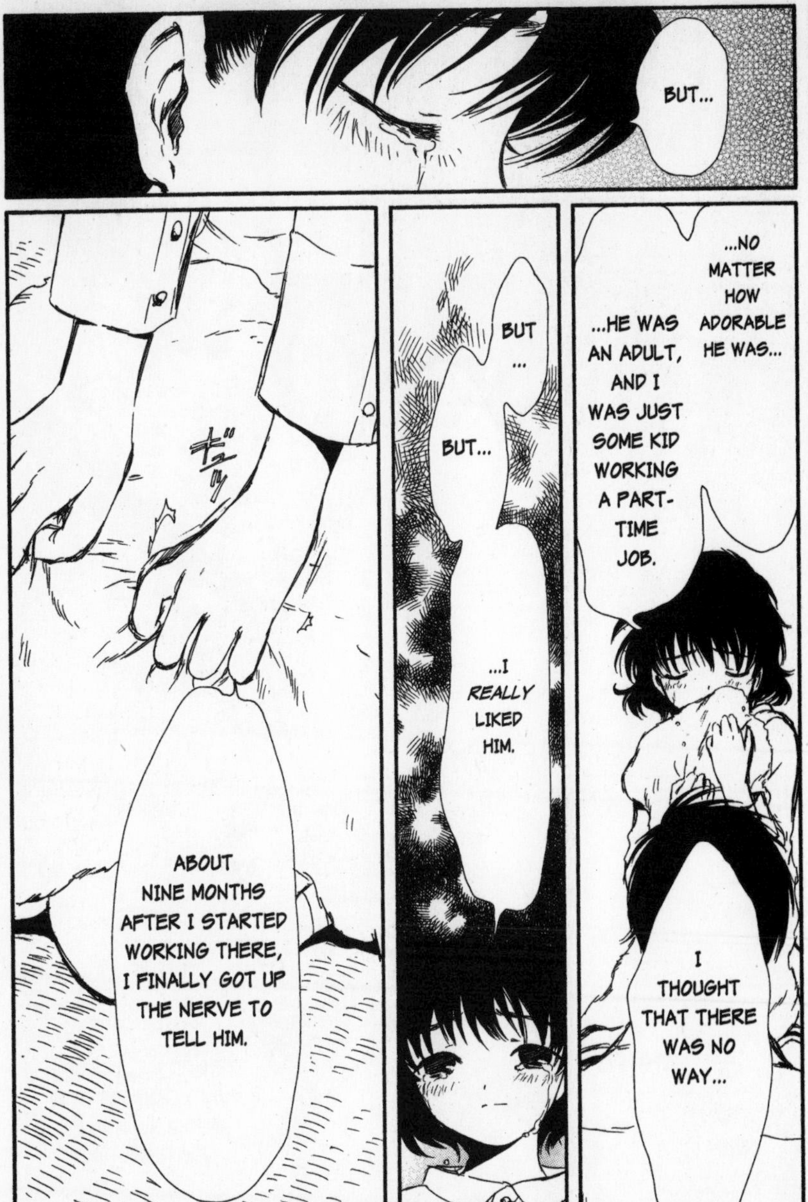
BUT...
...NO MATTER HOW ADORABLE HE WAS...
...HE WAS AN ADULT, AND I WAS JUST SOME KID WORKING A PART-TIME JOB.
I THOUGHT THAT THERE WAS NO WAY...
BUT ...
BUT...
...I *REALLY* LIKED HIM.
ギュッ
ABOUT NINE MONTHS AFTER I STARTED WORKING THERE, I FINALLY GOT UP THE NERVE TO TELL HIM.

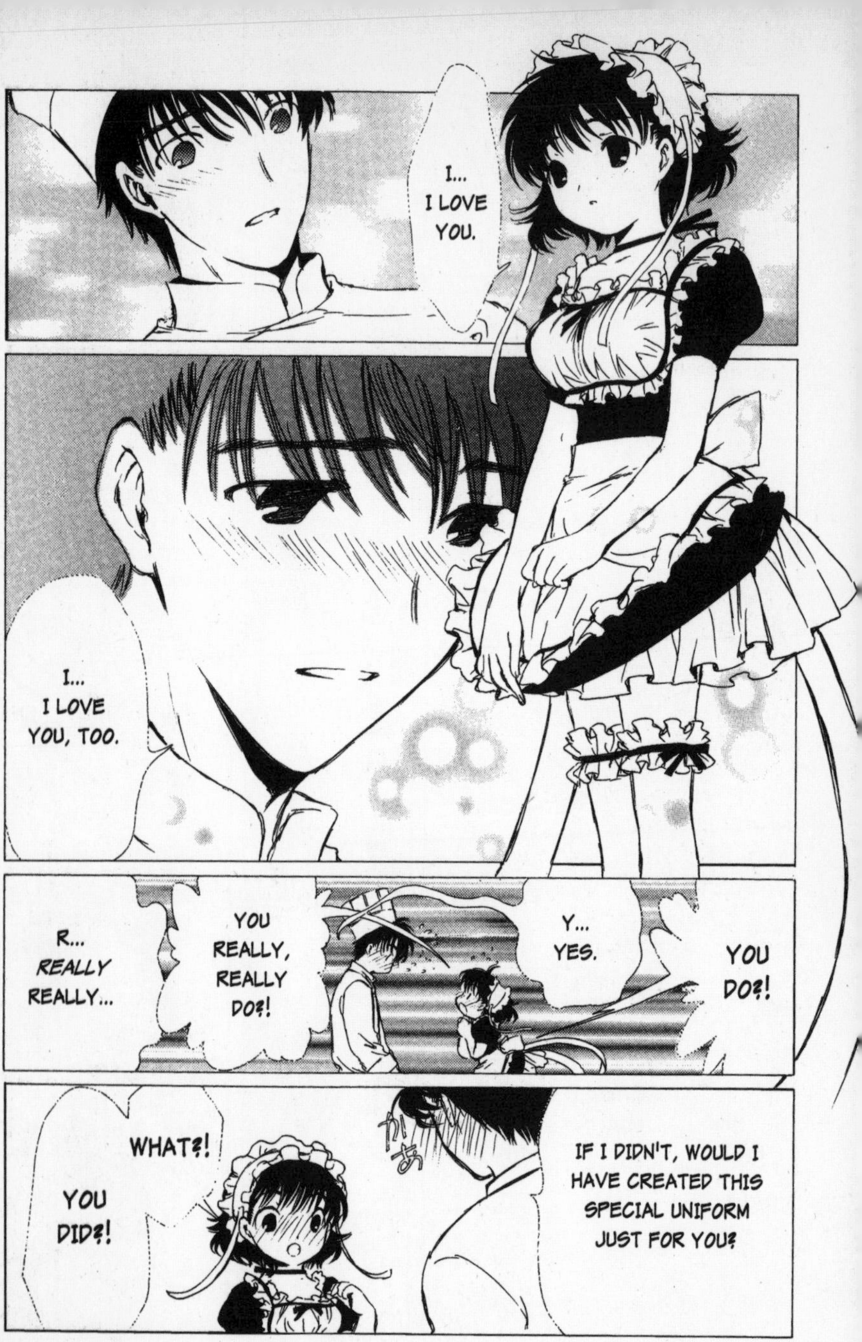
I...
I LOVE
YOU.
I...
I LOVE
YOU, TOO.
YOU
DO?!
Y...
YES.
YOU
REALLY,
REALLY
DO?!
R...
REALLY
REALLY...
IF I DIDN'T, WOULD I
HAVE CREATED THIS
SPECIAL UNIFORM
JUST FOR YOU?
かぁ
WHAT?!
YOU
DID?!

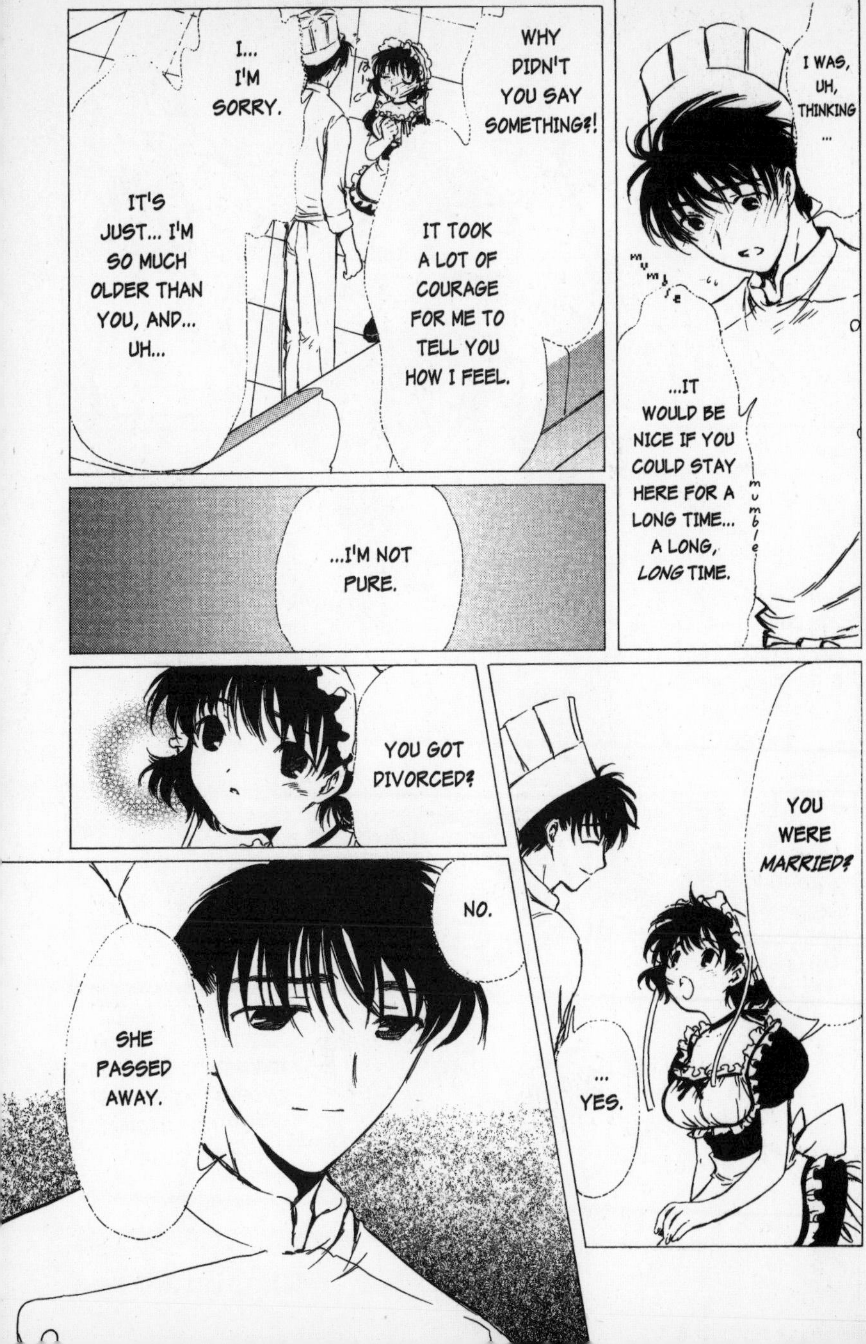
I WAS, UH, THINKING ...
mumble
...IT WOULD BE NICE IF YOU COULD STAY HERE FOR A LONG TIME... A LONG, *LONG* TIME.
mumble
WHY DIDN'T YOU SAY SOMETHING?!
I... I'M SORRY.
IT TOOK A LOT OF COURAGE FOR ME TO TELL YOU HOW I FEEL.
IT'S JUST... I'M SO MUCH OLDER THAN YOU, AND... UH...
...I'M NOT PURE.
YOU WERE *MARRIED*?
... YES.
YOU GOT DIVORCED?
NO.
SHE PASSED AWAY.

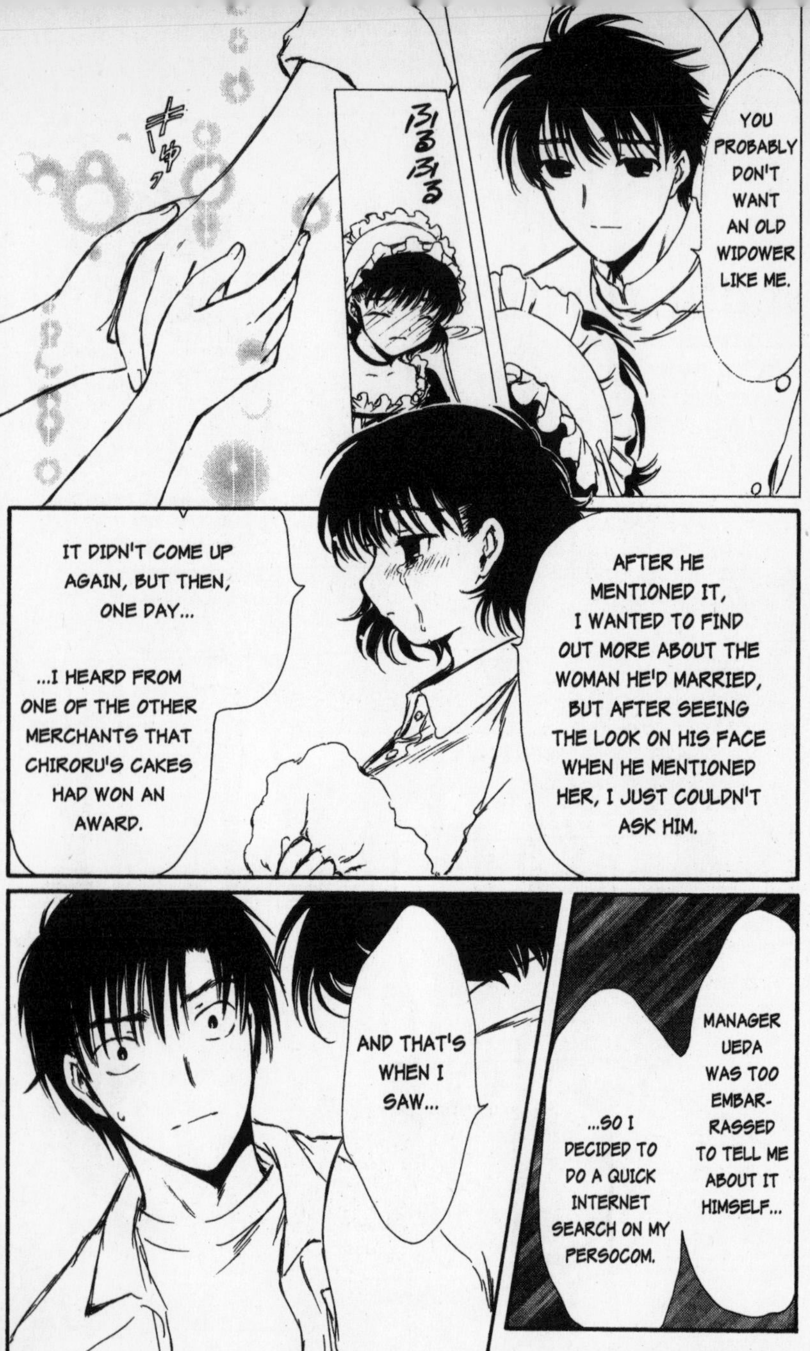
YOU PROBABLY DON'T WANT AN OLD WIDOWER LIKE ME.
ふるふる
キュッ
AFTER HE MENTIONED IT, I WANTED TO FIND OUT MORE ABOUT THE WOMAN HE'D MARRIED, BUT AFTER SEEING THE LOOK ON HIS FACE WHEN HE MENTIONED HER, I JUST COULDN'T ASK HIM.
IT DIDN'T COME UP AGAIN, BUT THEN, ONE DAY...
...I HEARD FROM ONE OF THE OTHER MERCHANTS THAT CHIRORU'S CAKES HAD WON AN AWARD.
MANAGER UEDA WAS TOO EMBAR-RASSED TO TELL ME ABOUT IT HIMSELF...
...SO I DECIDED TO DO A QUICK INTERNET SEARCH ON MY PERSOCOM.
AND THAT'S WHEN I SAW...

◀chapter.61▶ end

◀chapter.62▶

ちょびっツ

Chobits

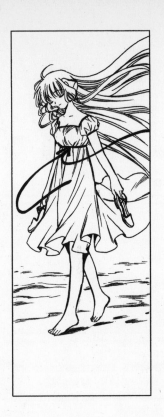

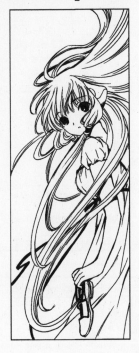

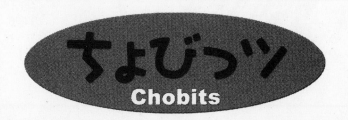

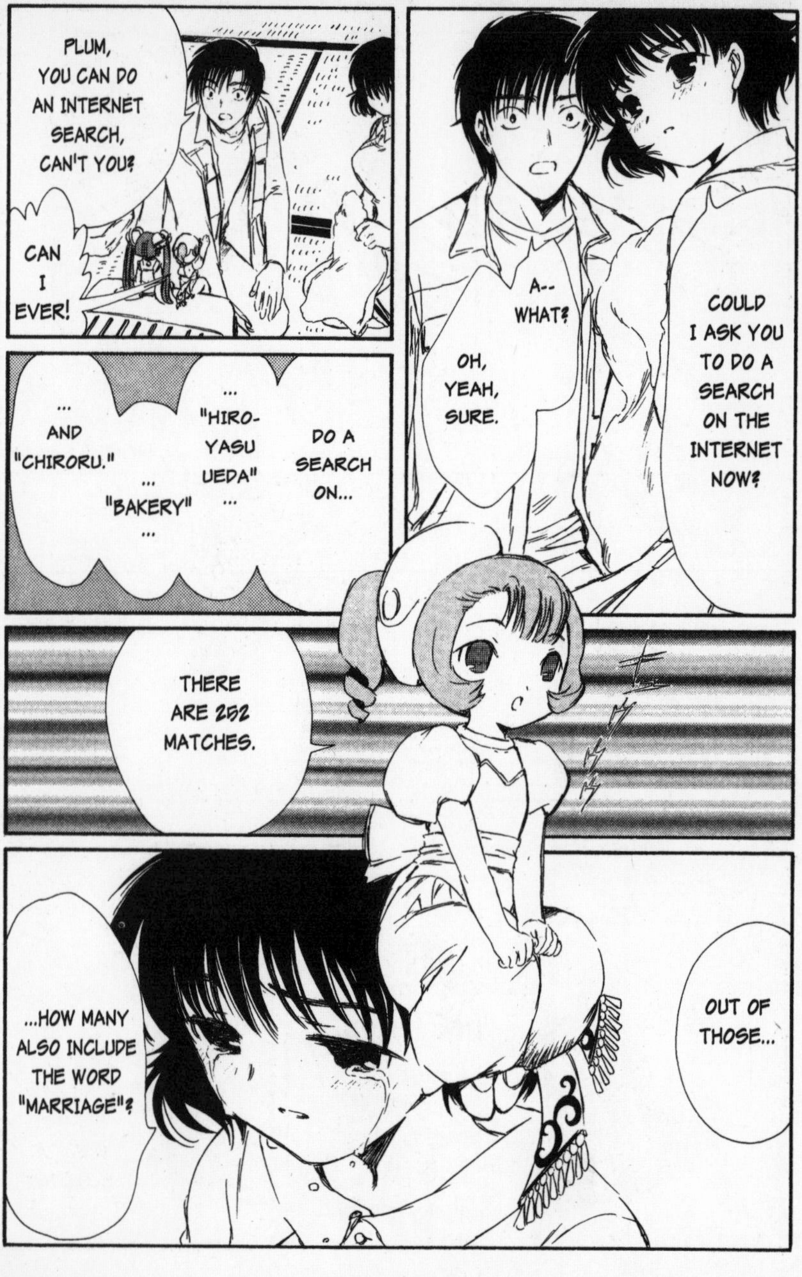
COULD I ASK YOU TO DO A SEARCH ON THE INTERNET NOW?
A-- WHAT?
OH, YEAH, SURE.
PLUM, YOU CAN DO AN INTERNET SEARCH, CAN'T YOU?
CAN I EVER!
DO A SEARCH ON...
... "HIRO-YASU UEDA" ...
... "BAKERY" ...
... AND "CHIRORU."
THERE ARE 252 MATCHES.
OUT OF THOSE...
...HOW MANY ALSO INCLUDE THE WORD "MARRIAGE"?

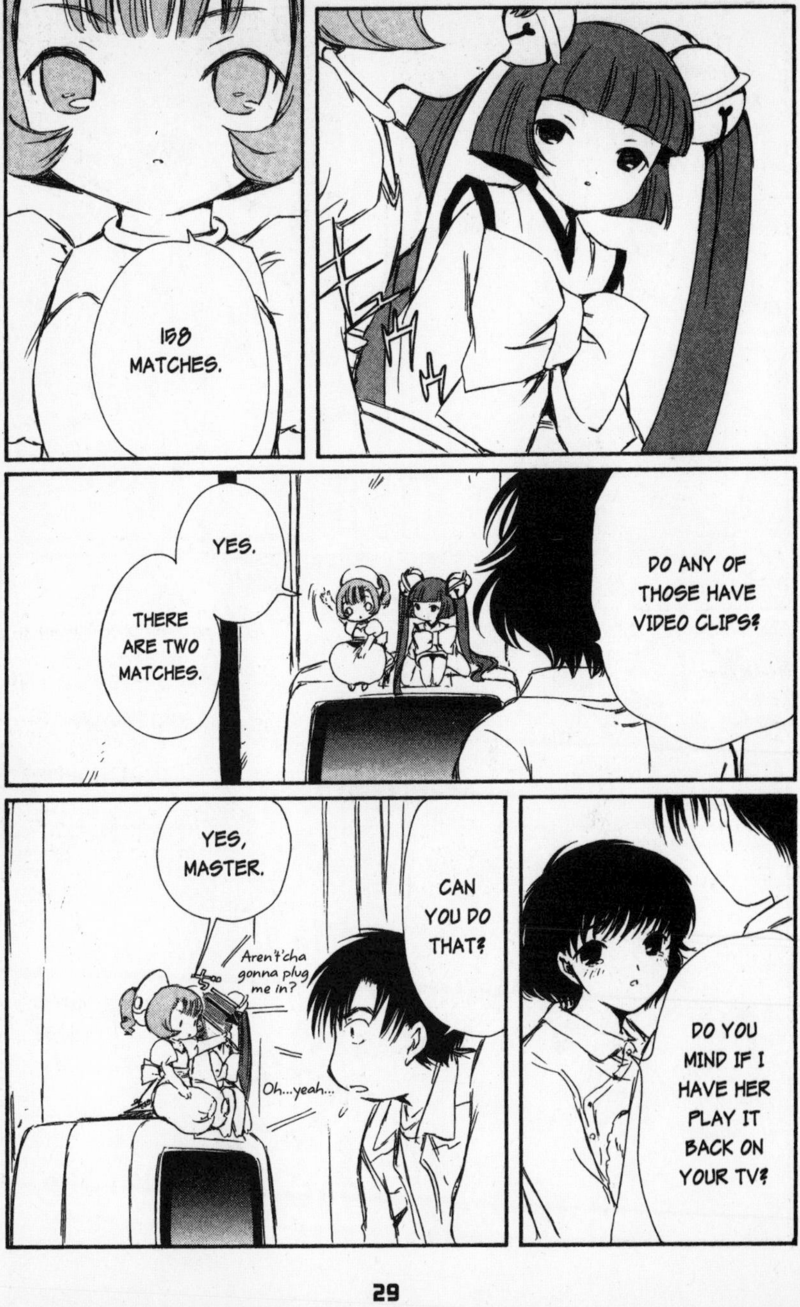
158 MATCHES.
DO ANY OF THOSE HAVE VIDEO CLIPS?
YES.
THERE ARE TWO MATCHES.
DO YOU MIND IF I HAVE HER PLAY IT BACK ON YOUR TV?
CAN YOU DO THAT?
YES, MASTER.
Aren't'cha gonna plug me in?
Oh...yeah...

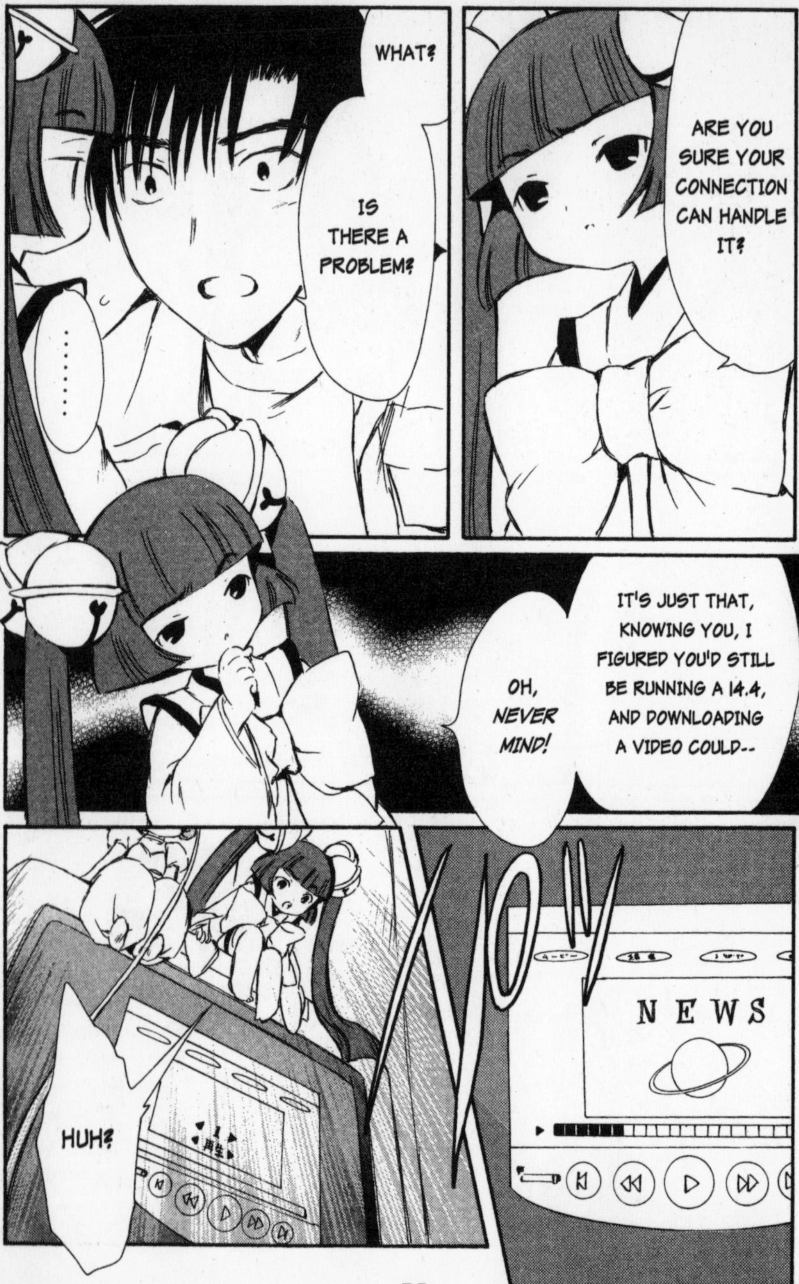
ARE YOU SURE YOUR CONNECTION CAN HANDLE IT?
WHAT?
IS THERE A PROBLEM?
......
IT'S JUST THAT, KNOWING YOU, I FIGURED YOU'D STILL BE RUNNING A 14.4, AND DOWNLOADING A VIDEO COULD--
OH, *NEVER MIND!*
NEWS
HUH?

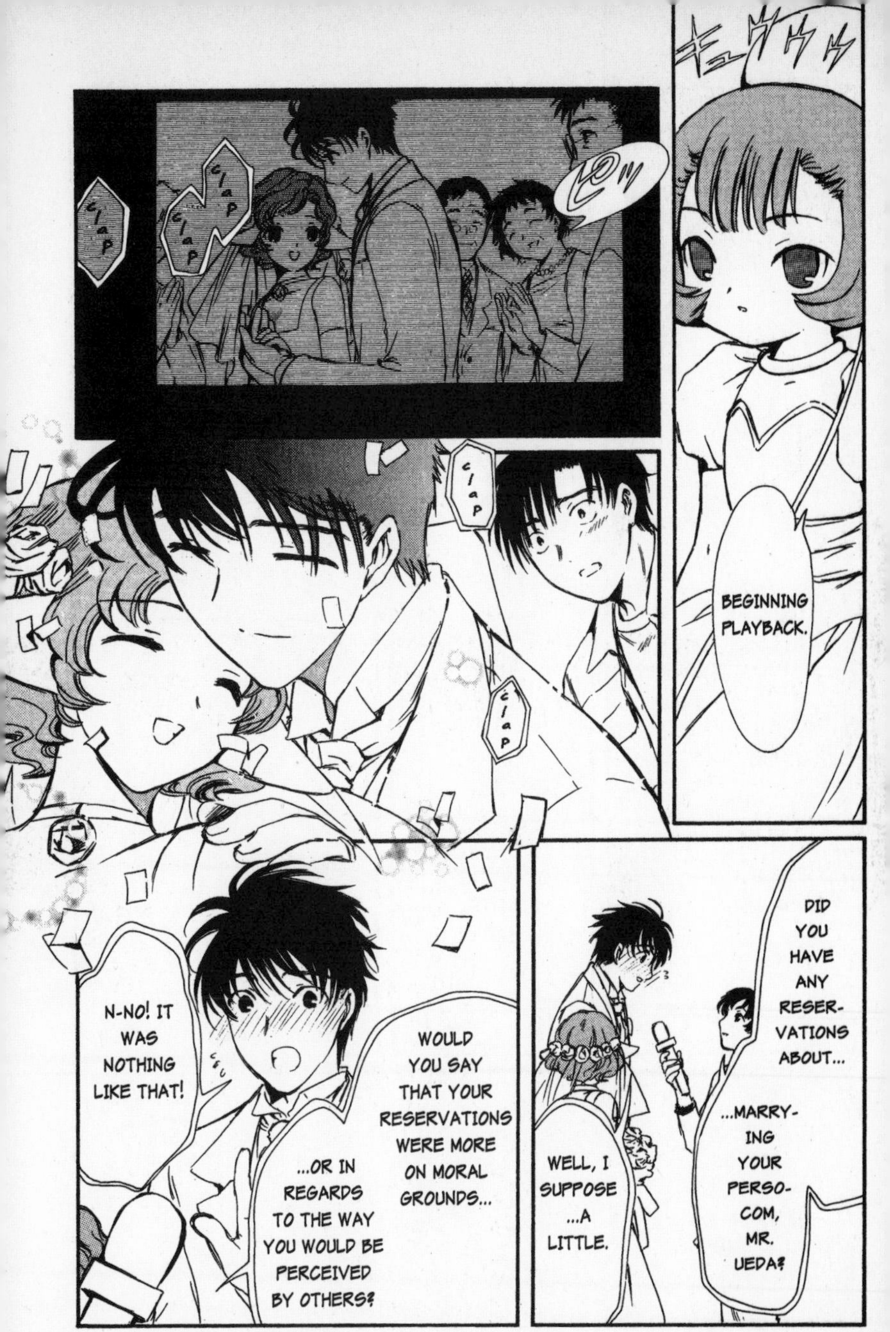
BEGINNING PLAYBACK.
clap
clap
clap
clap
clap
DID YOU HAVE ANY RESER-VATIONS ABOUT...
...MARRY-ING YOUR PERSO-COM, MR. UEDA?
WELL, I SUPPOSE ...A LITTLE.
WOULD YOU SAY THAT YOUR RESERVATIONS WERE MORE ON MORAL GROUNDS...
...OR IN REGARDS TO THE WAY YOU WOULD BE PERCEIVED BY OTHERS?
N-NO! IT WAS NOTHING LIKE THAT!

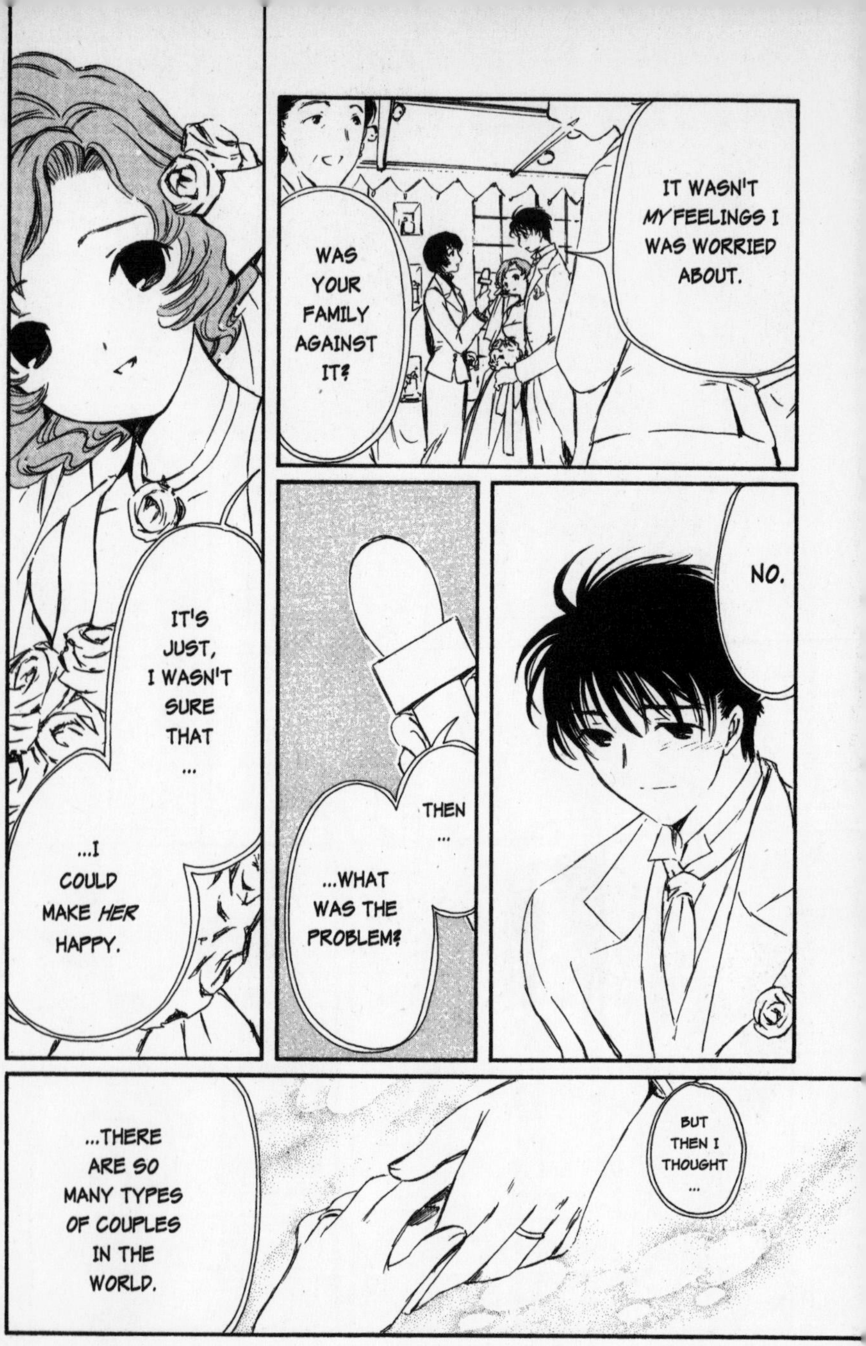
IT WASN'T *MY* FEELINGS I WAS WORRIED ABOUT.
WAS YOUR FAMILY AGAINST IT?
NO.
THEN ...
...WHAT WAS THE PROBLEM?
IT'S JUST, I WASN'T SURE THAT ...
...I COULD MAKE *HER* HAPPY.
BUT THEN I THOUGHT ...
...THERE ARE SO MANY TYPES OF COUPLES IN THE WORLD.

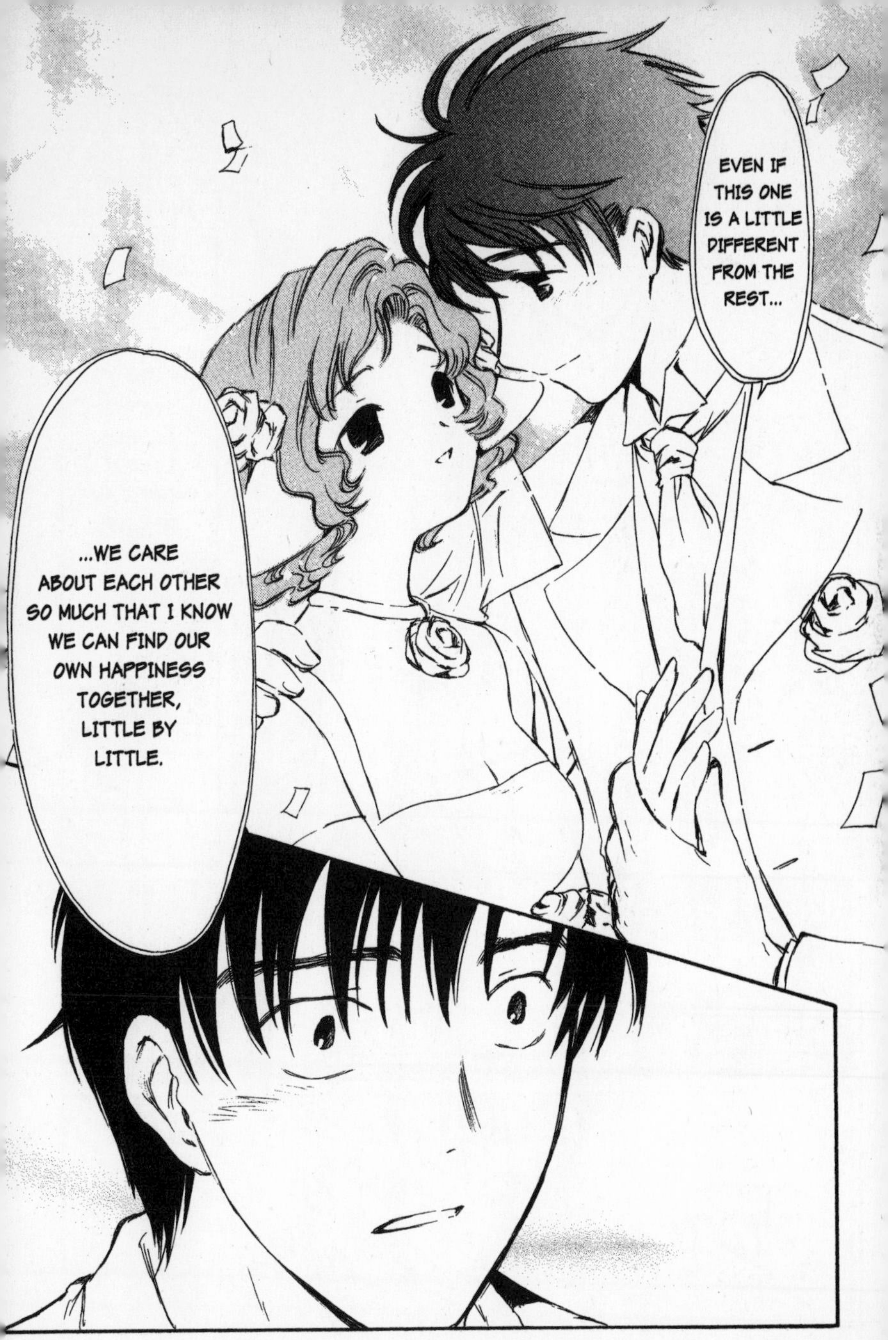
EVEN IF THIS ONE IS A LITTLE DIFFERENT FROM THE REST...
...WE CARE ABOUT EACH OTHER SO MUCH THAT I KNOW WE CAN FIND OUR OWN HAPPINESS TOGETHER, LITTLE BY LITTLE.

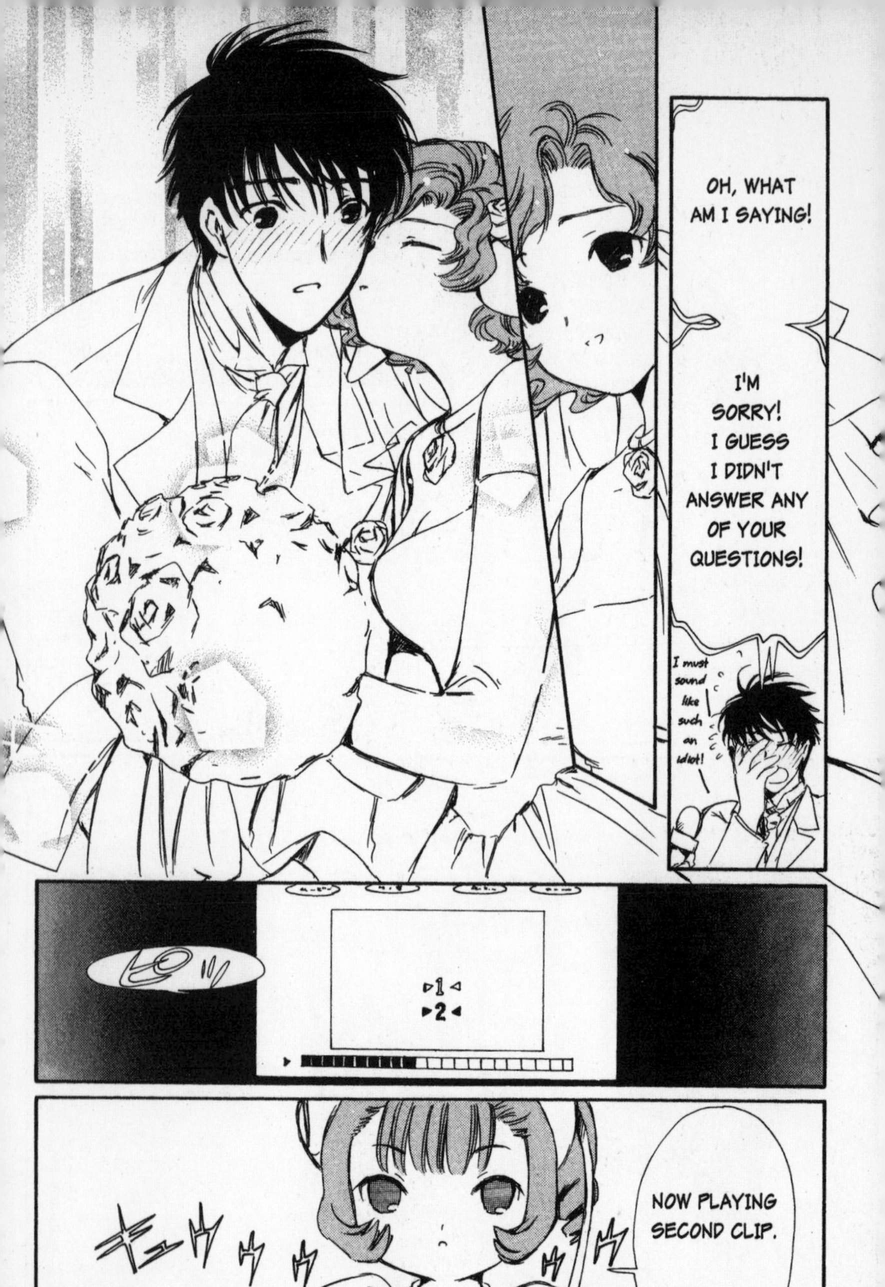
OH, WHAT AM I SAYING!
I'M SORRY! I GUESS I DIDN'T ANSWER ANY OF YOUR QUESTIONS!
I must sound like such an idiot!
1
2
NOW PLAYING SECOND CLIP.

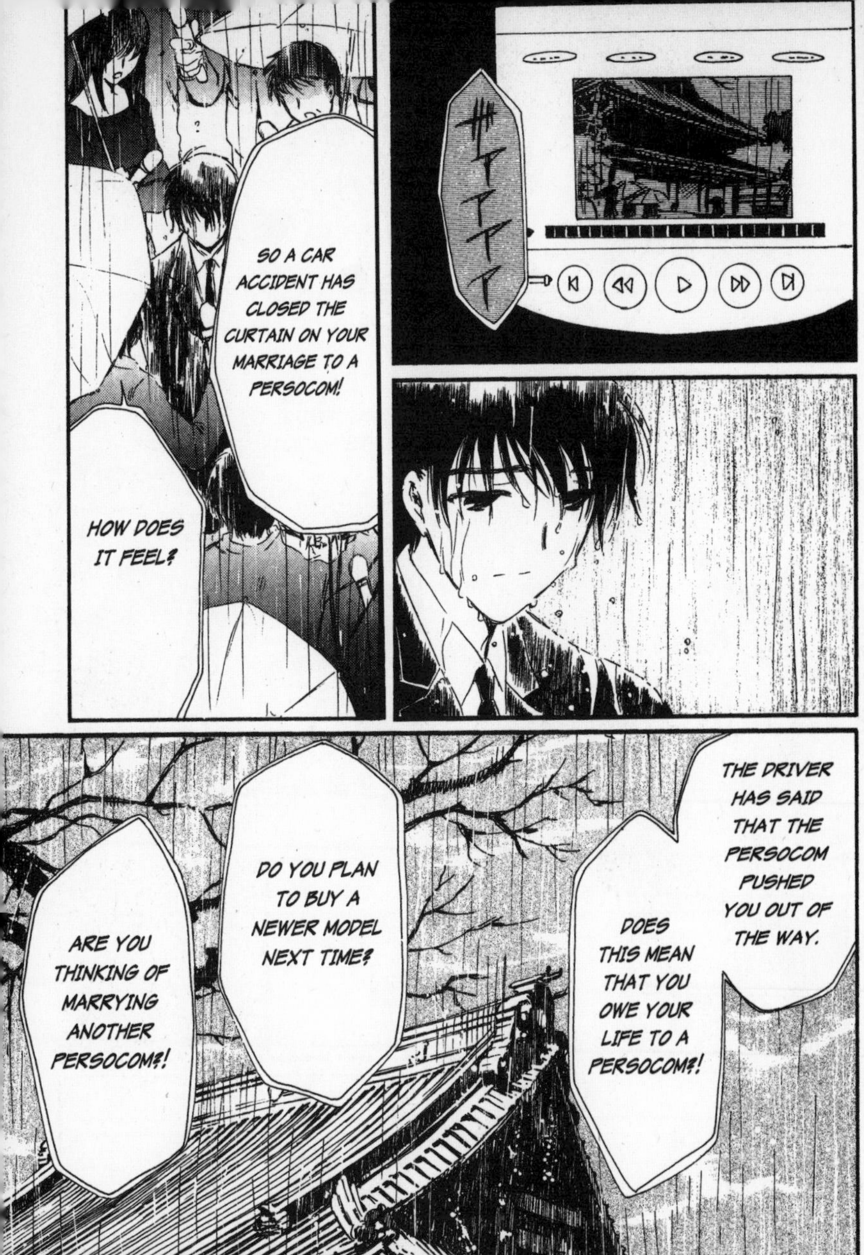
SO A CAR ACCIDENT HAS CLOSED THE CURTAIN ON YOUR MARRIAGE TO A PERSOCOM!
HOW DOES IT FEEL?
THE DRIVER HAS SAID THAT THE PERSOCOM PUSHED YOU OUT OF THE WAY.
DOES THIS MEAN THAT YOU OWE YOUR LIFE TO A PERSOCOM?!
DO YOU PLAN TO BUY A NEWER MODEL NEXT TIME?
ARE YOU THINKING OF MARRYING ANOTHER PERSOCOM?!

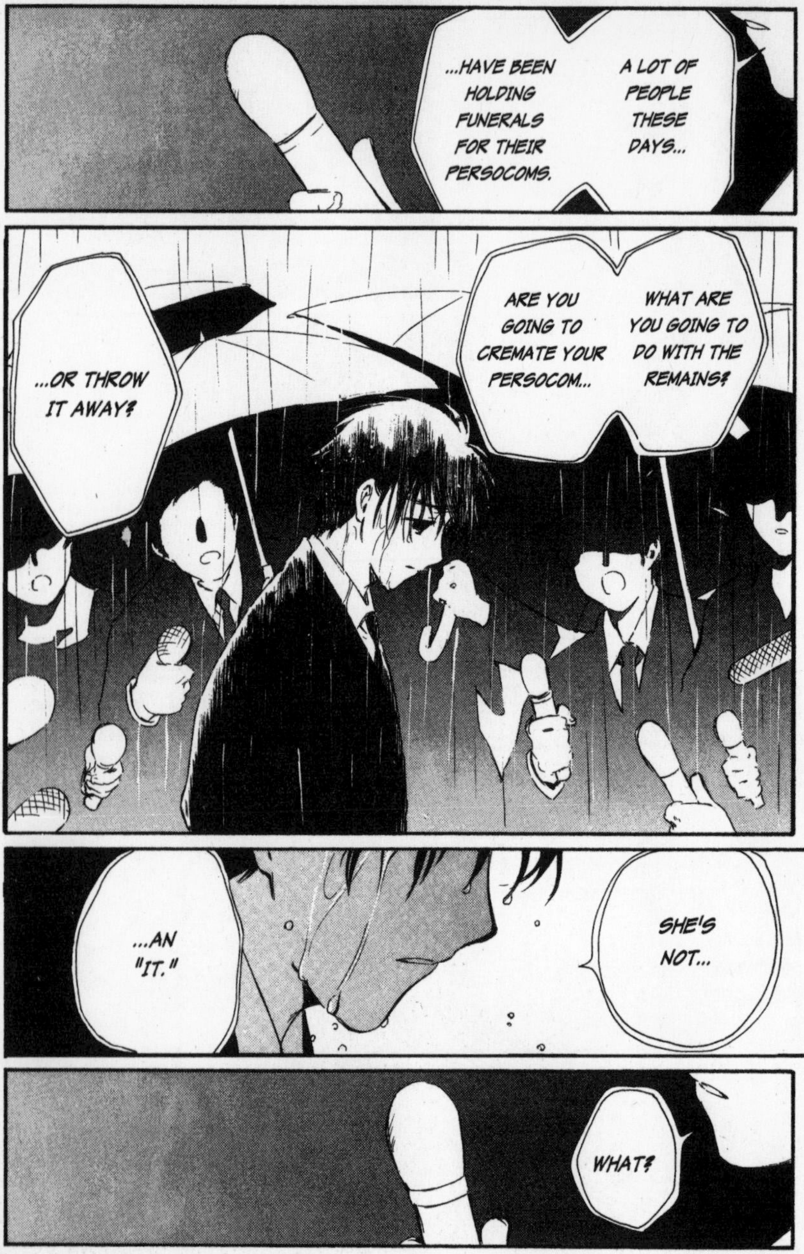
A LOT OF PEOPLE THESE DAYS...
...HAVE BEEN HOLDING FUNERALS FOR THEIR PERSOCOMS.
WHAT ARE YOU GOING TO DO WITH THE REMAINS?
ARE YOU GOING TO CREMATE YOUR PERSOCOM...
...OR THROW IT AWAY?
SHE'S NOT...
...AN "IT."
WHAT?

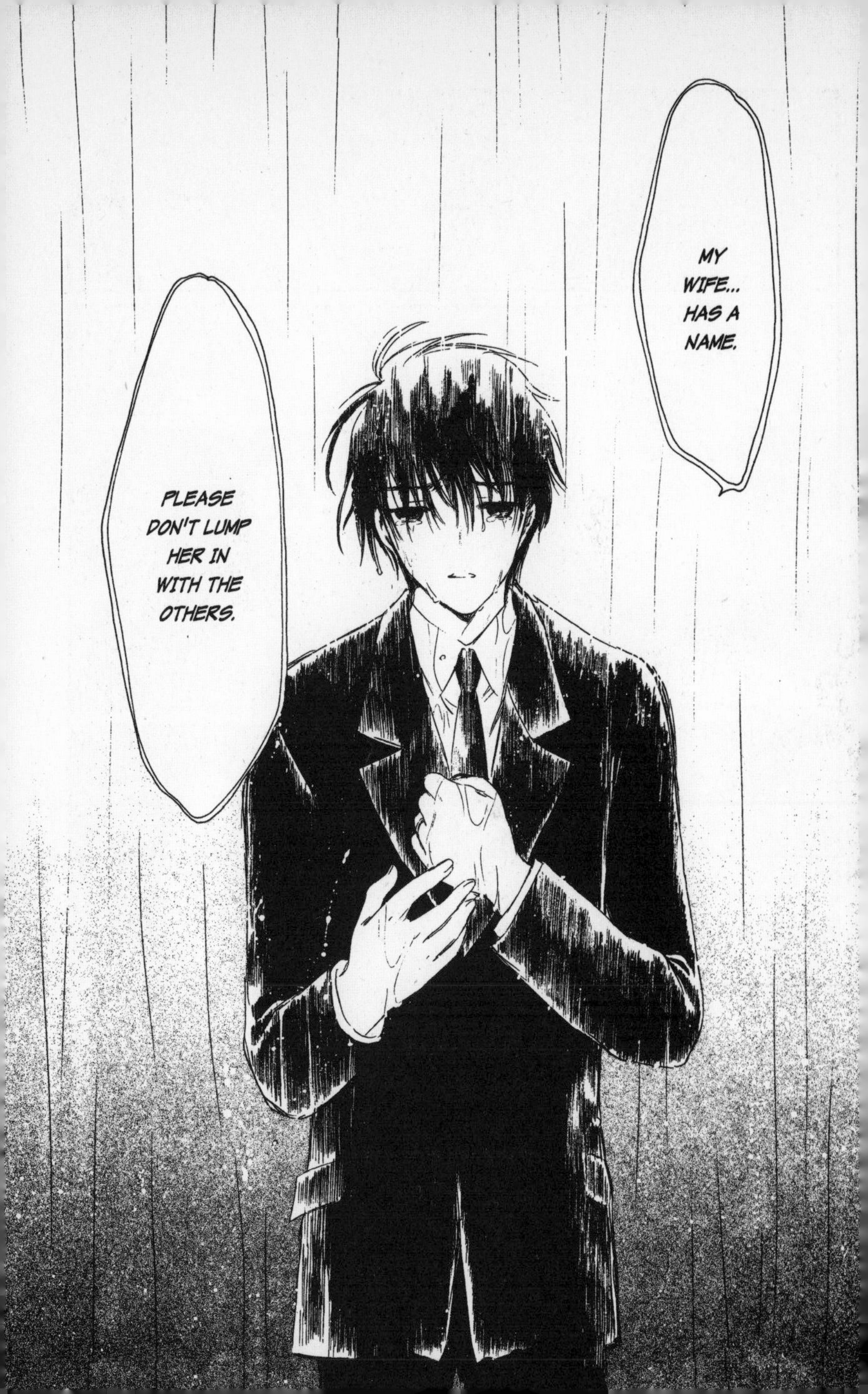
MY WIFE... HAS A NAME.
PLEASE DON'T LUMP HER IN WITH THE OTHERS.

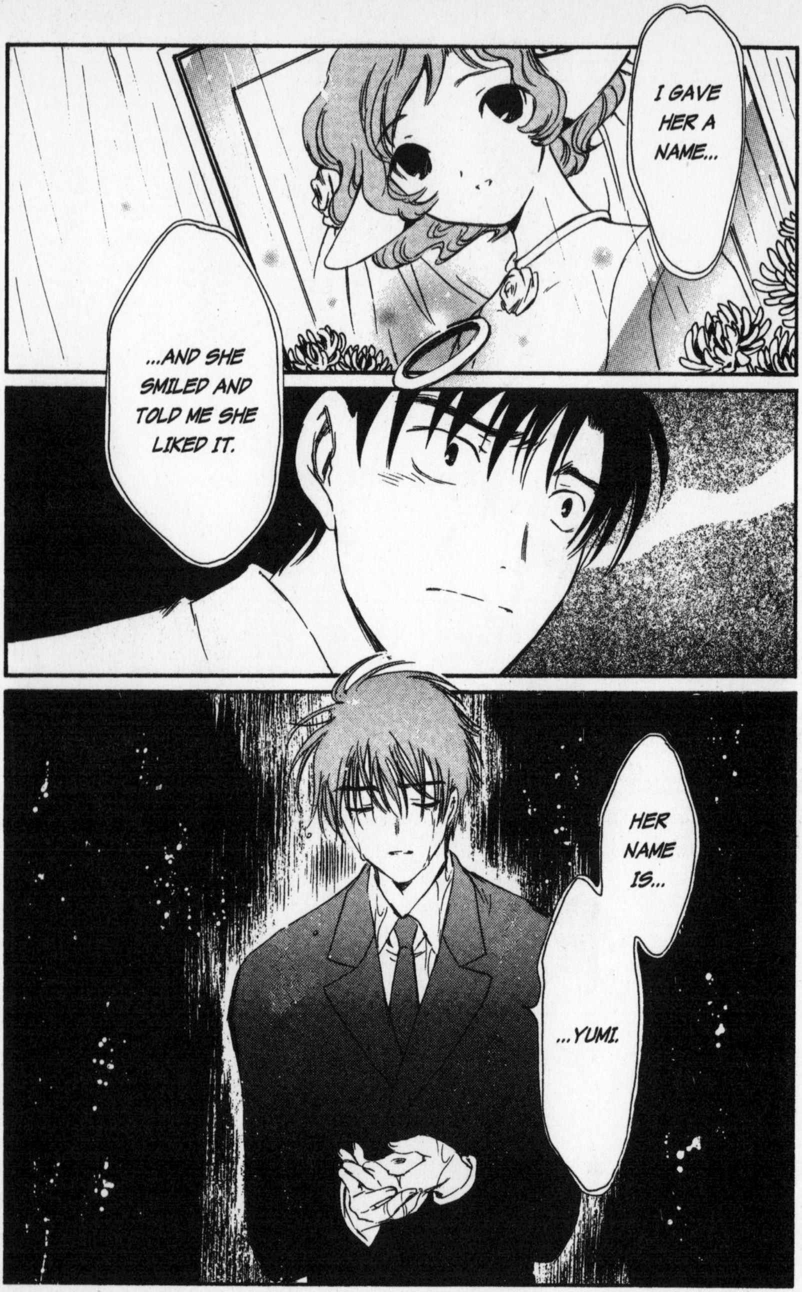
I GAVE HER A NAME...
...AND SHE SMILED AND TOLD ME SHE LIKED IT.
HER NAME IS...
...YUMI.

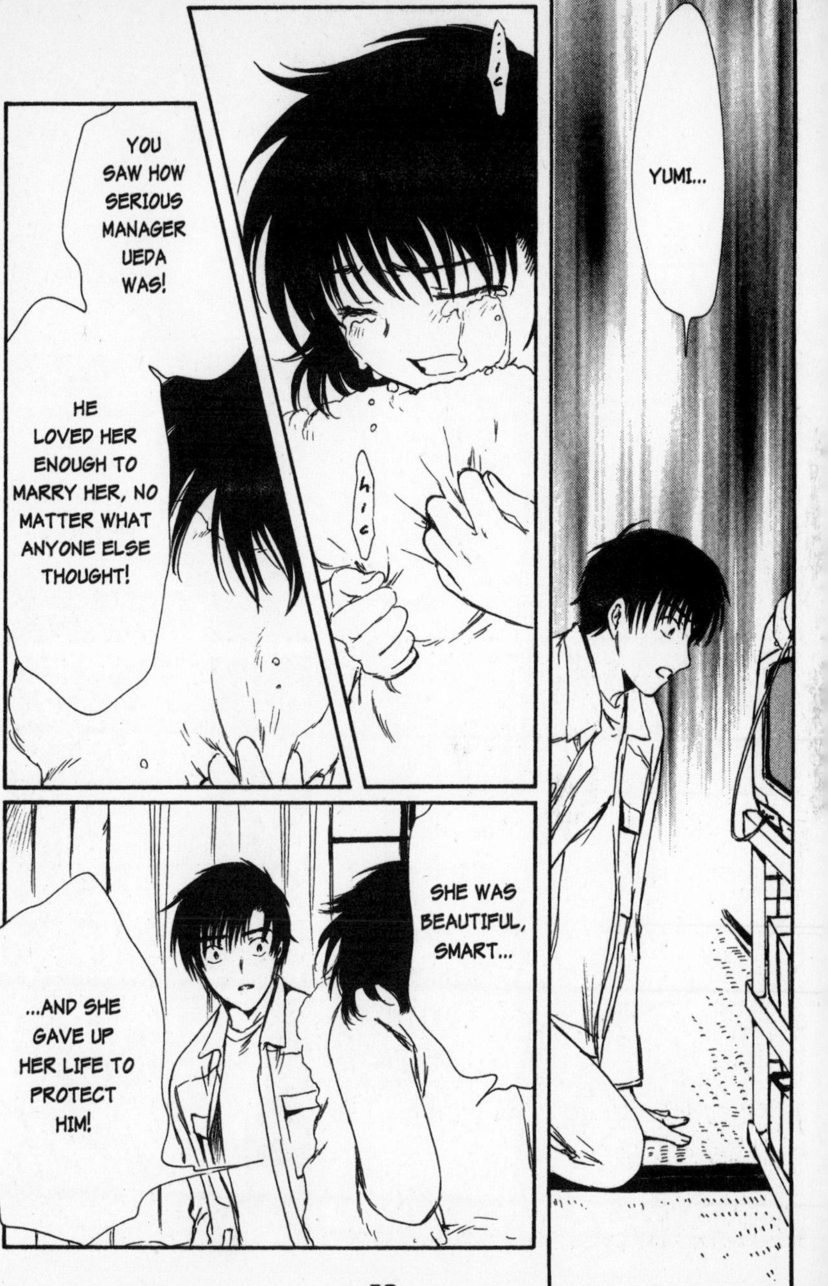
YUMI...
...ic
hic
YOU SAW HOW SERIOUS MANAGER UEDA WAS!
HE LOVED HER ENOUGH TO MARRY HER, NO MATTER WHAT ANYONE ELSE THOUGHT!
SHE WAS BEAUTIFUL, SMART...
...AND SHE GAVE UP HER LIFE TO PROTECT HIM!

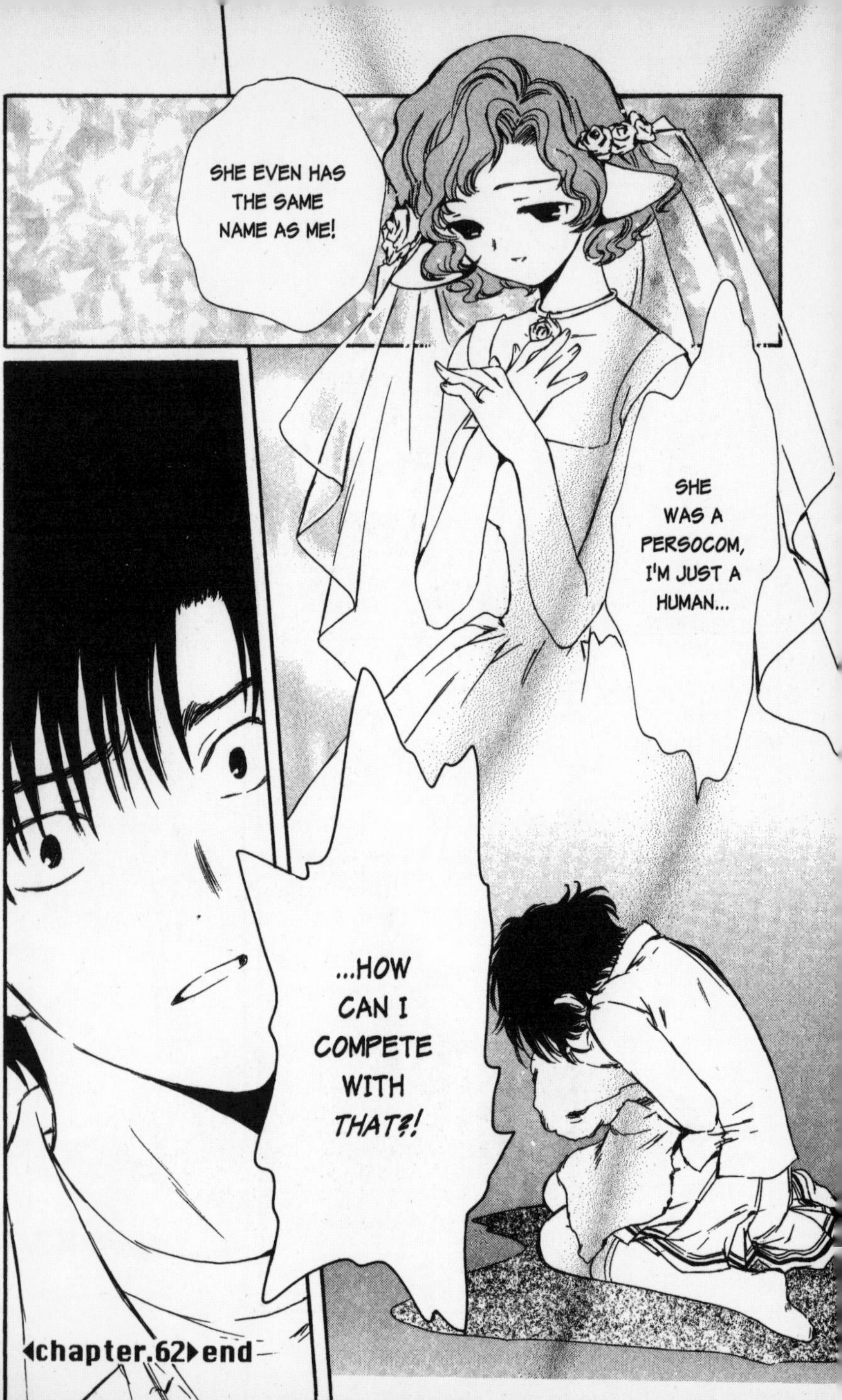
SHE EVEN HAS THE SAME NAME AS ME!
SHE WAS A PERSOCOM, I'M JUST A HUMAN...
...HOW CAN I COMPETE WITH *THAT?!*
chapter.62 end

ちょびっツ
Chobits

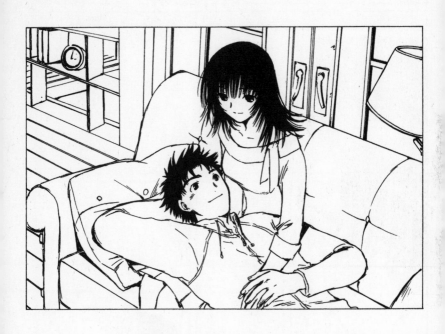

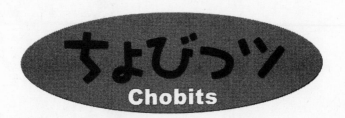

◀chapter.63▶

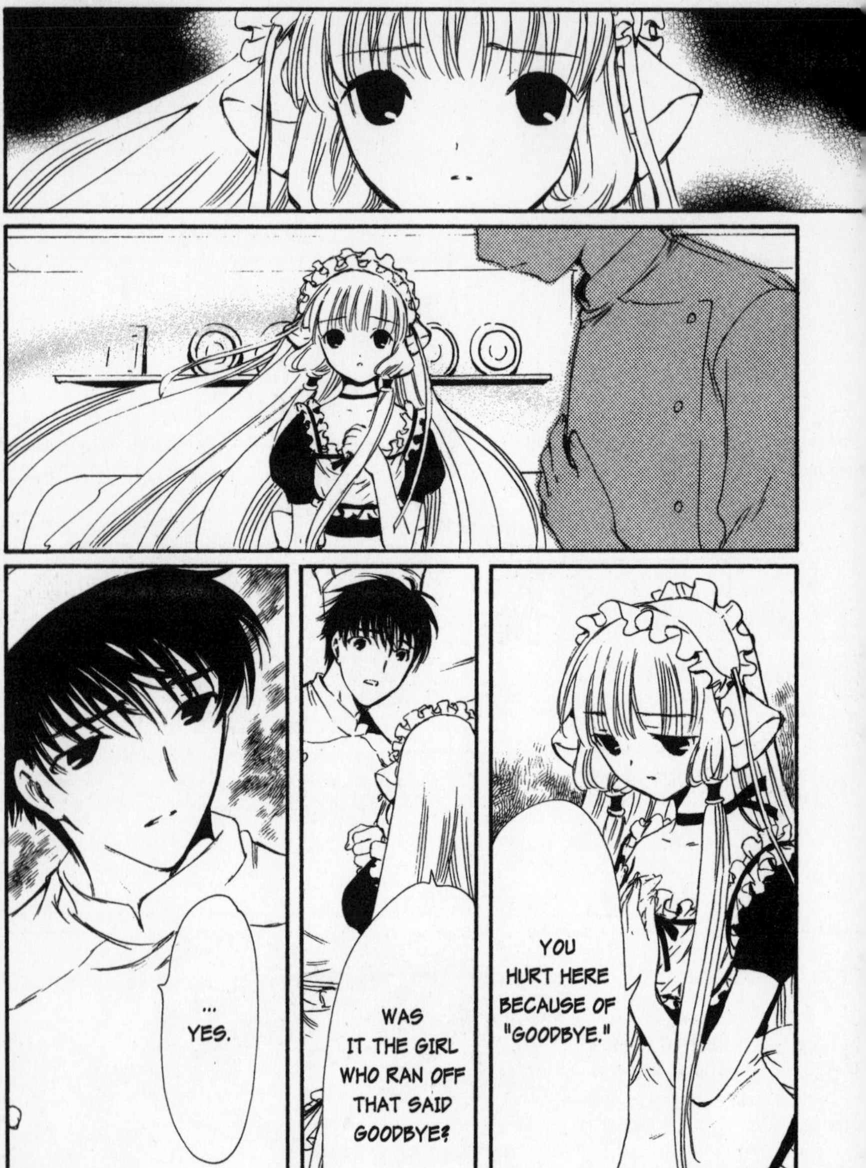
YOU HURT HERE BECAUSE OF "GOODBYE."
WAS IT THE GIRL WHO RAN OFF THAT SAID GOODBYE?
... YES.

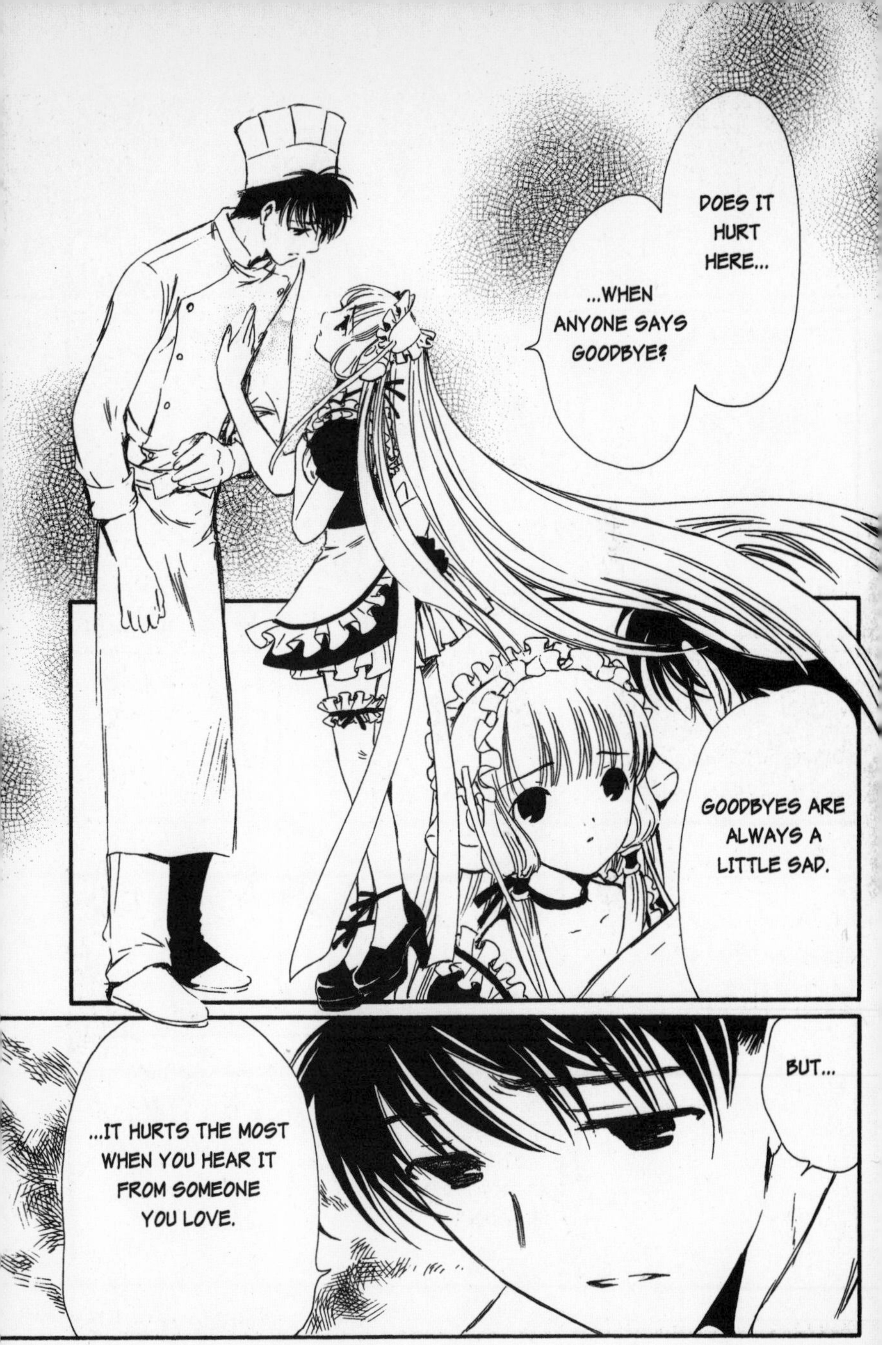
DOES IT HURT HERE...
...WHEN ANYONE SAYS GOODBYE?
GOODBYES ARE ALWAYS A LITTLE SAD.
BUT...
...IT HURTS THE MOST WHEN YOU HEAR IT FROM SOMEONE YOU LOVE.

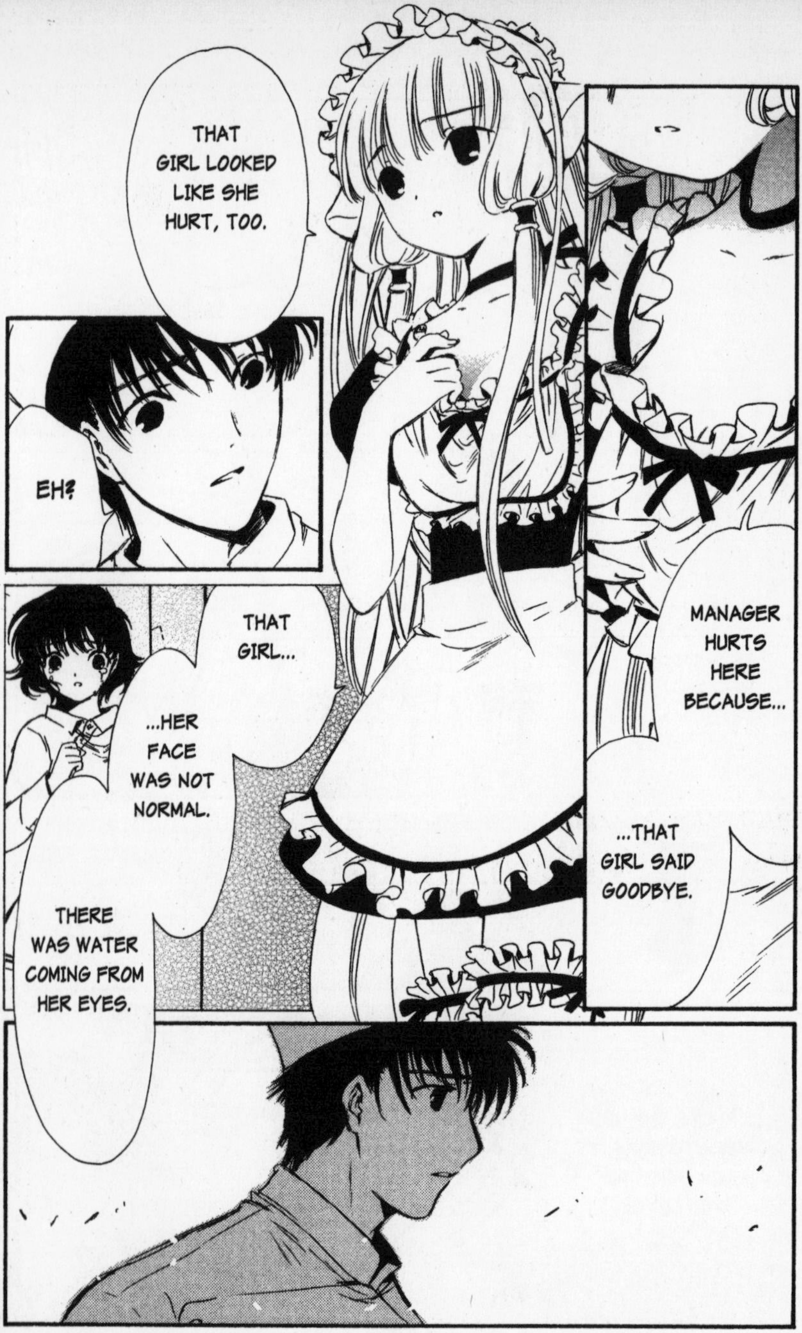
MANAGER HURTS HERE BECAUSE...
...THAT GIRL SAID GOODBYE.
THAT GIRL LOOKED LIKE SHE HURT, TOO.
EH?
THAT GIRL...
...HER FACE WAS NOT NORMAL.
THERE WAS WATER COMING FROM HER EYES.

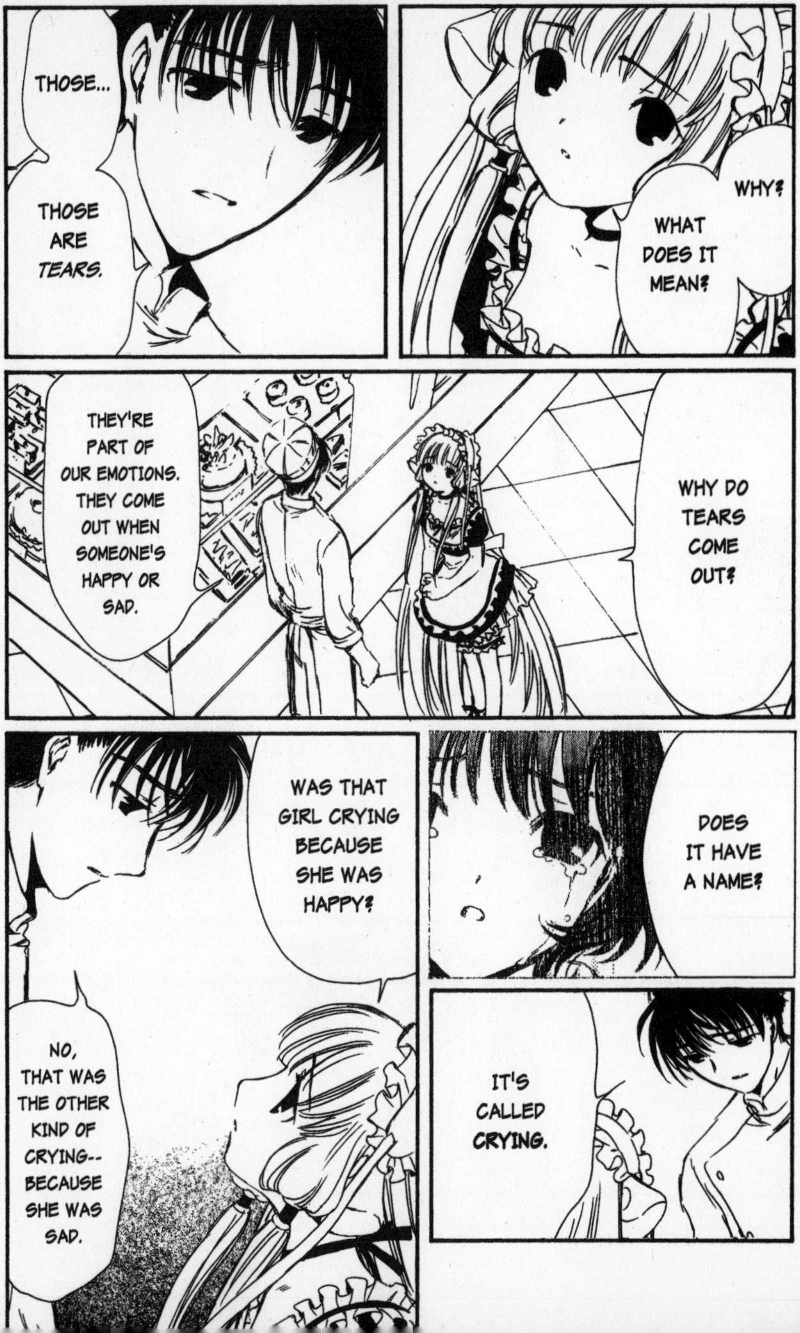
WHY?
WHAT DOES IT MEAN?
THOSE...
THOSE ARE *TEARS.*
WHY DO TEARS COME OUT?
THEY'RE PART OF OUR EMOTIONS. THEY COME OUT WHEN SOMEONE'S HAPPY OR SAD.
DOES IT HAVE A NAME?
IT'S CALLED CRYING.
WAS THAT GIRL CRYING BECAUSE SHE WAS HAPPY?
NO, THAT WAS THE OTHER KIND OF CRYING-- BECAUSE SHE WAS SAD.

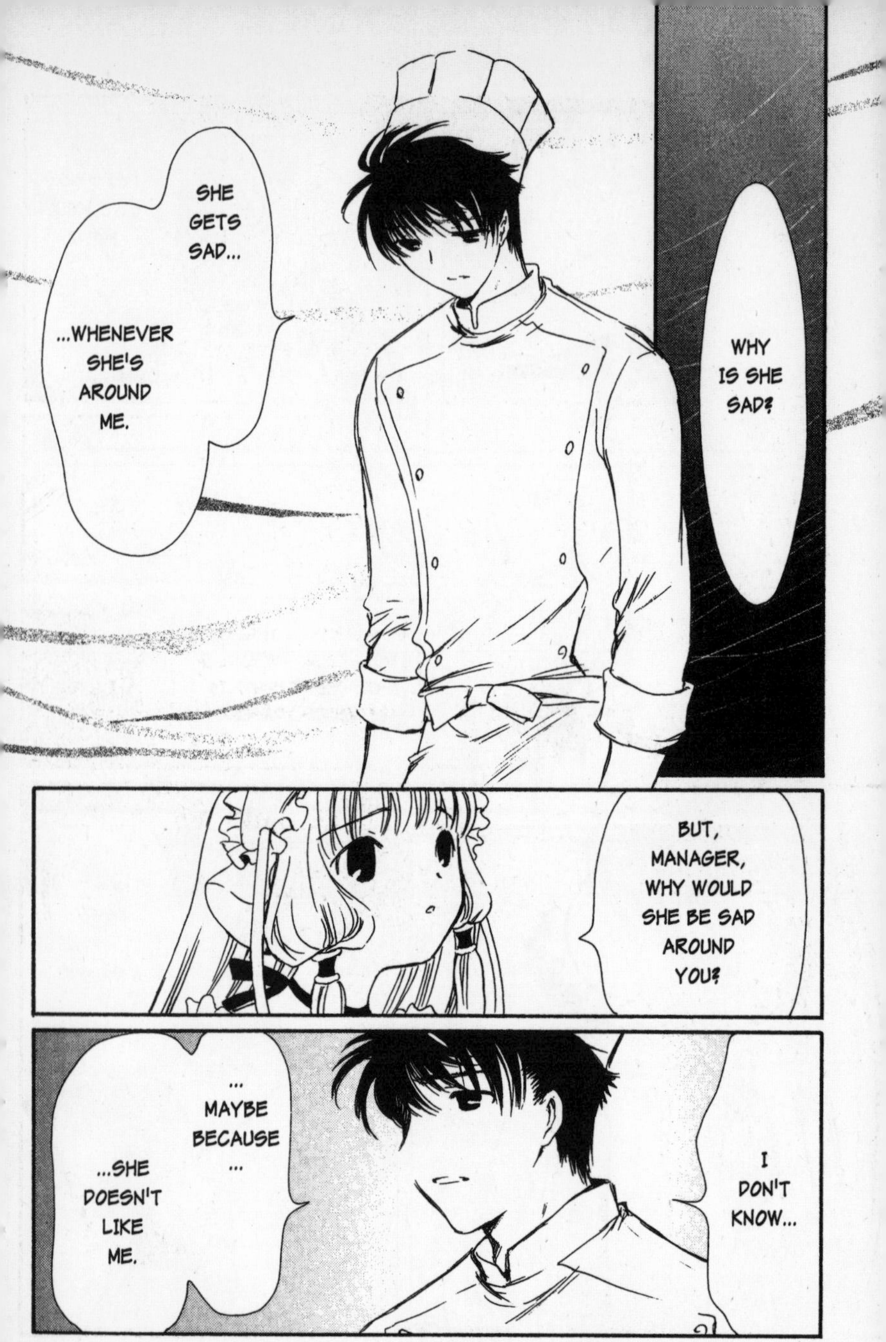
WHY IS SHE SAD?
SHE GETS SAD...
...WHENEVER SHE'S AROUND ME.
BUT, MANAGER, WHY WOULD SHE BE SAD AROUND YOU?
I DON'T KNOW...
... MAYBE BECAUSE ...
...SHE DOESN'T LIKE ME.

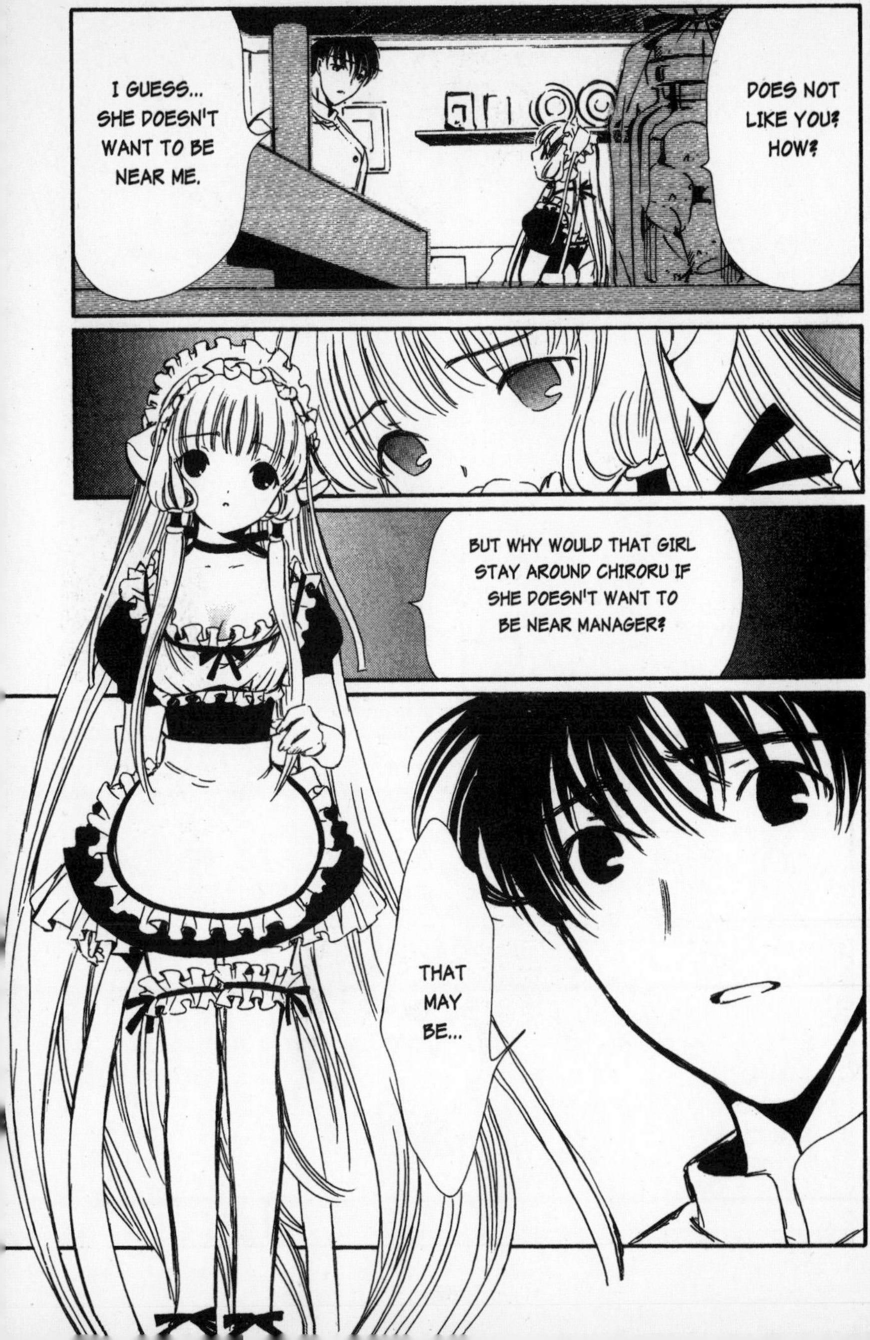
DOES NOT LIKE YOU? HOW?
I GUESS... SHE DOESN'T WANT TO BE NEAR ME.
BUT WHY WOULD THAT GIRL STAY AROUND CHIRORU IF SHE DOESN'T WANT TO BE NEAR MANAGER?
THAT MAY BE...

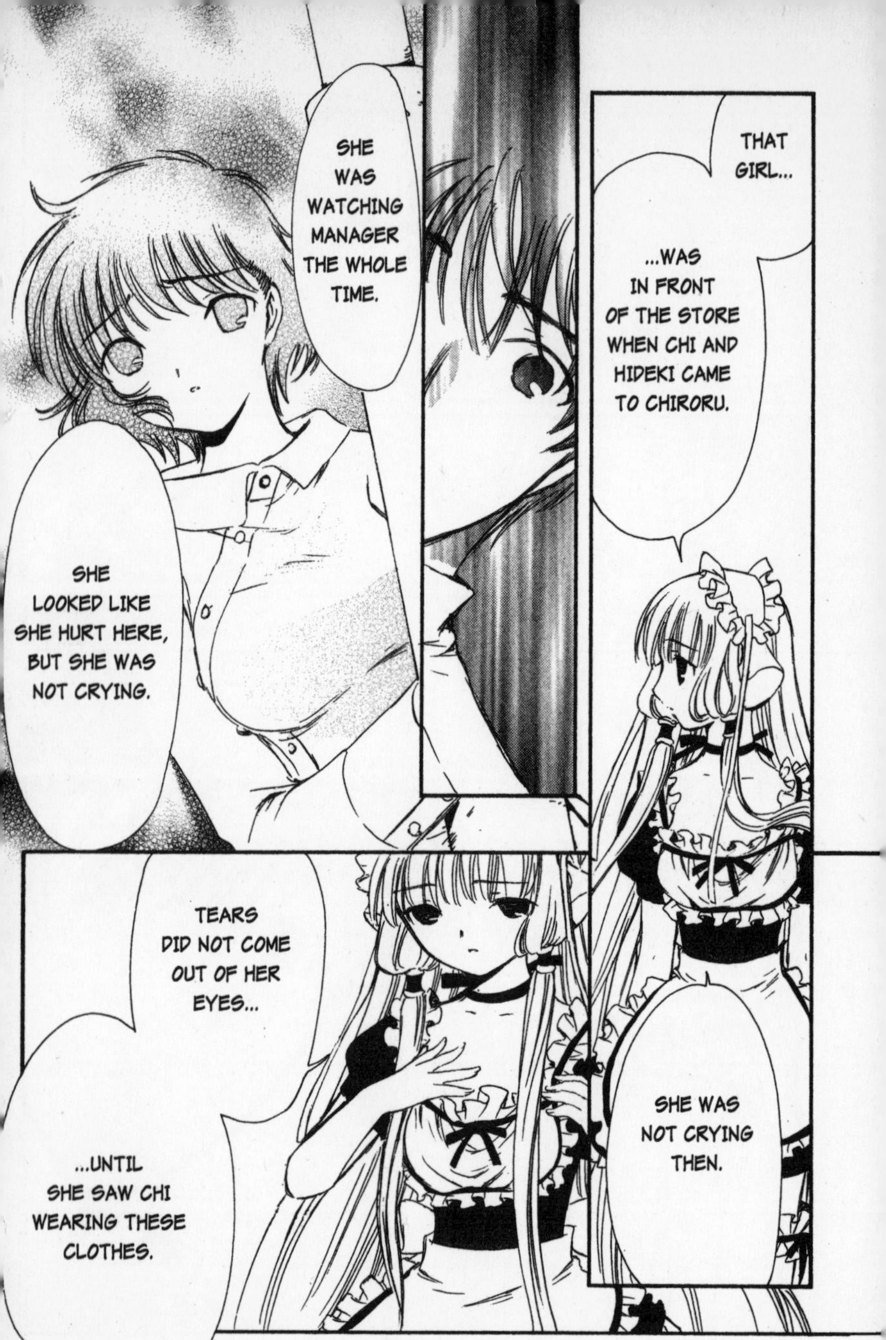
THAT GIRL...
...WAS IN FRONT OF THE STORE WHEN CHI AND HIDEKI CAME TO CHIRORU.
SHE WAS NOT CRYING THEN.
SHE WAS WATCHING MANAGER THE WHOLE TIME.
SHE LOOKED LIKE SHE HURT HERE, BUT SHE WAS NOT CRYING.
TEARS DID NOT COME OUT OF HER EYES...
...UNTIL SHE SAW CHI WEARING THESE CLOTHES.

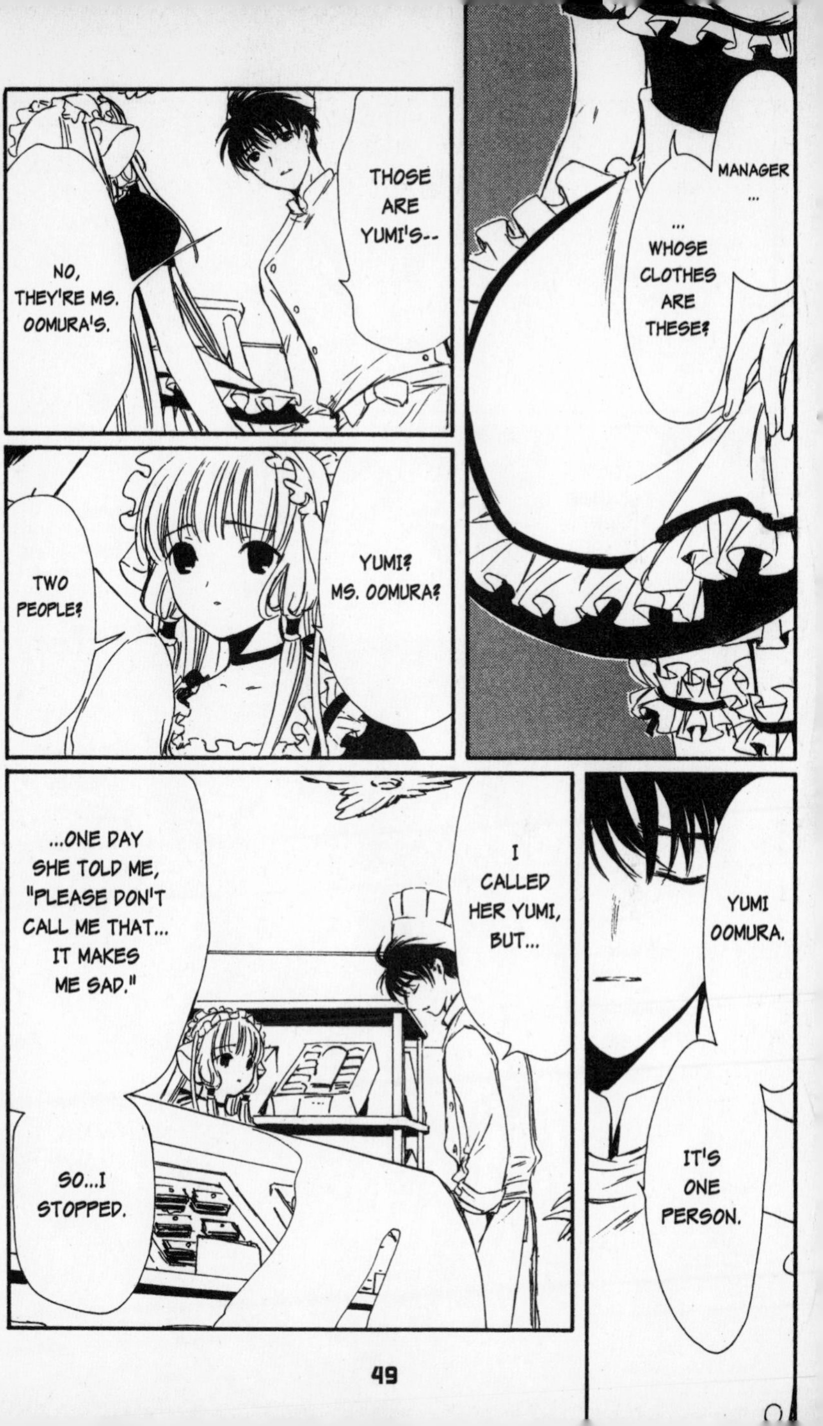
MANAGER ...
... WHOSE CLOTHES ARE THESE?
THOSE ARE YUMI'S--
NO, THEY'RE MS. OOMURA'S.
YUMI? MS. OOMURA?
TWO PEOPLE?
YUMI OOMURA.
IT'S ONE PERSON.
I CALLED HER YUMI, BUT...
...ONE DAY SHE TOLD ME, "PLEASE DON'T CALL ME THAT... IT MAKES ME SAD."
SO...I STOPPED.

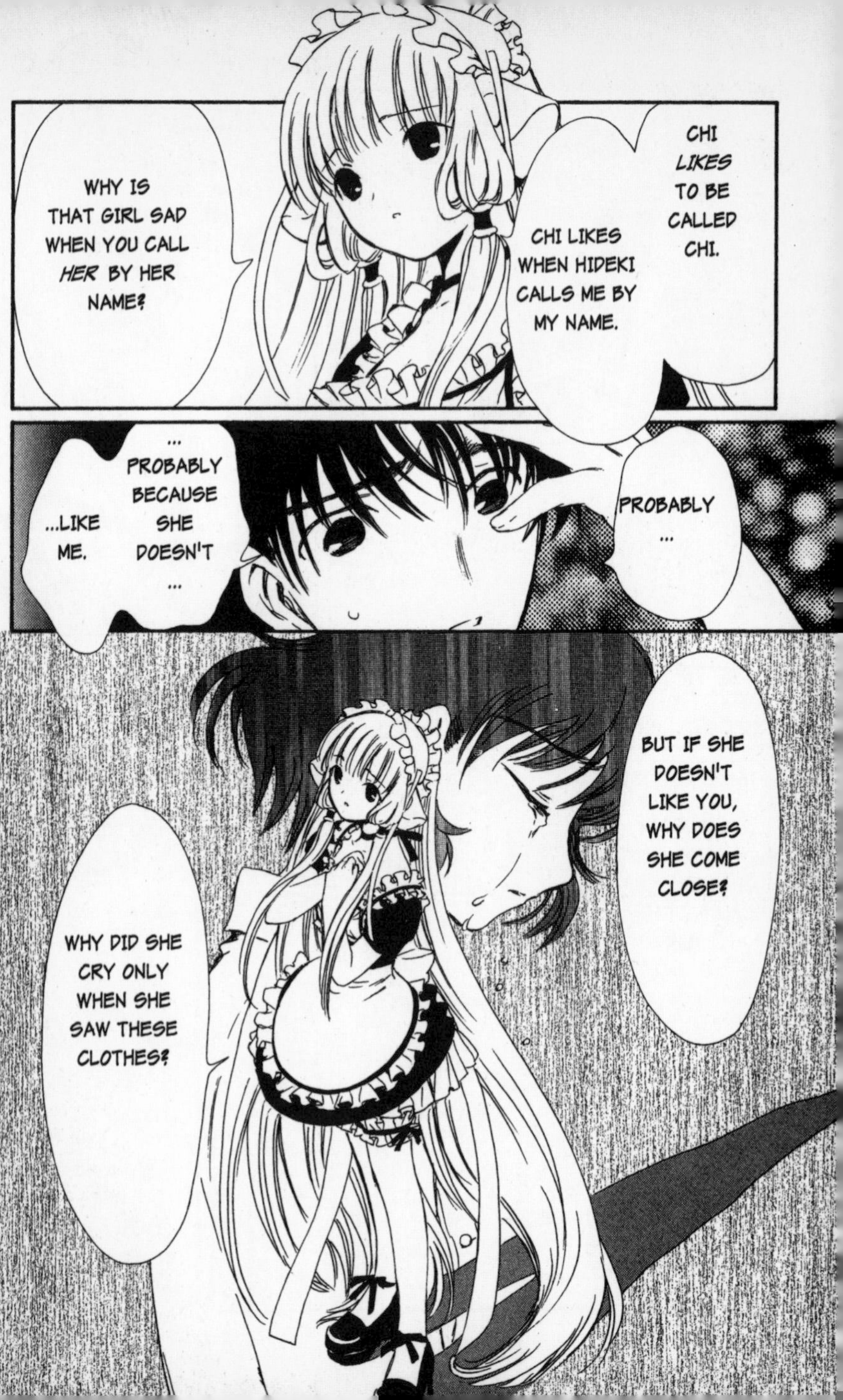
CHI *LIKES* TO BE CALLED CHI.
CHI LIKES WHEN HIDEKI CALLS ME BY MY NAME.
WHY IS THAT GIRL SAD WHEN YOU CALL *HER* BY HER NAME?
PROBABLY ...
... PROBABLY BECAUSE SHE DOESN'T ...
...LIKE ME.
BUT IF SHE DOESN'T LIKE YOU, WHY DOES SHE COME CLOSE?
WHY DID SHE CRY ONLY WHEN SHE SAW THESE CLOTHES?

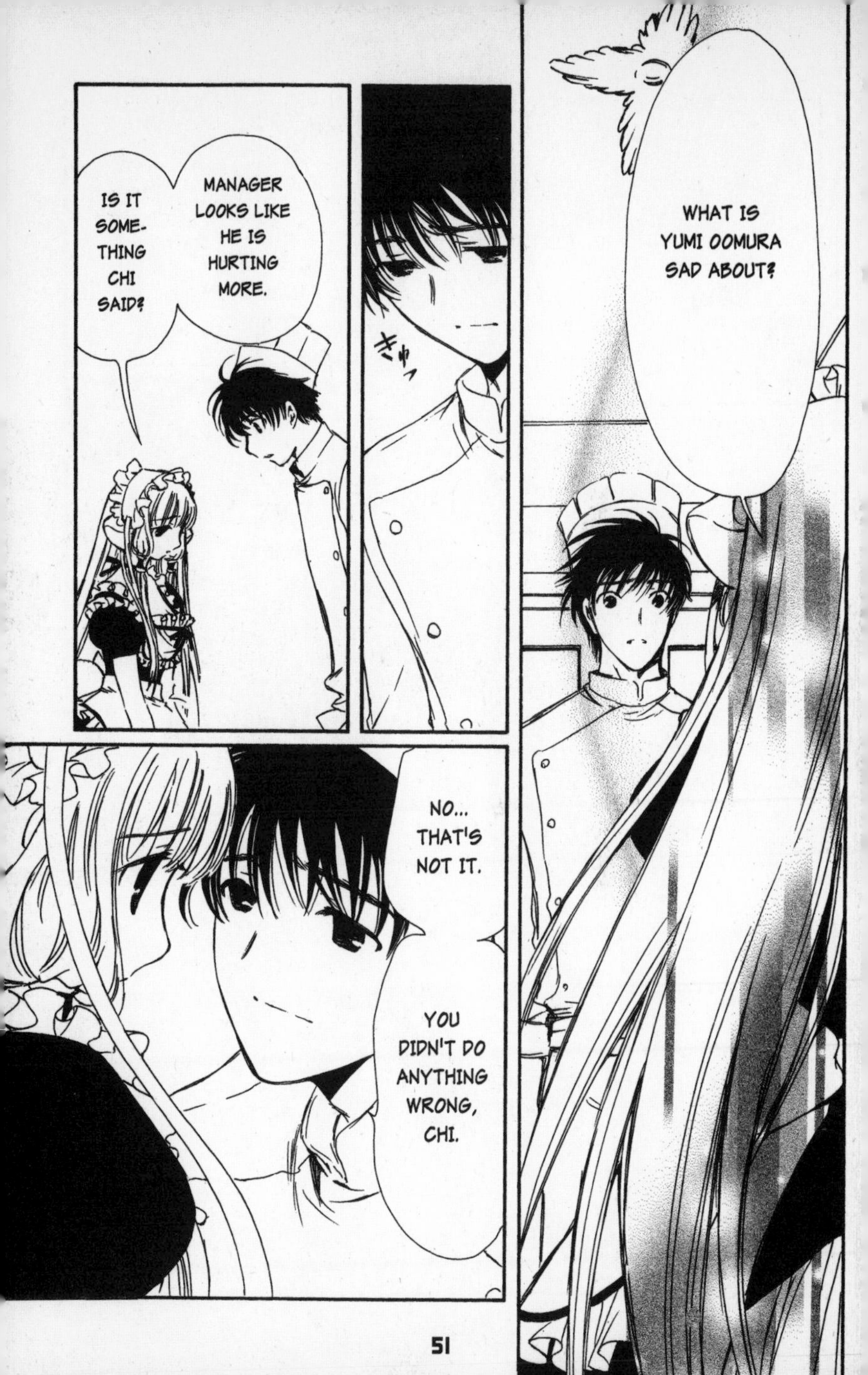
WHAT IS YUMI OOMURA SAD ABOUT?
きゅっ
MANAGER LOOKS LIKE HE IS HURTING MORE.
IS IT SOME-THING CHI SAID?
NO... THAT'S NOT IT.
YOU DIDN'T DO ANYTHING WRONG, CHI.

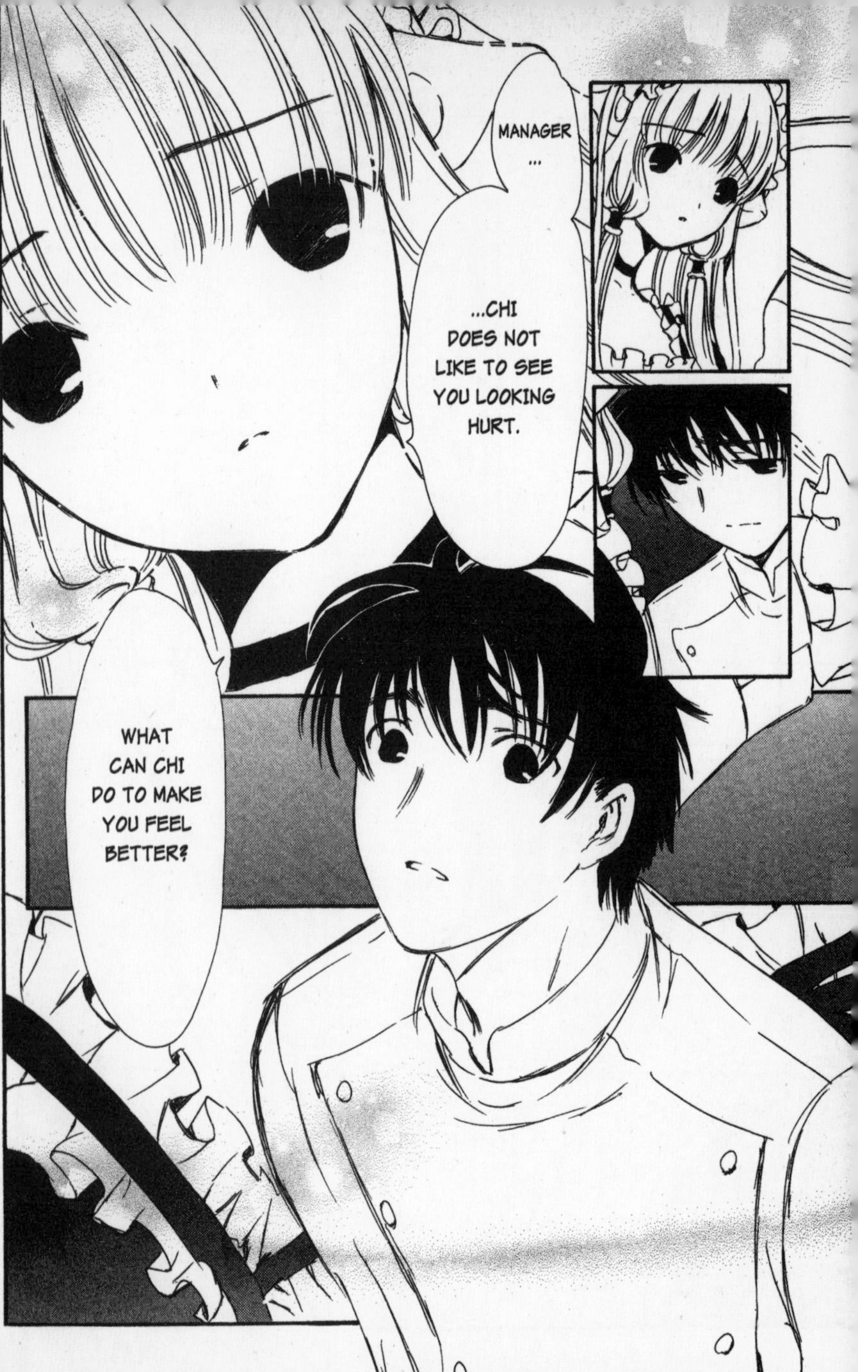
MANAGER ...
...CHI DOES NOT LIKE TO SEE YOU LOOKING HURT.
WHAT CAN CHI DO TO MAKE YOU FEEL BETTER?

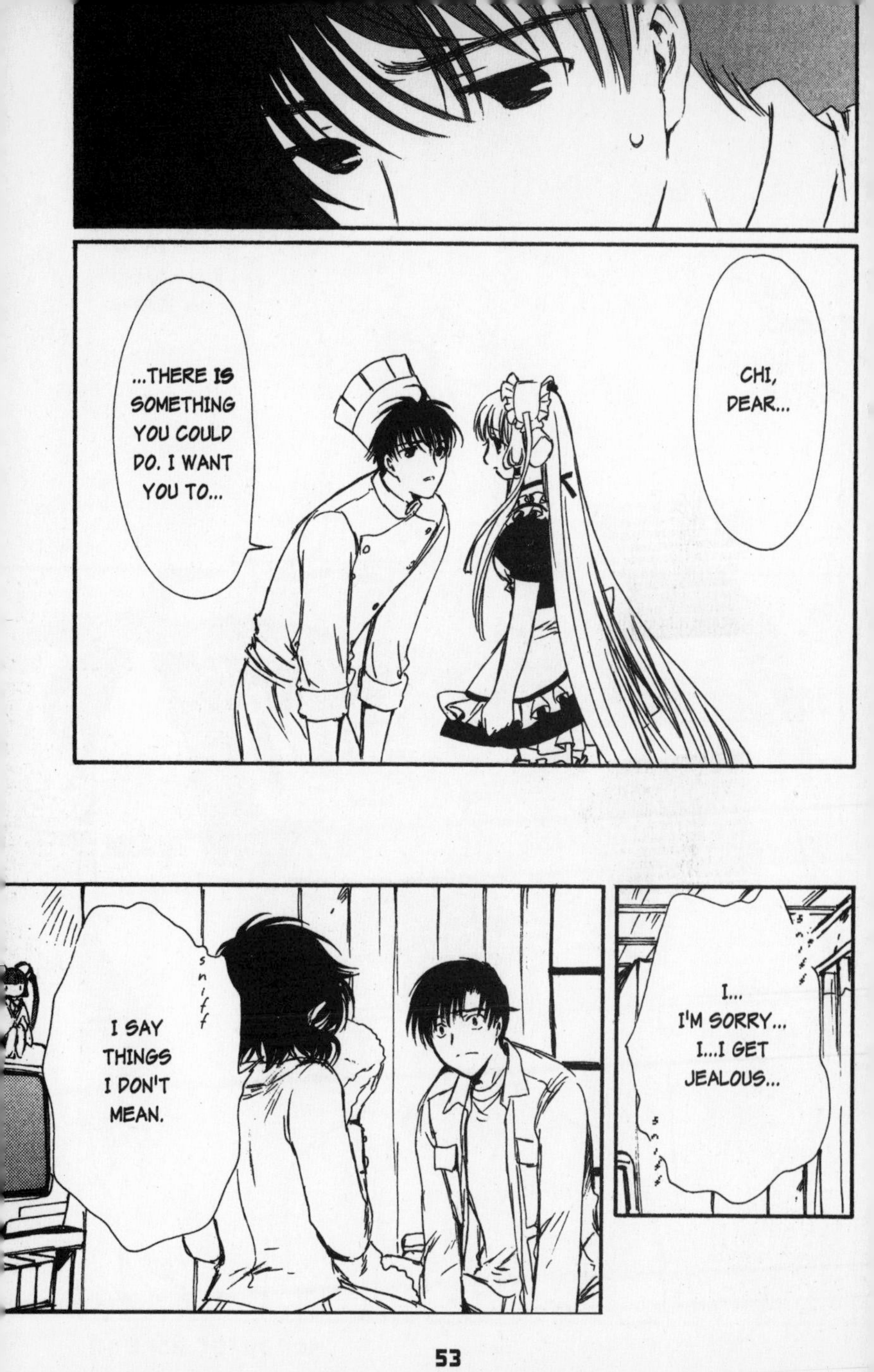
CHI, DEAR...
...THERE IS SOMETHING YOU COULD DO. I WANT YOU TO...
I... I'M SORRY... I...I GET JEALOUS...
sniff
I SAY THINGS I DON'T MEAN.

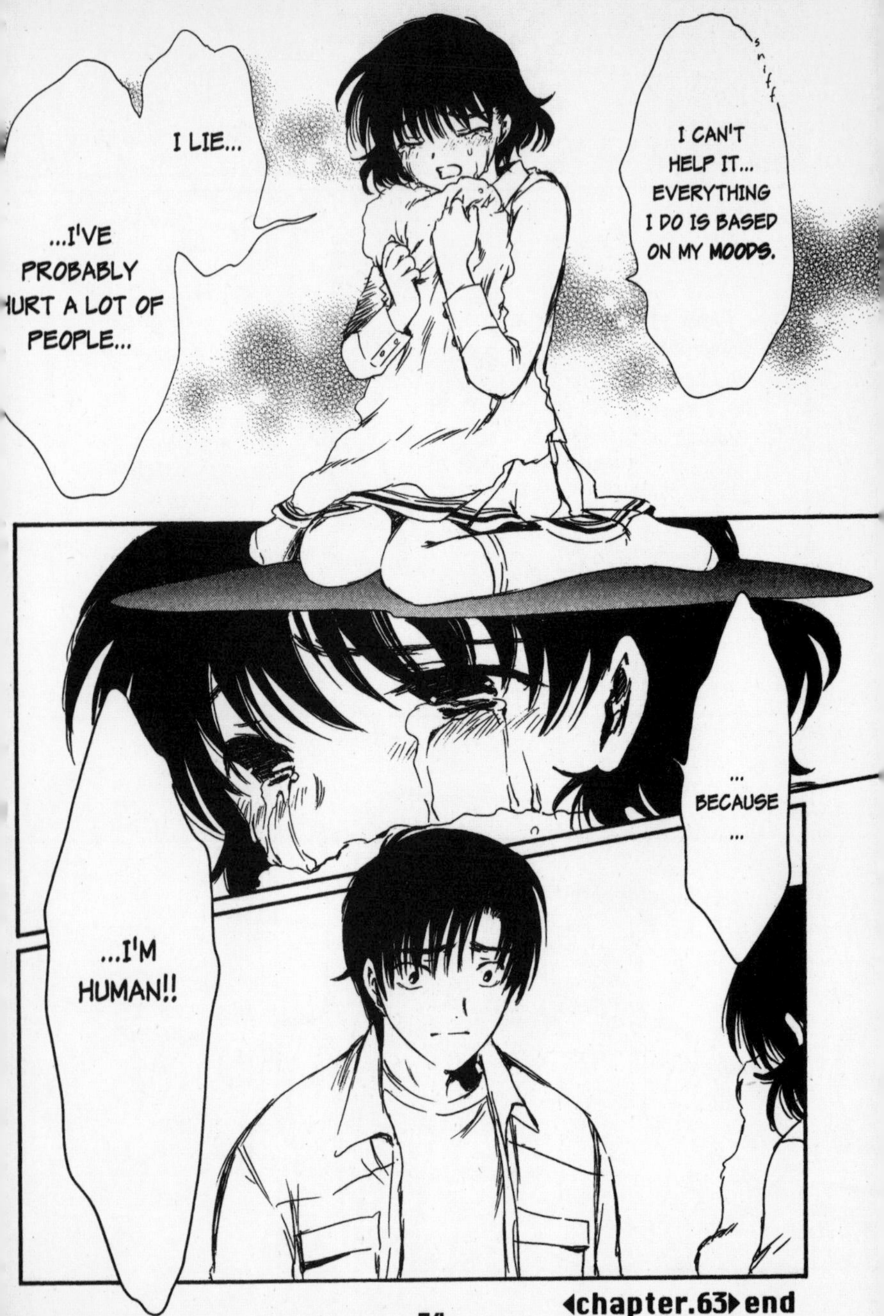
sniff
I CAN'T HELP IT... EVERYTHING I DO IS BASED ON MY MOODS.
I LIE...
...I'VE PROBABLY HURT A LOT OF PEOPLE...
... BECAUSE ...
...I'M HUMAN!!

<chapter.63> end

ちょびっツ

Chobits

◀chapter.64▶

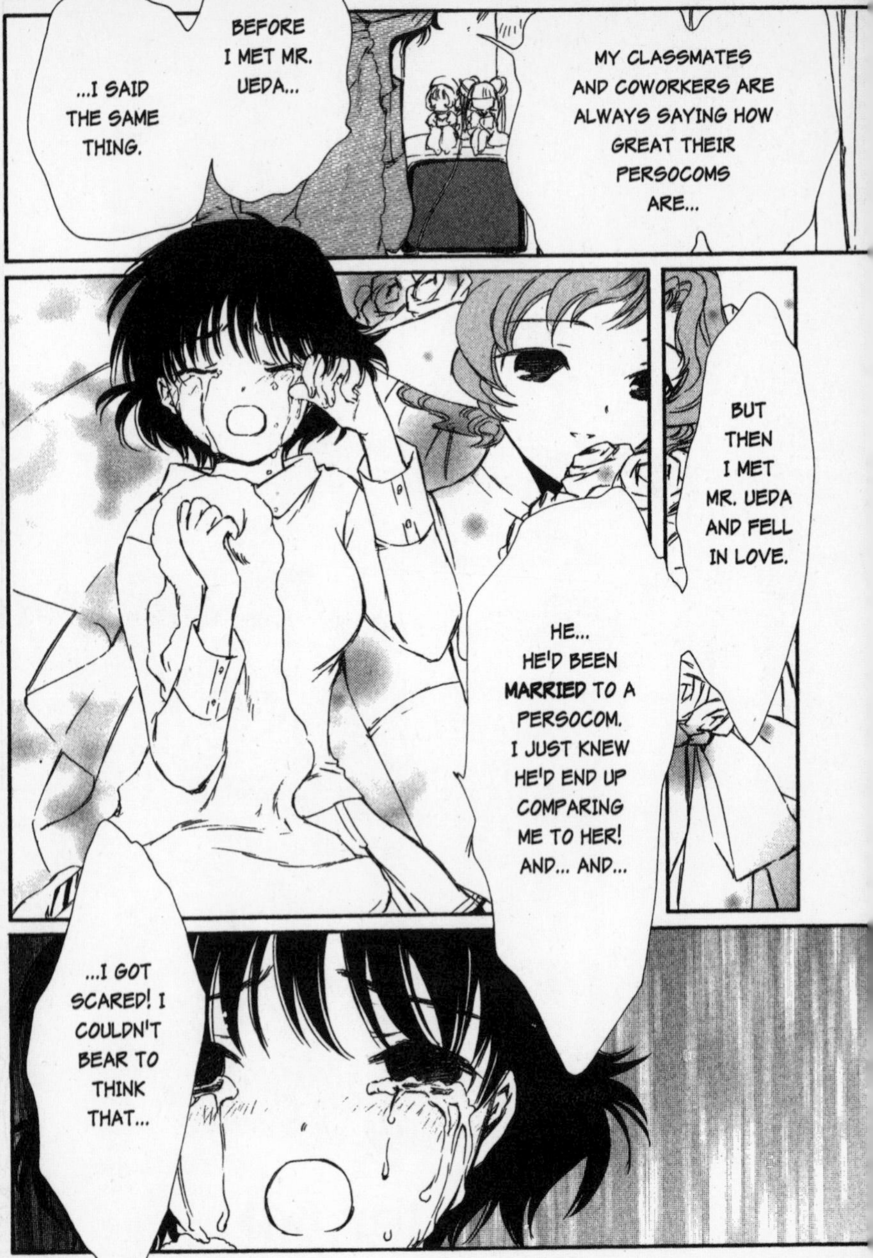
MY CLASSMATES AND COWORKERS ARE ALWAYS SAYING HOW GREAT THEIR PERSOCOMS ARE...
BEFORE I MET MR. UEDA...
...I SAID THE SAME THING.
BUT THEN I MET MR. UEDA AND FELL IN LOVE.
HE... HE'D BEEN **MARRIED** TO A PERSOCOM. I JUST KNEW HE'D END UP COMPARING ME TO HER! AND... AND...
...I GOT SCARED! I COULDN'T BEAR TO THINK THAT...

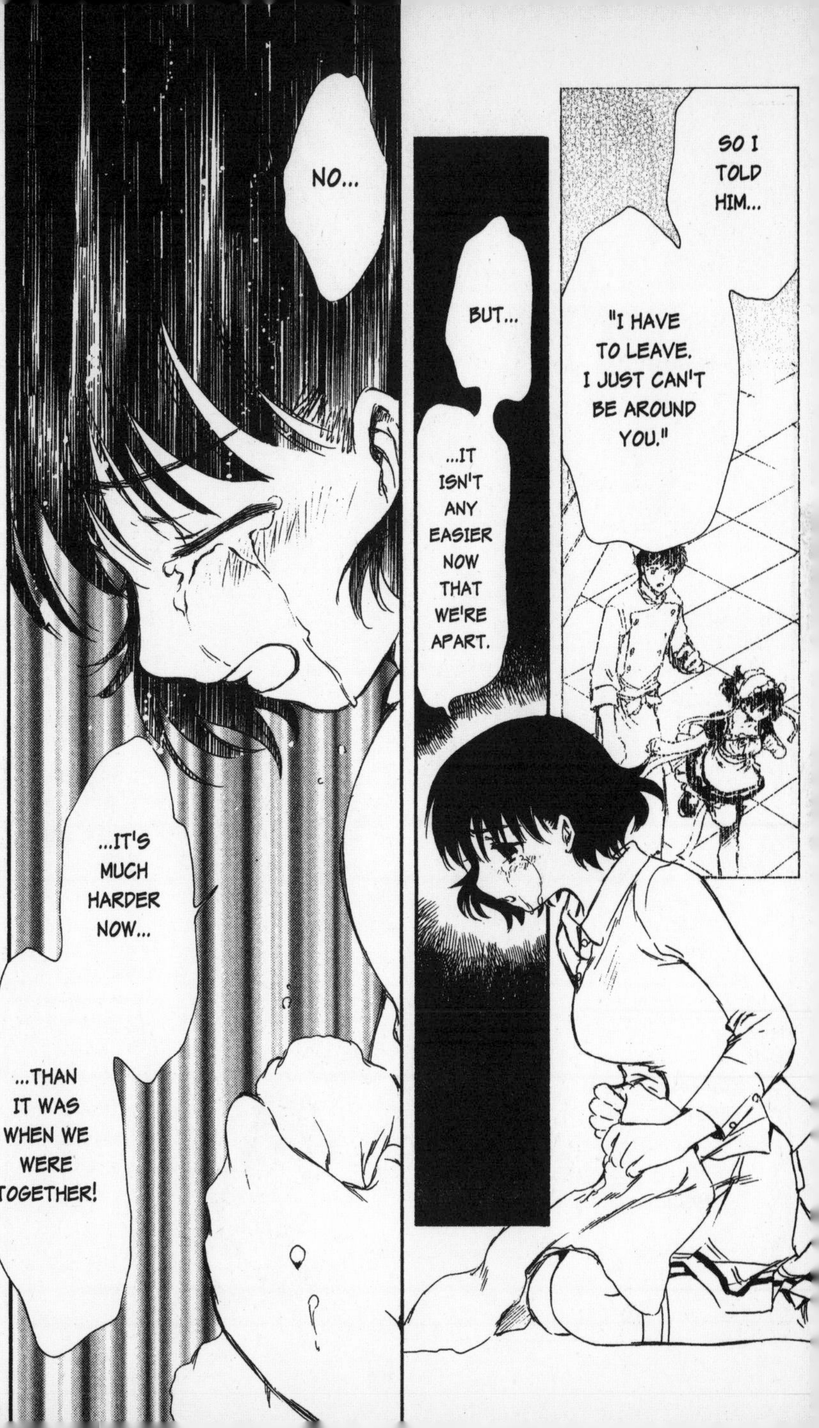
SO I TOLD HIM...
"I HAVE TO LEAVE. I JUST CAN'T BE AROUND YOU."
BUT...
...IT ISN'T ANY EASIER NOW THAT WE'RE APART.
NO...
...IT'S MUCH HARDER NOW...
...THAN IT WAS WHEN WE WERE TOGETHER!

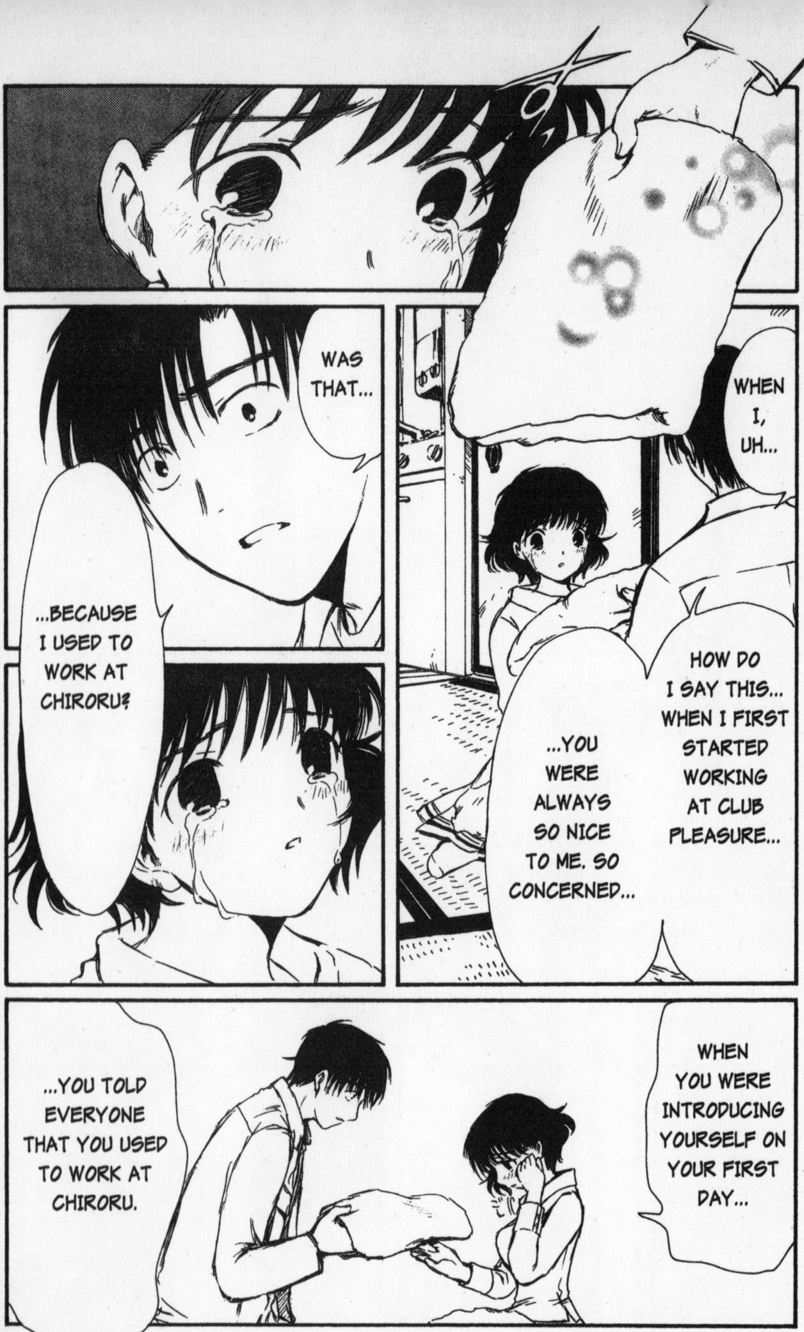
WHEN I, UH...
HOW DO I SAY THIS... WHEN I FIRST STARTED WORKING AT CLUB PLEASURE...
...YOU WERE ALWAYS SO NICE TO ME. SO CONCERNED...
WAS THAT...
...BECAUSE I USED TO WORK AT CHIRORU?
WHEN YOU WERE INTRODUCING YOURSELF ON YOUR FIRST DAY...
...YOU TOLD EVERYONE THAT YOU USED TO WORK AT CHIRORU.

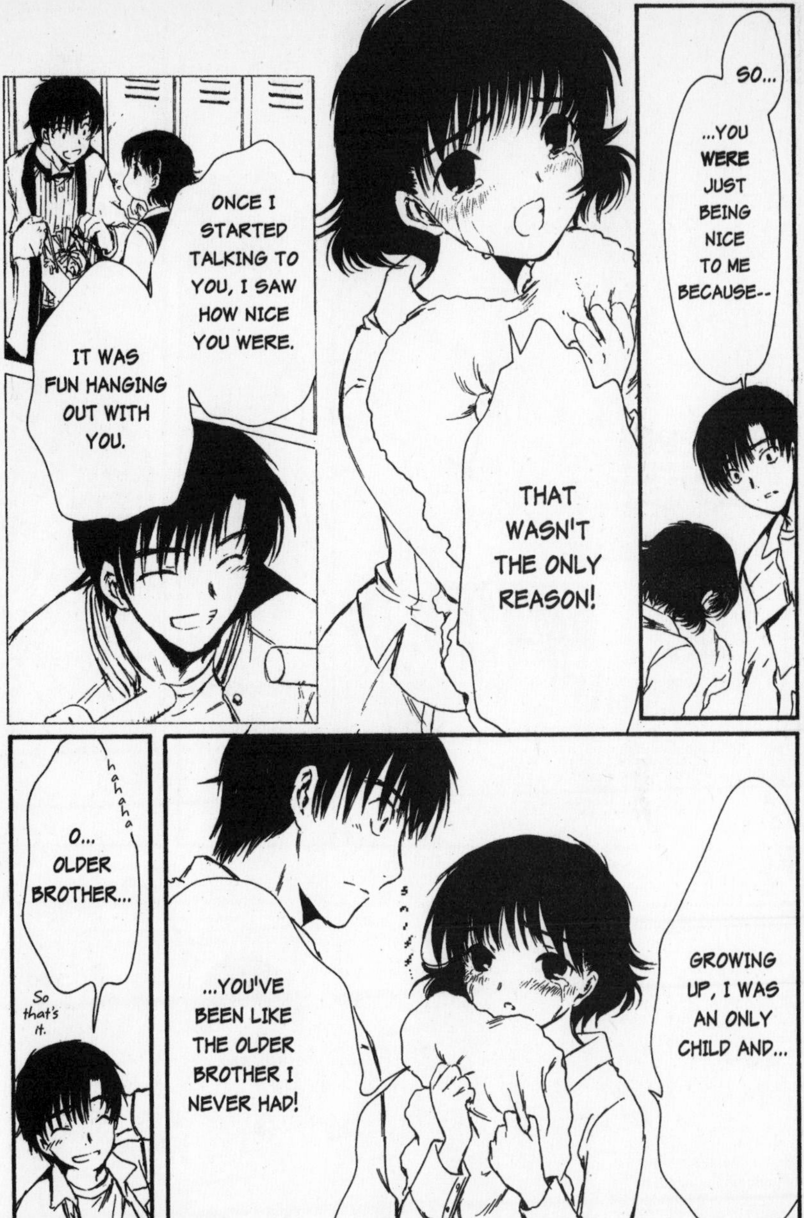

SO...
...YOU WERE JUST BEING NICE TO ME BECAUSE--
THAT WASN'T THE ONLY REASON!
ONCE I STARTED TALKING TO YOU, I SAW HOW NICE YOU WERE.
IT WAS FUN HANGING OUT WITH YOU.
GROWING UP, I WAS AN ONLY CHILD AND...
...YOU'VE BEEN LIKE THE OLDER BROTHER I NEVER HAD!
hahaha
O... OLDER BROTHER...
So that's it.

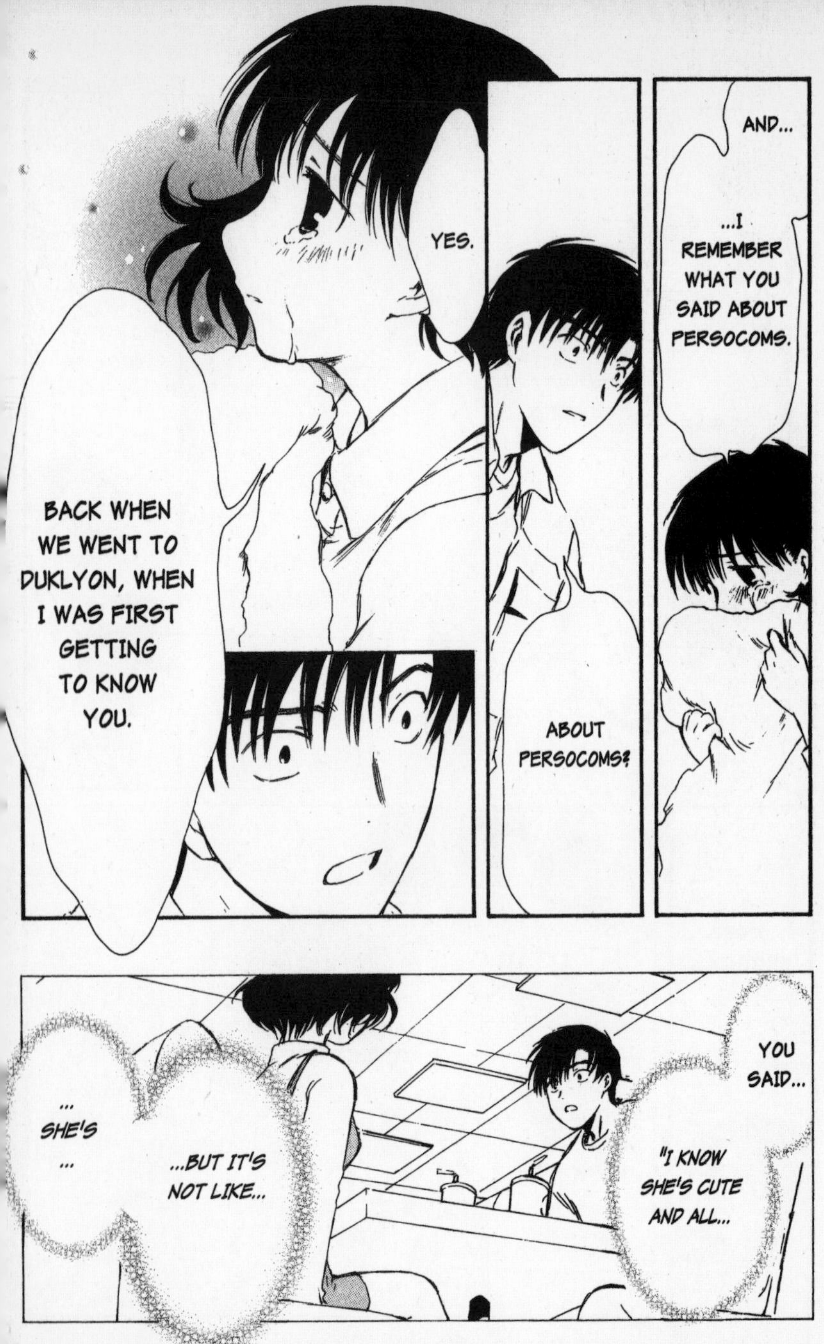
AND...
...I REMEMBER WHAT YOU SAID ABOUT PERSOCOMS.
ABOUT PERSOCOMS?
YES.
BACK WHEN WE WENT TO DUKLYON, WHEN I WAS FIRST GETTING TO KNOW YOU.
YOU SAID...
"I KNOW SHE'S CUTE AND ALL...
...BUT IT'S NOT LIKE...
... SHE'S ...

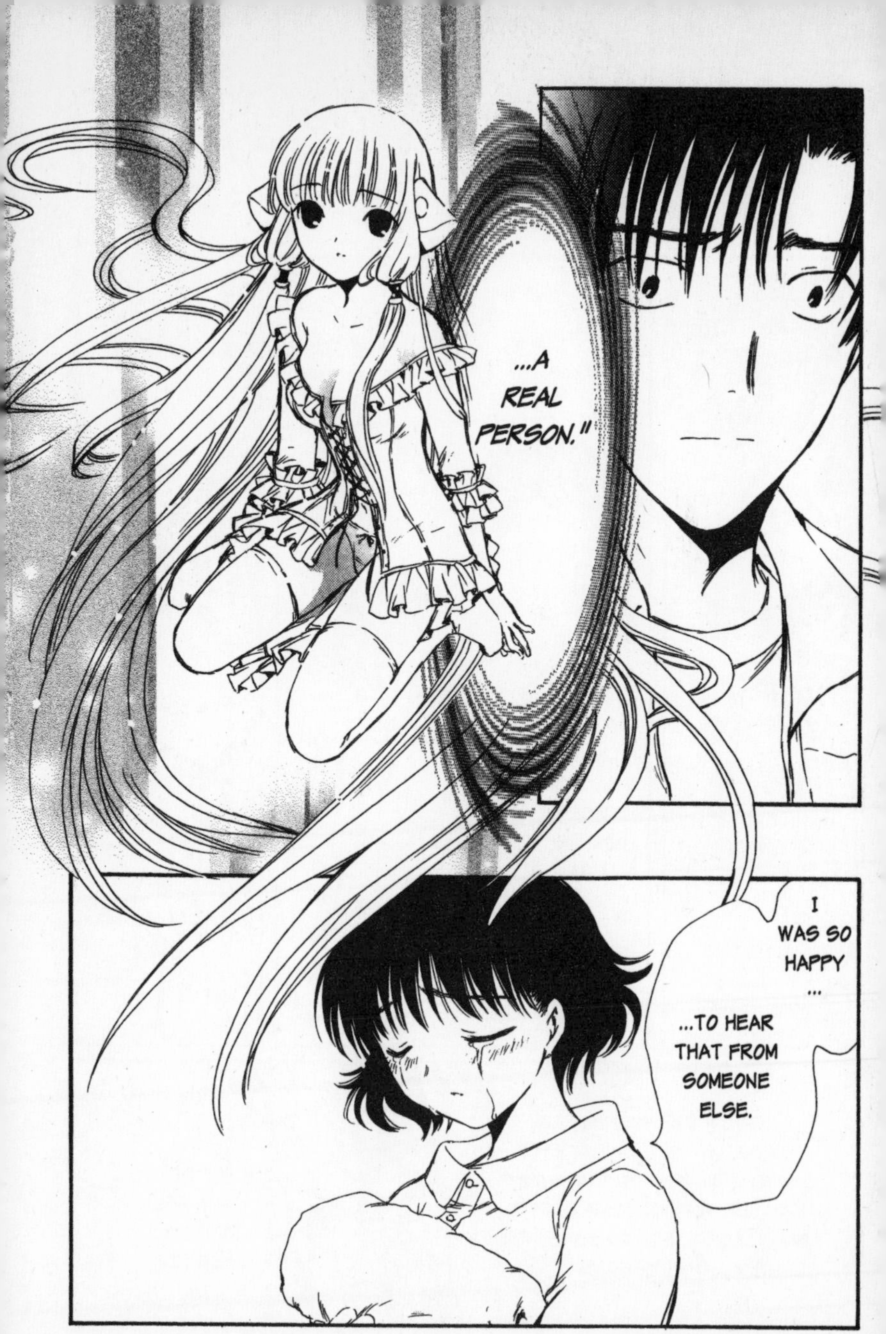
...A REAL PERSON."
I WAS SO HAPPY ...
...TO HEAR THAT FROM SOMEONE ELSE.

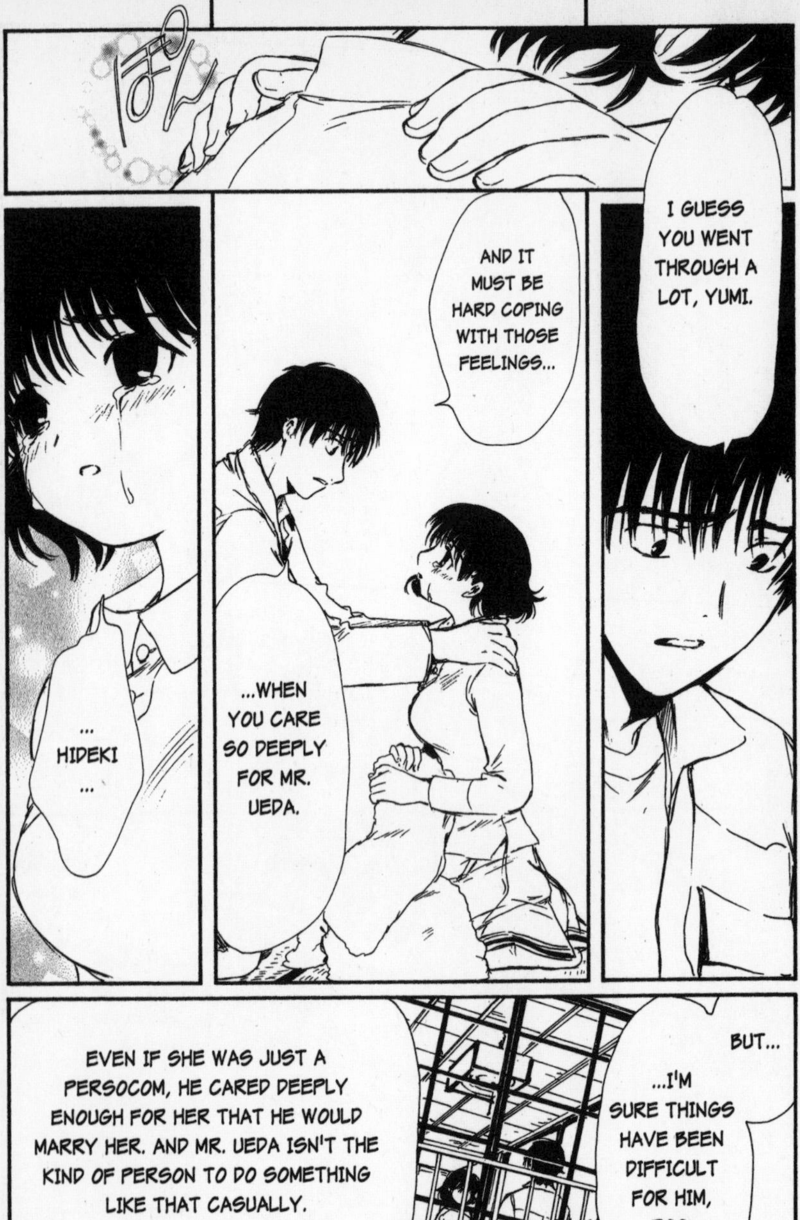
ぽん
I GUESS YOU WENT THROUGH A LOT, YUMI.
AND IT MUST BE HARD COPING WITH THOSE FEELINGS...
...WHEN YOU CARE SO DEEPLY FOR MR. UEDA.
... HIDEKI ...
BUT...
...I'M SURE THINGS HAVE BEEN DIFFICULT FOR HIM, TOO.
EVEN IF SHE WAS JUST A PERSOCOM, HE CARED DEEPLY ENOUGH FOR HER THAT HE WOULD MARRY HER. AND MR. UEDA ISN'T THE KIND OF PERSON TO DO SOMETHING LIKE THAT CASUALLY.

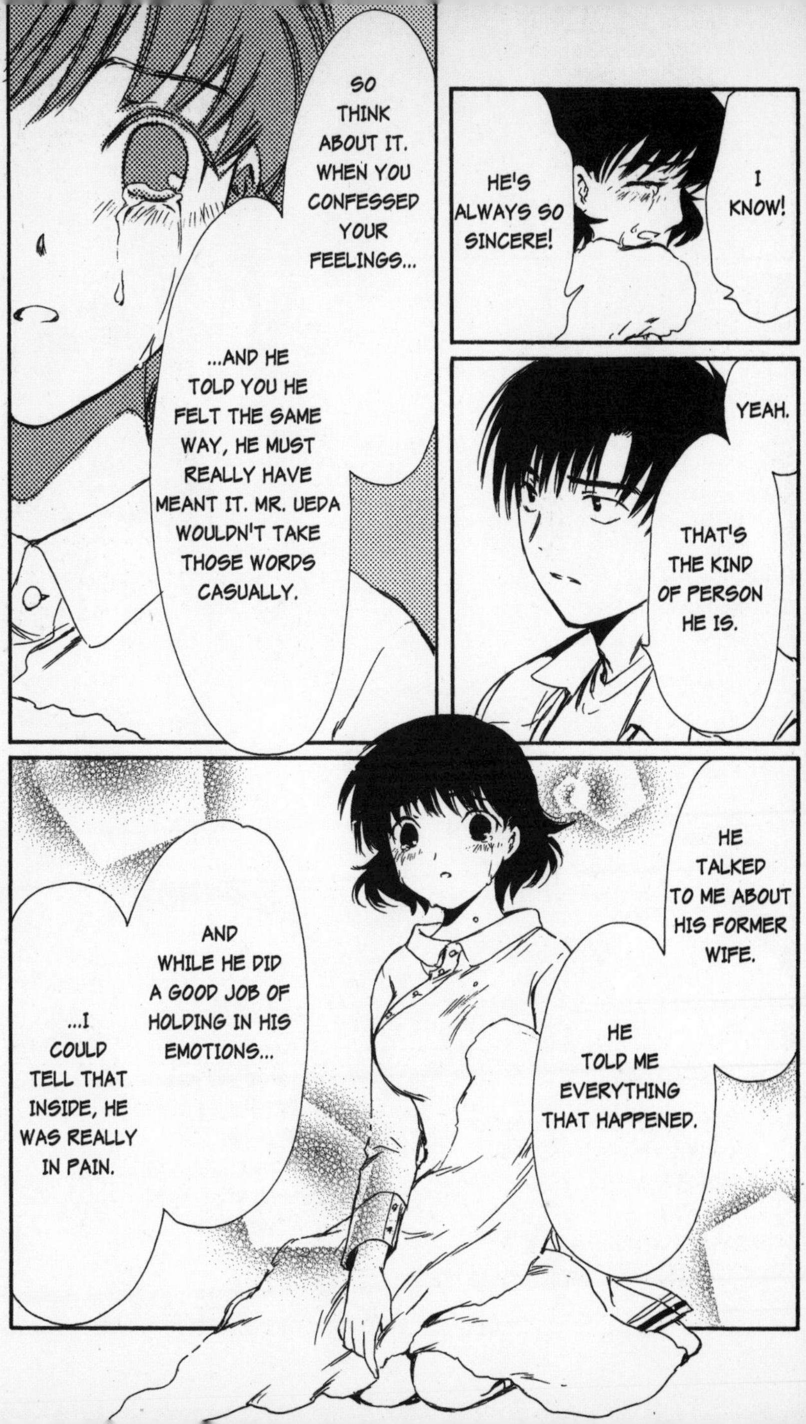
I KNOW!
HE'S ALWAYS SO SINCERE!
YEAH.
THAT'S THE KIND OF PERSON HE IS.
SO THINK ABOUT IT. WHEN YOU CONFESSED YOUR FEELINGS...
...AND HE TOLD YOU HE FELT THE SAME WAY, HE MUST REALLY HAVE MEANT IT. MR. UEDA WOULDN'T TAKE THOSE WORDS CASUALLY.
HE TALKED TO ME ABOUT HIS FORMER WIFE.
HE TOLD ME EVERYTHING THAT HAPPENED.
AND WHILE HE DID A GOOD JOB OF HOLDING IN HIS EMOTIONS...
...I COULD TELL THAT INSIDE, HE WAS REALLY IN PAIN.

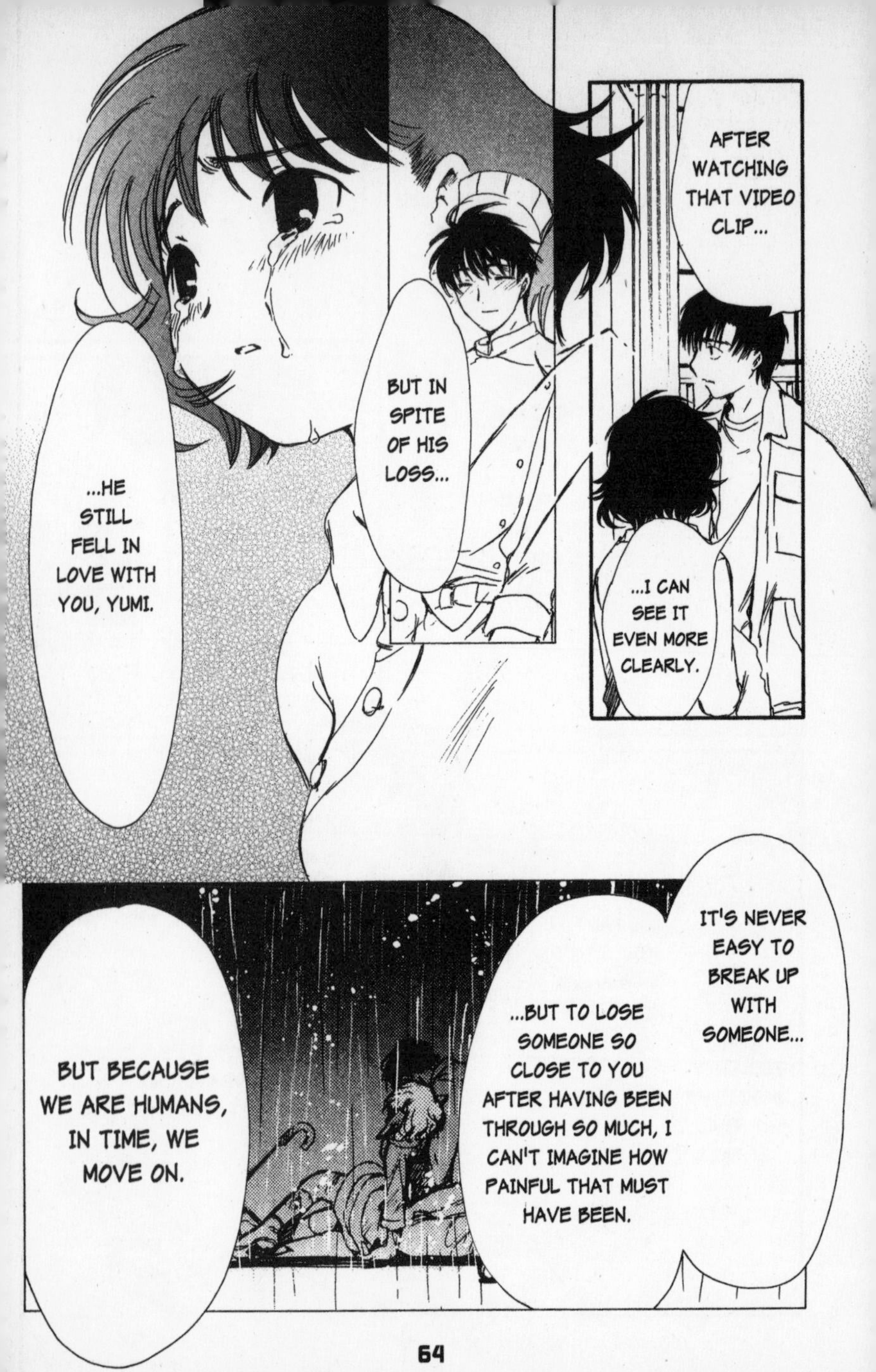
AFTER WATCHING THAT VIDEO CLIP...
...I CAN SEE IT EVEN MORE CLEARLY.
BUT IN SPITE OF HIS LOSS...
...HE STILL FELL IN LOVE WITH YOU, YUMI.
IT'S NEVER EASY TO BREAK UP WITH SOMEONE...
...BUT TO LOSE SOMEONE SO CLOSE TO YOU AFTER HAVING BEEN THROUGH SO MUCH, I CAN'T IMAGINE HOW PAINFUL THAT MUST HAVE BEEN.
BUT BECAUSE WE ARE HUMANS, IN TIME, WE MOVE ON.

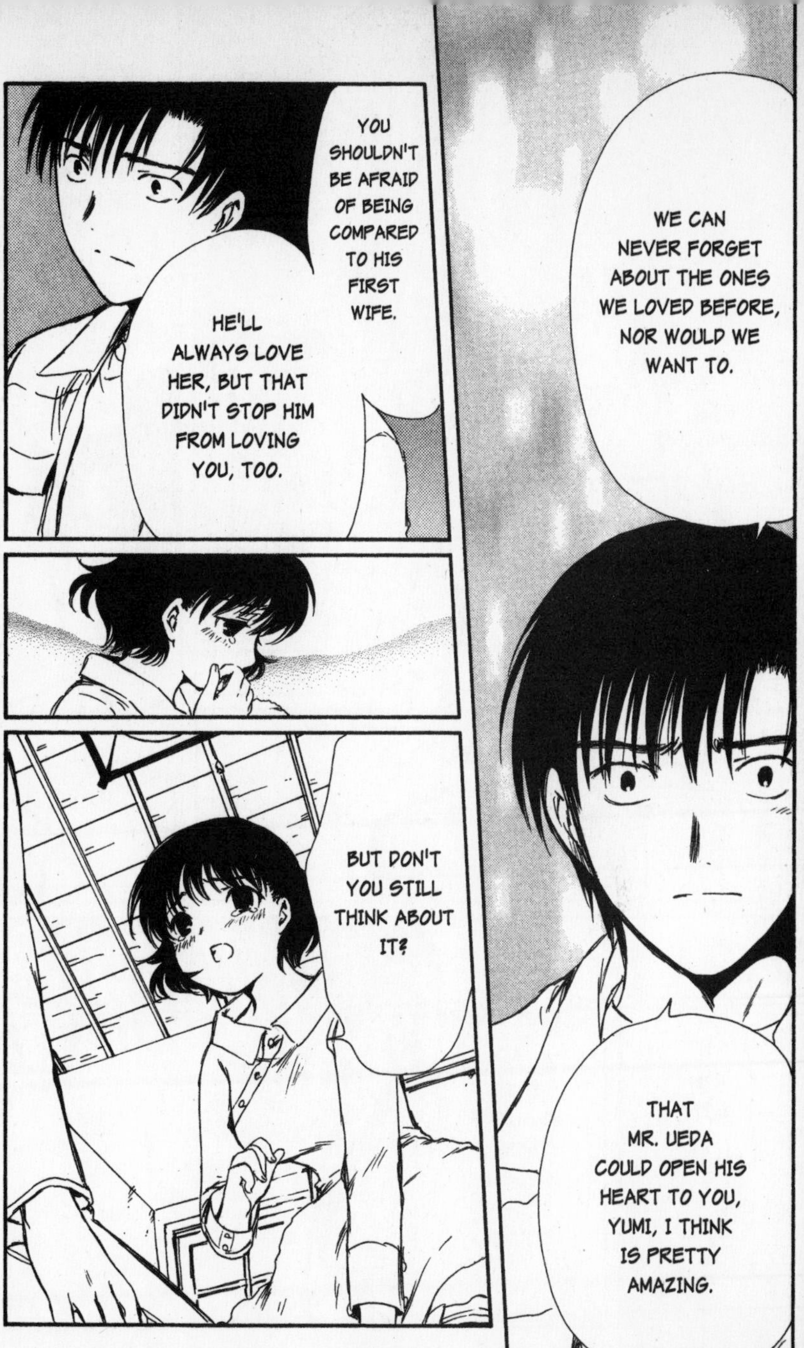
YOU SHOULDN'T BE AFRAID OF BEING COMPARED TO HIS FIRST WIFE.
HE'LL ALWAYS LOVE HER, BUT THAT DIDN'T STOP HIM FROM LOVING YOU, TOO.
BUT DON'T YOU STILL THINK ABOUT IT?
WE CAN NEVER FORGET ABOUT THE ONES WE LOVED BEFORE, NOR WOULD WE WANT TO.
THAT MR. UEDA COULD OPEN HIS HEART TO YOU, YUMI, I THINK IS PRETTY AMAZING.

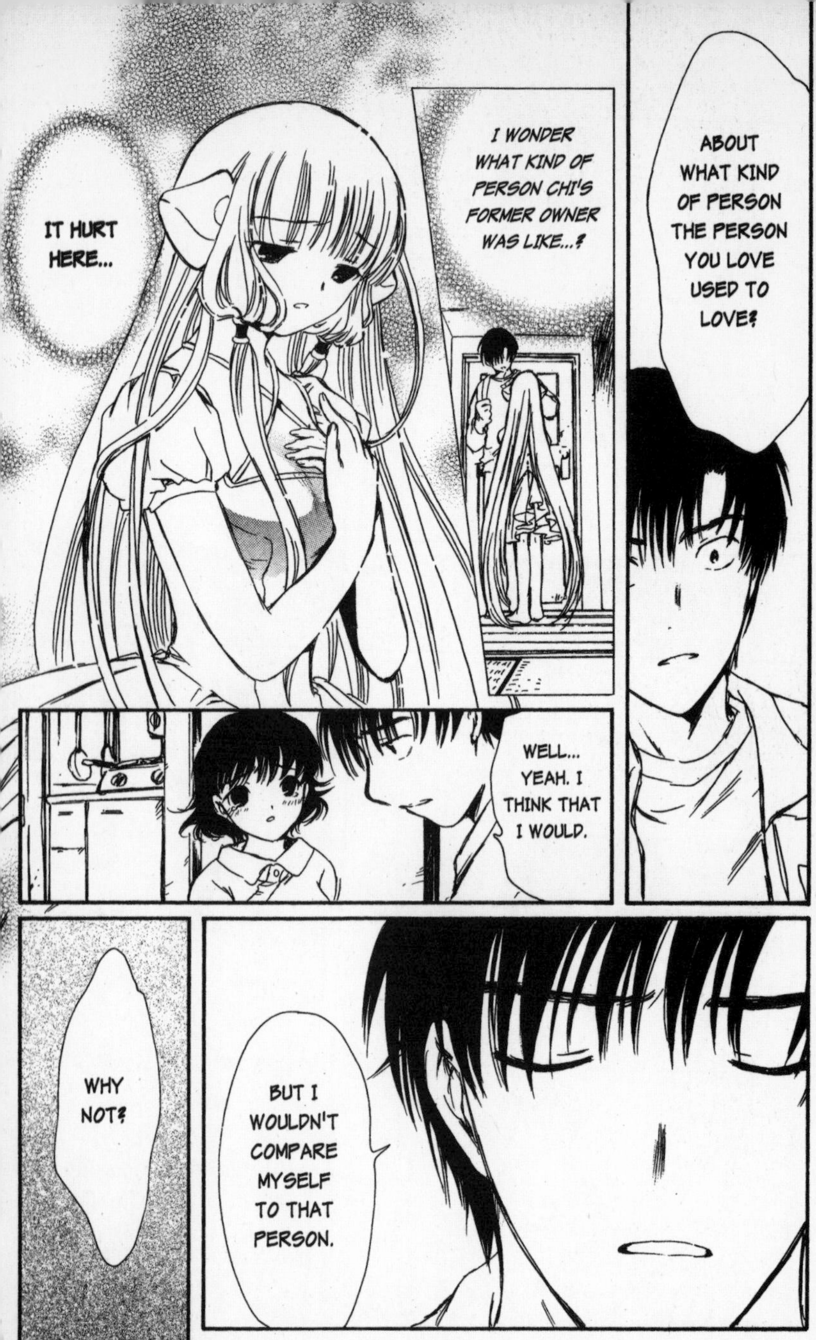
ABOUT WHAT KIND OF PERSON THE PERSON YOU LOVE USED TO LOVE?
I WONDER WHAT KIND OF PERSON CHI'S FORMER OWNER WAS LIKE...?
IT HURT HERE...
WELL... YEAH. I THINK THAT I WOULD.
BUT I WOULDN'T COMPARE MYSELF TO THAT PERSON.
WHY NOT?

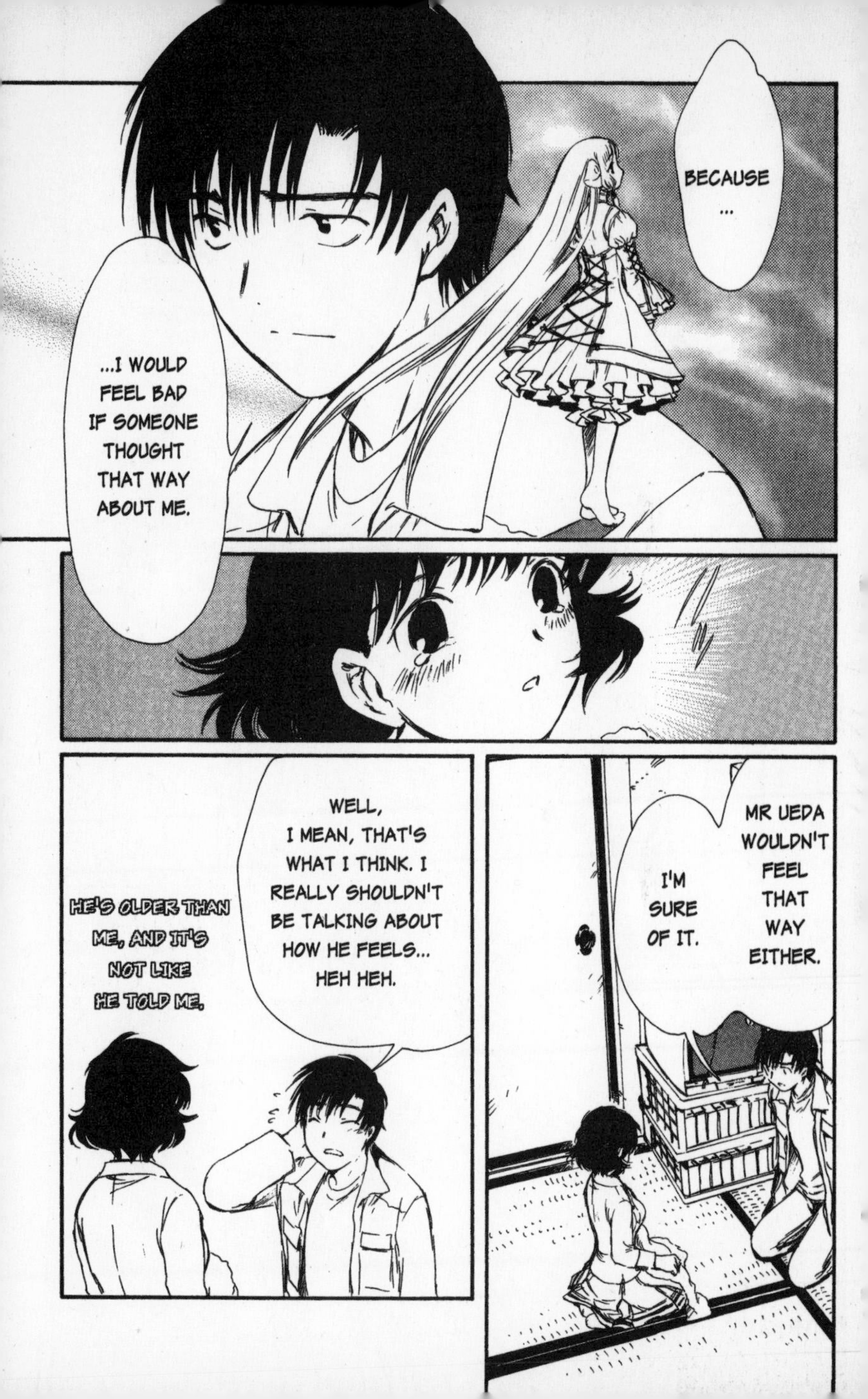
BECAUSE ...
...I WOULD FEEL BAD IF SOMEONE THOUGHT THAT WAY ABOUT ME.
MR UEDA WOULDN'T FEEL THAT WAY EITHER.
I'M SURE OF IT.
WELL, I MEAN, THAT'S WHAT I THINK. I REALLY SHOULDN'T BE TALKING ABOUT HOW HE FEELS... HEH HEH.
HE'S OLDER THAN ME, AND IT'S NOT LIKE HE TOLD ME.

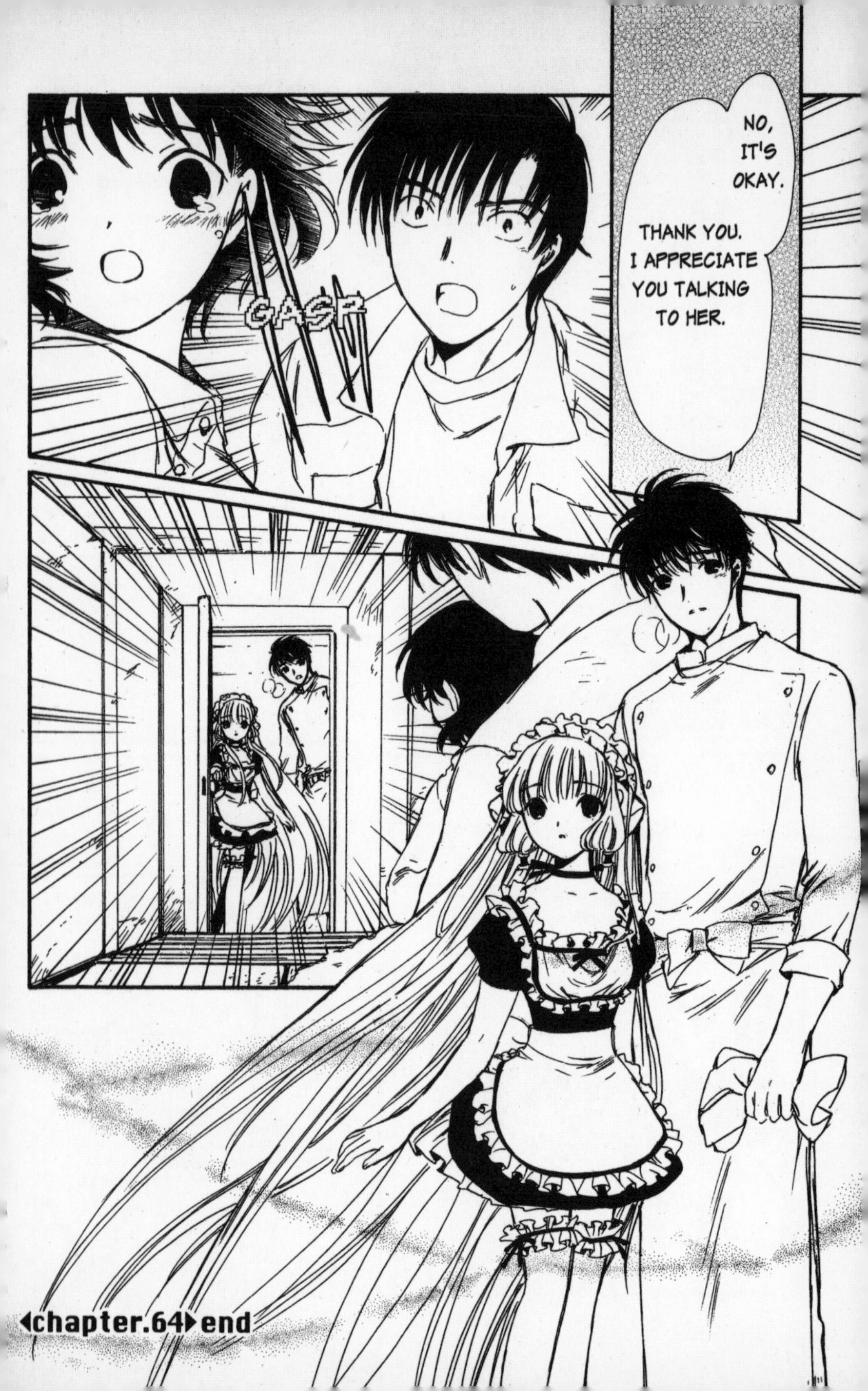
NO, IT'S OKAY.
THANK YOU. I APPRECIATE YOU TALKING TO HER.
GASP
◀chapter.64▶end

ちょびっツ

Chobits

◀chapter.65▶

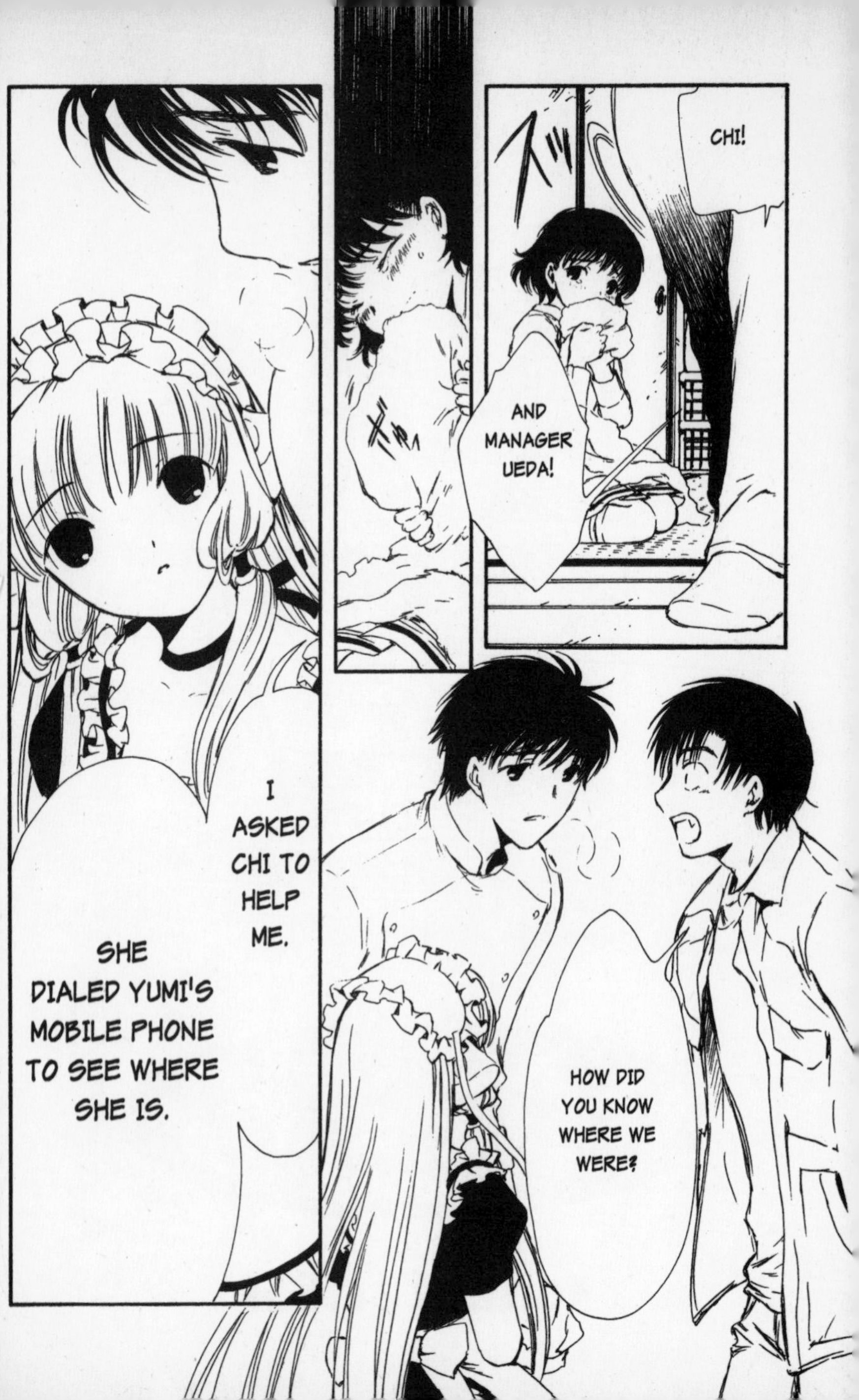
CHI!
AND MANAGER UEDA!
HOW DID YOU KNOW WHERE WE WERE?
I ASKED CHI TO HELP ME.
SHE DIALED YUMI'S MOBILE PHONE TO SEE WHERE SHE IS.

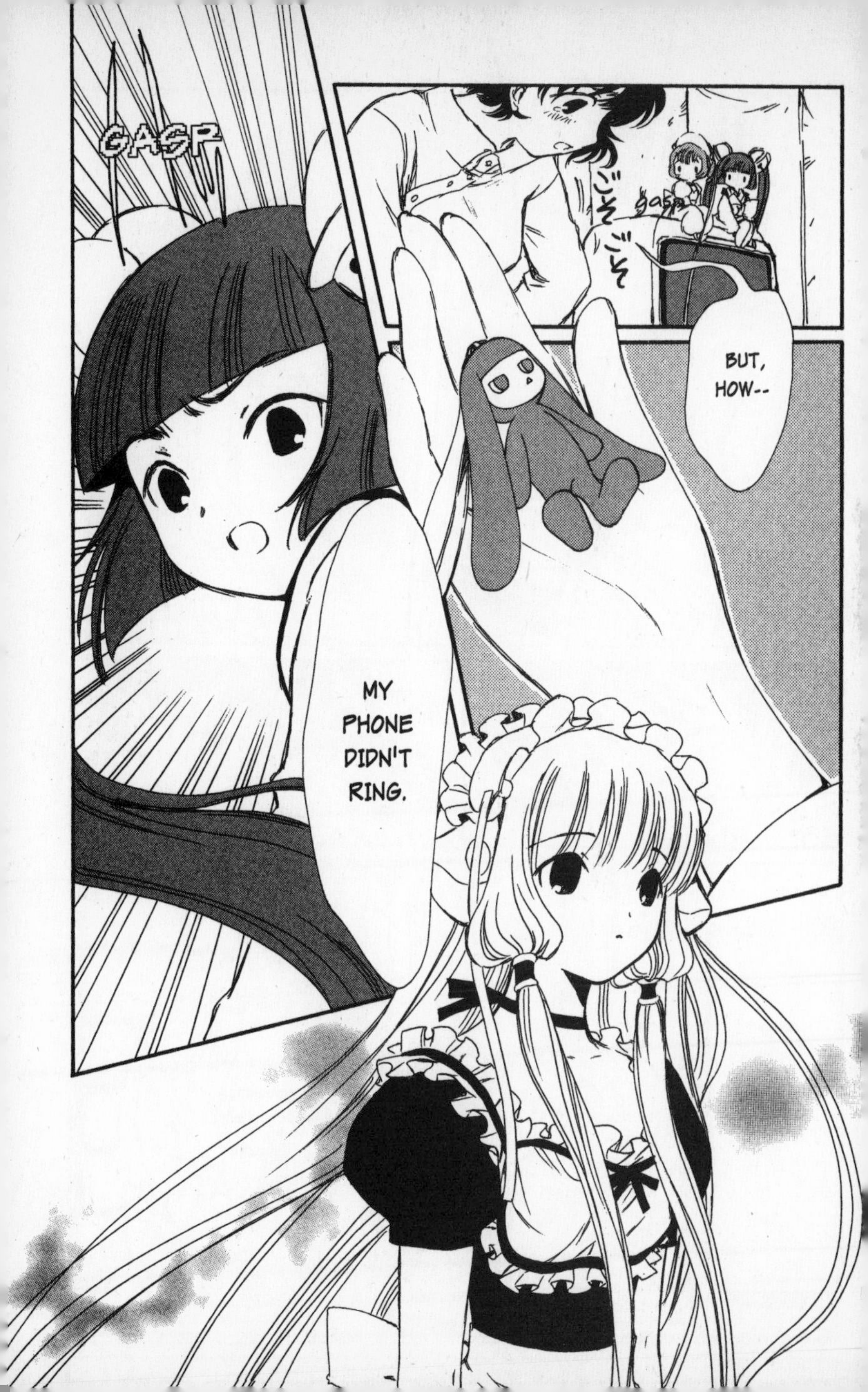
ごそごそ
gasp
BUT, HOW--
GASP
MY PHONE DIDN'T RING.

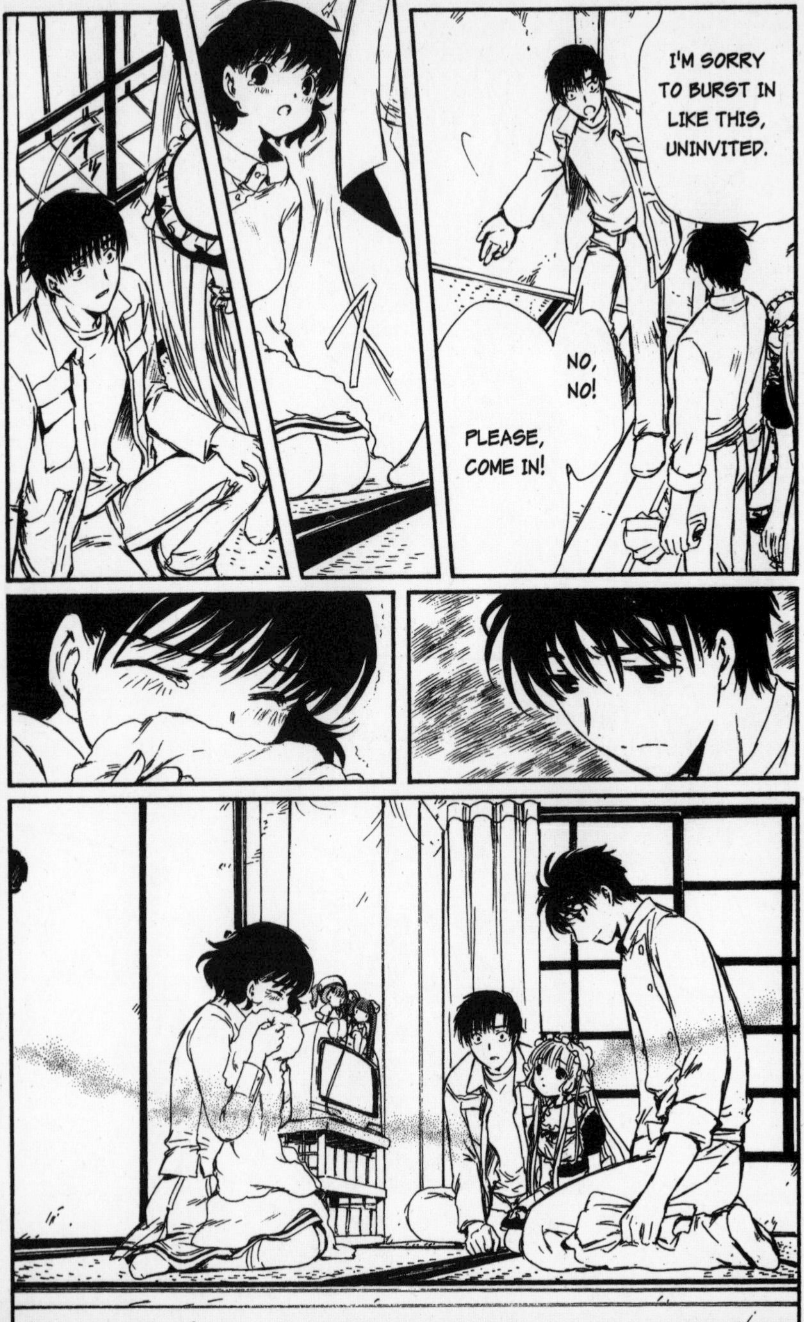
I'M SORRY TO BURST IN LIKE THIS, UNINVITED.
NO, NO!
PLEASE, COME IN!
は

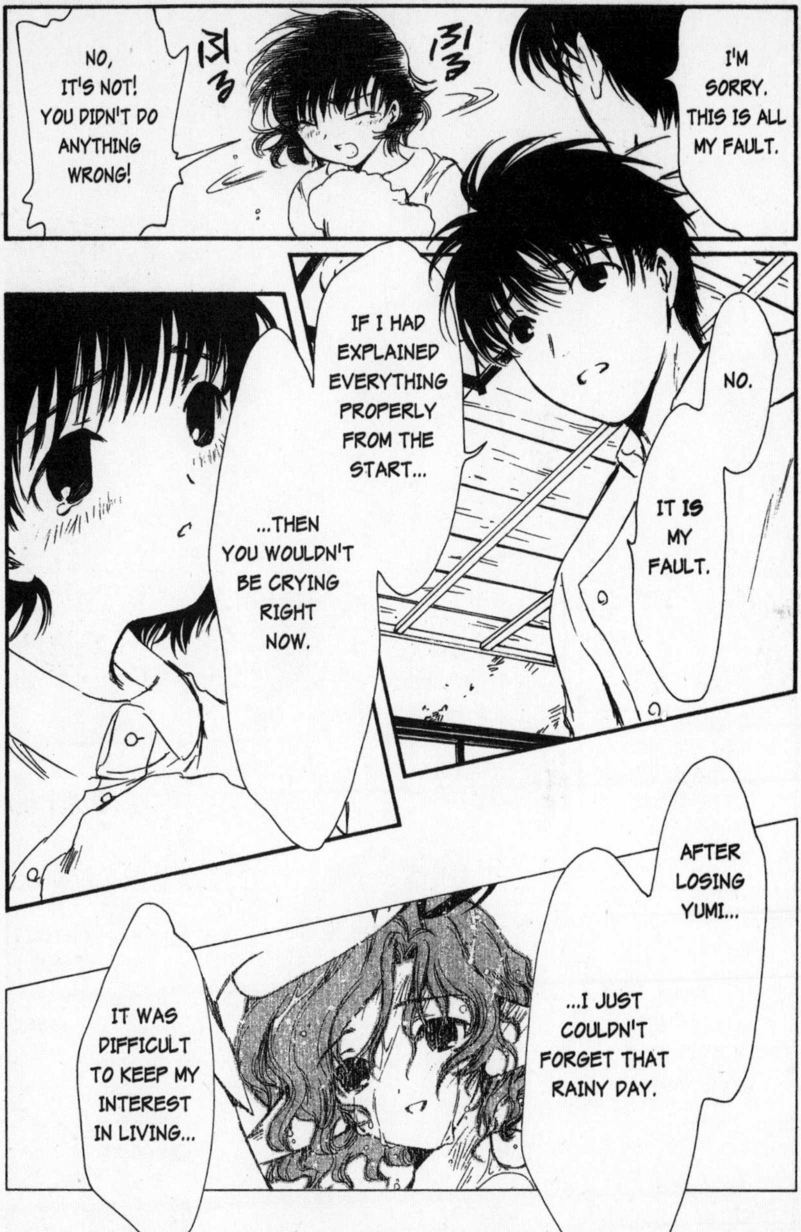
I'M SORRY. THIS IS ALL MY FAULT.
NO, IT'S NOT! YOU DIDN'T DO ANYTHING WRONG!
NO.
IT IS MY FAULT.
IF I HAD EXPLAINED EVERYTHING PROPERLY FROM THE START...
...THEN YOU WOULDN'T BE CRYING RIGHT NOW.
AFTER LOSING YUMI...
...I JUST COULDN'T FORGET THAT RAINY DAY.
IT WAS DIFFICULT TO KEEP MY INTEREST IN LIVING...

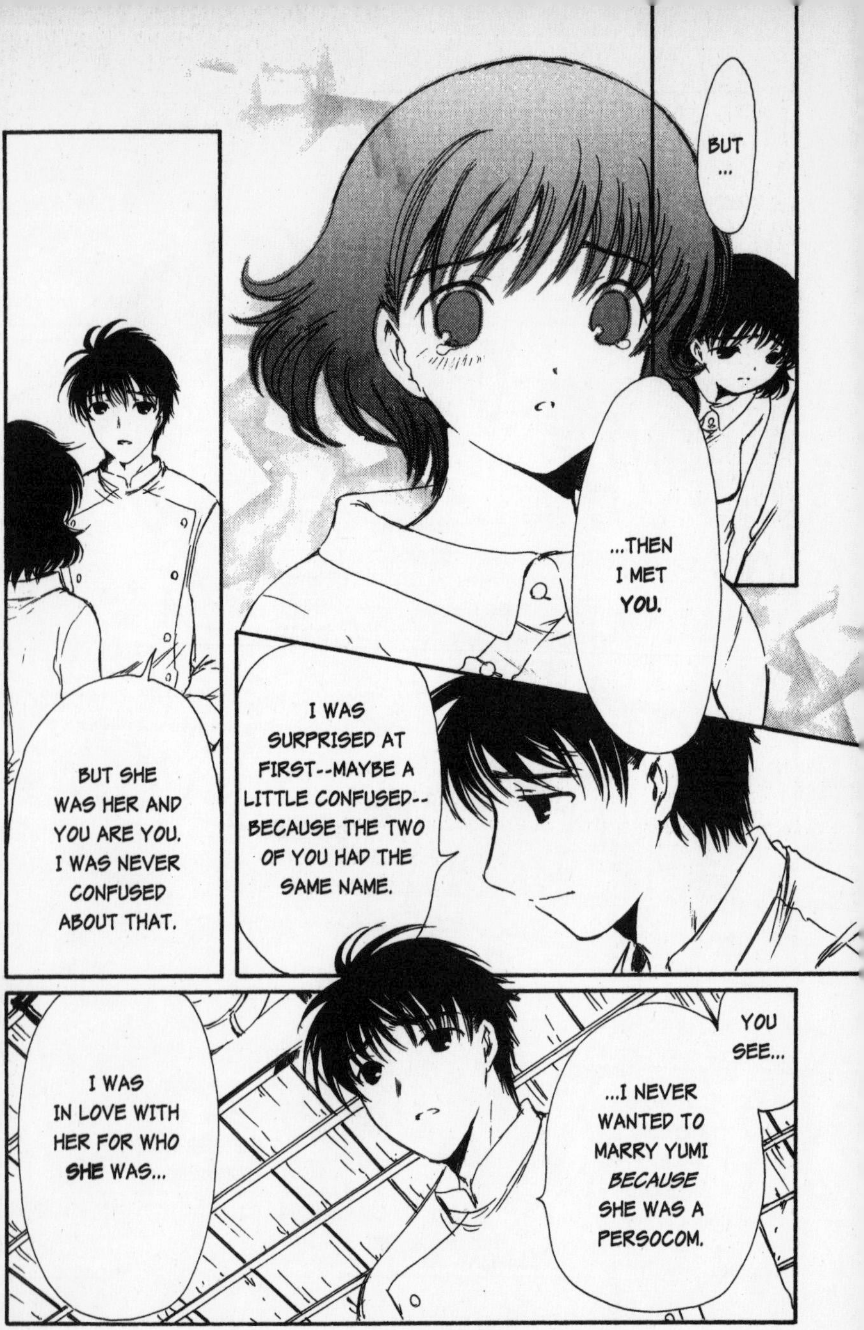
BUT ...
...THEN I MET YOU.
I WAS SURPRISED AT FIRST--MAYBE A LITTLE CONFUSED--BECAUSE THE TWO OF YOU HAD THE SAME NAME.
BUT SHE WAS HER AND YOU ARE YOU. I WAS NEVER CONFUSED ABOUT THAT.
YOU SEE...
...I NEVER WANTED TO MARRY YUMI *BECAUSE* SHE WAS A PERSOCOM.
I WAS IN LOVE WITH HER FOR WHO SHE WAS...

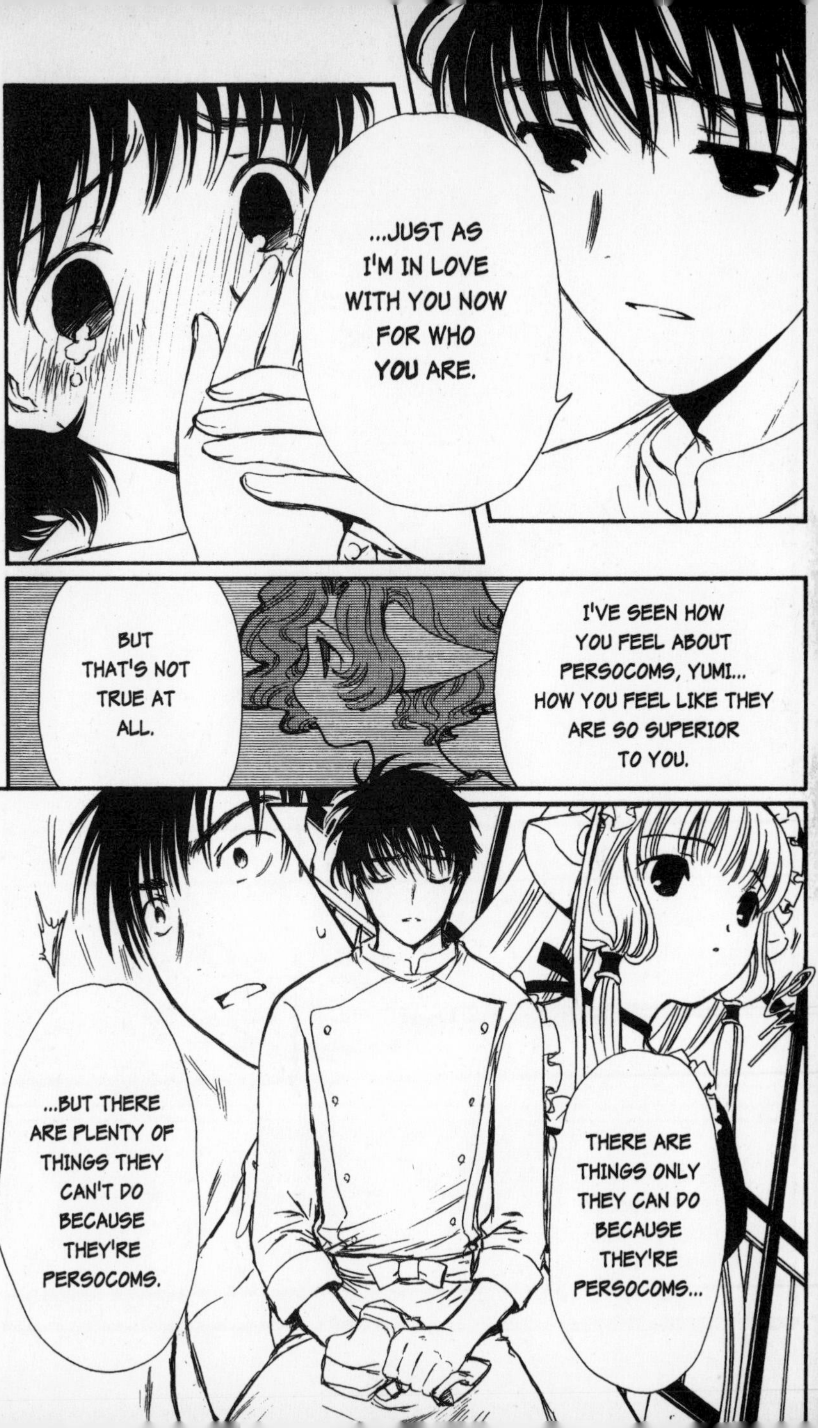
...JUST AS I'M IN LOVE WITH YOU NOW FOR WHO YOU ARE.
I'VE SEEN HOW YOU FEEL ABOUT PERSOCOMS, YUMI... HOW YOU FEEL LIKE THEY ARE SO SUPERIOR TO YOU.
BUT THAT'S NOT TRUE AT ALL.
THERE ARE THINGS ONLY THEY CAN DO BECAUSE THEY'RE PERSOCOMS...
...BUT THERE ARE PLENTY OF THINGS THEY CAN'T DO BECAUSE THEY'RE PERSOCOMS.

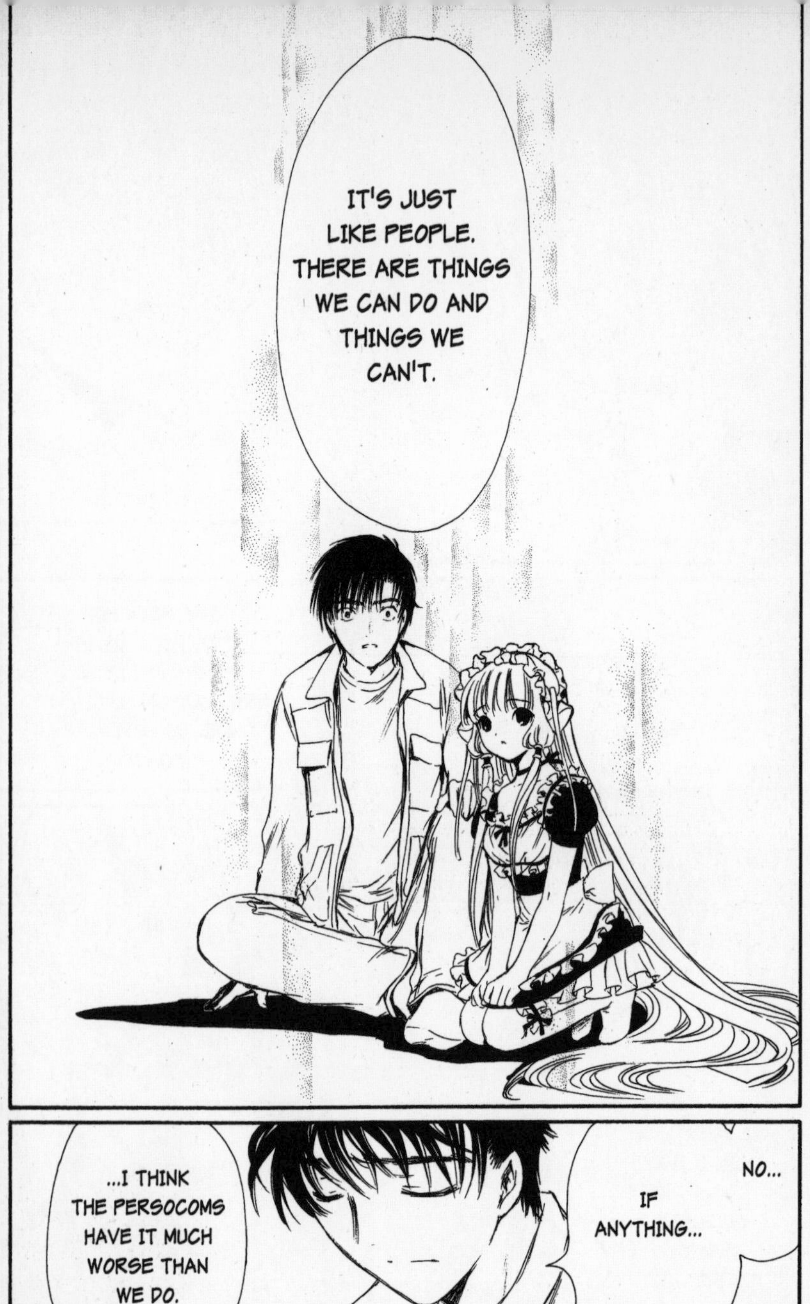
IT'S JUST LIKE PEOPLE. THERE ARE THINGS WE CAN DO AND THINGS WE CAN'T.
NO...
IF ANYTHING...
...I THINK THE PERSOCOMS HAVE IT MUCH WORSE THAN WE DO.

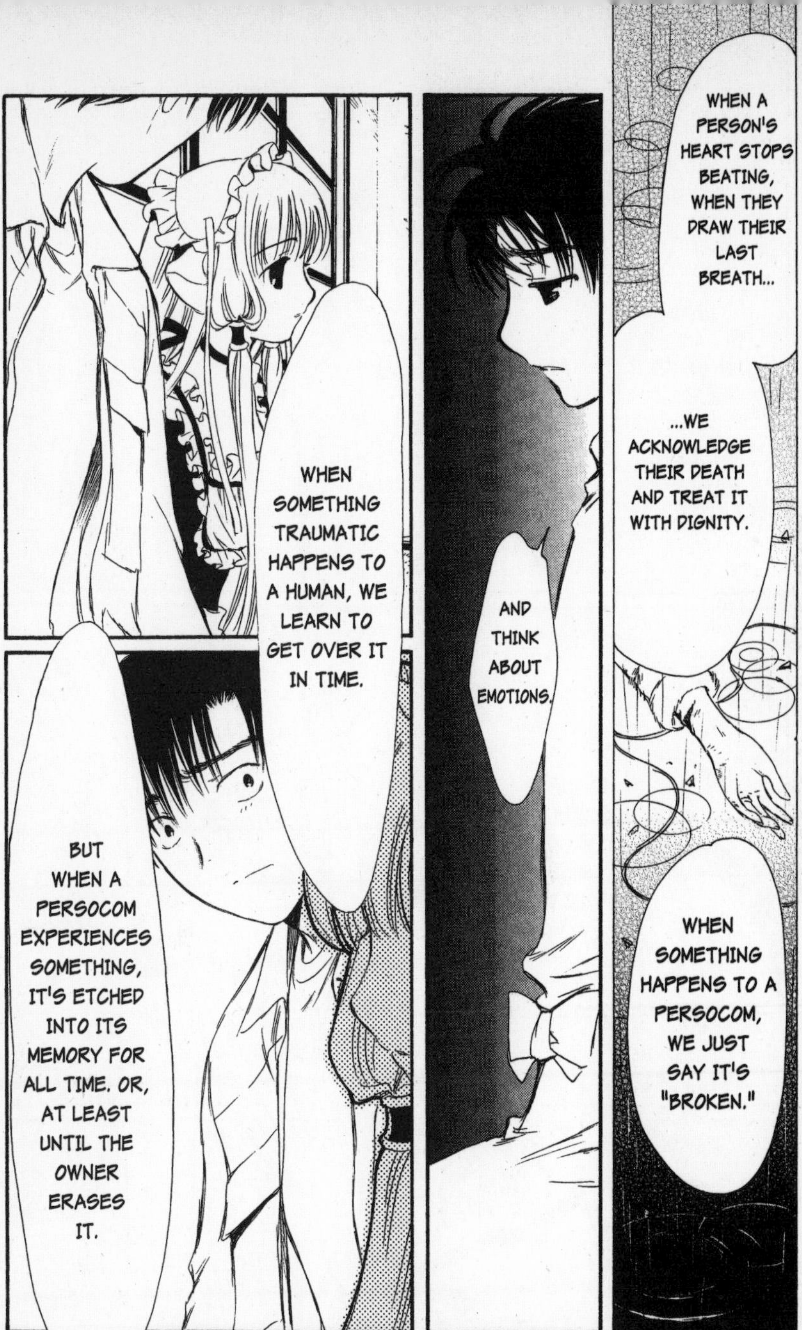
WHEN A PERSON'S HEART STOPS BEATING, WHEN THEY DRAW THEIR LAST BREATH...
...WE ACKNOWLEDGE THEIR DEATH AND TREAT IT WITH DIGNITY.
WHEN SOMETHING HAPPENS TO A PERSOCOM, WE JUST SAY IT'S "BROKEN."
AND THINK ABOUT EMOTIONS.
WHEN SOMETHING TRAUMATIC HAPPENS TO A HUMAN, WE LEARN TO GET OVER IT IN TIME.
BUT WHEN A PERSOCOM EXPERIENCES SOMETHING, IT'S ETCHED INTO ITS MEMORY FOR ALL TIME. OR, AT LEAST UNTIL THE OWNER ERASES IT.

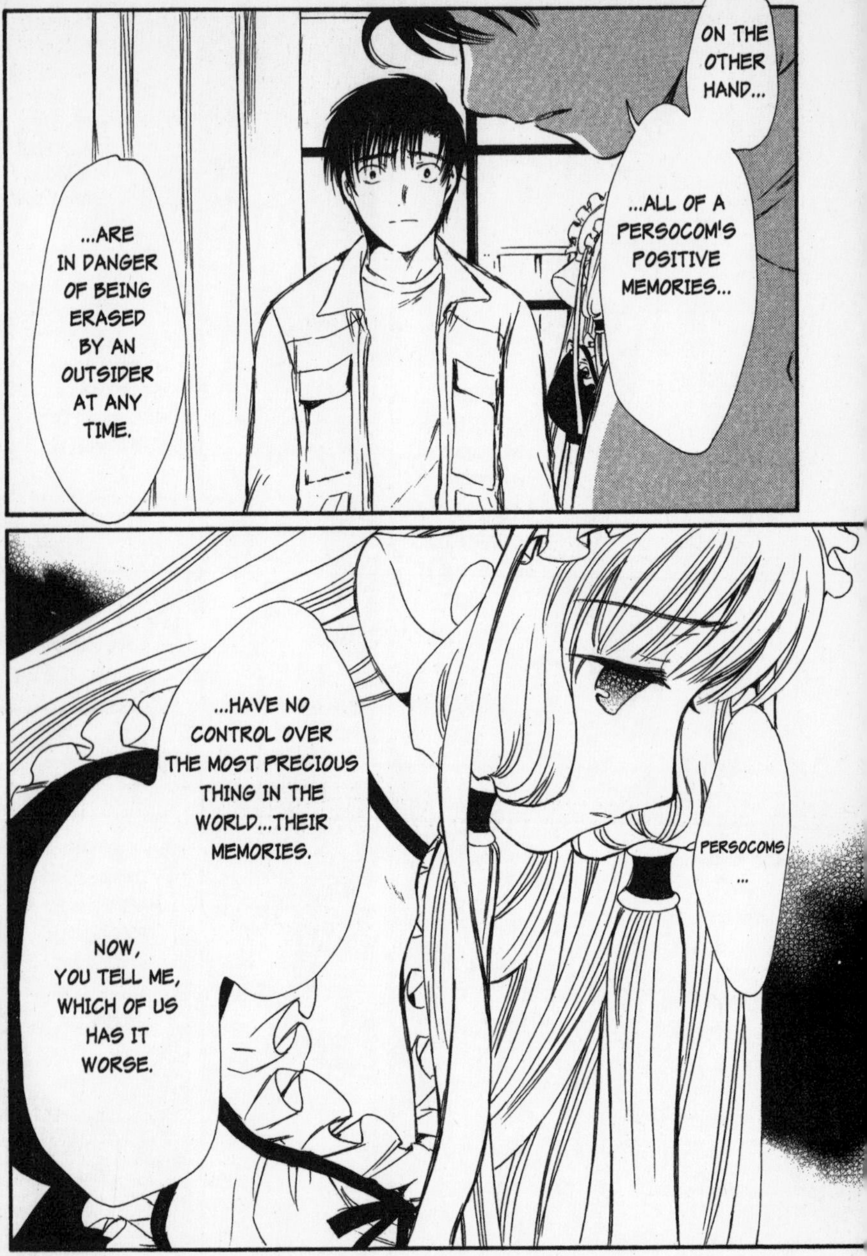
ON THE OTHER HAND...
...ALL OF A PERSOCOM'S POSITIVE MEMORIES...
...ARE IN DANGER OF BEING ERASED BY AN OUTSIDER AT ANY TIME.
PERSOCOMS ...
...HAVE NO CONTROL OVER THE MOST PRECIOUS THING IN THE WORLD...THEIR MEMORIES.
NOW, YOU TELL ME, WHICH OF US HAS IT WORSE.

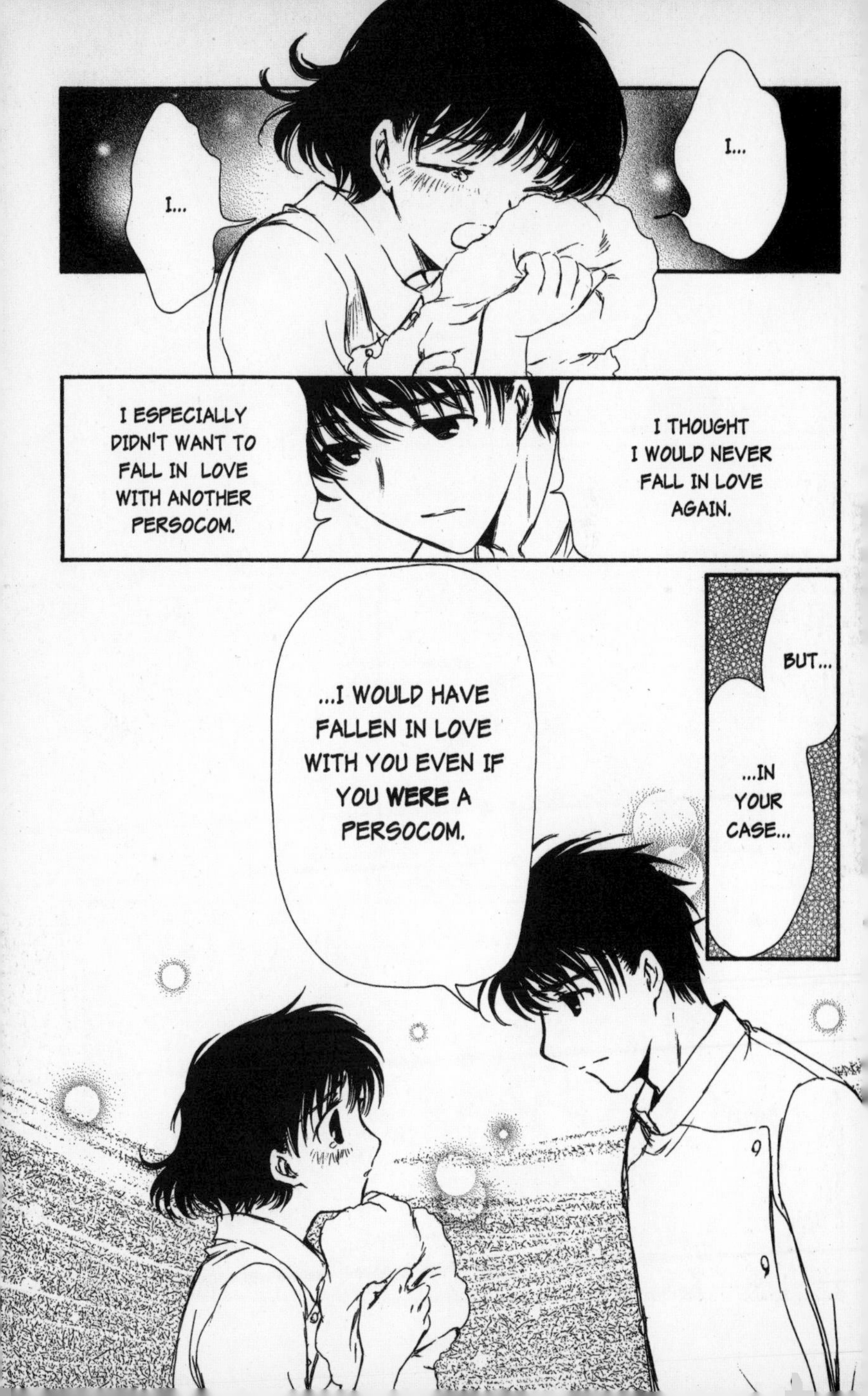
I...
I...
I THOUGHT I WOULD NEVER FALL IN LOVE AGAIN.
I ESPECIALLY DIDN'T WANT TO FALL IN LOVE WITH ANOTHER PERSOCOM.
BUT...
...IN YOUR CASE...
...I WOULD HAVE FALLEN IN LOVE WITH YOU EVEN IF YOU WERE A PERSOCOM.

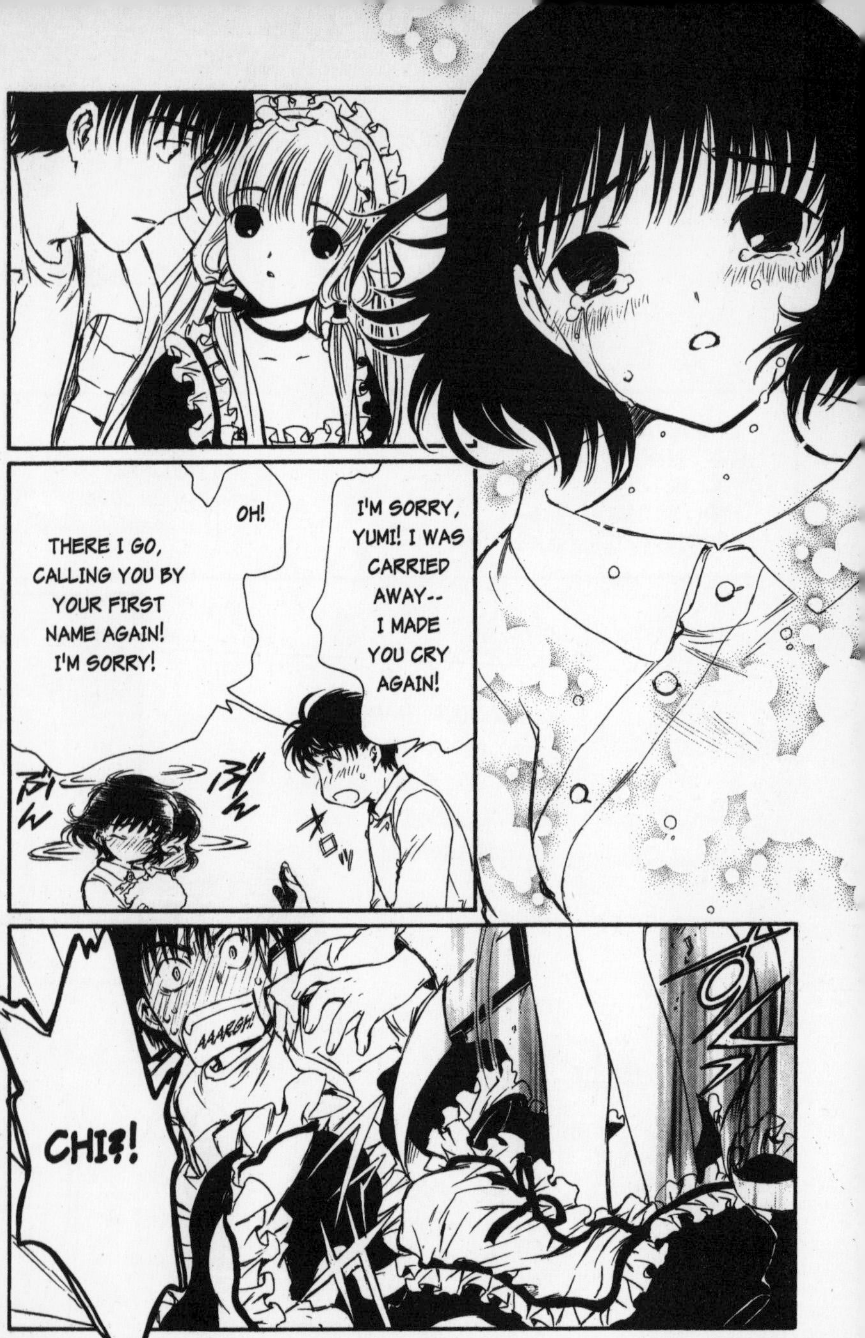
I'M SORRY, YUMI! I WAS CARRIED AWAY-- I MADE YOU CRY AGAIN!
OH!
THERE I GO, CALLING YOU BY YOUR FIRST NAME AGAIN! I'M SORRY!
AAARGH!
CHI?!

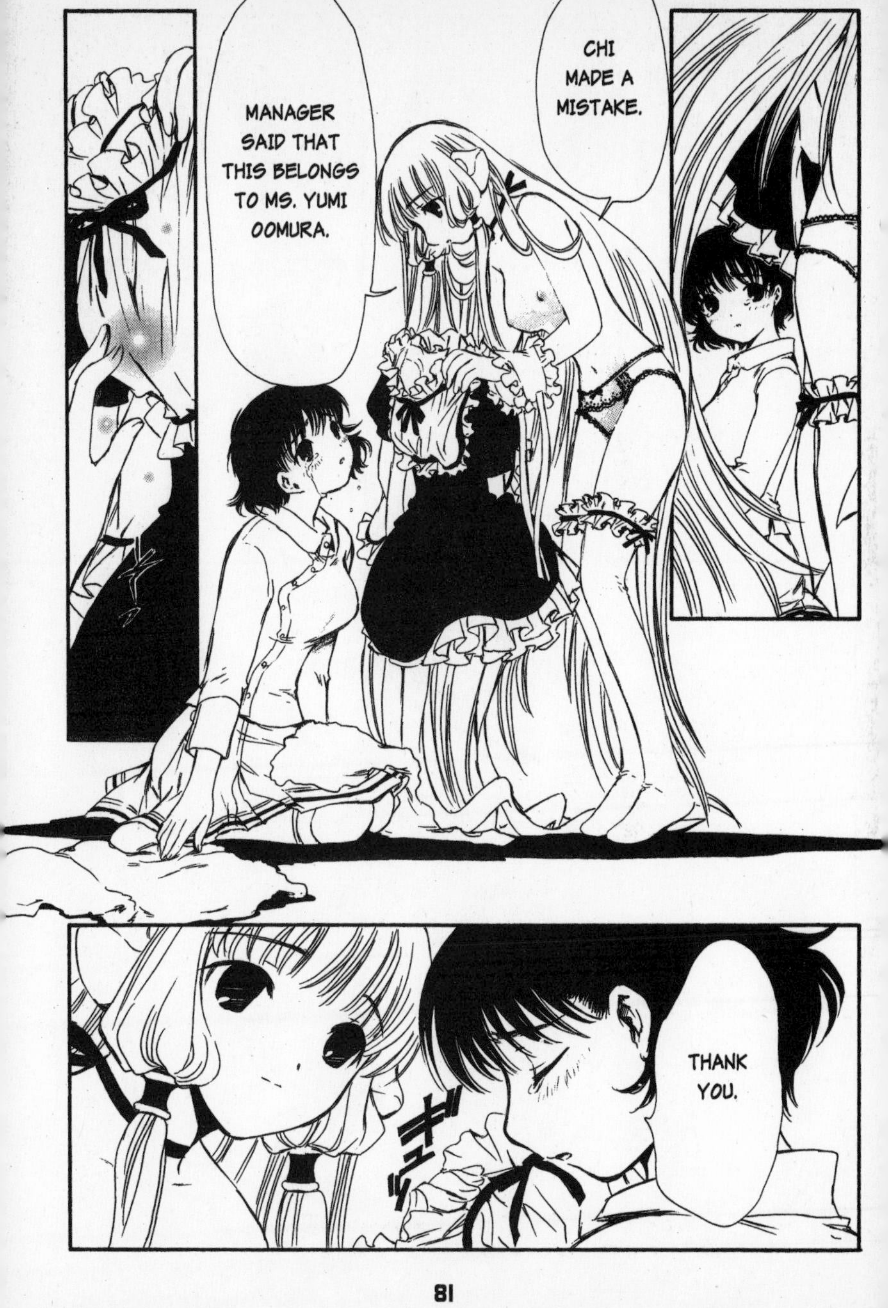
CHI MADE A MISTAKE.
MANAGER SAID THAT THIS BELONGS TO MS. YUMI OOMURA.
THANK YOU.
ギュッ

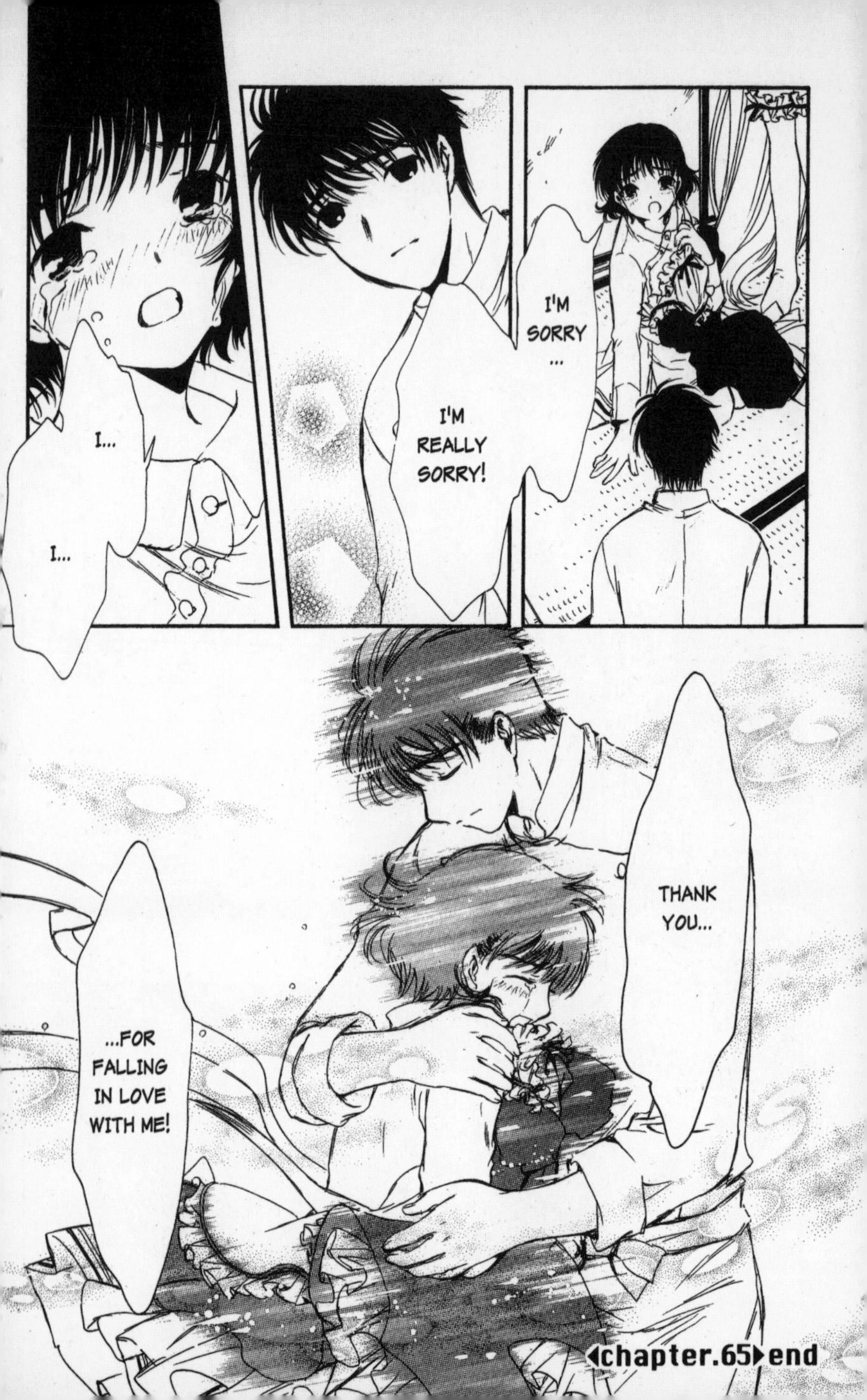
I'M SORRY ...
I'M REALLY SORRY!
I...
I...
THANK YOU...
...FOR FALLING IN LOVE WITH ME!
chapter.65 end

◂chapter.66▸

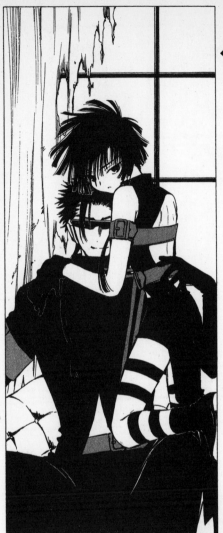

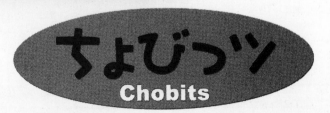

ちょびっツ

Chobits

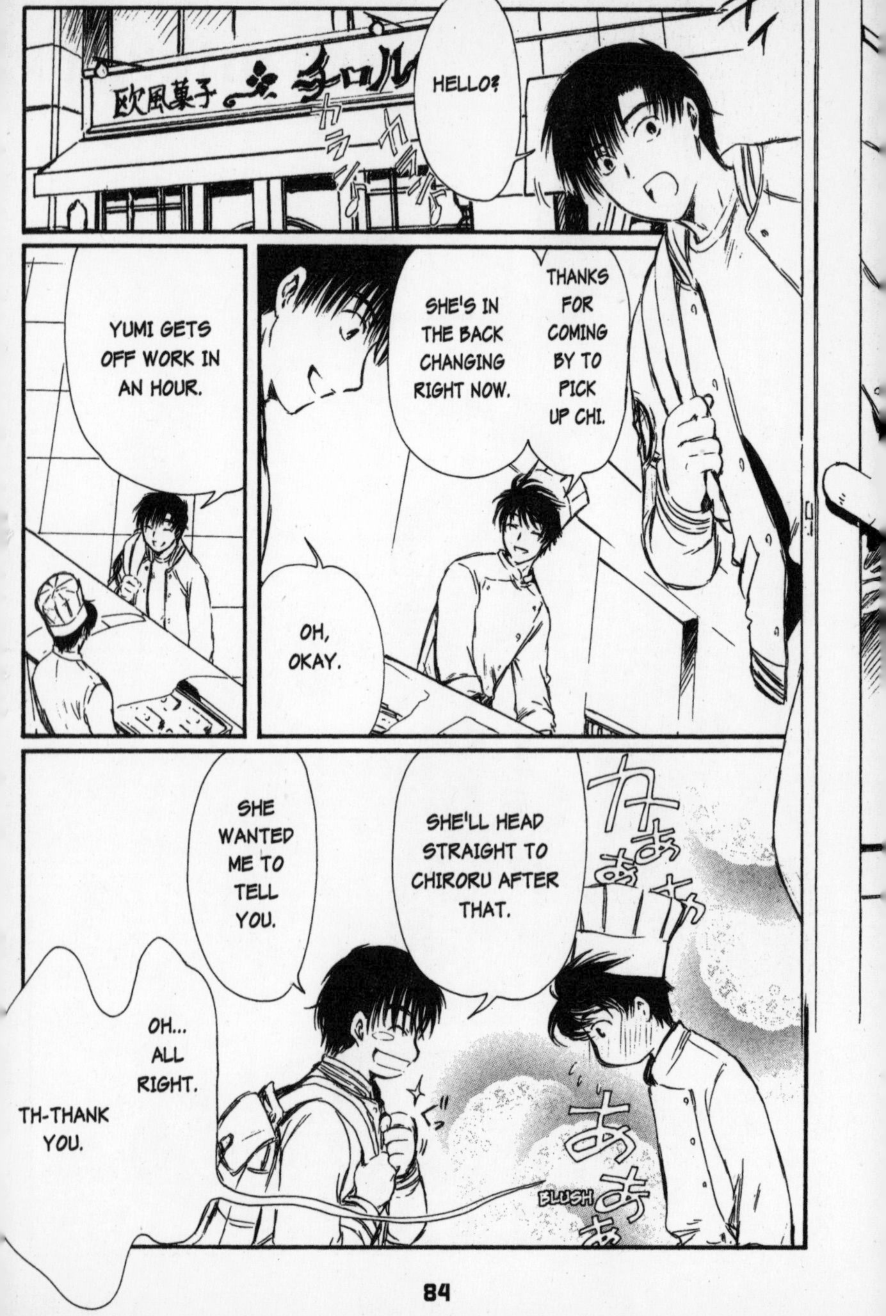
欧風菓子 チロル
カラン カラン
HELLO?
キィ
THANKS FOR COMING BY TO PICK UP CHI.
SHE'S IN THE BACK CHANGING RIGHT NOW.
OH, OKAY.
YUMI GETS OFF WORK IN AN HOUR.
SHE'LL HEAD STRAIGHT TO CHIRORU AFTER THAT.
SHE WANTED ME TO TELL YOU.
かああああ
あああ
BLUSH
OH... ALL RIGHT.
TH-THANK YOU.

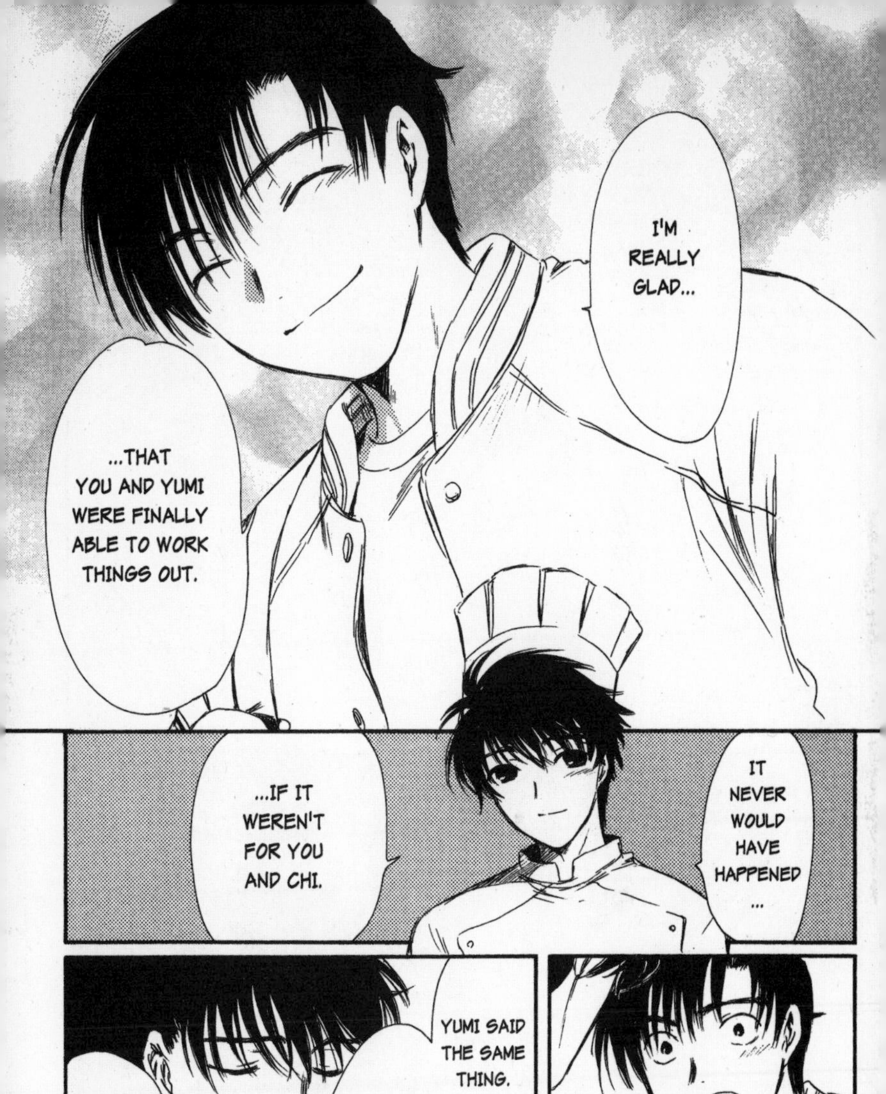
I'M REALLY GLAD...
...THAT YOU AND YUMI WERE FINALLY ABLE TO WORK THINGS OUT.
IT NEVER WOULD HAVE HAPPENED ...
...IF IT WEREN'T FOR YOU AND CHI.
NO, I DIDN'T...!
YUMI SAID THE SAME THING.
SHE NEVER WOULD HAVE BEEN ABLE TO FACE HER FEARS IF YOU HADN'T CHASED HER THAT DAY.
SHE'S VERY GRATEFUL.

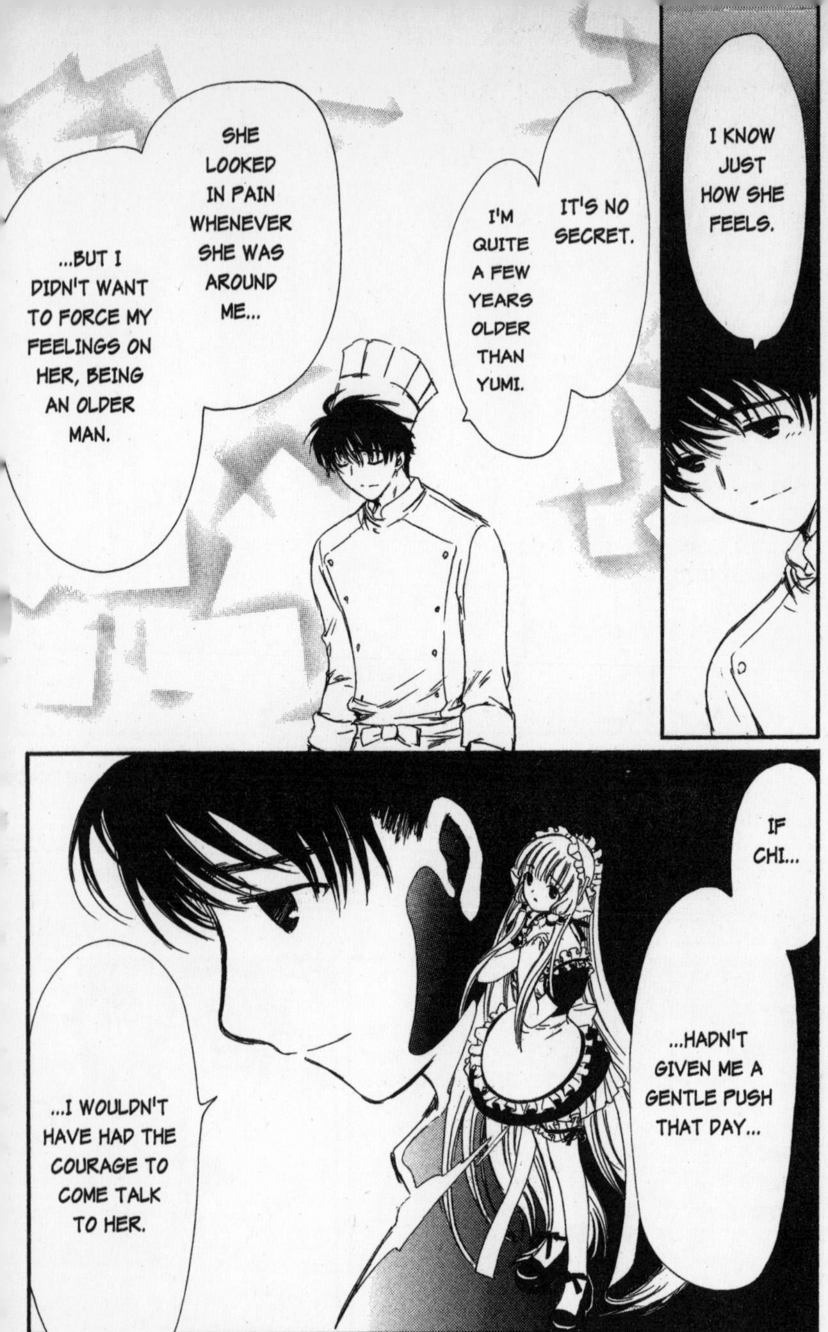
I KNOW JUST HOW SHE FEELS.
IT'S NO SECRET.
I'M QUITE A FEW YEARS OLDER THAN YUMI.
SHE LOOKED IN PAIN WHENEVER SHE WAS AROUND ME...
...BUT I DIDN'T WANT TO FORCE MY FEELINGS ON HER, BEING AN OLDER MAN.
IF CHI...
...HADN'T GIVEN ME A GENTLE PUSH THAT DAY...
...I WOULDN'T HAVE HAD THE COURAGE TO COME TALK TO HER.

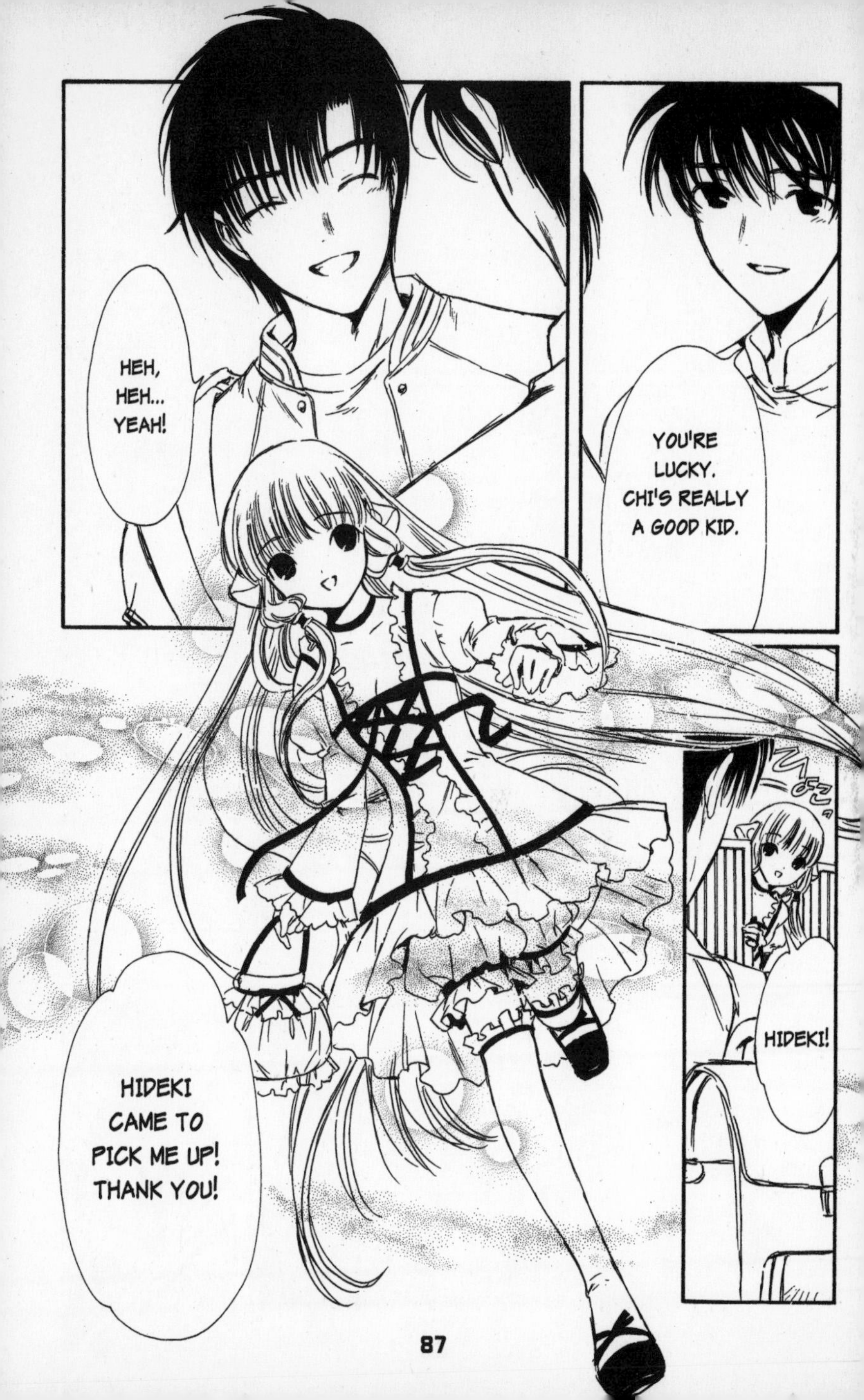

YOU'RE LUCKY. CHI'S REALLY A GOOD KID.
HEH, HEH... YEAH!
HIDEKI!
HIDEKI CAME TO PICK ME UP! THANK YOU!

SHALL WE GO...

...CHI?

OKAY!

THANK YOU VERY MUCH.

THANK YOU VERY MUCH FOR ALL YOUR HARD WORK.

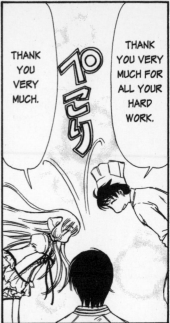

CHI WILL SEE THE MANAGER TOMORROW?

YES, CHI, I'LL SEE YOU TOMORROW.

HM?

HIDEKI!

HIDEKI!

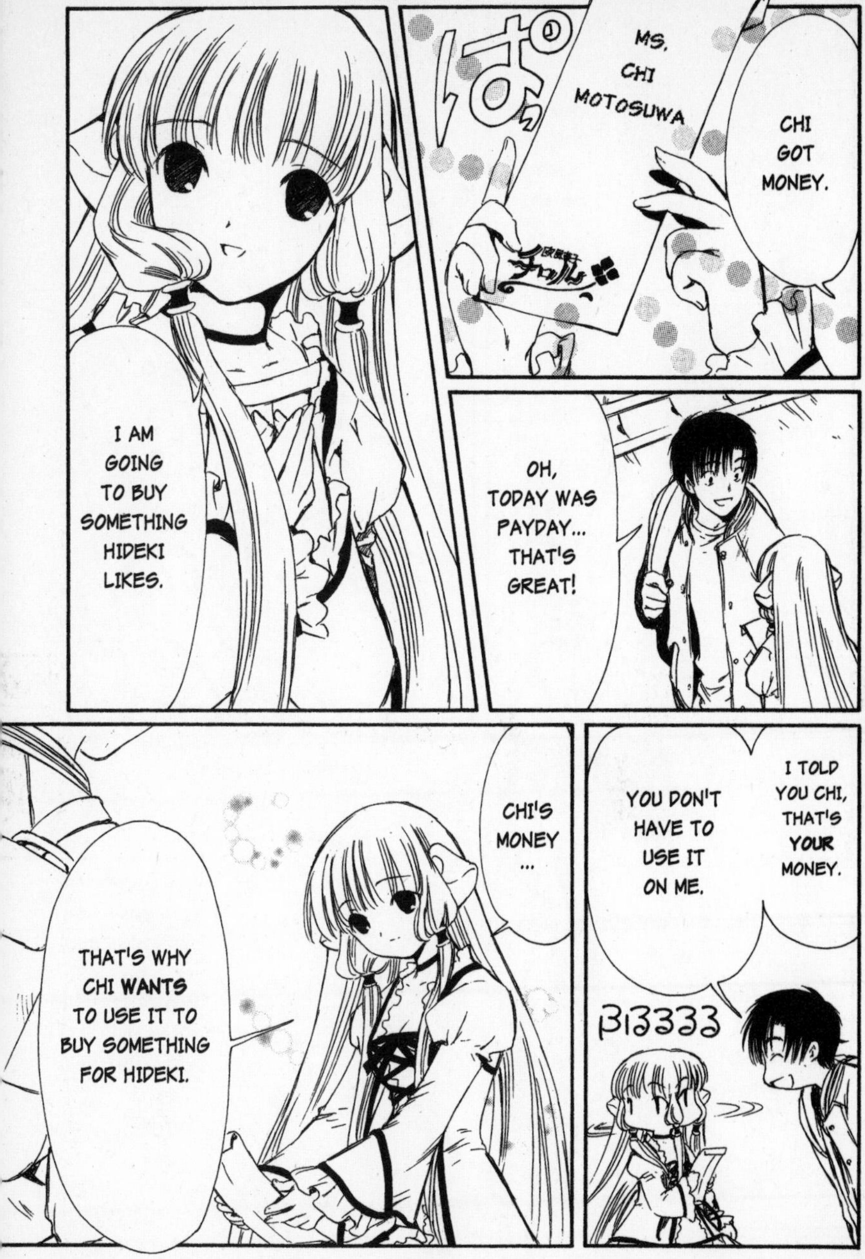
ぱっ
MS. CHI MOTOSUWA
CHI GOT MONEY.
OH, TODAY WAS PAYDAY... THAT'S GREAT!
I AM GOING TO BUY SOMETHING HIDEKI LIKES.
I TOLD YOU CHI, THAT'S **YOUR** MONEY.
YOU DON'T HAVE TO USE IT ON ME.
ふるるるる
CHI'S MONEY ...
THAT'S WHY CHI **WANTS** TO USE IT TO BUY SOMETHING FOR HIDEKI.

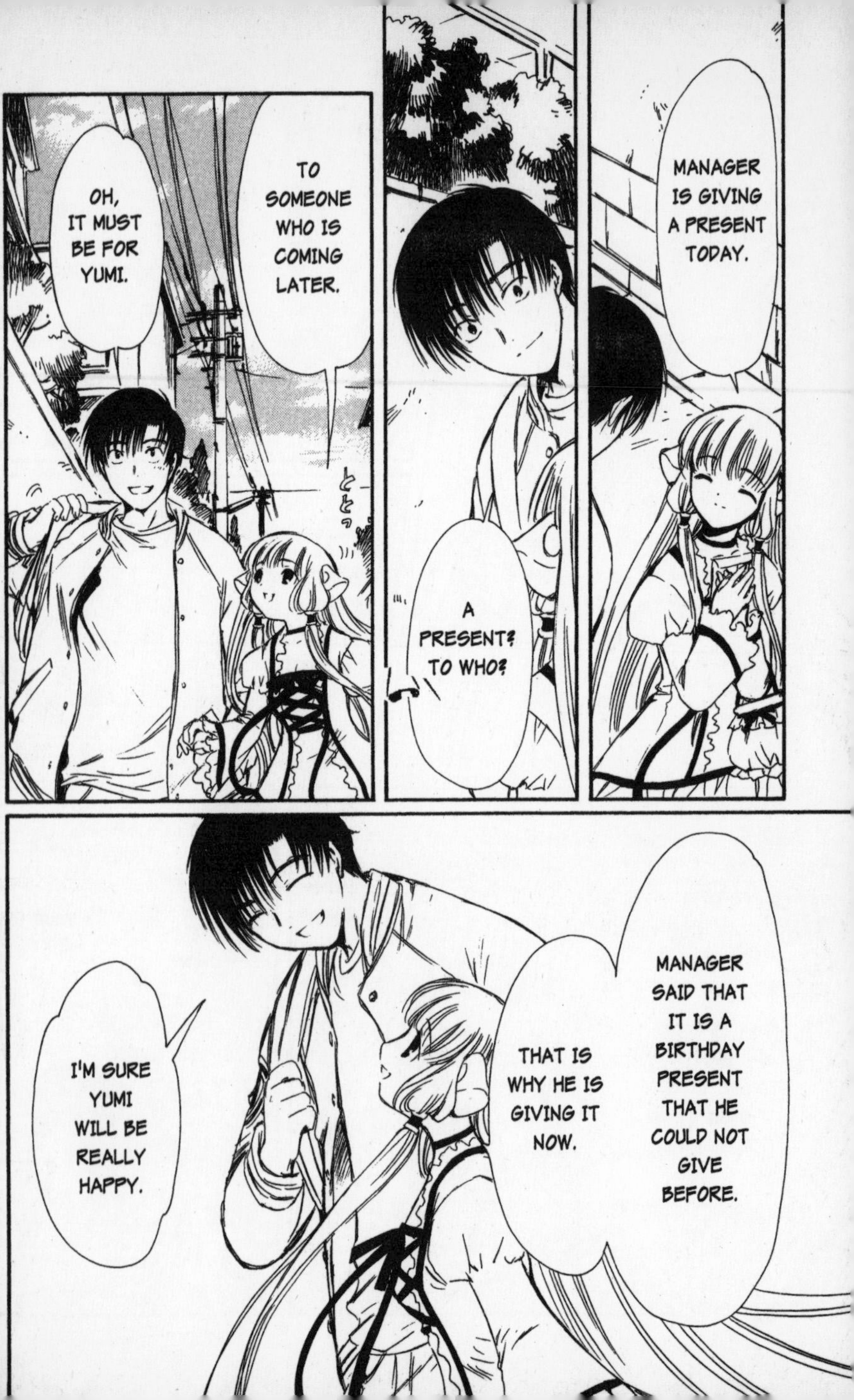
MANAGER IS GIVING A PRESENT TODAY.
A PRESENT? TO WHO?
TO SOMEONE WHO IS COMING LATER.
OH, IT MUST BE FOR YUMI.
MANAGER SAID THAT IT IS A BIRTHDAY PRESENT THAT HE COULD NOT GIVE BEFORE.
THAT IS WHY HE IS GIVING IT NOW.
I'M SURE YUMI WILL BE REALLY HAPPY.

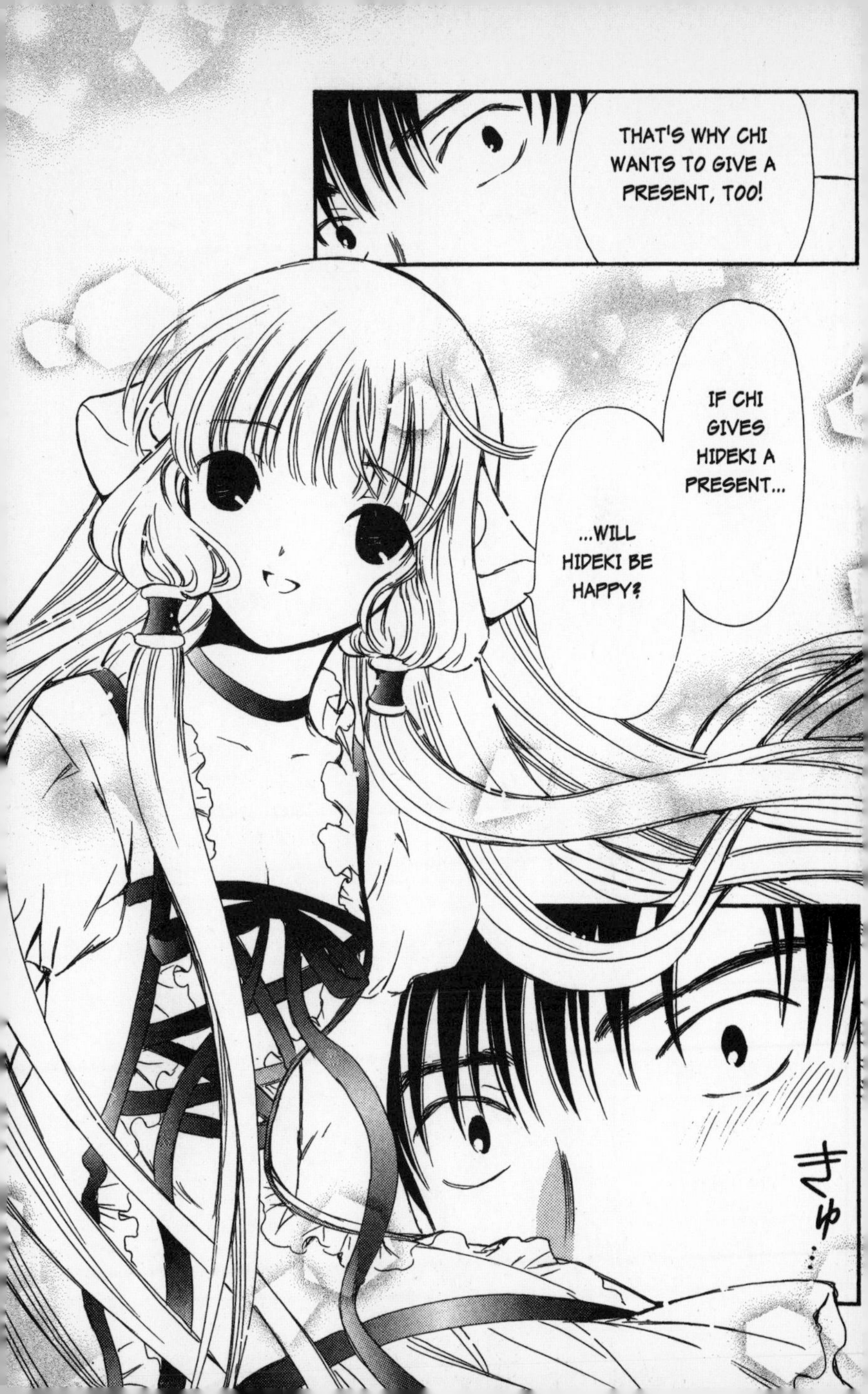
THAT'S WHY CHI WANTS TO GIVE A PRESENT, TOO!
IF CHI GIVES HIDEKI A PRESENT...
...WILL HIDEKI BE HAPPY?
きゅ...

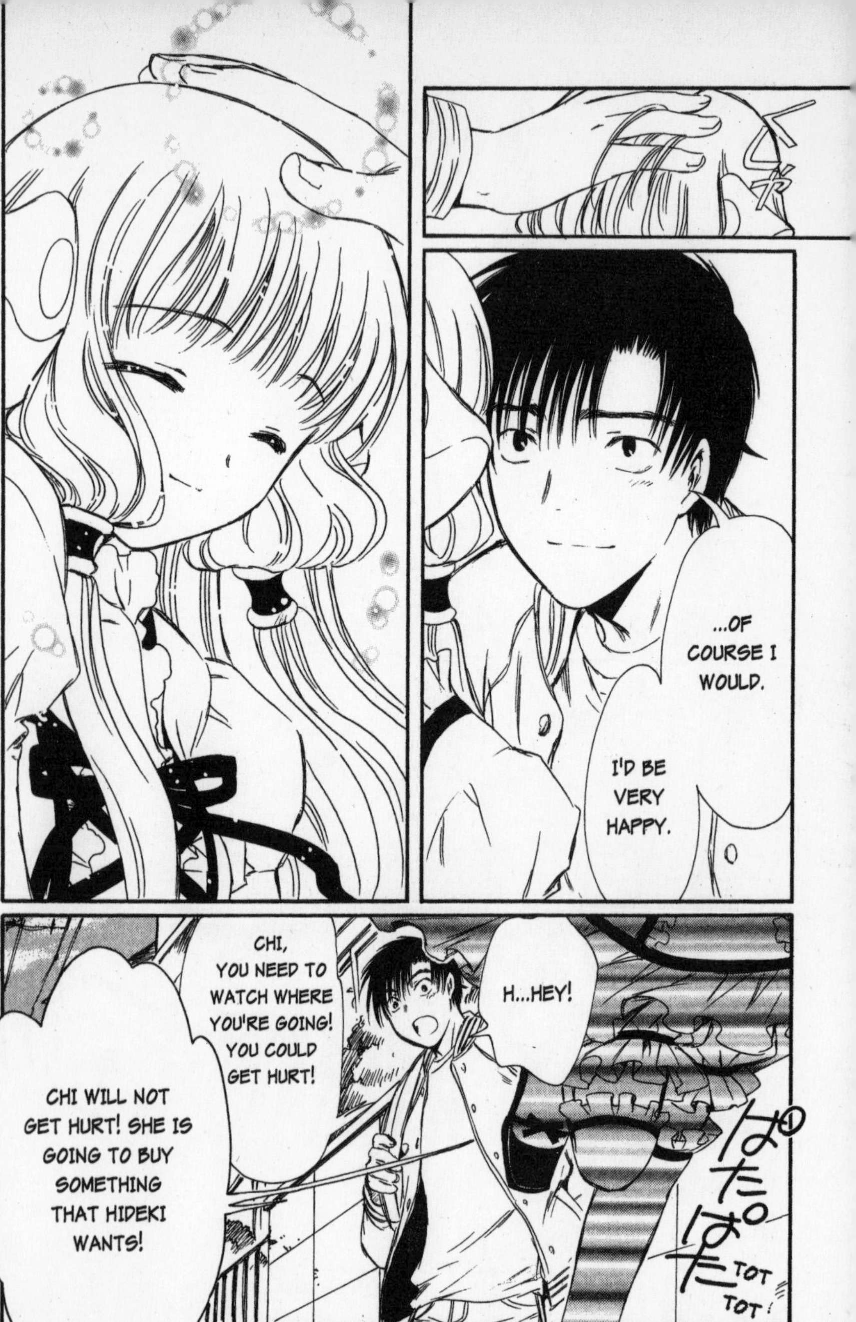
くしゃ
...OF COURSE I WOULD.
I'D BE VERY HAPPY.
H...HEY!
ぱたぱた
TOT TOT
CHI, YOU NEED TO WATCH WHERE YOU'RE GOING! YOU COULD GET HURT!
CHI WILL NOT GET HURT! SHE IS GOING TO BUY SOMETHING THAT HIDEKI WANTS!

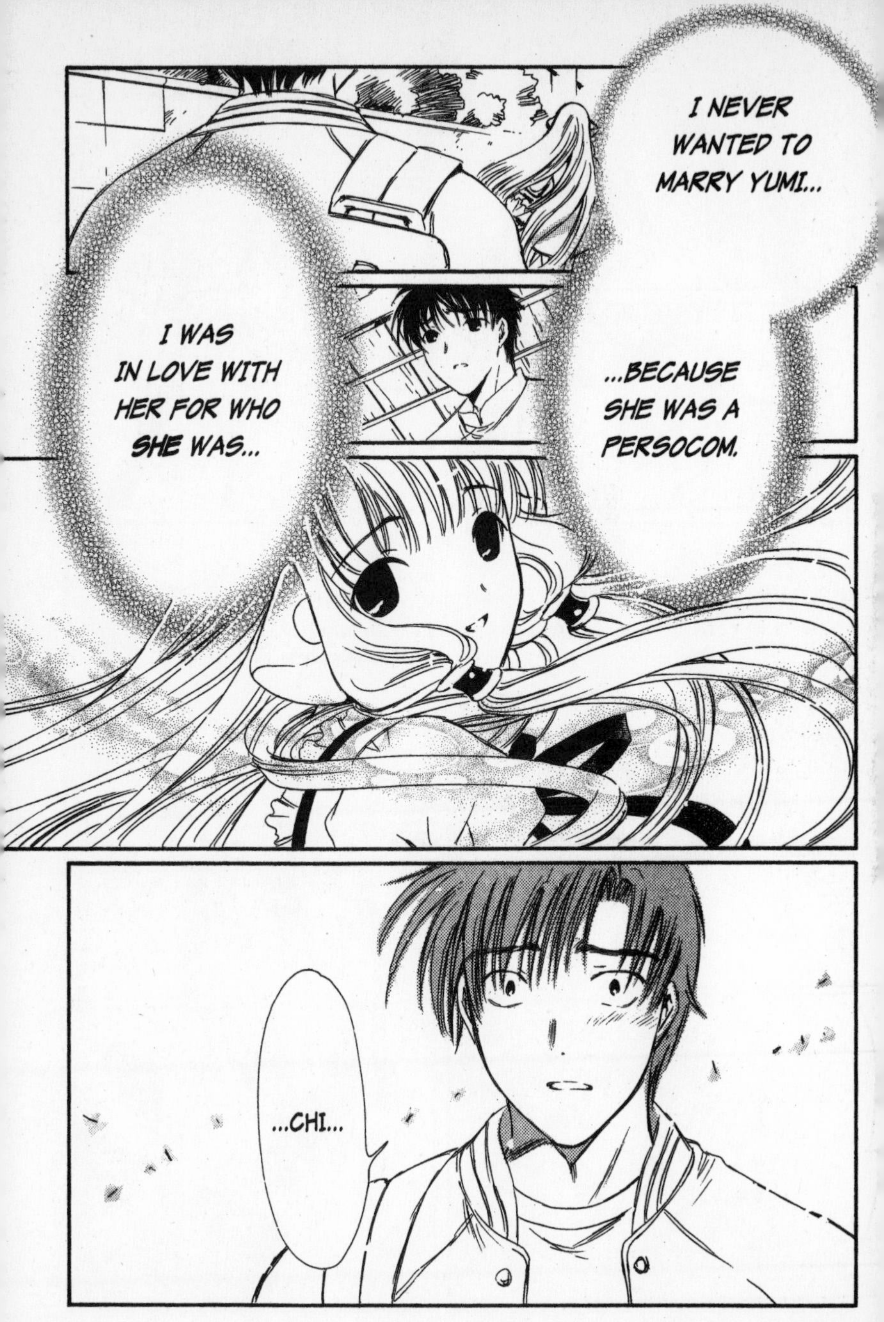
I NEVER WANTED TO MARRY YUMI...
...BECAUSE SHE WAS A PERSOCOM.
I WAS IN LOVE WITH HER FOR WHO SHE WAS...
...CHI...

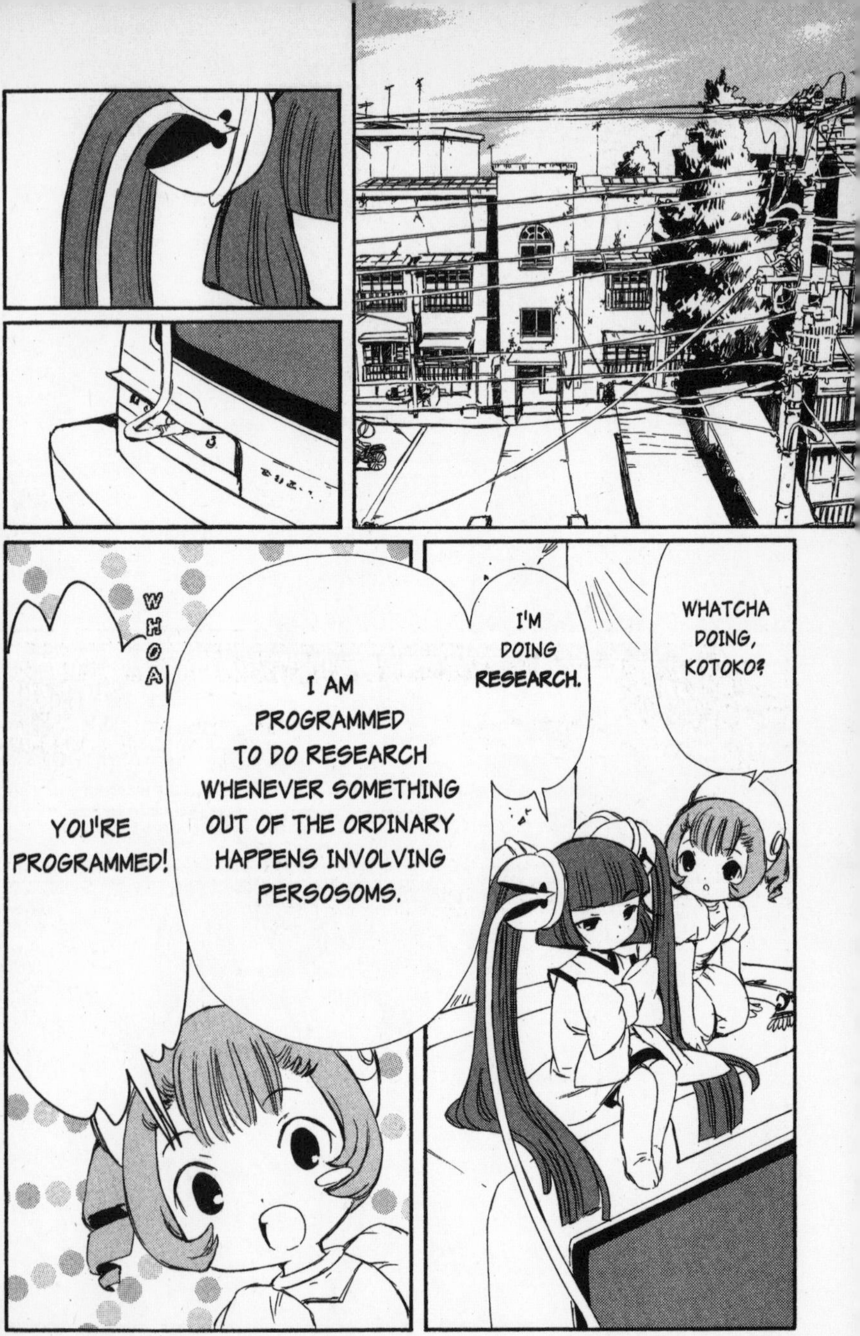
WHATCHA DOING, KOTOKO?
I'M DOING RESEARCH.
I AM PROGRAMMED TO DO RESEARCH WHENEVER SOMETHING OUT OF THE ORDINARY HAPPENS INVOLVING PERSOSOMS.
WHOA
YOU'RE PROGRAMMED!

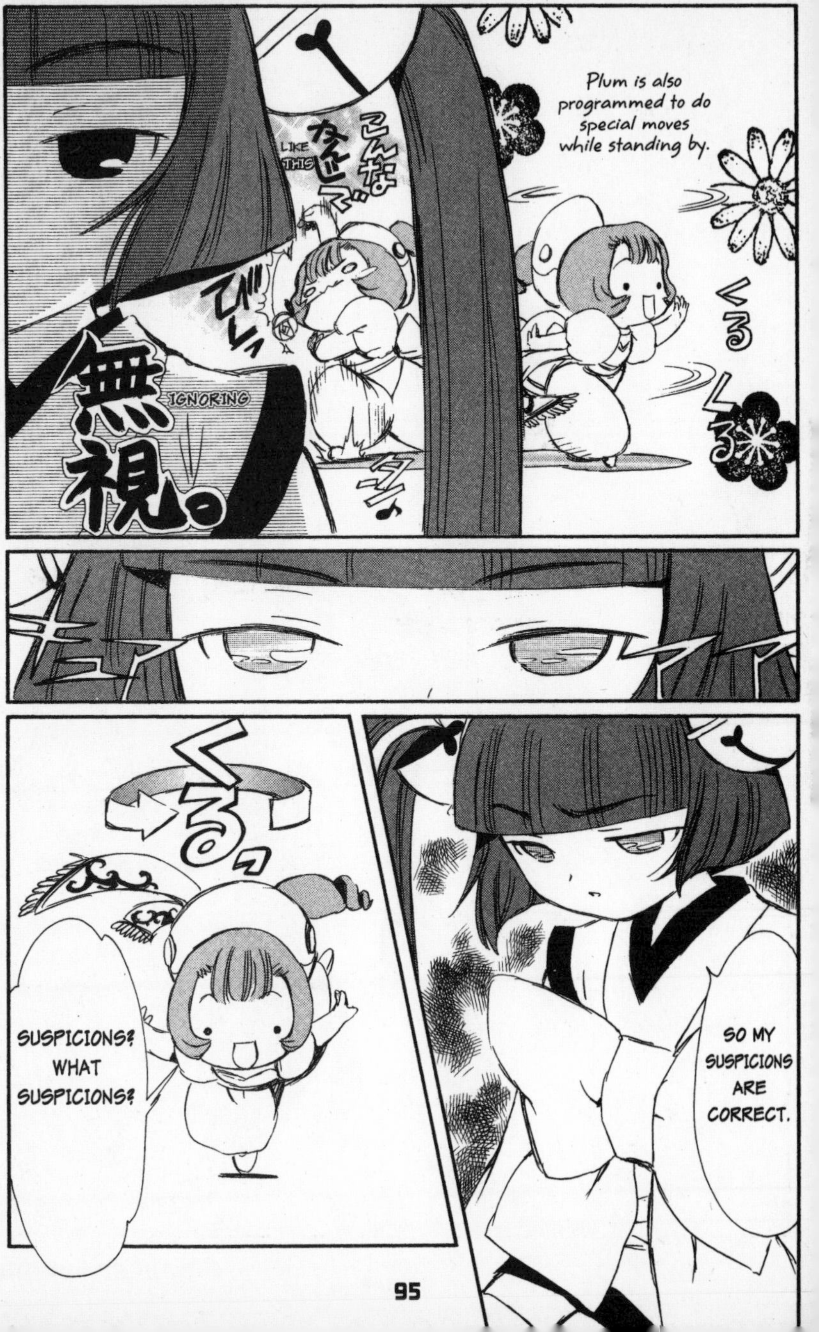
Plum is also programmed to do special moves while standing by.
くるくる
こんなかんじで
LIKE THIS
無視。
IGNORING
SO MY SUSPICIONS ARE CORRECT.
くるっ
SUSPICIONS? WHAT SUSPICIONS?

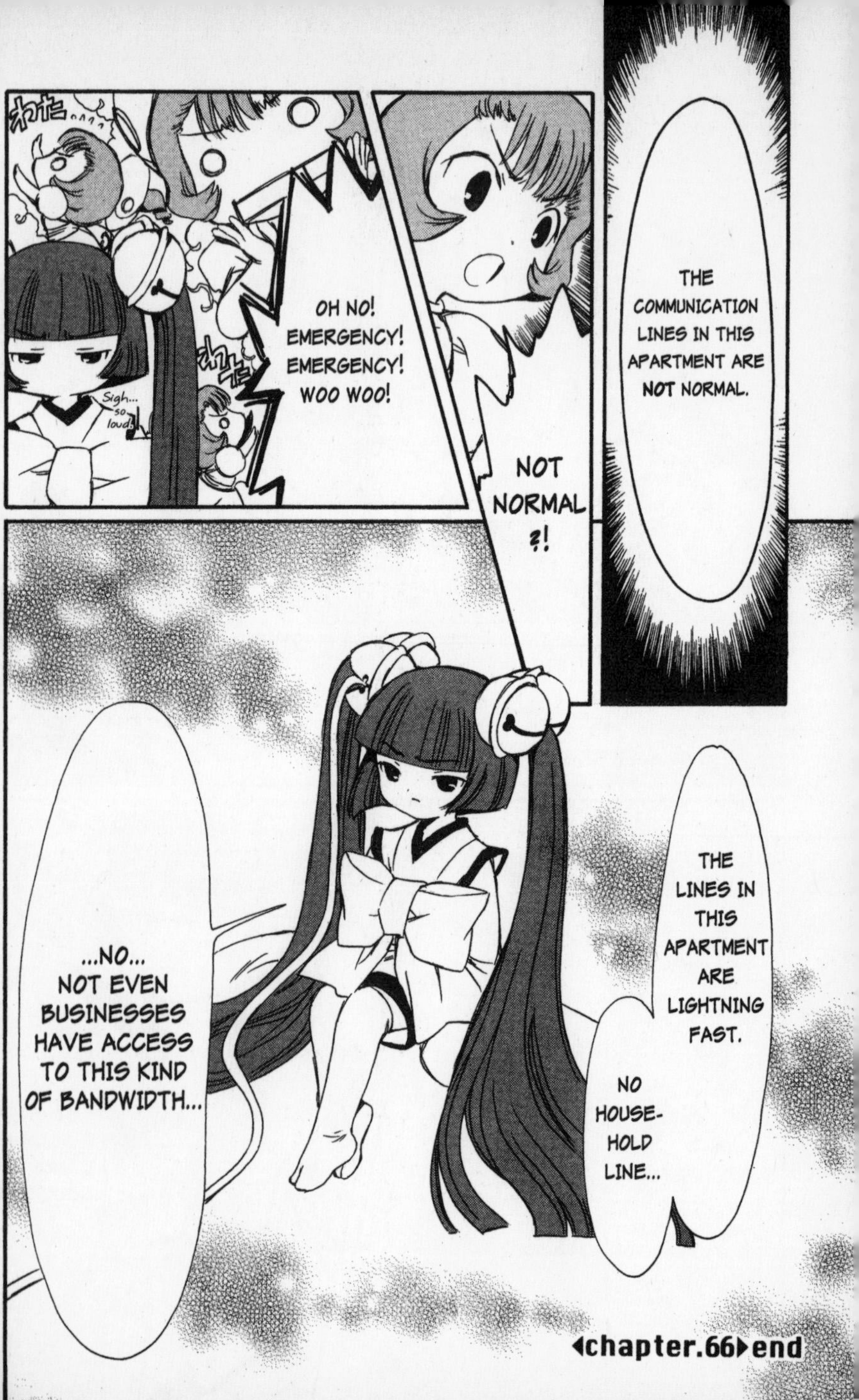
THE COMMUNICATION LINES IN THIS APARTMENT ARE NOT NORMAL.
NOT NORMAL ?!
OH NO! EMERGENCY! EMERGENCY! WOO WOO!
Sigh... so loud.
THE LINES IN THIS APARTMENT ARE LIGHTNING FAST.
NO HOUSE-HOLD LINE...
...NO... NOT EVEN BUSINESSES HAVE ACCESS TO THIS KIND OF BANDWIDTH...
◀chapter.66▶end

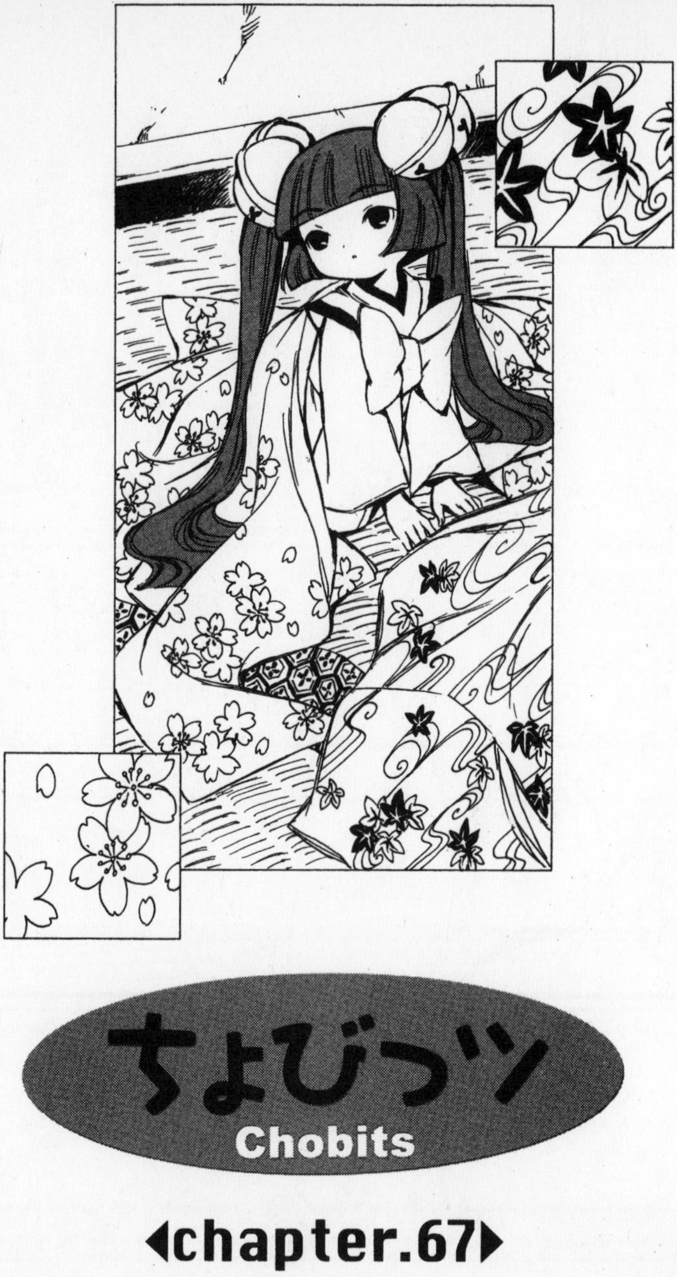

ちょびっツ
Chobits

◀chapter.67▶

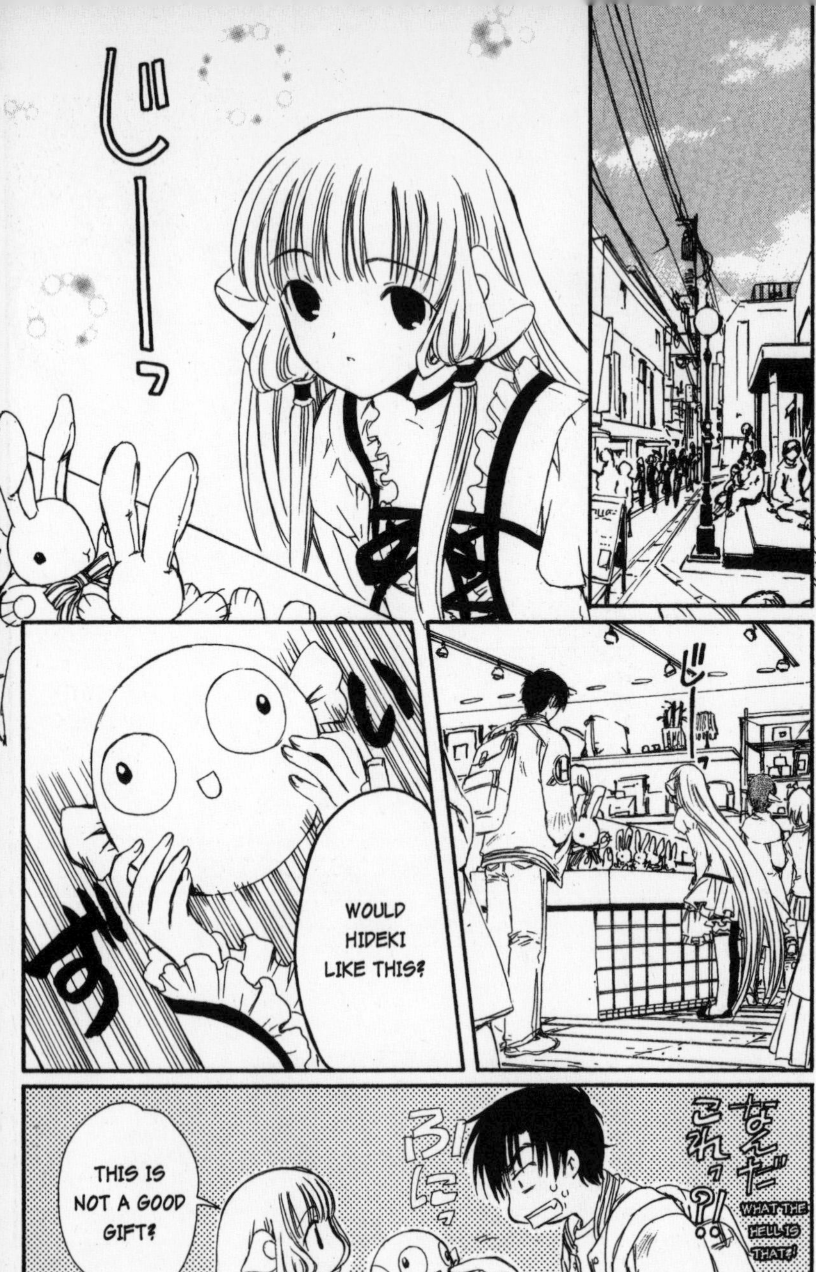

じーっ
WOULD HIDEKI LIKE THIS?
なんだこれっ?!
WHAT THE HELL IS THAT?!
THIS IS NOT A GOOD GIFT?

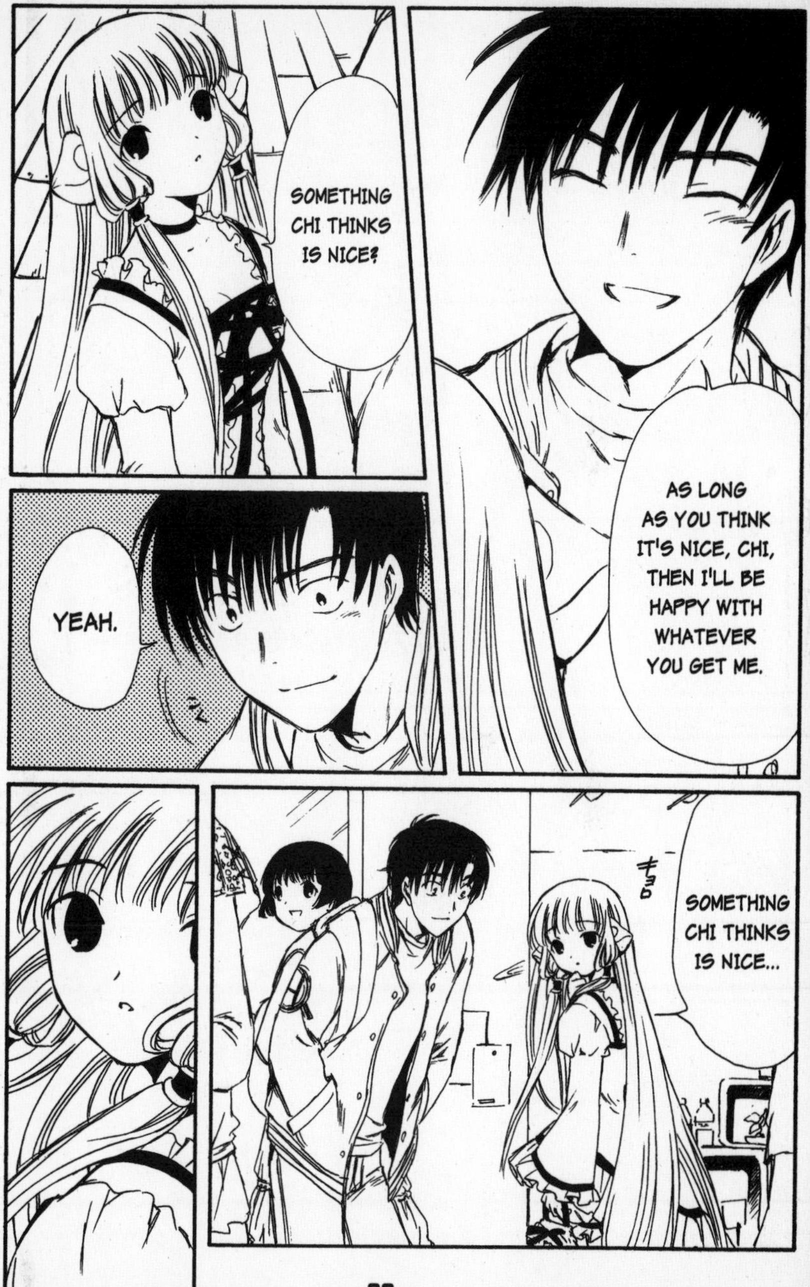
AS LONG AS YOU THINK IT'S NICE, CHI, THEN I'LL BE HAPPY WITH WHATEVER YOU GET ME.
SOMETHING CHI THINKS IS NICE?
YEAH.
キョロ
SOMETHING CHI THINKS IS NICE...

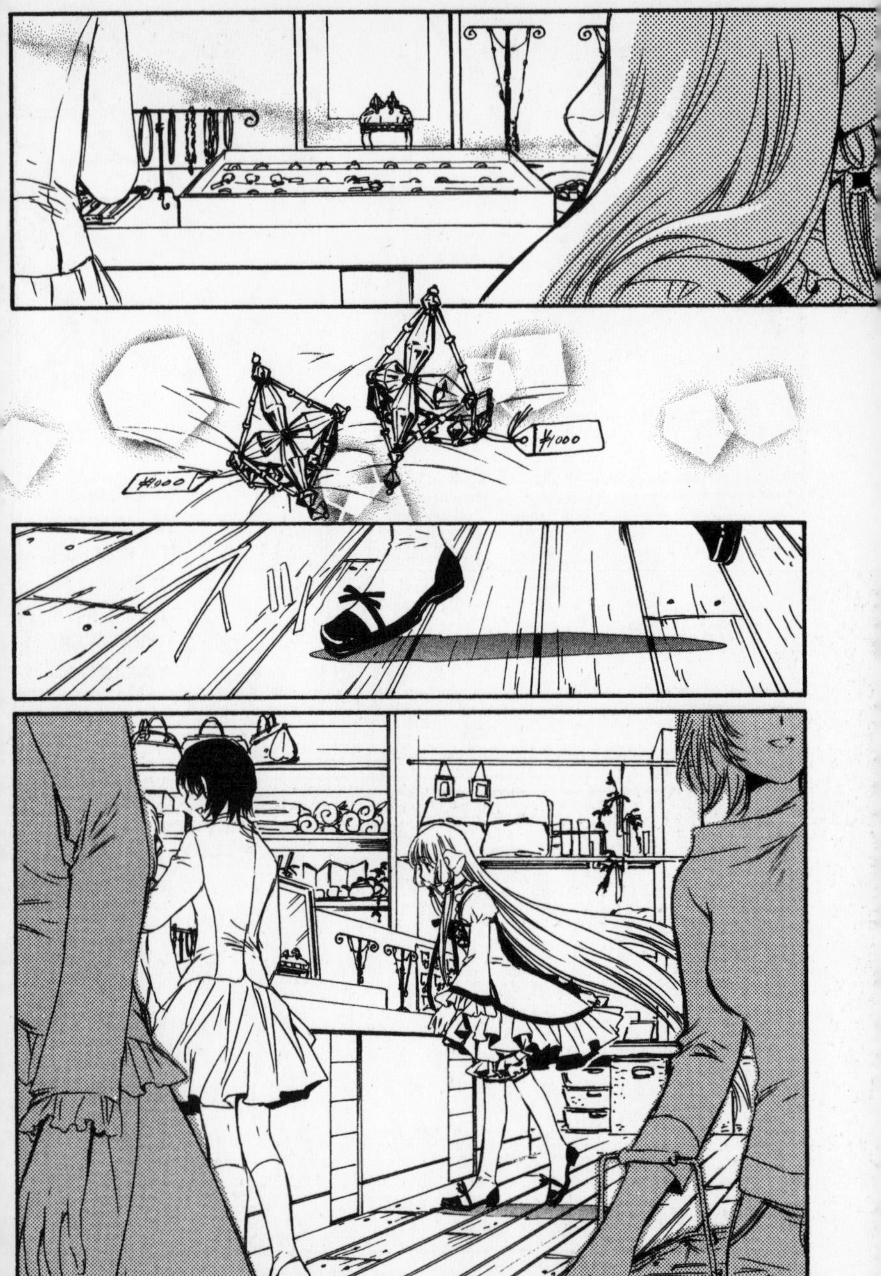
¥1000
¥1000

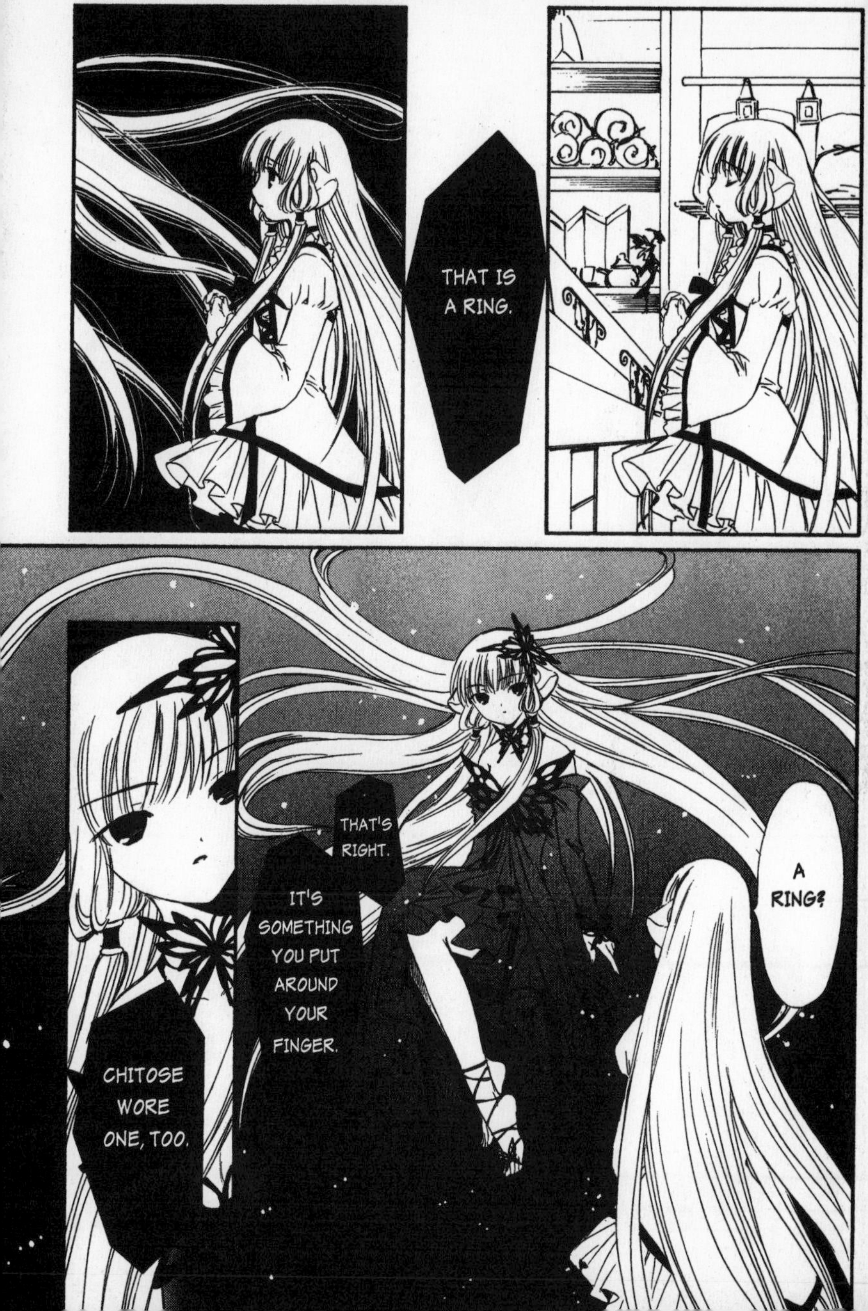
THAT IS A RING.
A RING?
THAT'S RIGHT.
IT'S SOMETHING YOU PUT AROUND YOUR FINGER.
CHITOSE WORE ONE, TOO.

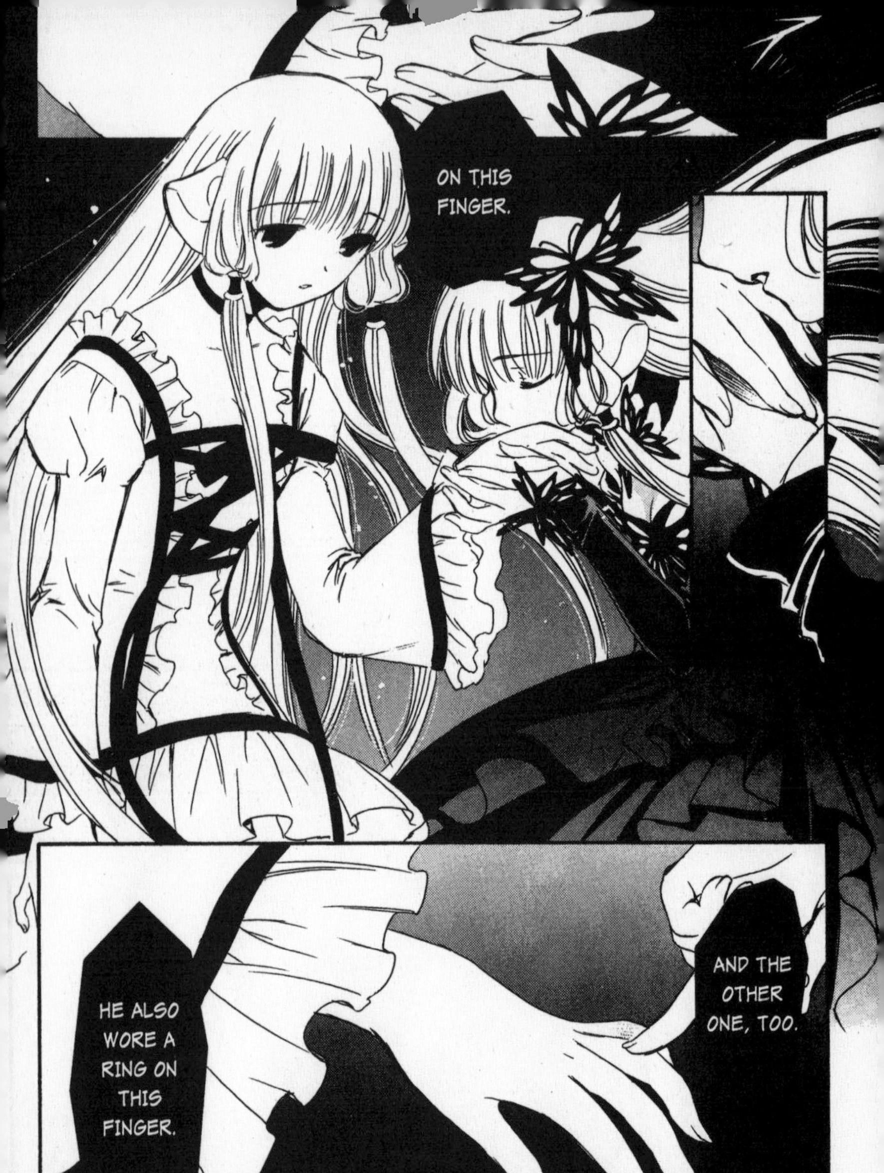
ON THIS FINGER.
AND THE OTHER ONE, TOO.
HE ALSO WORE A RING ON THIS FINGER.

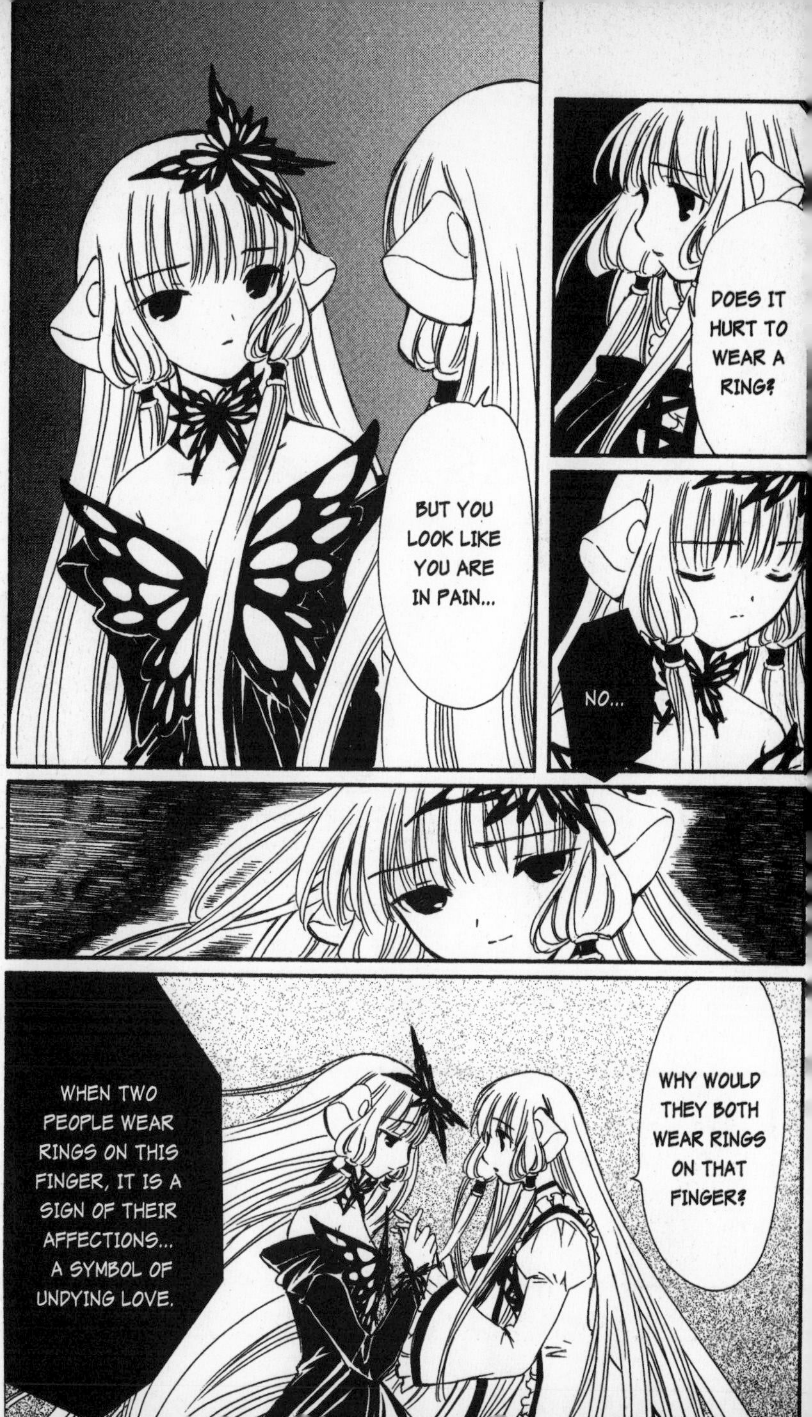
DOES IT HURT TO WEAR A RING?
NO...
BUT YOU LOOK LIKE YOU ARE IN PAIN...
WHY WOULD THEY BOTH WEAR RINGS ON THAT FINGER?
WHEN TWO PEOPLE WEAR RINGS ON THIS FINGER, IT IS A SIGN OF THEIR AFFECTIONS... A SYMBOL OF UNDYING LOVE.

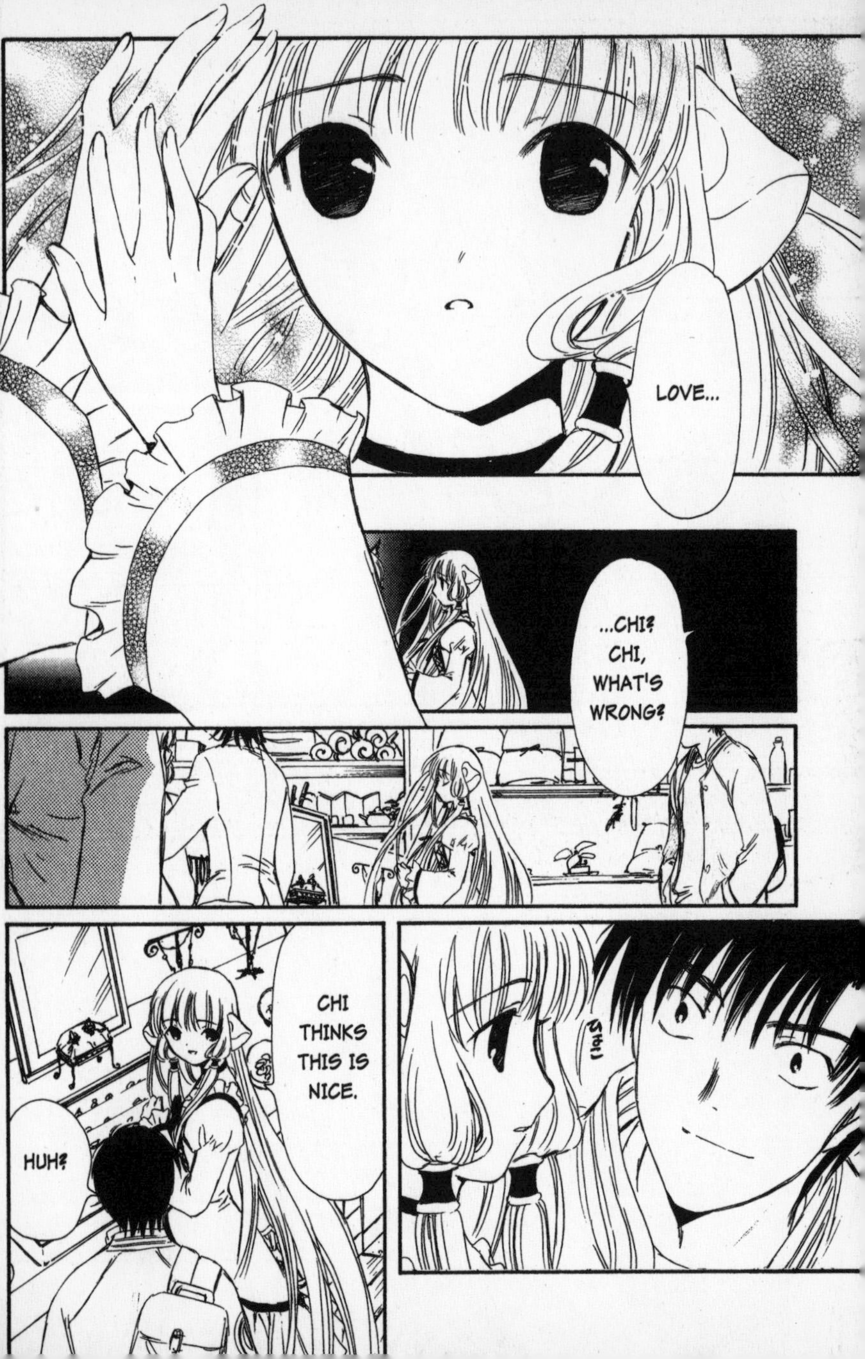
LOVE...
...CHI? CHI, WHAT'S WRONG?
CHI THINKS THIS IS NICE.
HUH?

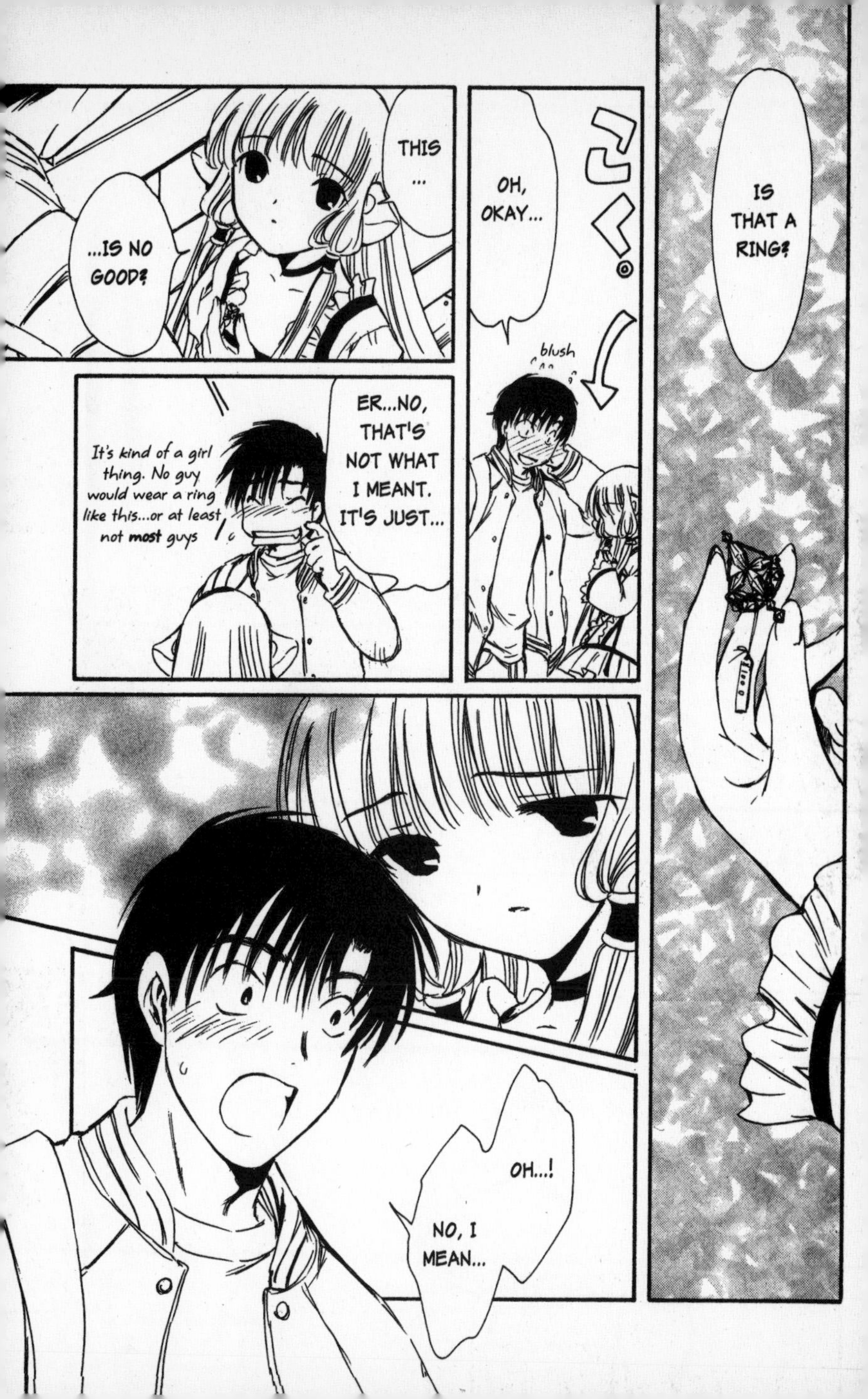
IS THAT A RING?
OH, OKAY...
blush
THIS ...
...IS NO GOOD?
ER...NO, THAT'S NOT WHAT I MEANT. IT'S JUST...
It's kind of a girl thing. No guy would wear a ring like this...or at least not **most** guys
OH...!
NO, I MEAN...

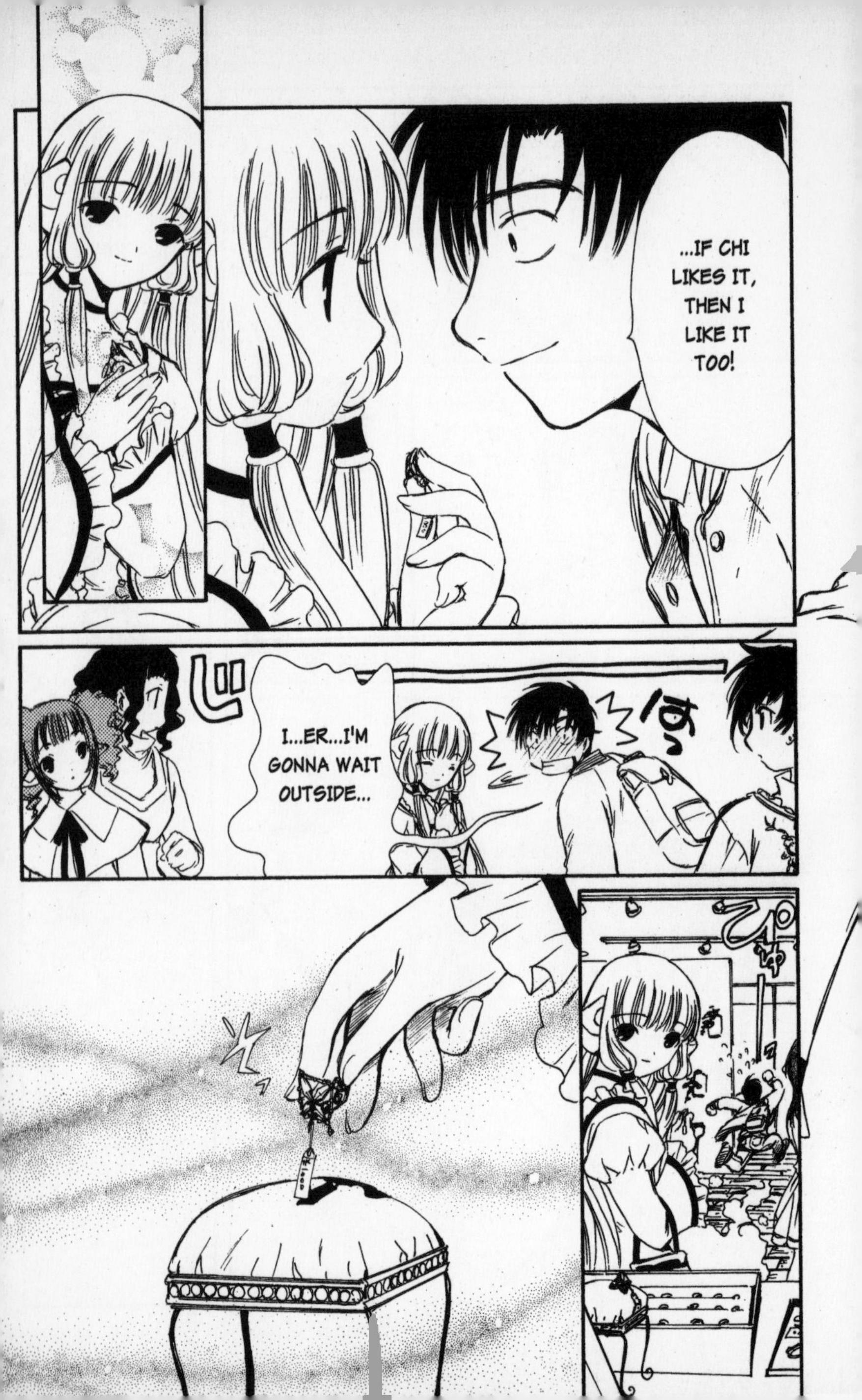
...IF CHI LIKES IT, THEN I LIKE IT TOO!
I...ER...I'M GONNA WAIT OUTSIDE...

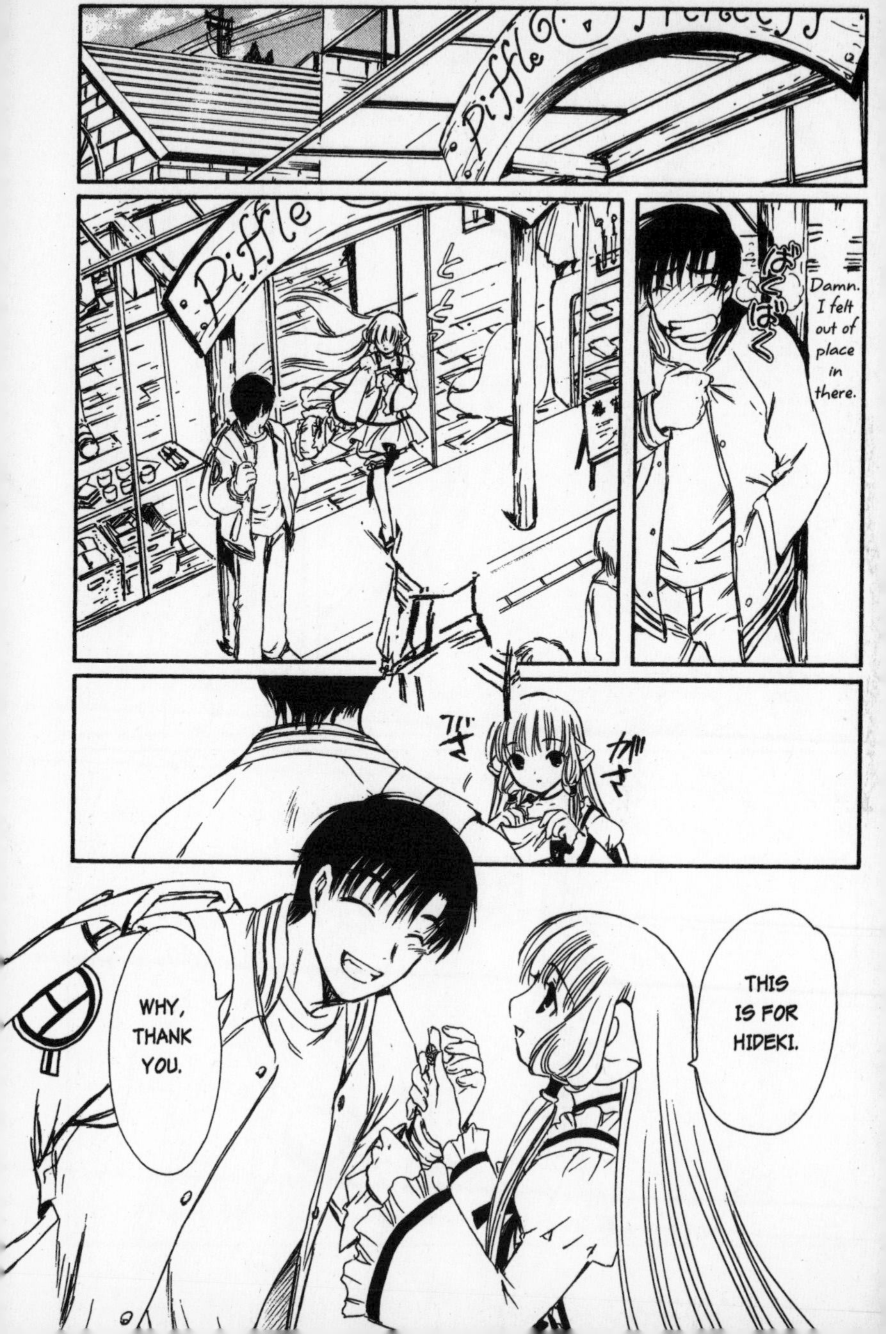
Piffle
ばくばく
Damn. I felt out of place in there.
Piffle
とと
がさ
THIS IS FOR HIDEKI.
WHY, THANK YOU.

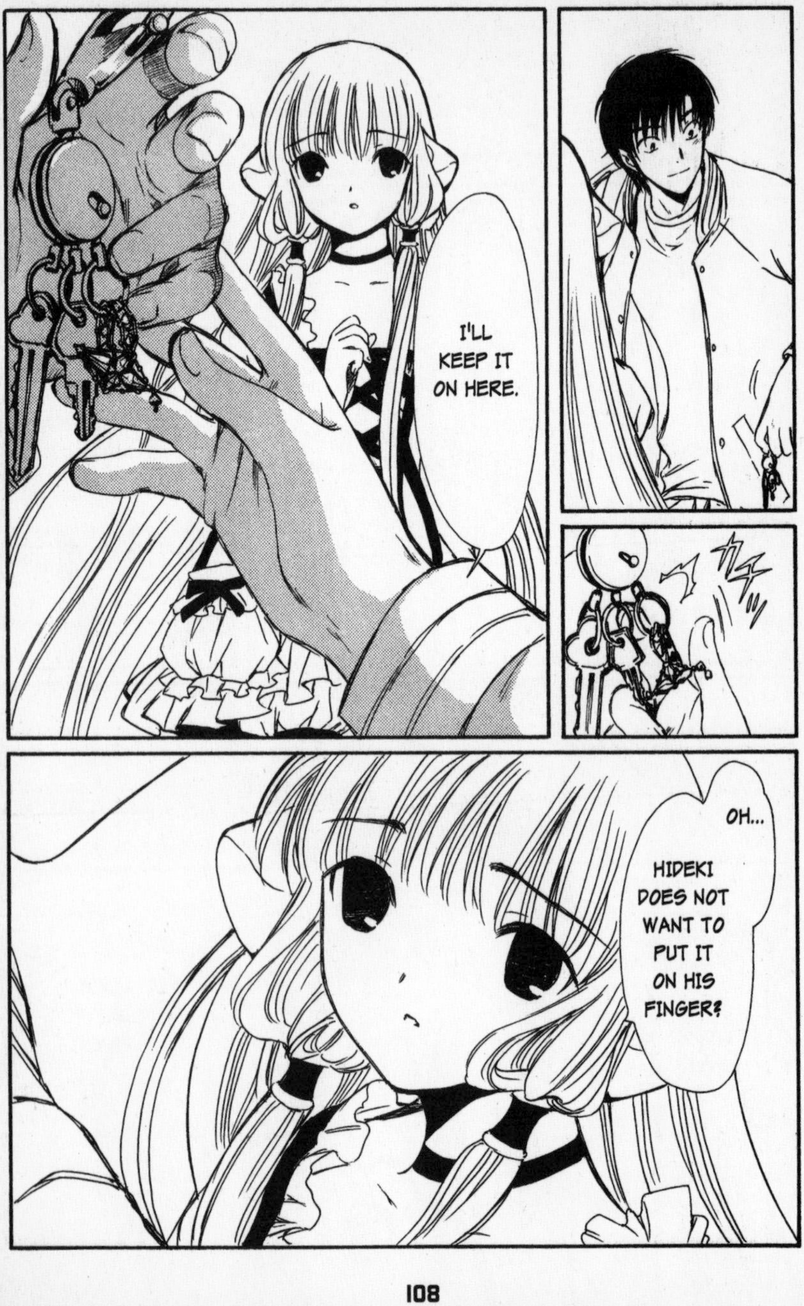
カチ
I'LL KEEP IT ON HERE.
OH...
HIDEKI DOES NOT WANT TO PUT IT ON HIS FINGER?

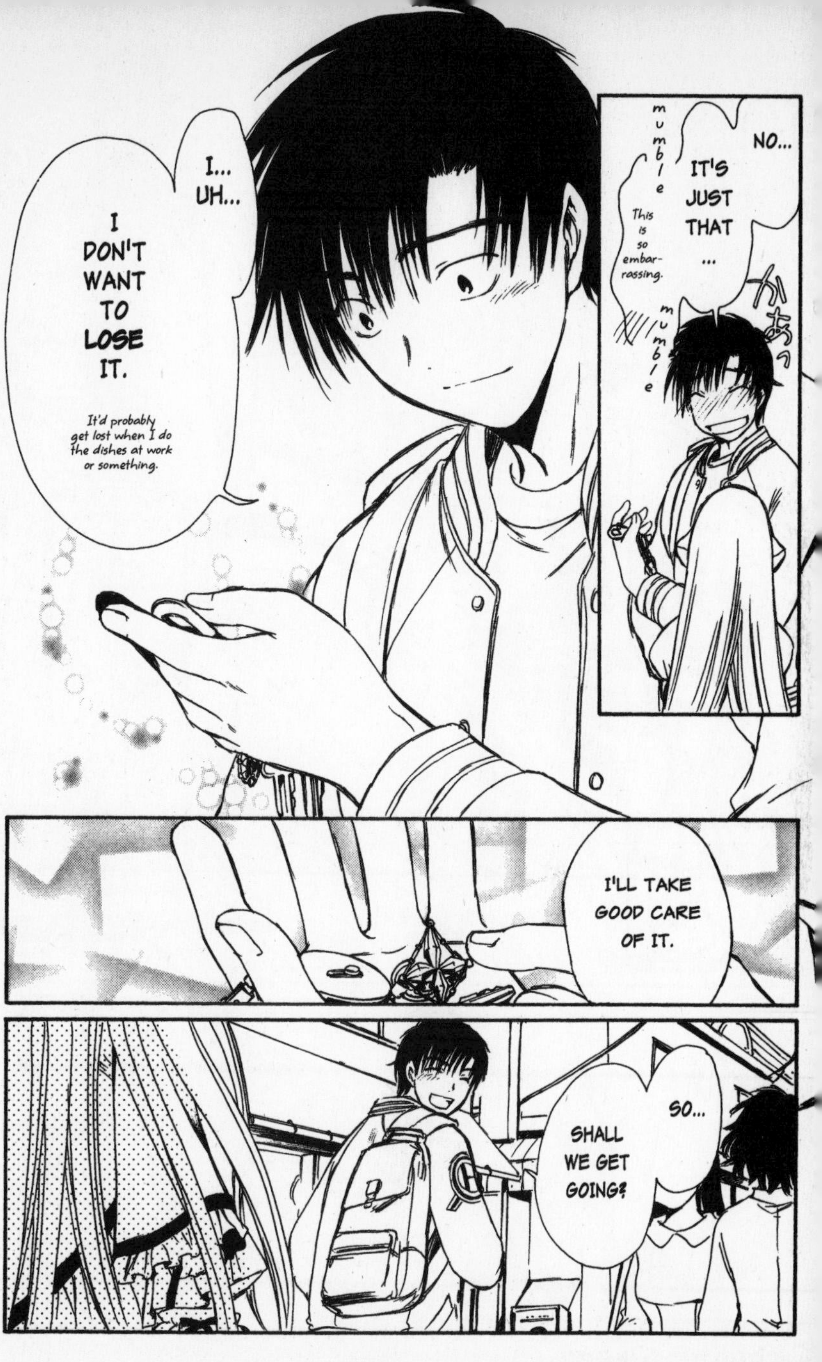
NO... IT'S JUST THAT ...
mumble
This is so embarrassing.
mumble
かあっ
I... UH...
I DON'T WANT TO LOSE IT.
It'd probably get lost when I do the dishes at work or something.
I'LL TAKE GOOD CARE OF IT.
SO...
SHALL WE GET GOING?

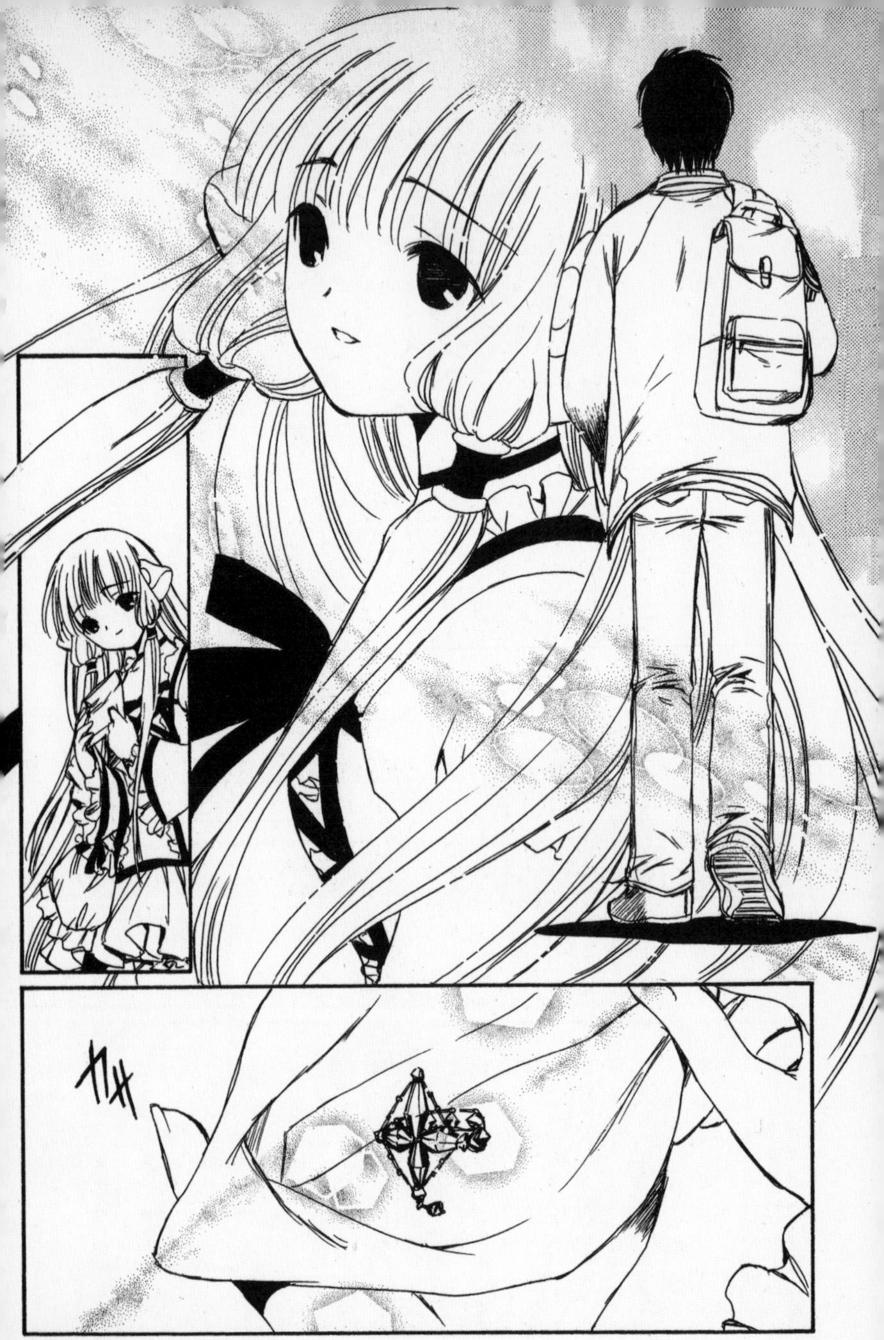
カサ

◂chapter.67▸ end

ちょびっツ

Chobits

◀chapter.68▶

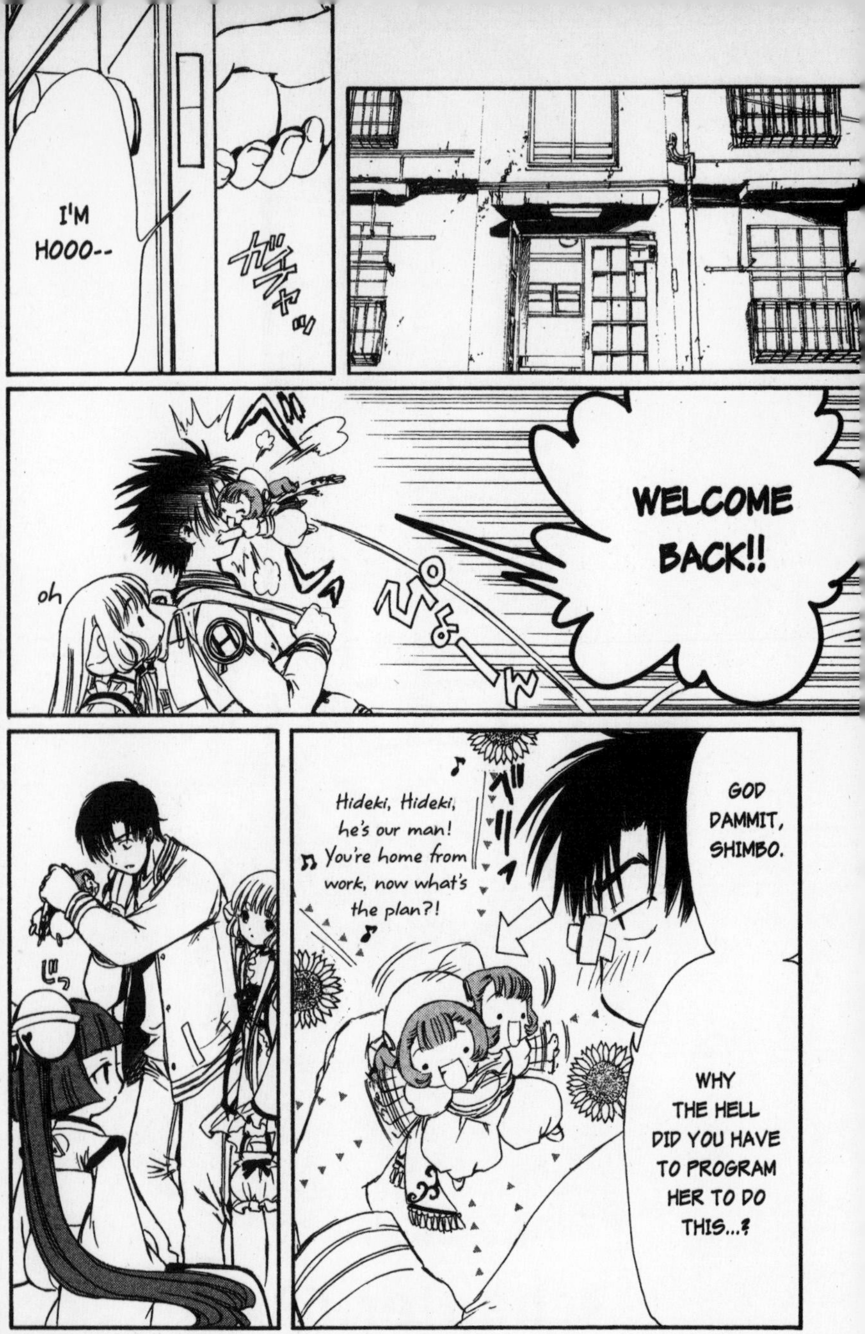

I'M HOOO--
WELCOME BACK!!
oh
GOD DAMMIT, SHIMBO.
Hideki, Hideki, he's our man! You're home from work, now what's the plan?!
WHY THE HELL DID YOU HAVE TO PROGRAM HER TO DO THIS...?

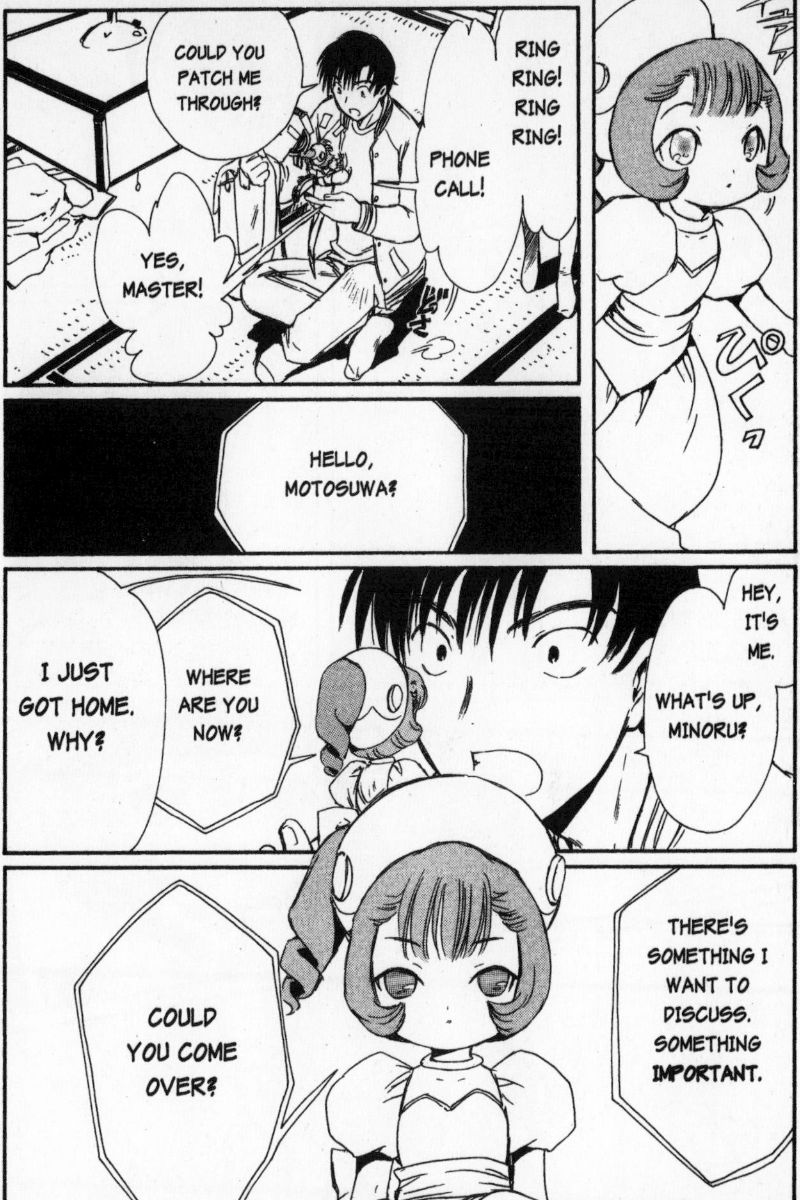
RING RING! RING RING!
PHONE CALL!
COULD YOU PATCH ME THROUGH?
YES, MASTER!
HELLO, MOTOSUWA?
HEY, IT'S ME.
WHAT'S UP, MINORU?
WHERE ARE YOU NOW?
I JUST GOT HOME. WHY?
THERE'S SOMETHING I WANT TO DISCUSS. SOMETHING IMPORTANT.
COULD YOU COME OVER?

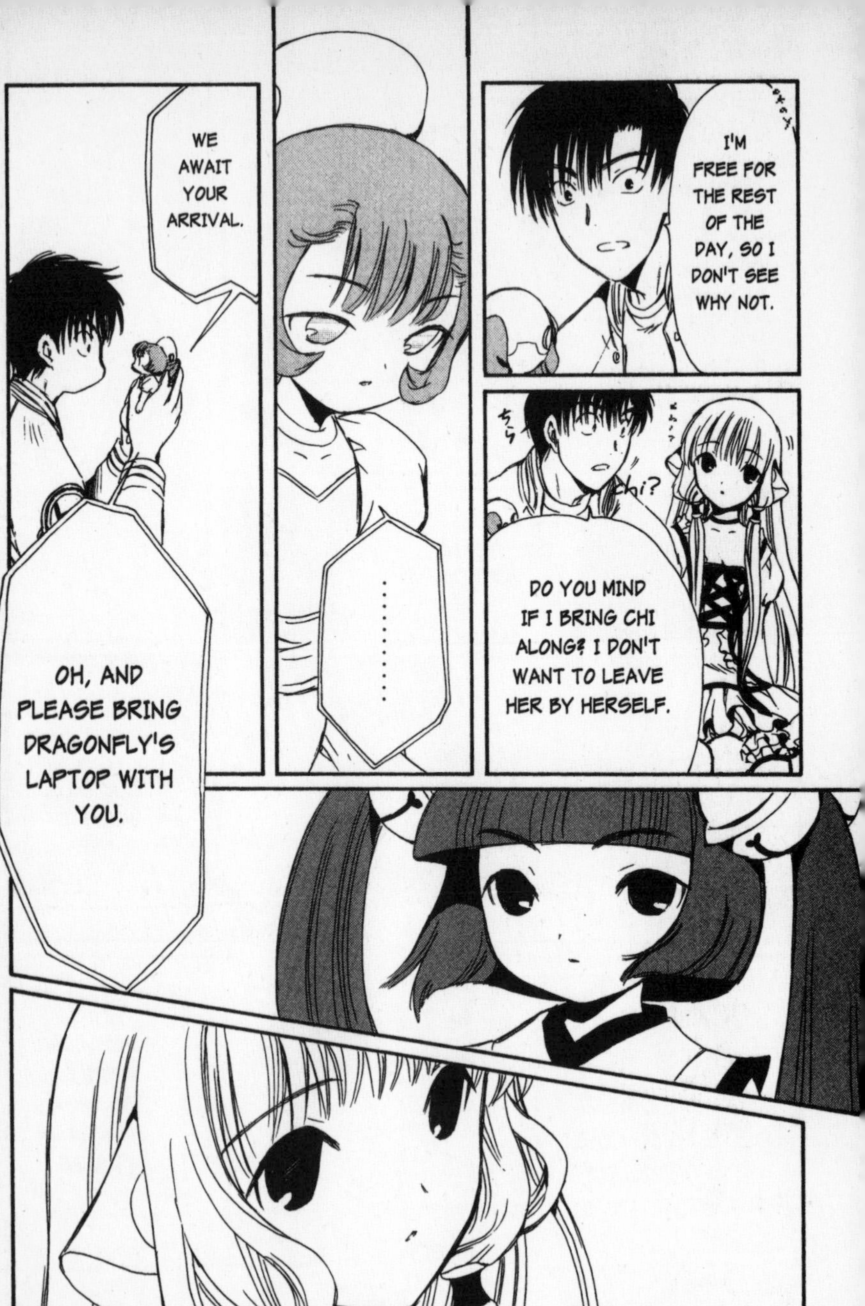
I'M FREE FOR THE REST OF THE DAY, SO I DON'T SEE WHY NOT.
chi?
DO YOU MIND IF I BRING CHI ALONG? I DON'T WANT TO LEAVE HER BY HERSELF.
....
WE AWAIT YOUR ARRIVAL.
OH, AND PLEASE BRING DRAGONFLY'S LAPTOP WITH YOU.

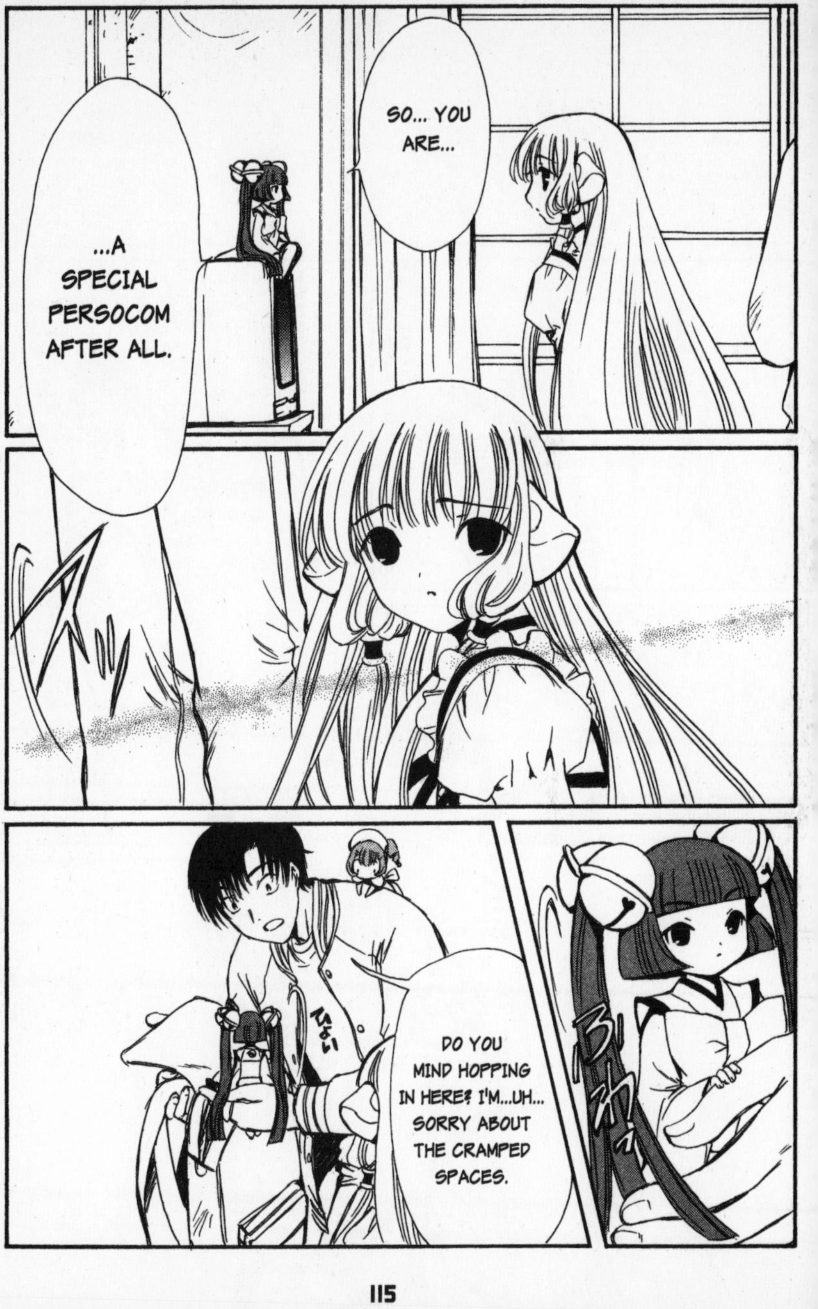
SO... YOU ARE...
...A SPECIAL PERSOCOM AFTER ALL.
DO YOU MIND HOPPING IN HERE? I'M...UH... SORRY ABOUT THE CRAMPED SPACES.

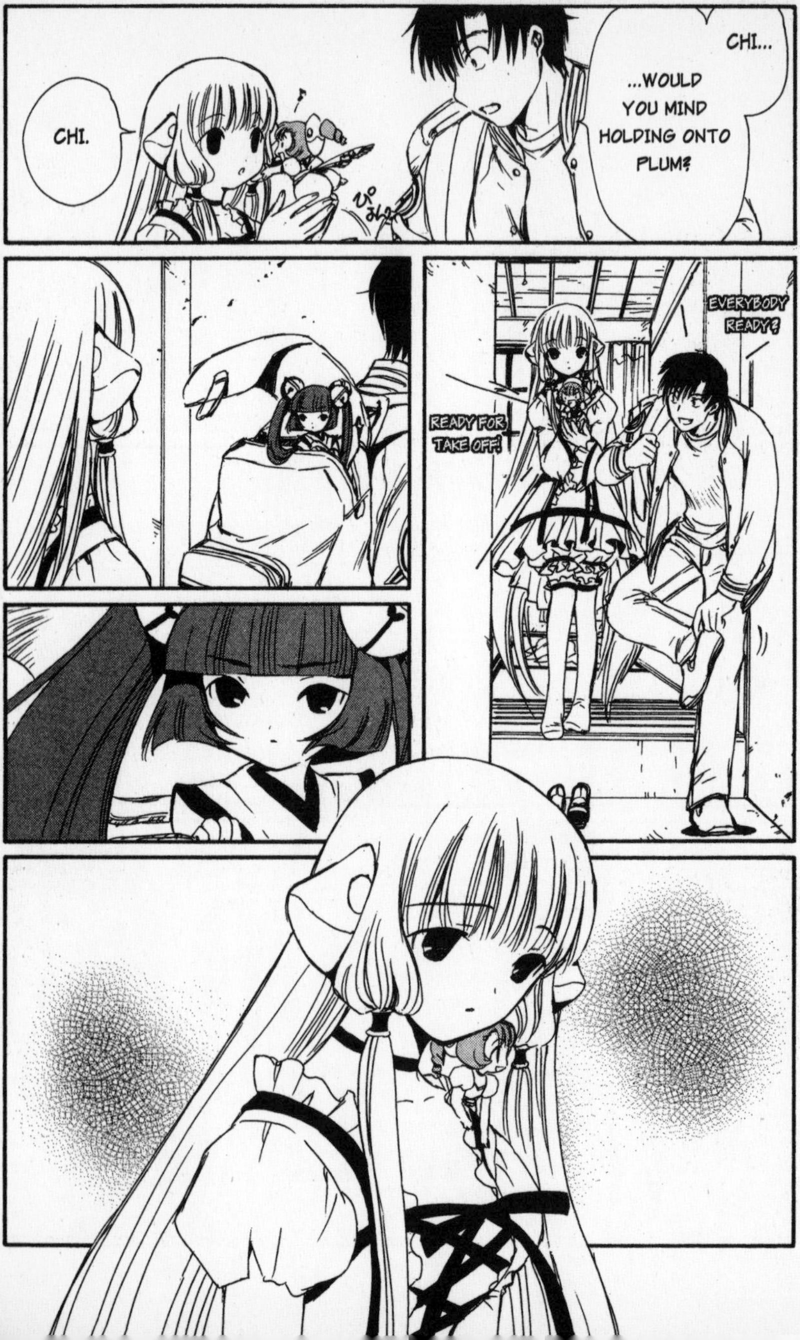
CHI...
...WOULD YOU MIND HOLDING ONTO PLUM?
CHI.
EVERYBODY READY?
READY FOR TAKE OFF!

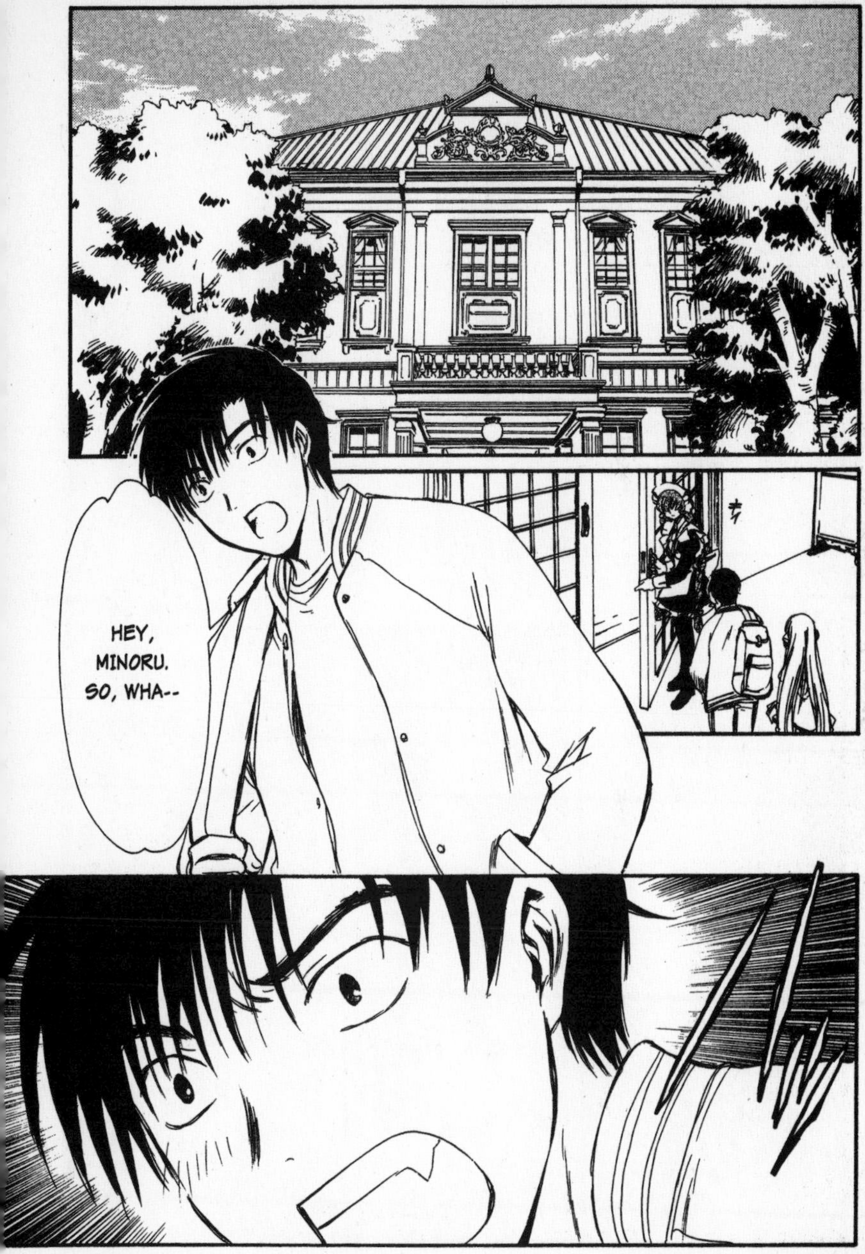
HEY, MINORU. SO, WHA--

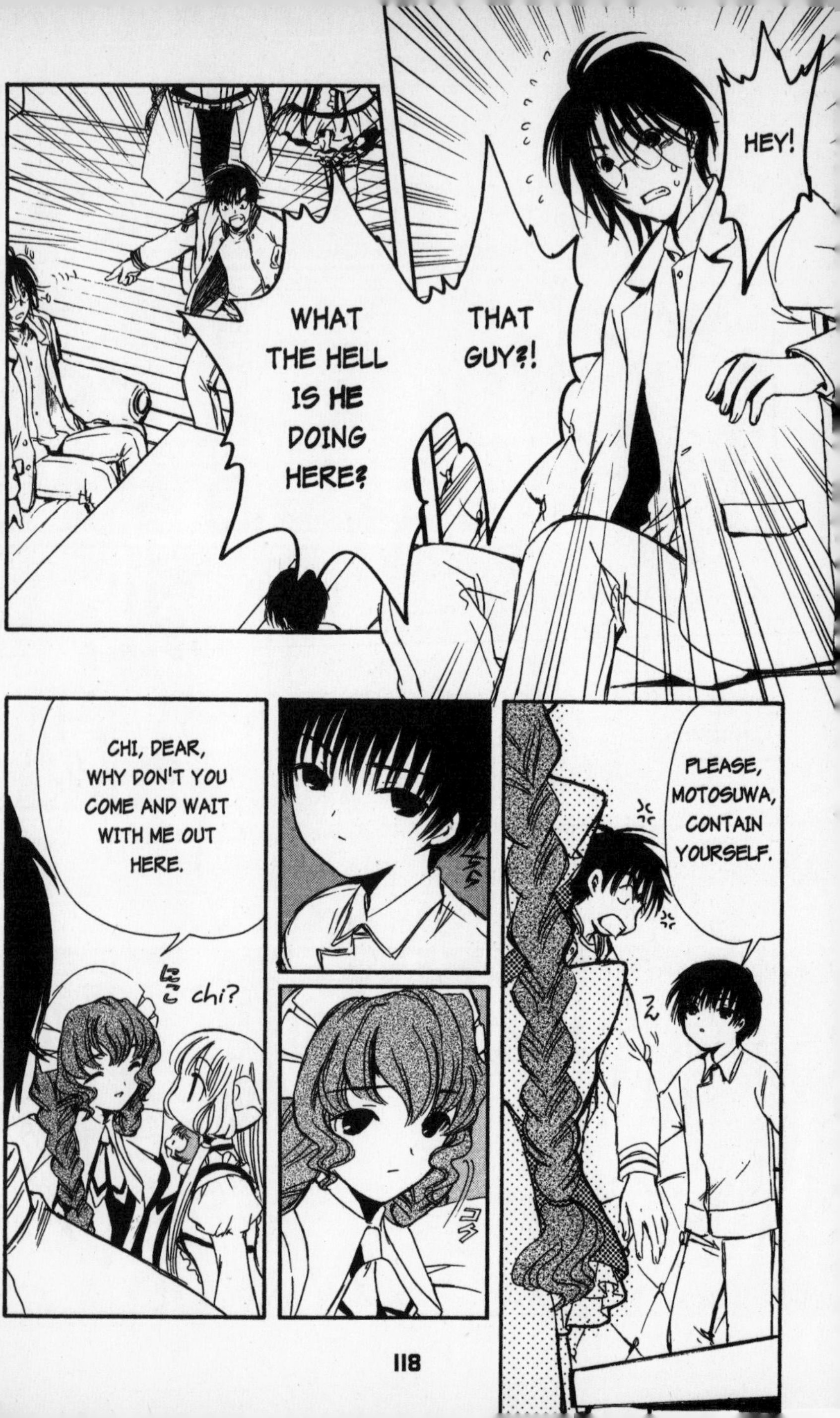
HEY!
WHAT THE HELL IS HE DOING HERE? THAT GUY?!
PLEASE, MOTOSUWA, CONTAIN YOURSELF.
CHI, DEAR, WHY DON'T YOU COME AND WAIT WITH ME OUT HERE.
chi?

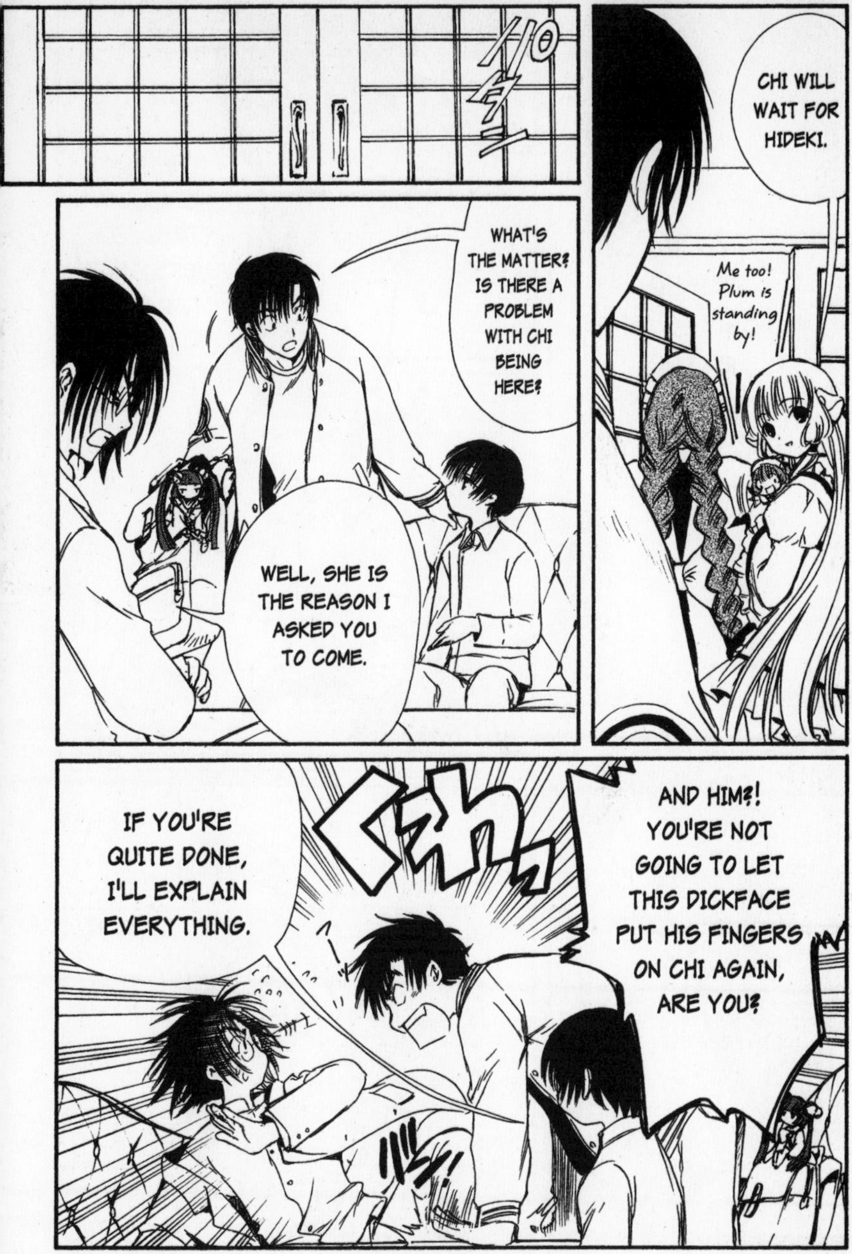
CHI WILL WAIT FOR HIDEKI.
Me too! Plum is standing by!
WHAT'S THE MATTER? IS THERE A PROBLEM WITH CHI BEING HERE?
WELL, SHE IS THE REASON I ASKED YOU TO COME.
AND HIM?! YOU'RE NOT GOING TO LET THIS DICKFACE PUT HIS FINGERS ON CHI AGAIN, ARE YOU?
IF YOU'RE QUITE DONE, I'LL EXPLAIN EVERYTHING.

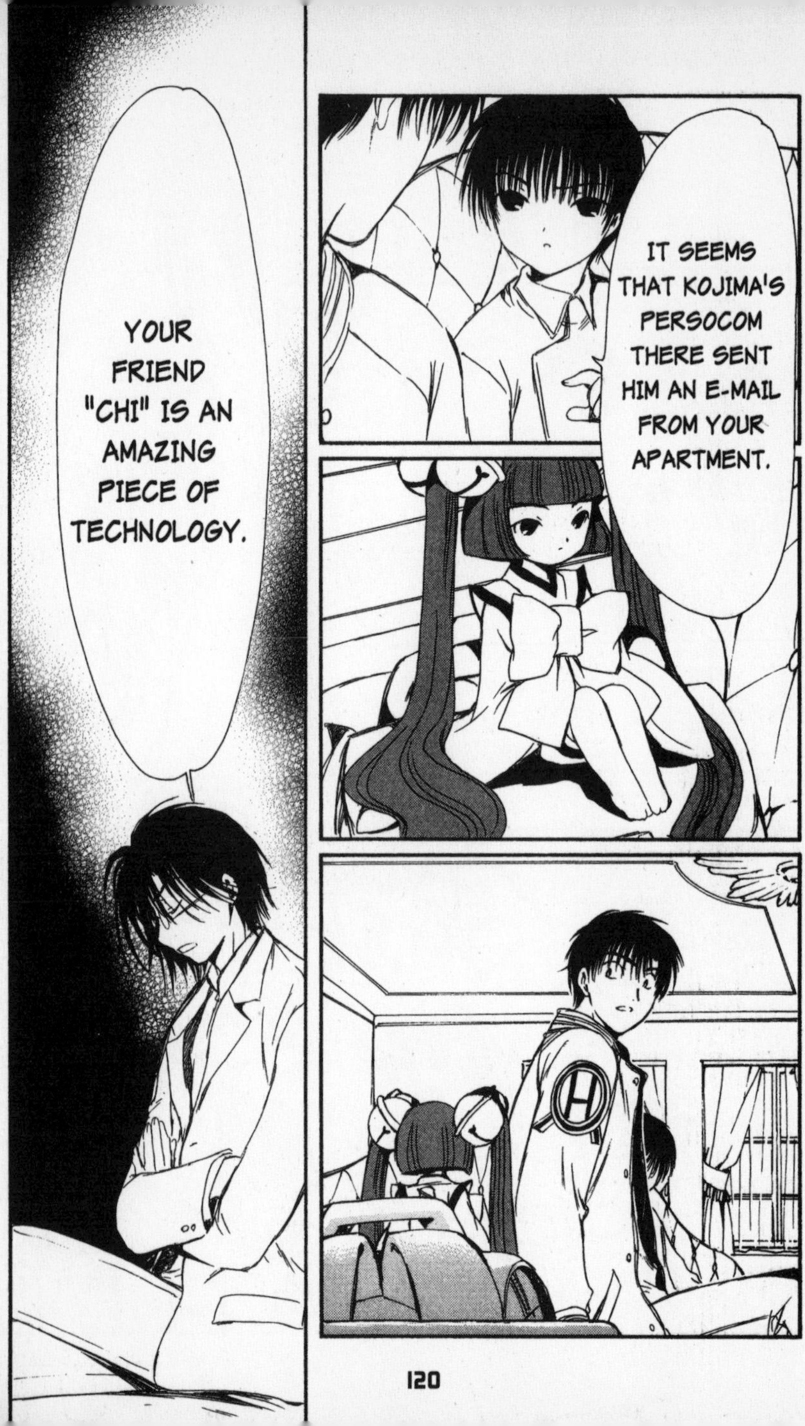
IT SEEMS THAT KOJIMA'S PERSOCOM THERE SENT HIM AN E-MAIL FROM YOUR APARTMENT.
YOUR FRIEND "CHI" IS AN AMAZING PIECE OF TECHNOLOGY.

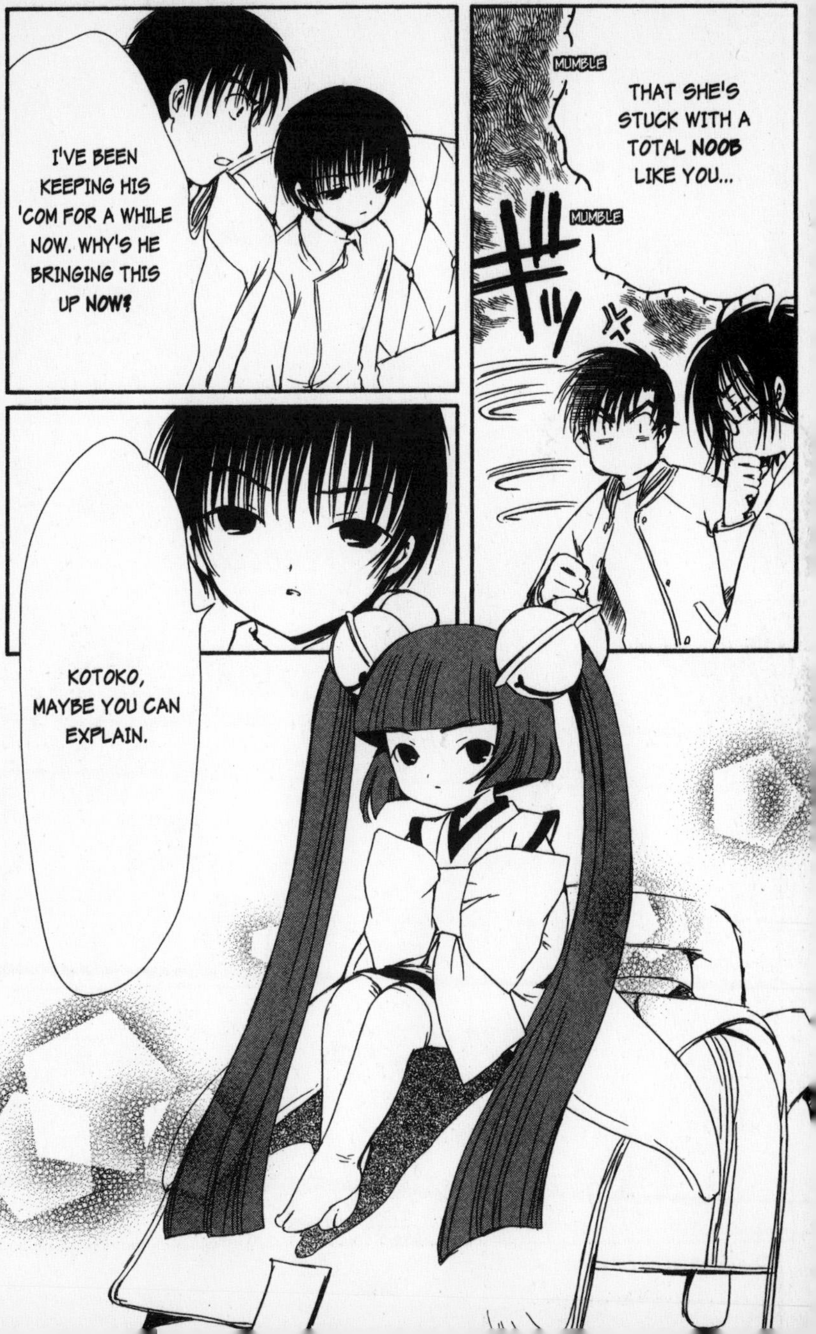
MUMBLE
THAT SHE'S STUCK WITH A TOTAL NOOB LIKE YOU...
MUMBLE
ギッ
I'VE BEEN KEEPING HIS 'COM FOR A WHILE NOW. WHY'S HE BRINGING THIS UP NOW?
KOTOKO, MAYBE YOU CAN EXPLAIN.

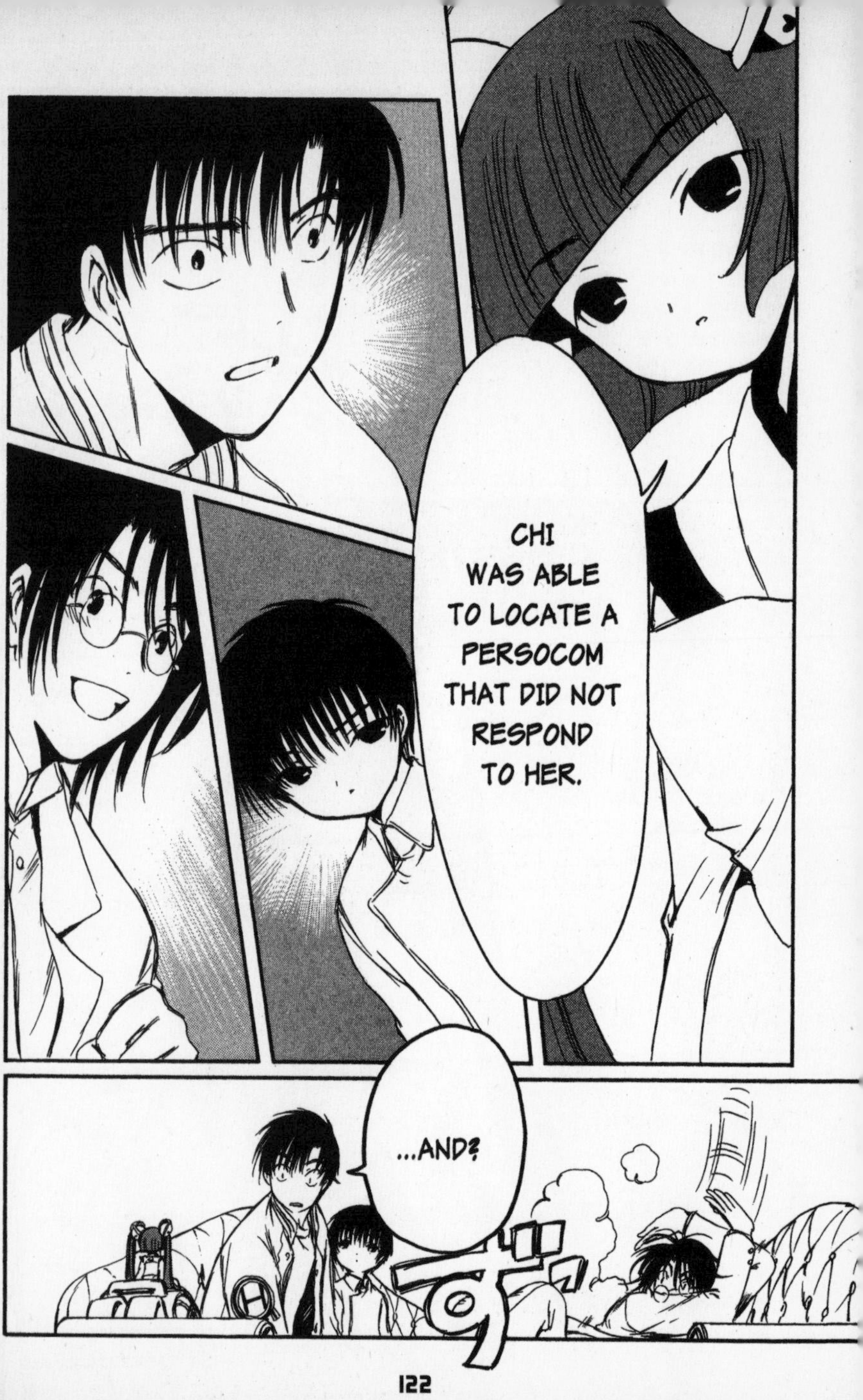
CHI WAS ABLE TO LOCATE A PERSOCOM THAT DID NOT RESPOND TO HER.
...AND?

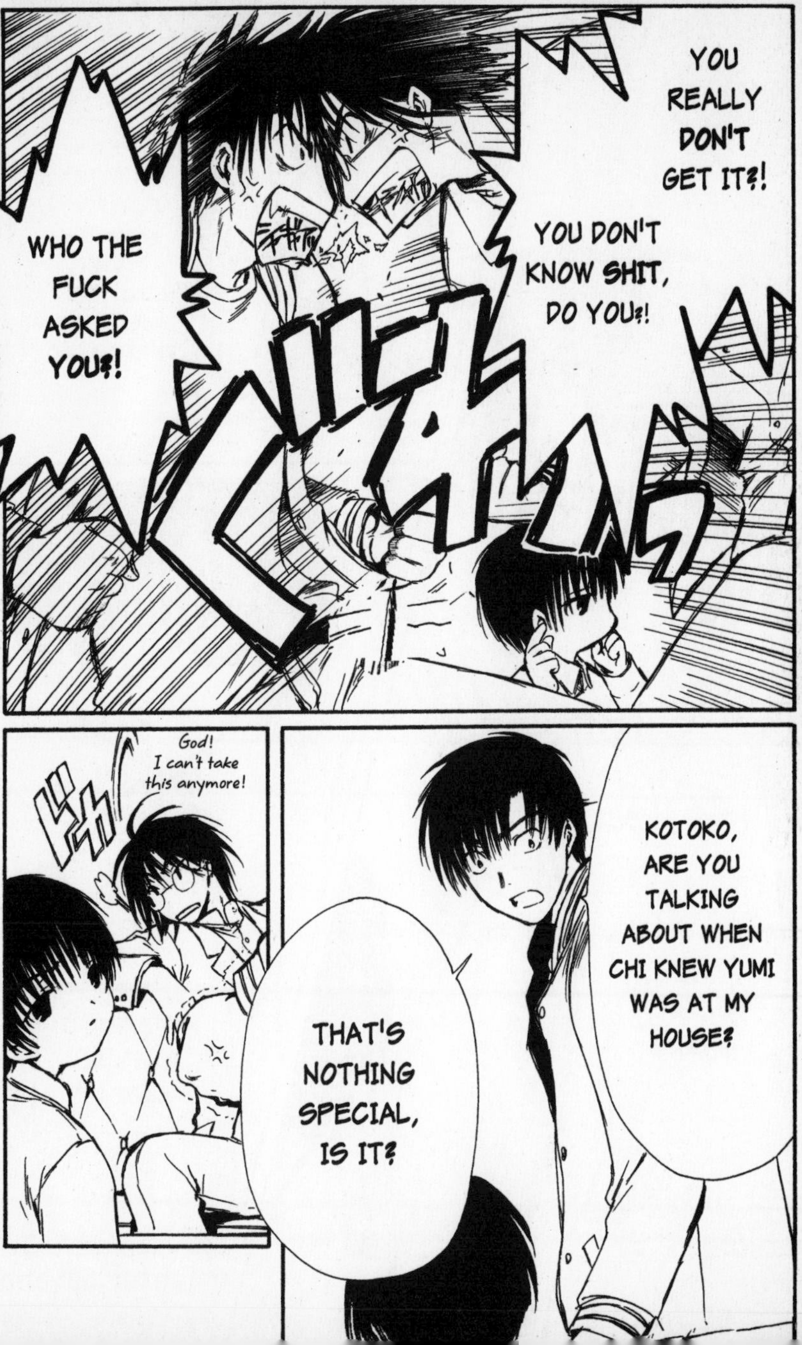
YOU REALLY DON'T GET IT?!
YOU DON'T KNOW SHIT, DO YOU?!
WHO THE FUCK ASKED YOU?!
KOTOKO, ARE YOU TALKING ABOUT WHEN CHI KNEW YUMI WAS AT MY HOUSE?
THAT'S NOTHING SPECIAL, IS IT?
God! I can't take this anymore!

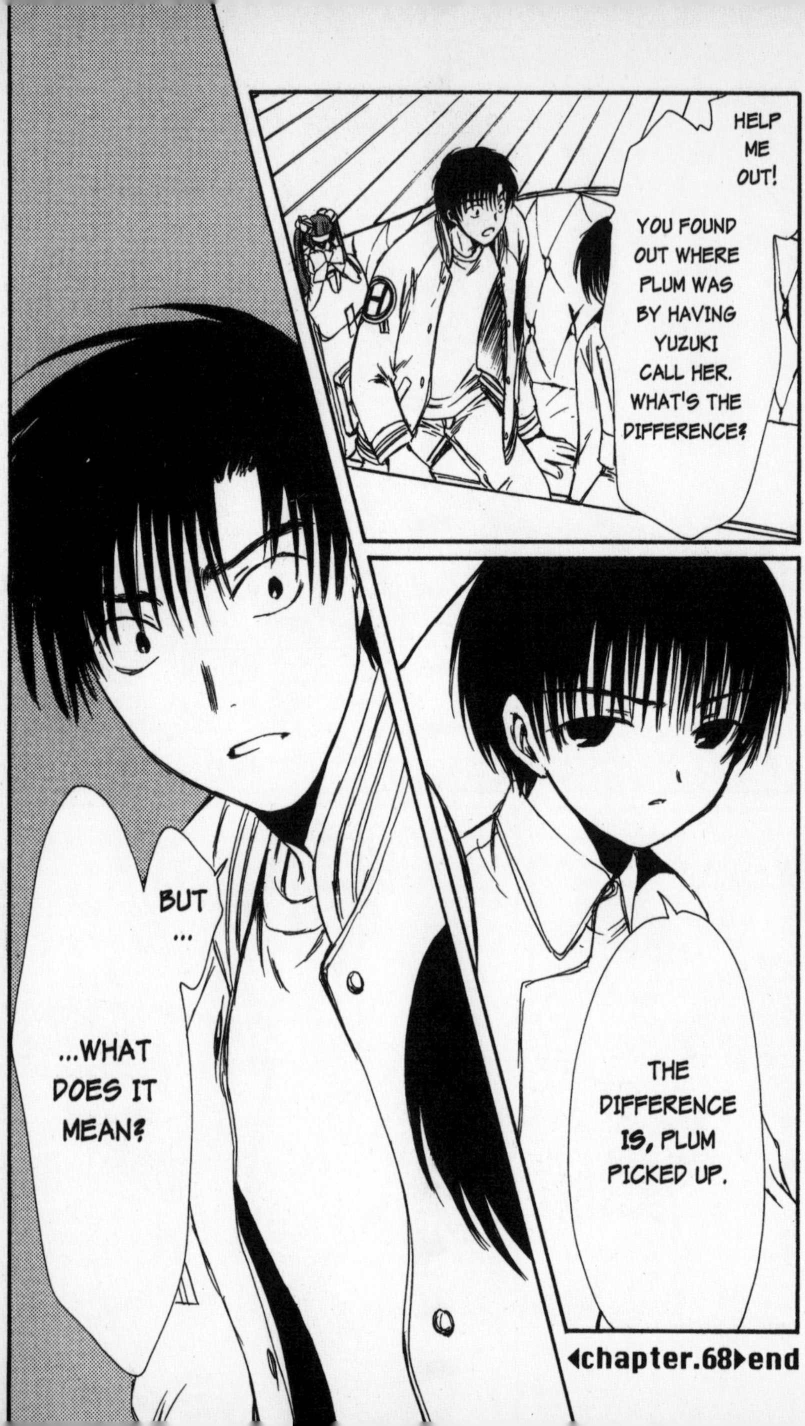
HELP ME OUT!
YOU FOUND OUT WHERE PLUM WAS BY HAVING YUZUKI CALL HER. WHAT'S THE DIFFERENCE?
THE DIFFERENCE IS, PLUM PICKED UP.
BUT ...
...WHAT DOES IT MEAN?
◂chapter.68▸end

ちょびッツ
Chobits

◀chapter.69▶

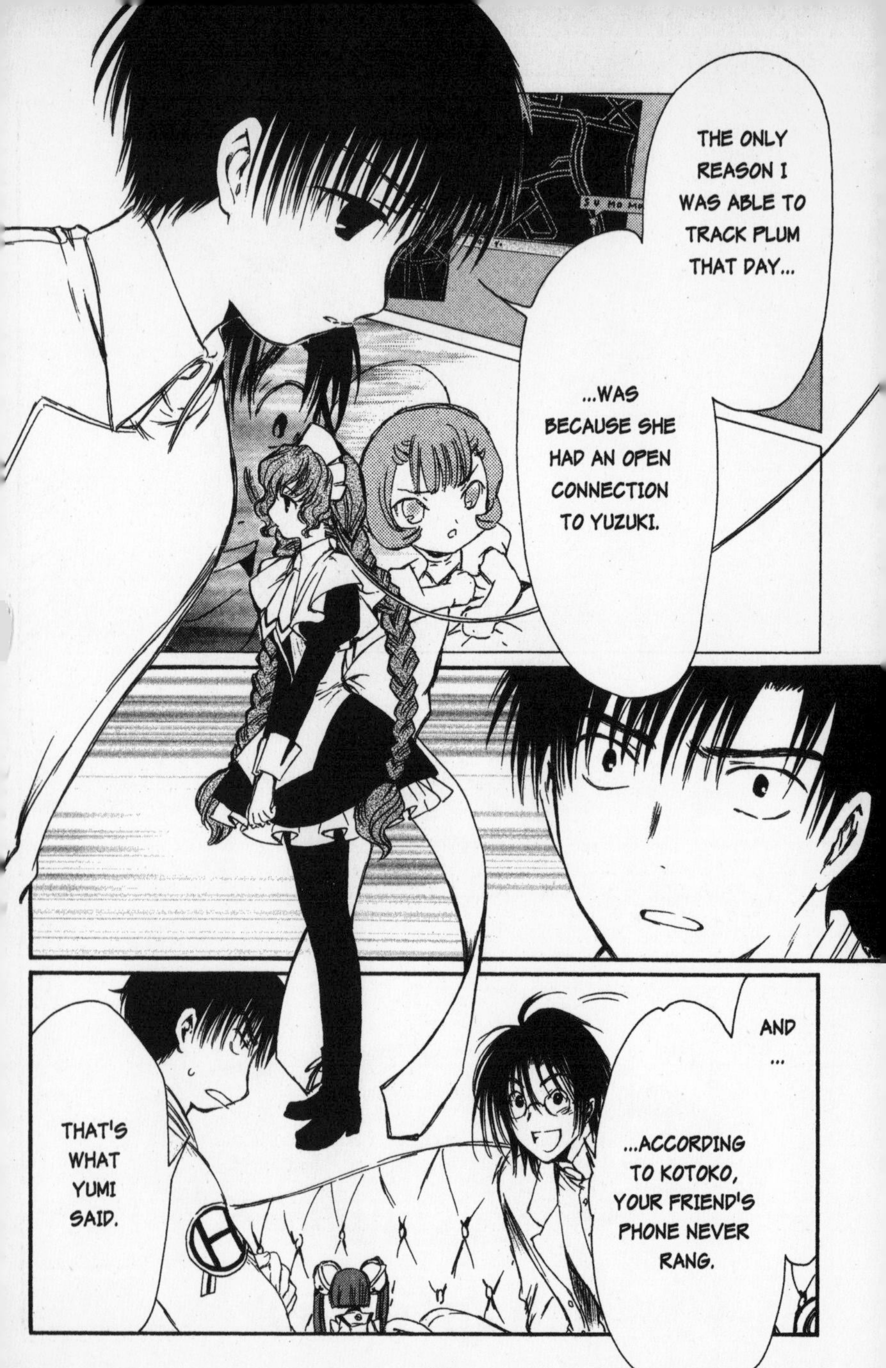
THE ONLY REASON I WAS ABLE TO TRACK PLUM THAT DAY...
...WAS BECAUSE SHE HAD AN OPEN CONNECTION TO YUZUKI.
AND ...
...ACCORDING TO KOTOKO, YOUR FRIEND'S PHONE NEVER RANG.
THAT'S WHAT YUMI SAID.

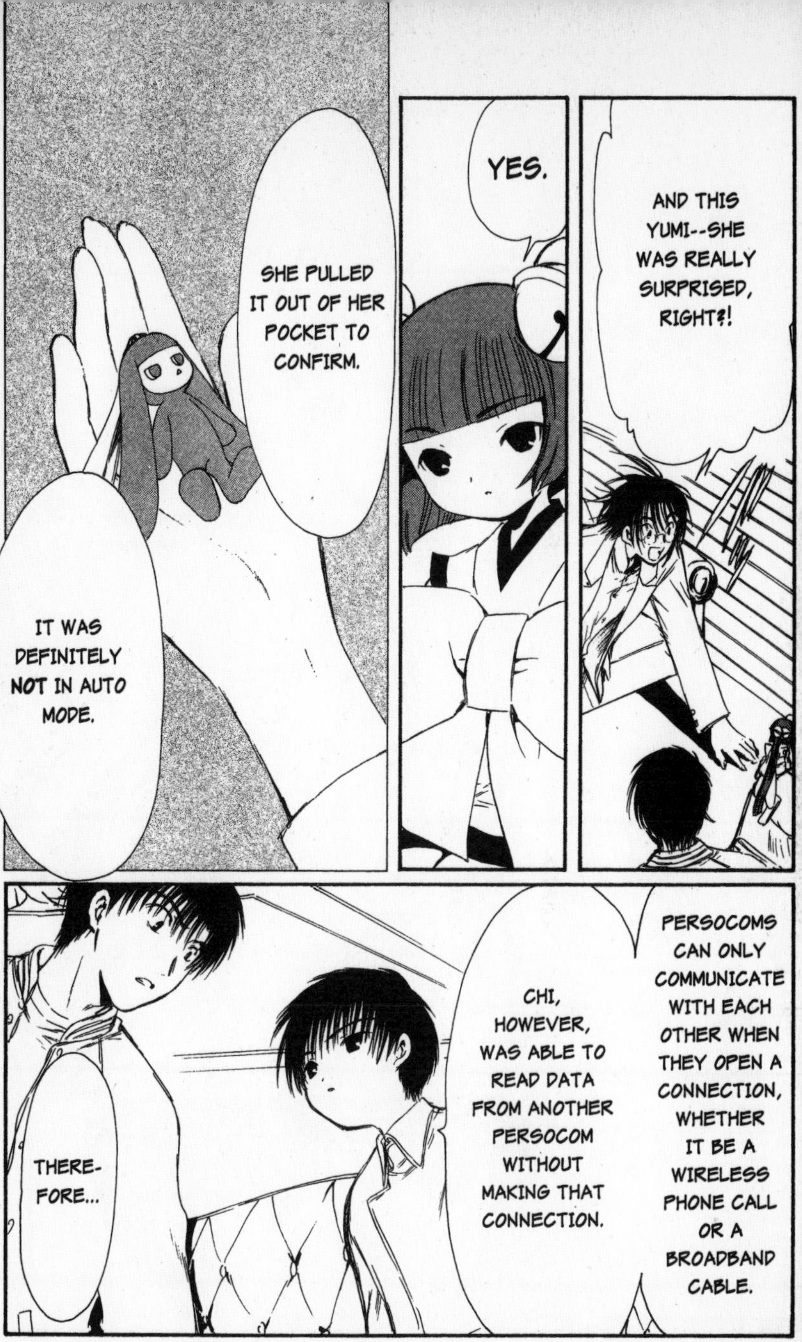
AND THIS YUMI--SHE WAS REALLY SURPRISED, RIGHT?!
YES.
SHE PULLED IT OUT OF HER POCKET TO CONFIRM.
IT WAS DEFINITELY NOT IN AUTO MODE.
PERSOCOMS CAN ONLY COMMUNICATE WITH EACH OTHER WHEN THEY OPEN A CONNECTION, WHETHER IT BE A WIRELESS PHONE CALL OR A BROADBAND CABLE.
CHI, HOWEVER, WAS ABLE TO READ DATA FROM ANOTHER PERSOCOM WITHOUT MAKING THAT CONNECTION.
THERE-FORE...

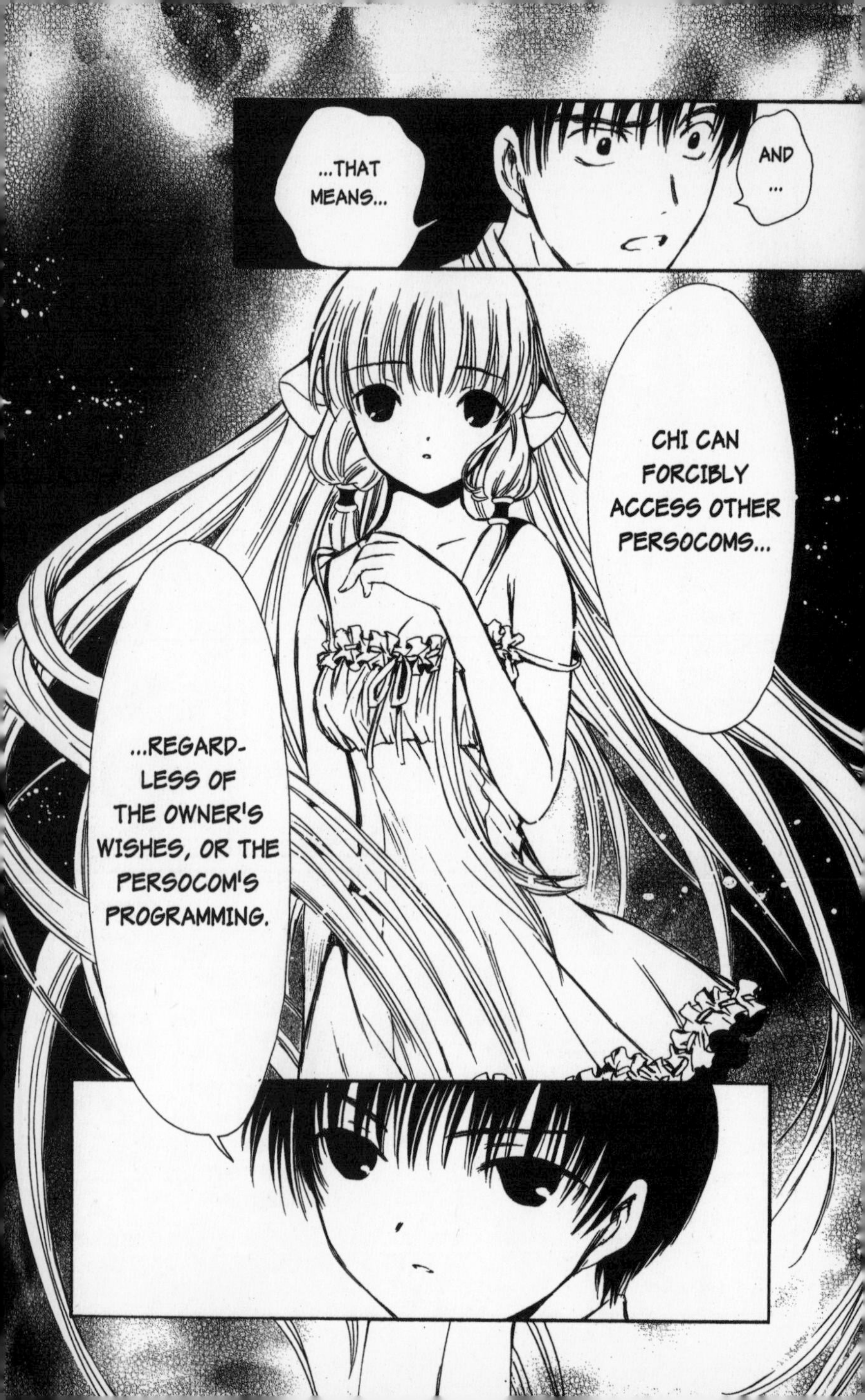
AND ...
...THAT MEANS...
CHI CAN FORCIBLY ACCESS OTHER PERSOCOMS...
...REGARD- LESS OF THE OWNER'S WISHES, OR THE PERSOCOM'S PROGRAMMING.

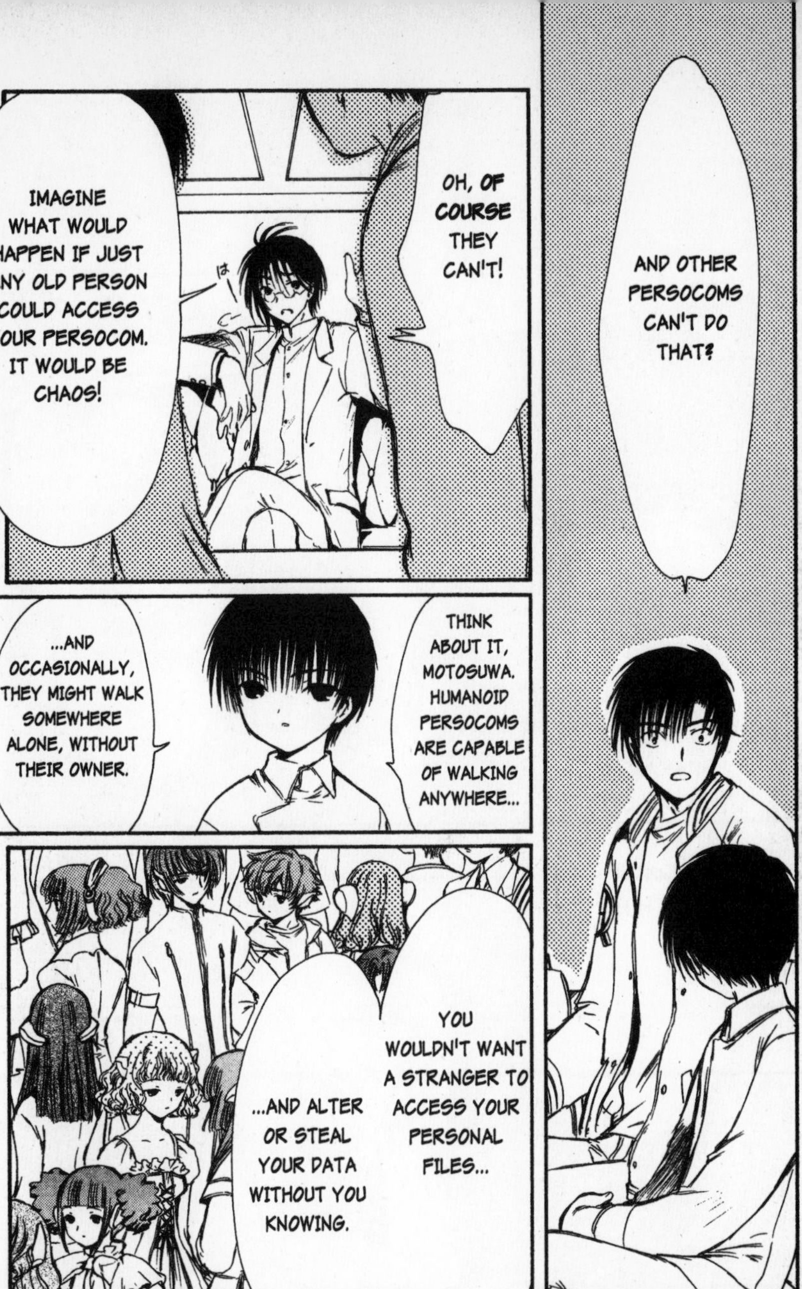
AND OTHER PERSOCOMS CAN'T DO THAT?
OH, OF COURSE THEY CAN'T!
は
IMAGINE WHAT WOULD HAPPEN IF JUST ANY OLD PERSON COULD ACCESS YOUR PERSOCOM. IT WOULD BE CHAOS!
THINK ABOUT IT, MOTOSUWA. HUMANOID PERSOCOMS ARE CAPABLE OF WALKING ANYWHERE...
...AND OCCASIONALLY, THEY MIGHT WALK SOMEWHERE ALONE, WITHOUT THEIR OWNER.
YOU WOULDN'T WANT A STRANGER TO ACCESS YOUR PERSONAL FILES...
...AND ALTER OR STEAL YOUR DATA WITHOUT YOU KNOWING.

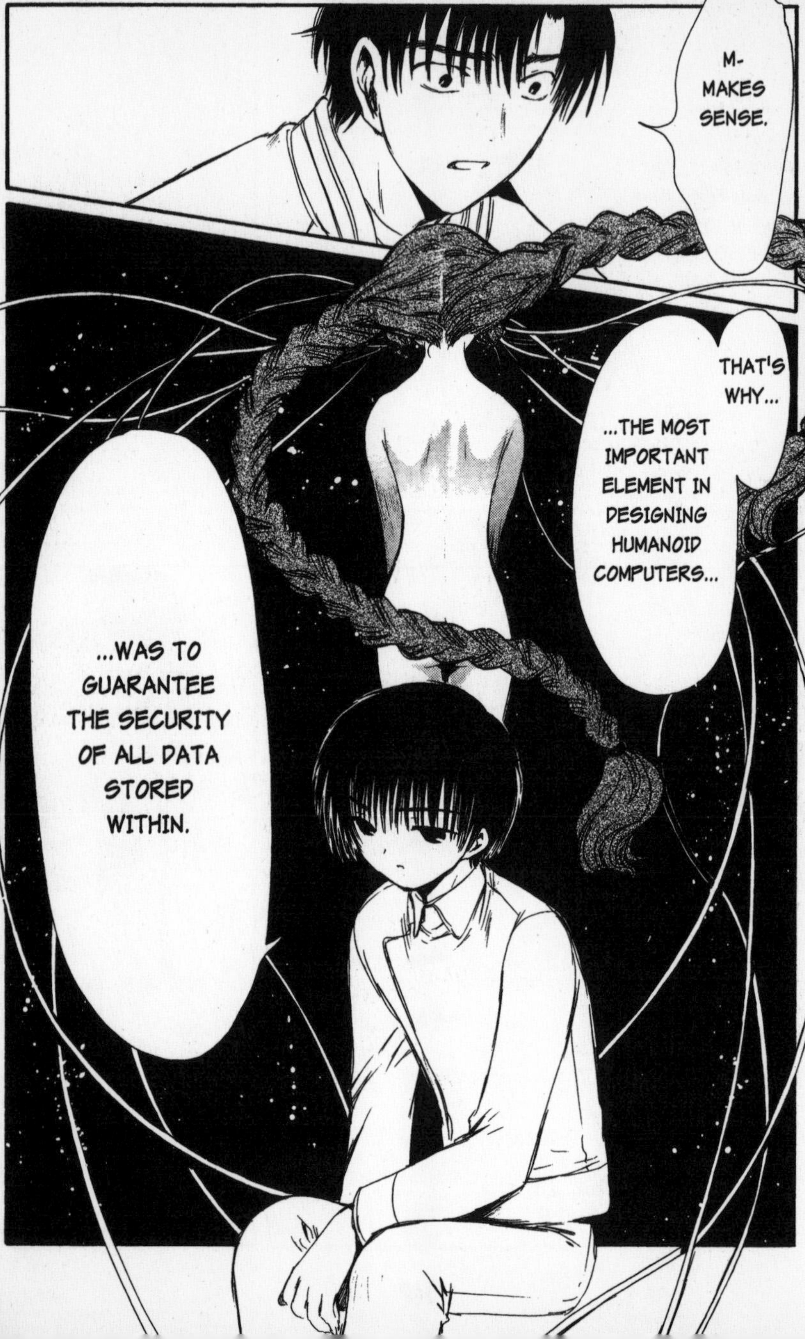
M-MAKES SENSE.
THAT'S WHY...
...THE MOST IMPORTANT ELEMENT IN DESIGNING HUMANOID COMPUTERS...
...WAS TO GUARANTEE THE SECURITY OF ALL DATA STORED WITHIN.

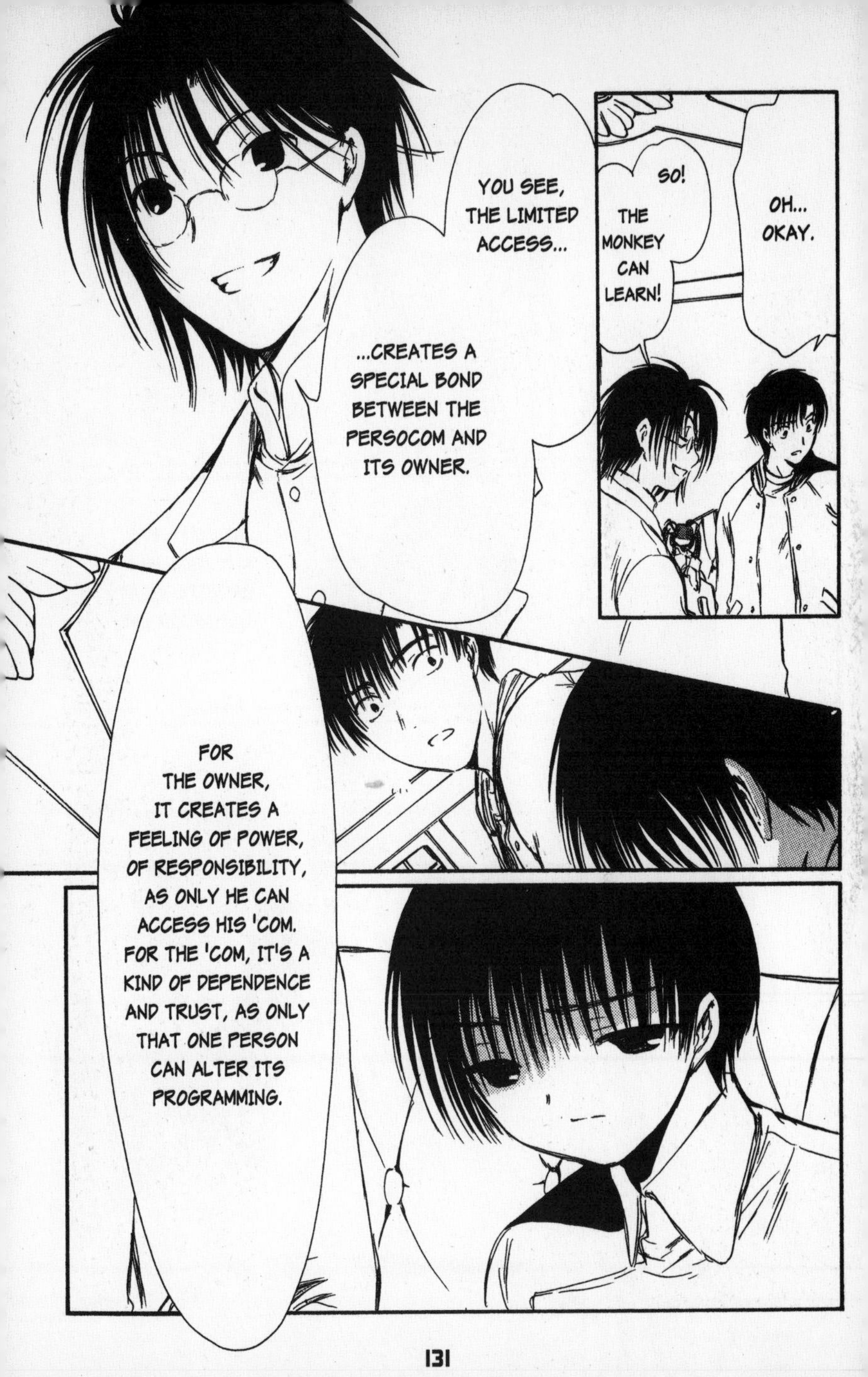
OH... OKAY.
SO! THE MONKEY CAN LEARN!
YOU SEE, THE LIMITED ACCESS...
...CREATES A SPECIAL BOND BETWEEN THE PERSOCOM AND ITS OWNER.
FOR THE OWNER, IT CREATES A FEELING OF POWER, OF RESPONSIBILITY, AS ONLY HE CAN ACCESS HIS 'COM. FOR THE 'COM, IT'S A KIND OF DEPENDENCE AND TRUST, AS ONLY THAT ONE PERSON CAN ALTER ITS PROGRAMMING.

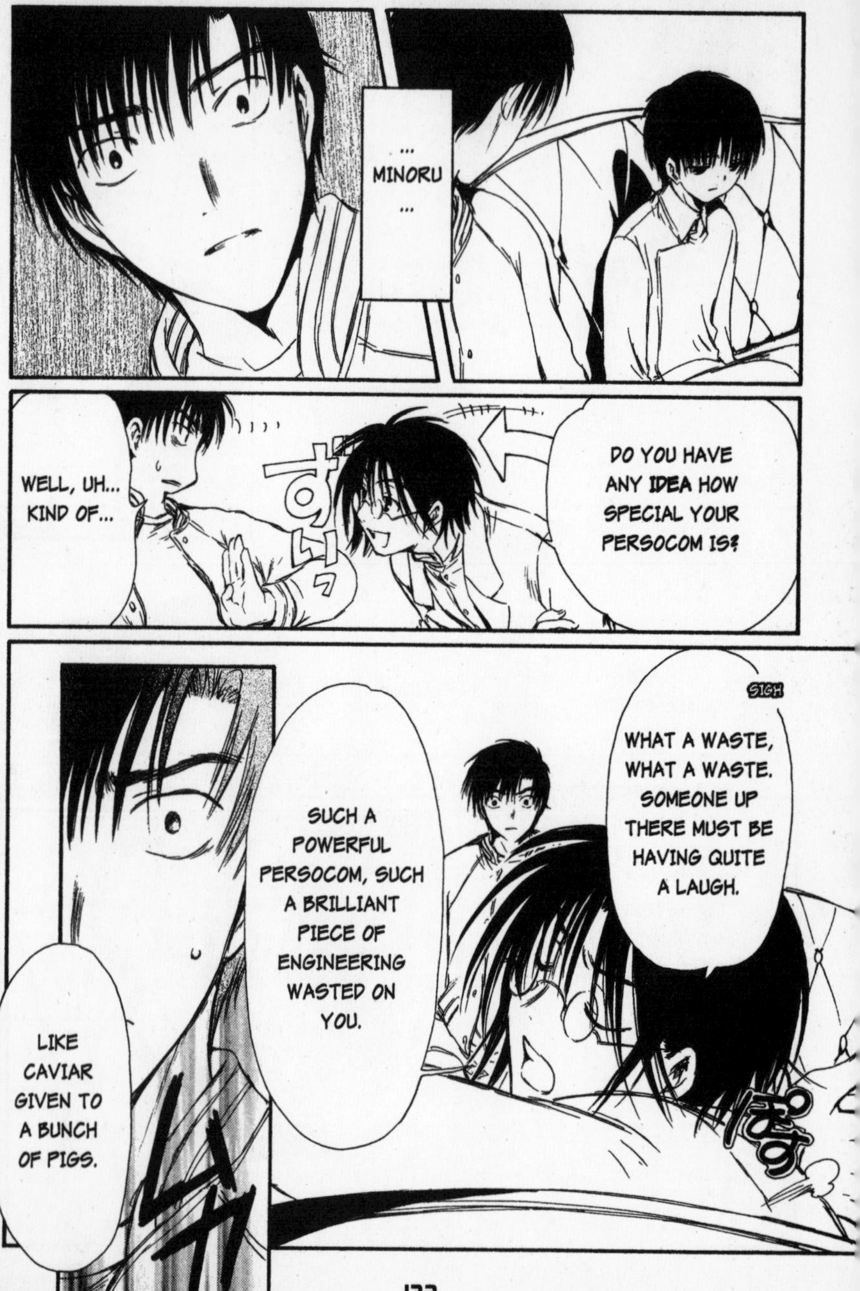
... MINORU ...
DO YOU HAVE ANY IDEA HOW SPECIAL YOUR PERSOCOM IS?
WELL, UH... KIND OF...
SIGH
WHAT A WASTE, WHAT A WASTE. SOMEONE UP THERE MUST BE HAVING QUITE A LAUGH.
SUCH A POWERFUL PERSOCOM, SUCH A BRILLIANT PIECE OF ENGINEERING WASTED ON YOU.
LIKE CAVIAR GIVEN TO A BUNCH OF PIGS.

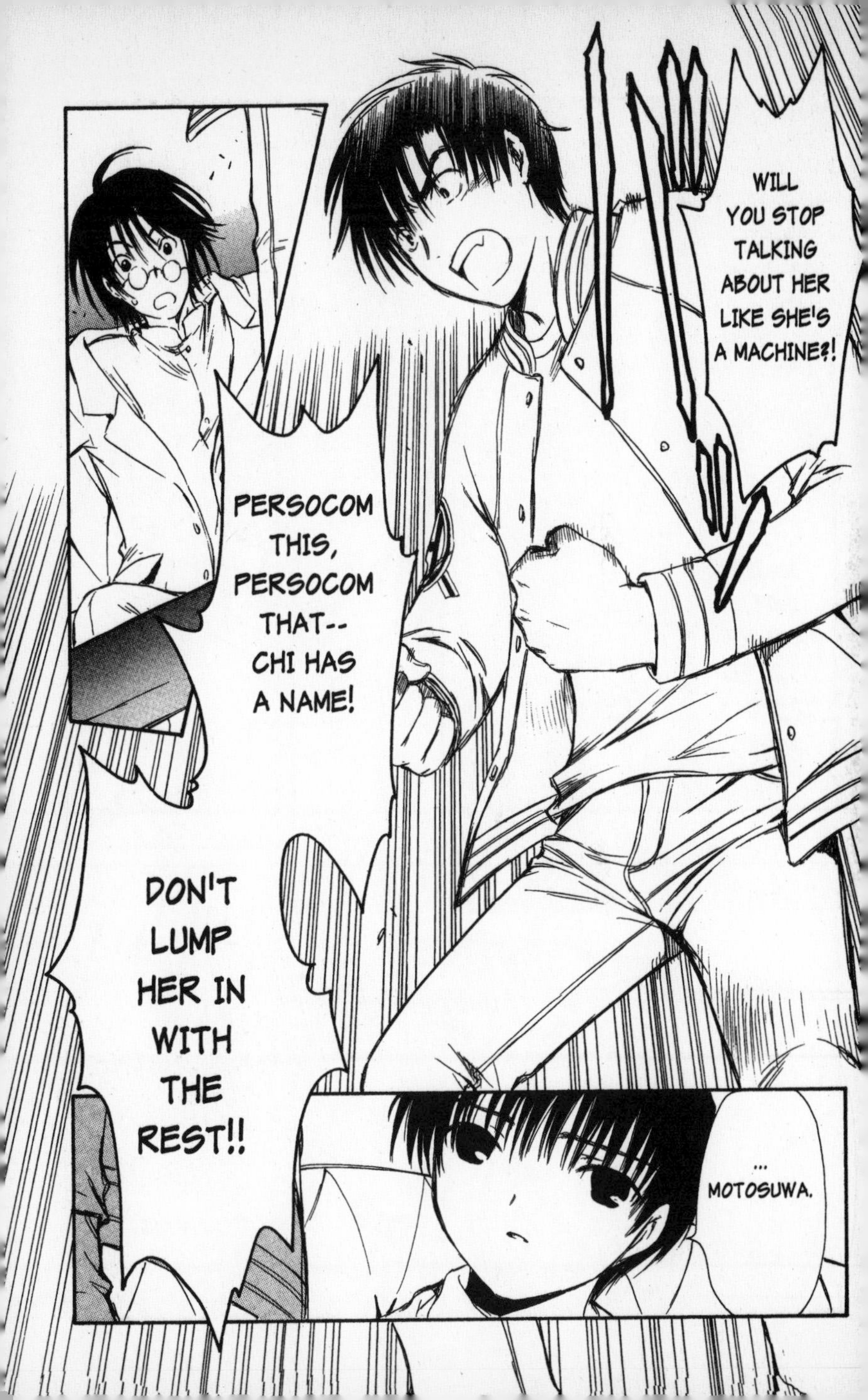
WILL YOU STOP TALKING ABOUT HER LIKE SHE'S A MACHINE?!
PERSOCOM THIS, PERSOCOM THAT-- CHI HAS A NAME!
DON'T LUMP HER IN WITH THE REST!!
... MOTOSUWA.

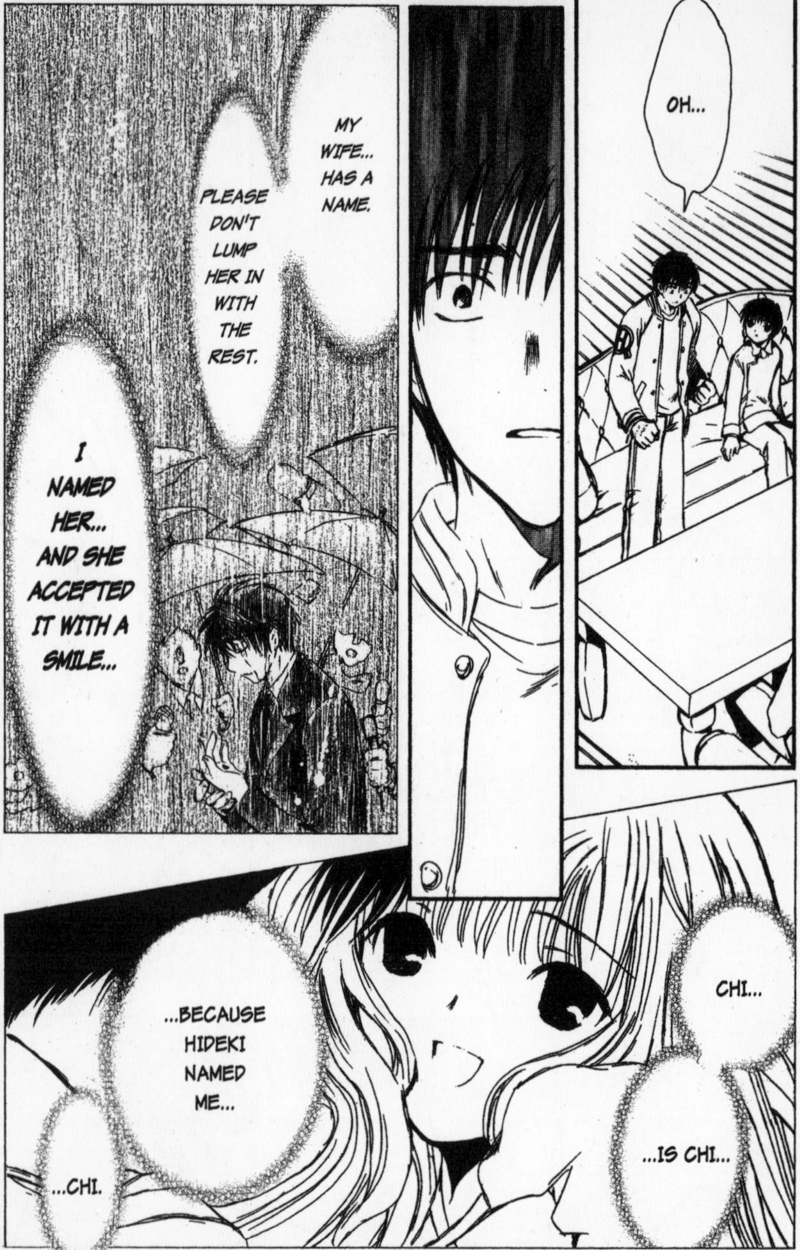
OH...
MY WIFE... HAS A NAME.
PLEASE DON'T LUMP HER IN WITH THE REST.
I NAMED HER... AND SHE ACCEPTED IT WITH A SMILE...
CHI...
...IS CHI...
...BECAUSE HIDEKI NAMED ME...
...CHI.

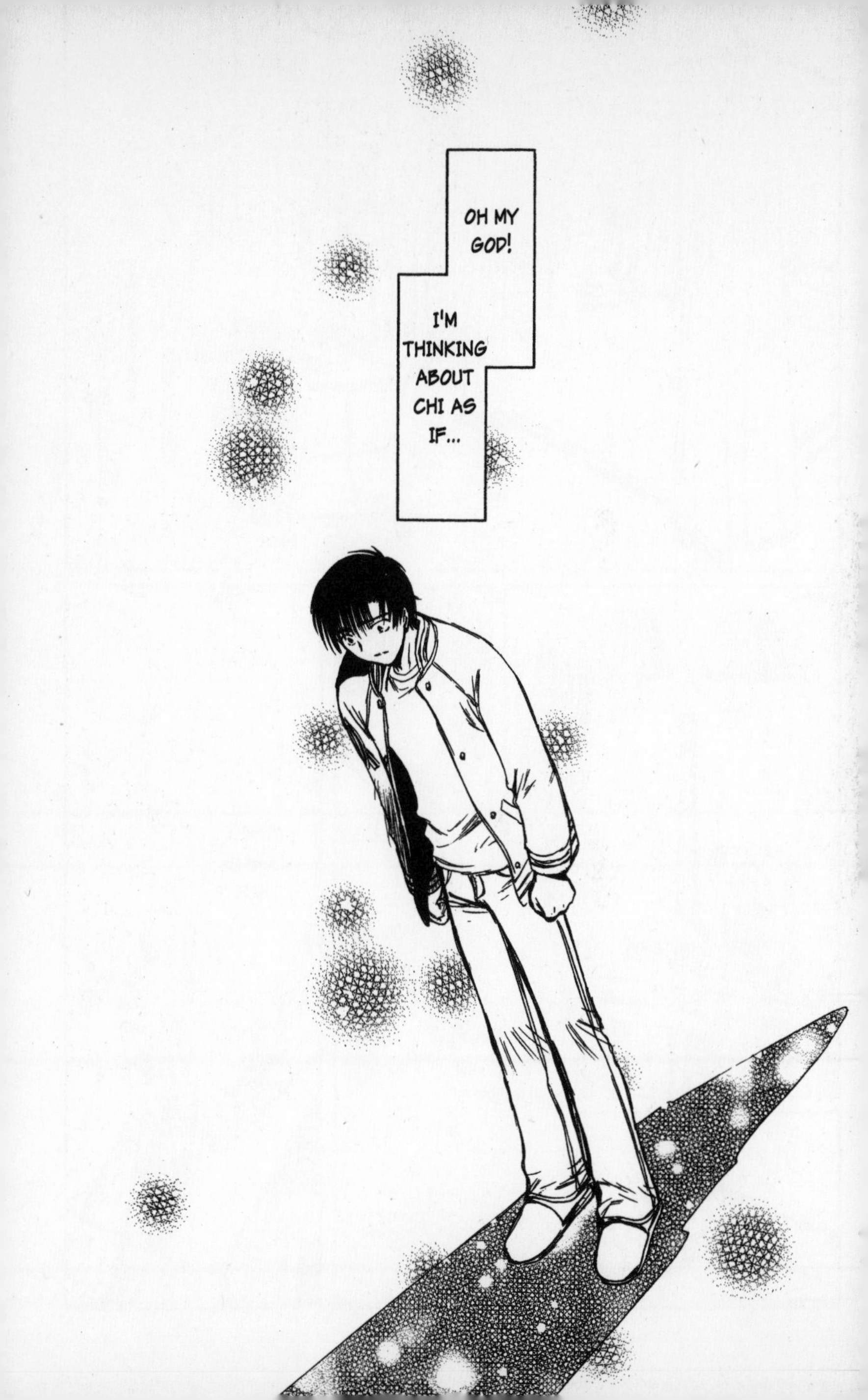
OH MY GOD!
I'M THINKING ABOUT CHI AS IF...

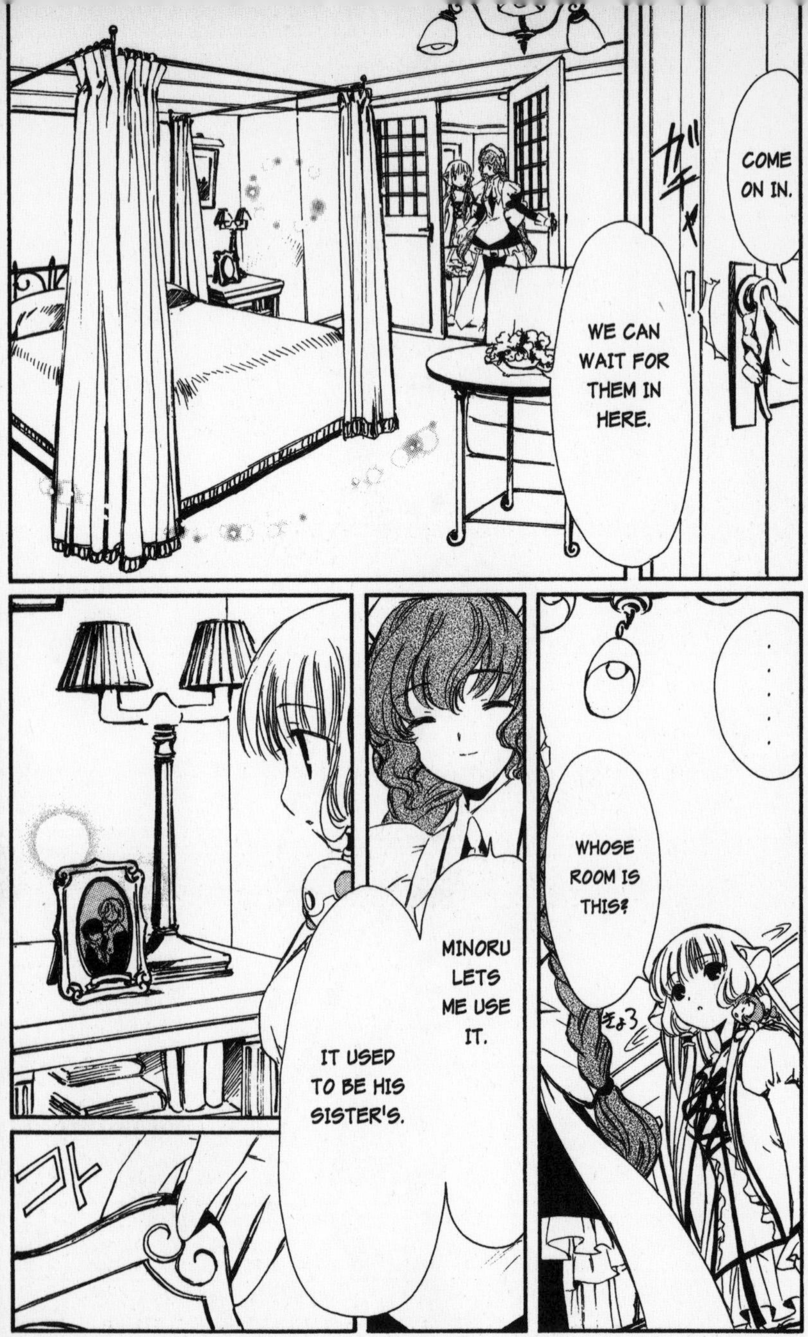
COME ON IN.
ガチャ
WE CAN WAIT FOR THEM IN HERE.
......
WHOSE ROOM IS THIS?
MINORU LETS ME USE IT.
IT USED TO BE HIS SISTER'S.

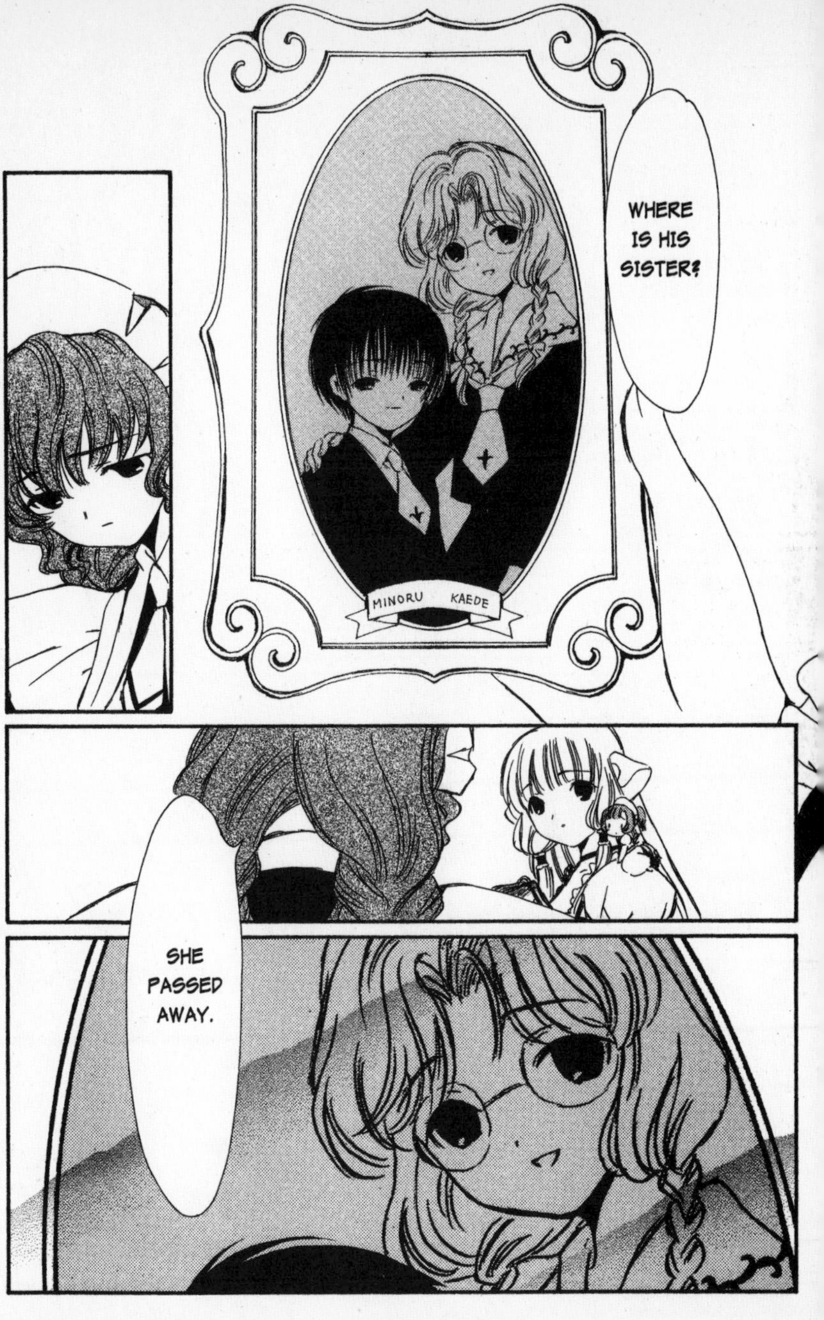
WHERE IS HIS SISTER?
MINORU KAEDE
SHE PASSED AWAY.

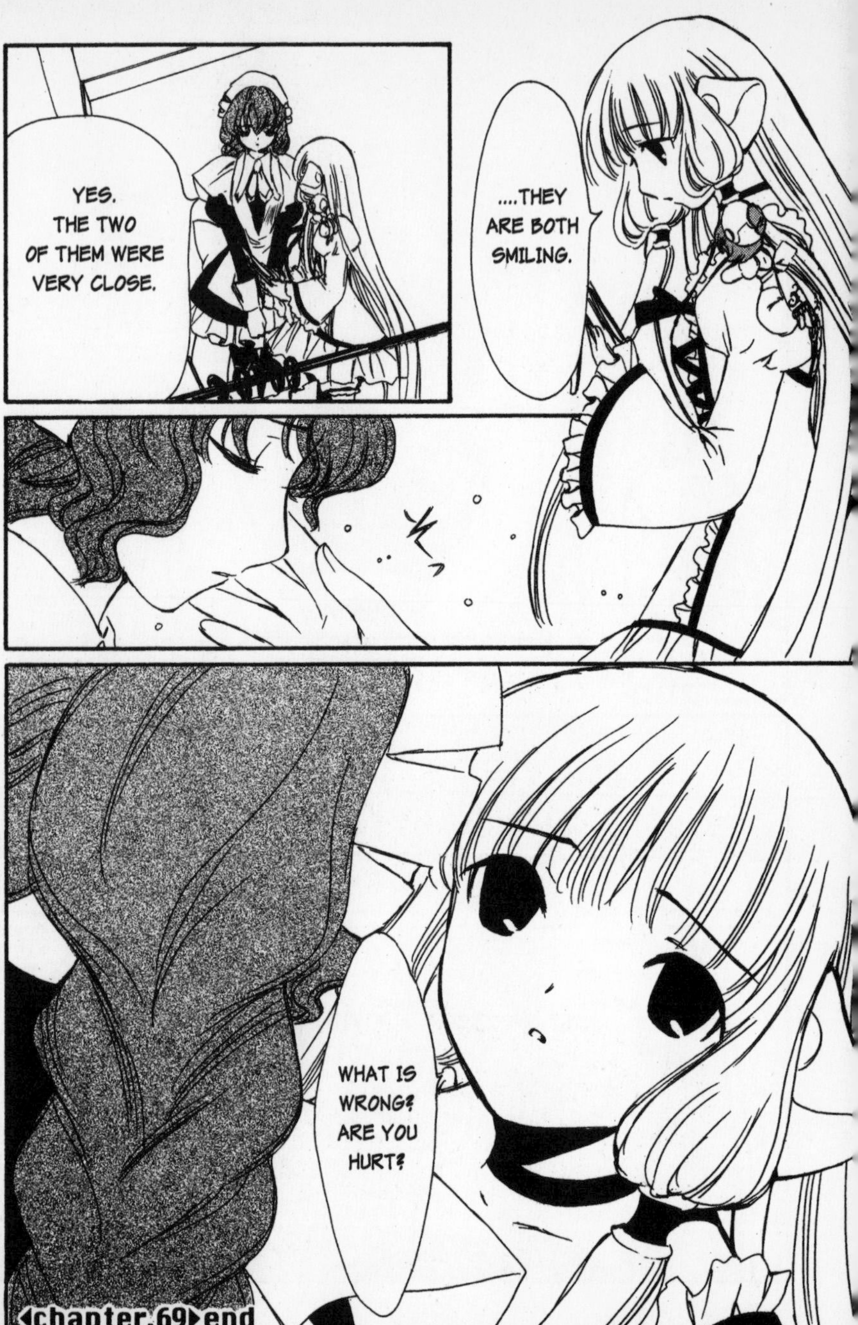
....THEY ARE BOTH SMILING.
YES. THE TWO OF THEM WERE VERY CLOSE.
WHAT IS WRONG? ARE YOU HURT?
chapter.69 end

ちょびっツ

Chobits

◀chapter.70▶

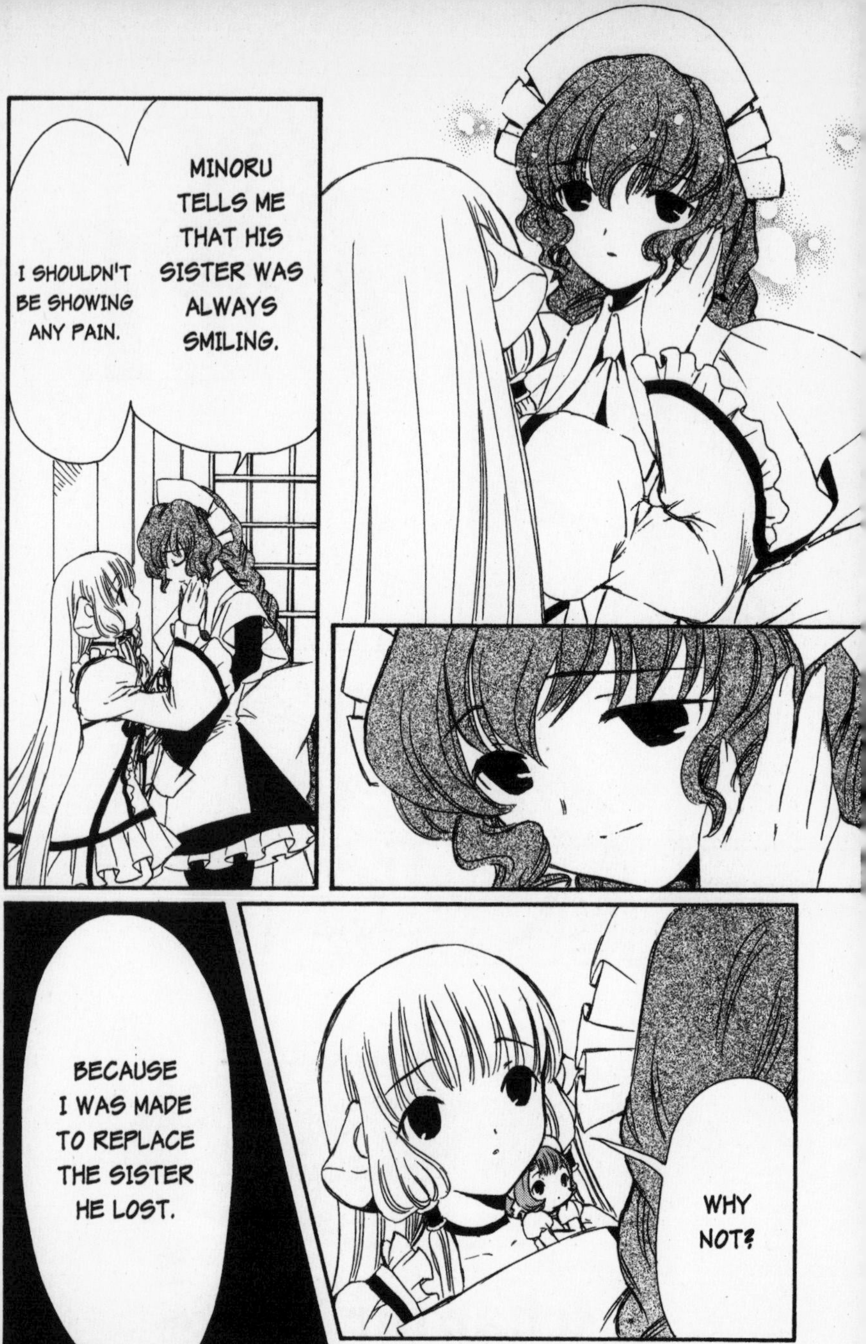
MINORU TELLS ME THAT HIS SISTER WAS ALWAYS SMILING.
I SHOULDN'T BE SHOWING ANY PAIN.
WHY NOT?
BECAUSE I WAS MADE TO REPLACE THE SISTER HE LOST.

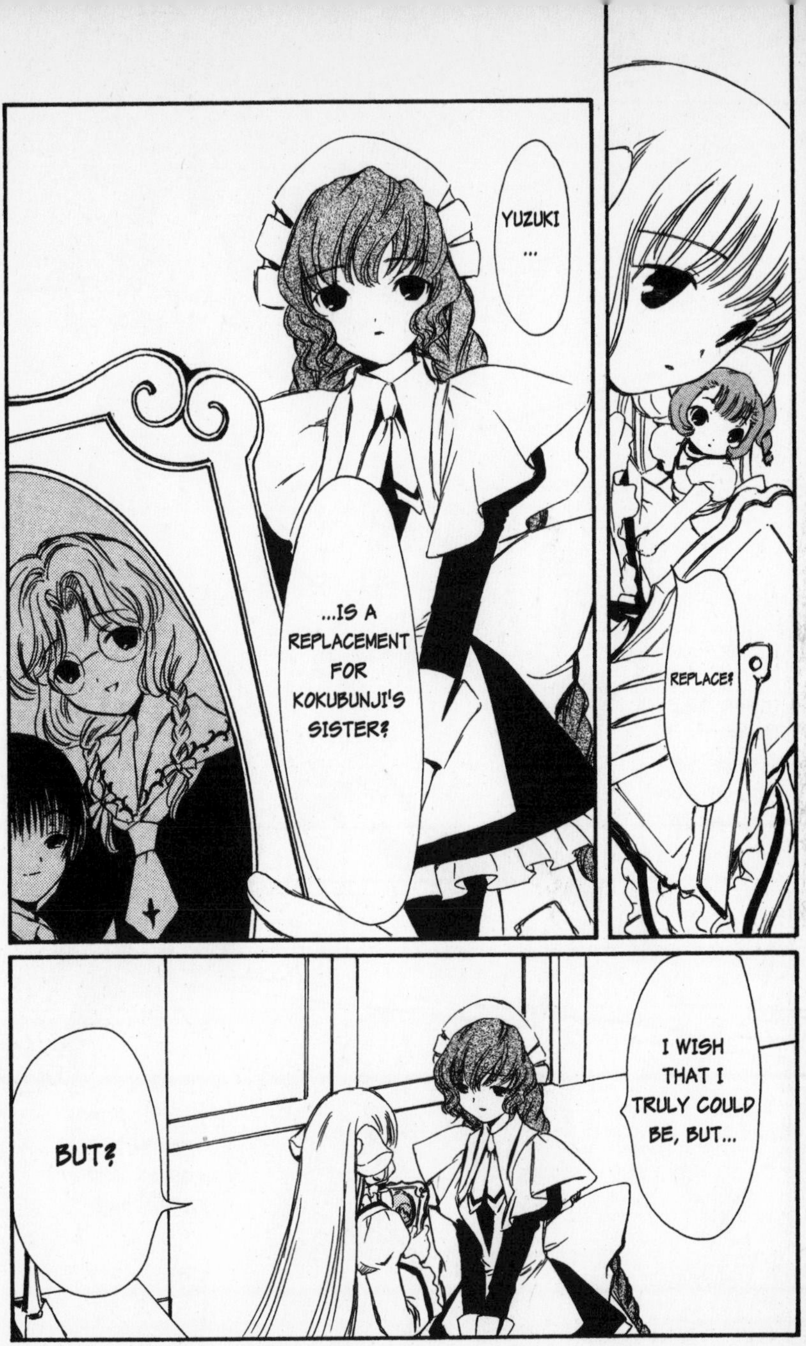
REPLACE?
YUZUKI ...
...IS A REPLACEMENT FOR KOKUBUNJI'S SISTER?
I WISH THAT I TRULY COULD BE, BUT...
BUT?

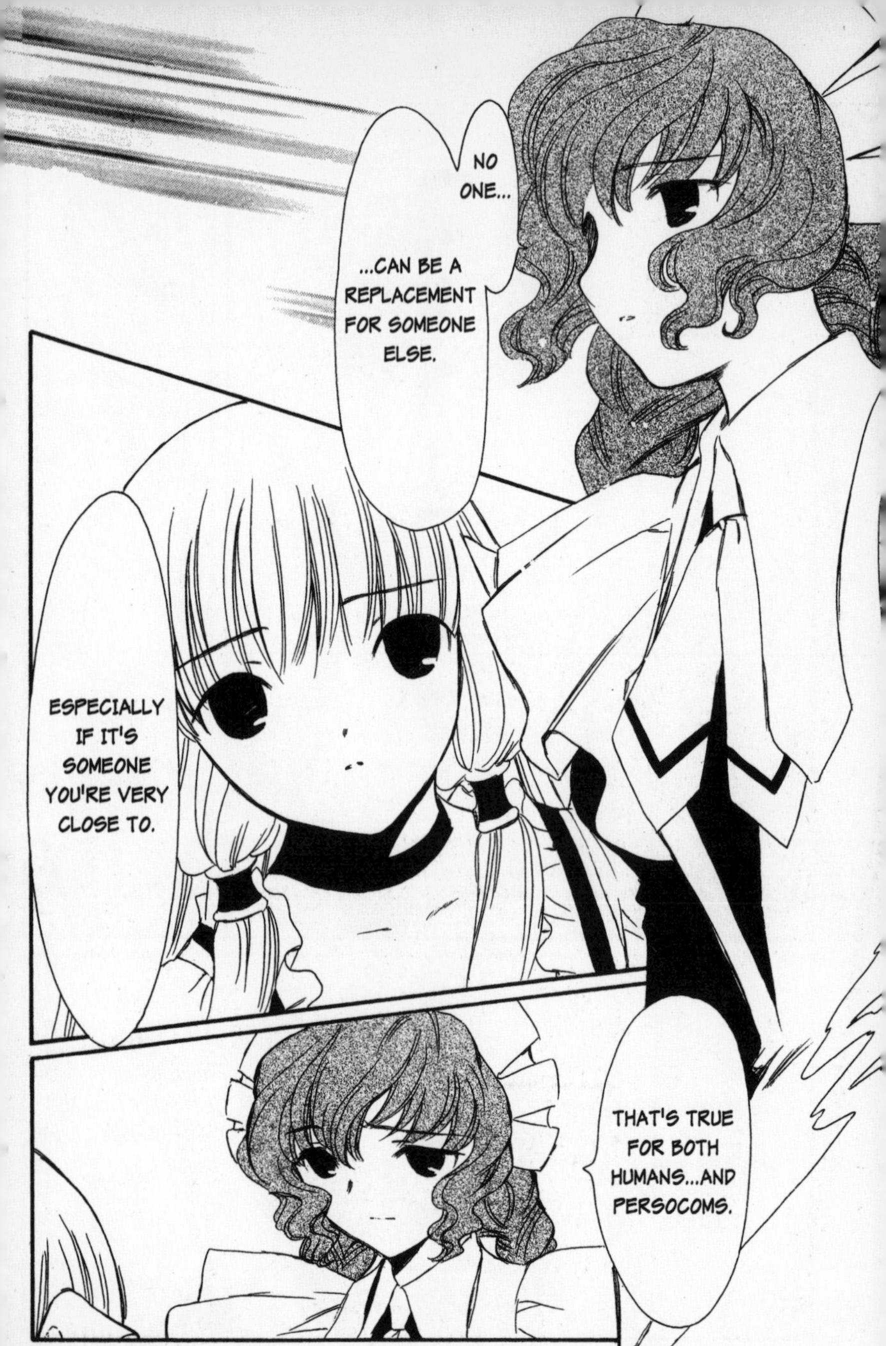
NO ONE...
...CAN BE A REPLACEMENT FOR SOMEONE ELSE.
ESPECIALLY IF IT'S SOMEONE YOU'RE VERY CLOSE TO.
THAT'S TRUE FOR BOTH HUMANS...AND PERSOCOMS.

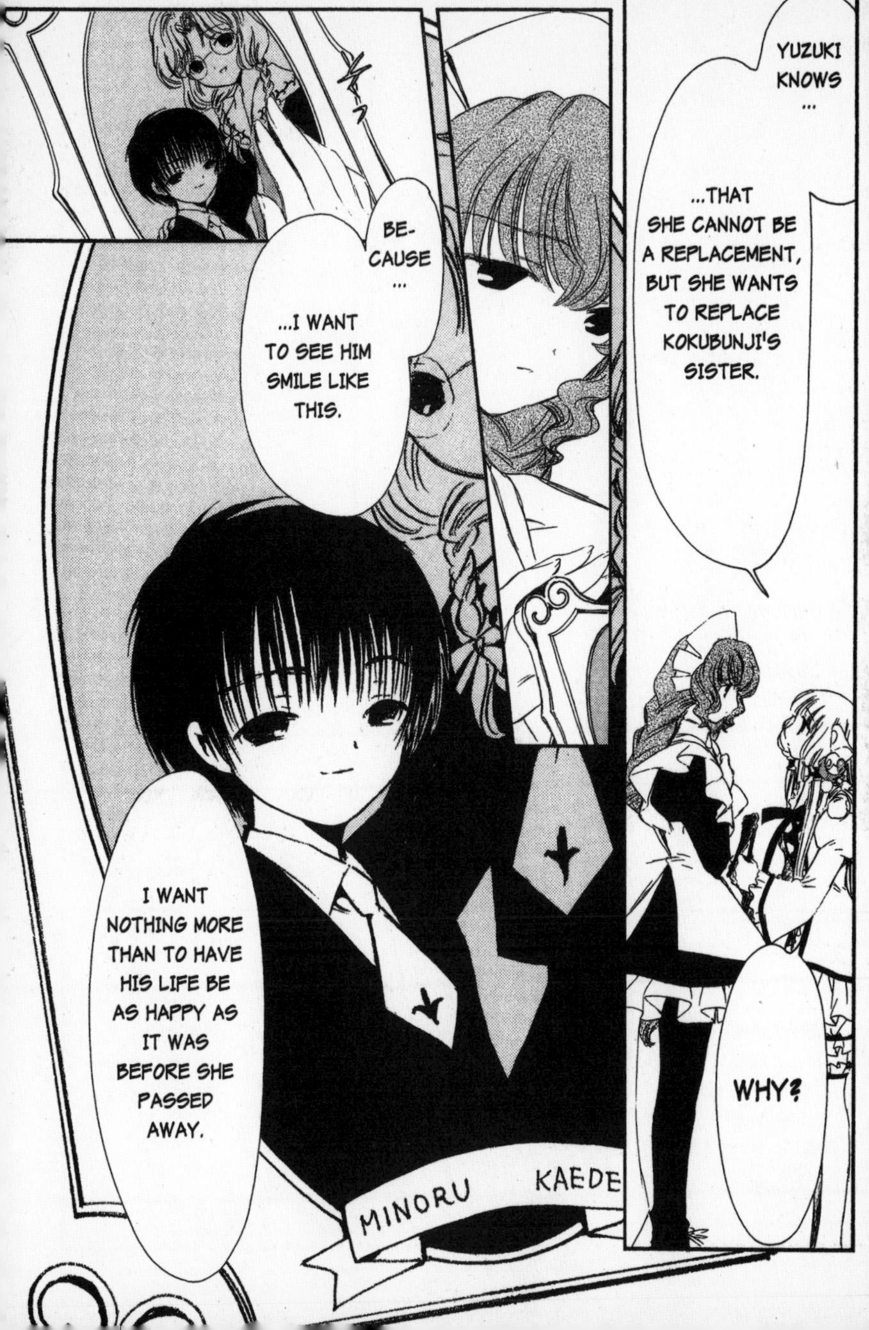
YUZUKI KNOWS ...
...THAT SHE CANNOT BE A REPLACEMENT, BUT SHE WANTS TO REPLACE KOKUBUNJI'S SISTER.
WHY?
BE-CAUSE ...
...I WANT TO SEE HIM SMILE LIKE THIS.
I WANT NOTHING MORE THAN TO HAVE HIS LIFE BE AS HAPPY AS IT WAS BEFORE SHE PASSED AWAY.
MINORU KAEDE

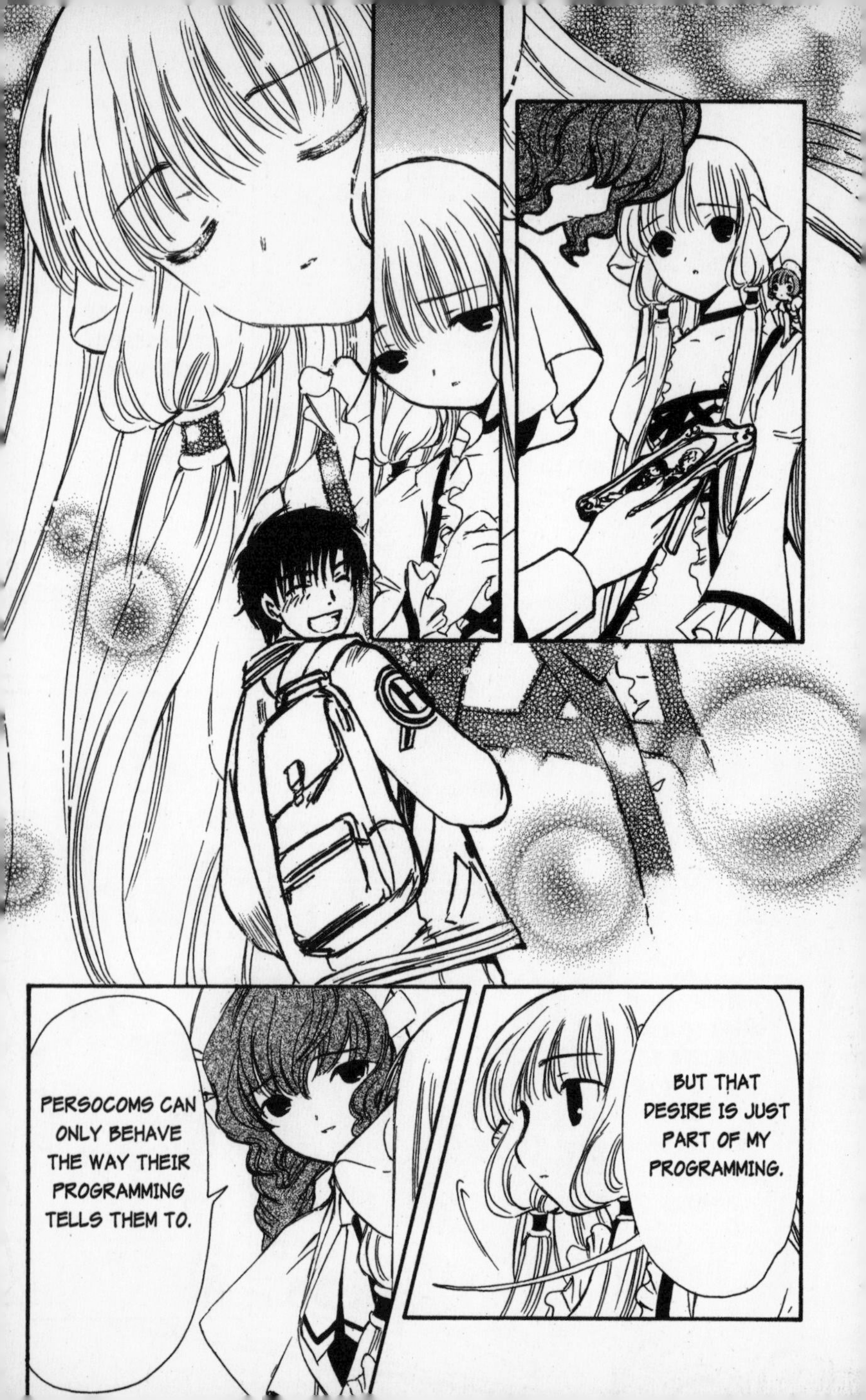
BUT THAT DESIRE IS JUST PART OF MY PROGRAMMING.
PERSOCOMS CAN ONLY BEHAVE THE WAY THEIR PROGRAMMING TELLS THEM TO.

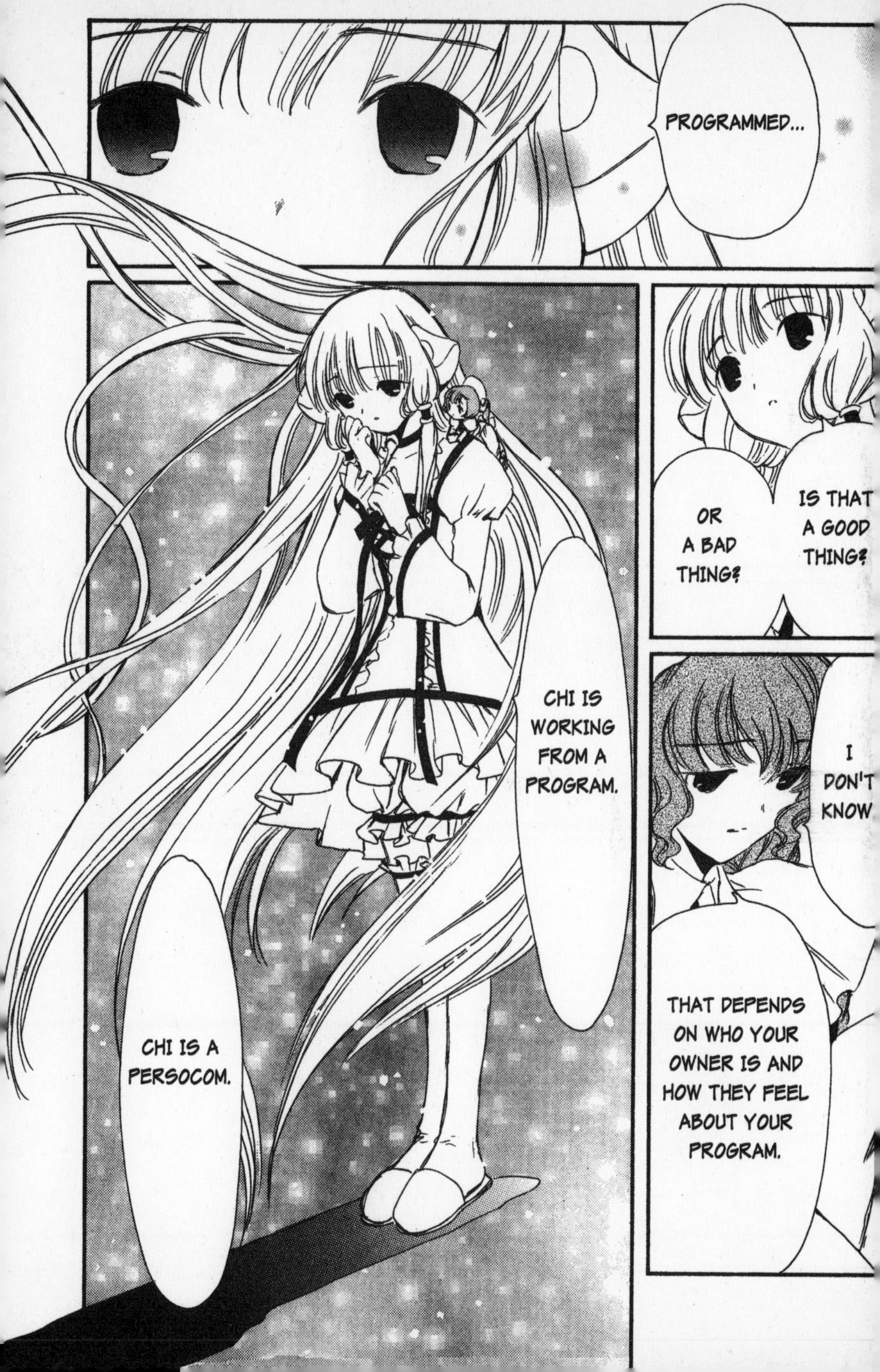
PROGRAMMED...
IS THAT A GOOD THING?
OR A BAD THING?
I DON'T KNOW
THAT DEPENDS ON WHO YOUR OWNER IS AND HOW THEY FEEL ABOUT YOUR PROGRAM.
CHI IS WORKING FROM A PROGRAM.
CHI IS A PERSOCOM.

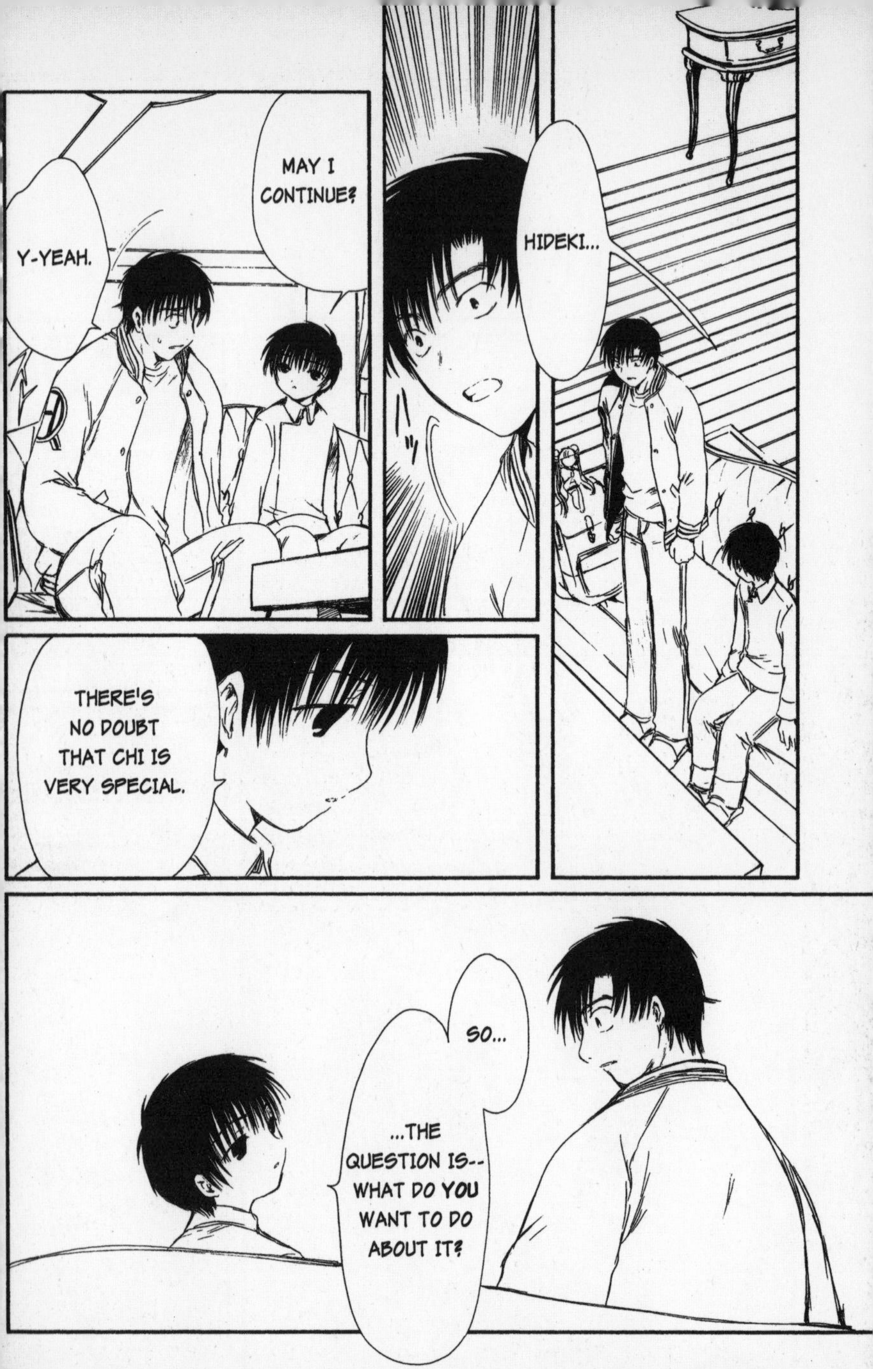
HIDEKI...
MAY I CONTINUE?
Y-YEAH.
THERE'S NO DOUBT THAT CHI IS VERY SPECIAL.
SO...
...THE QUESTION IS-- WHAT DO YOU WANT TO DO ABOUT IT?

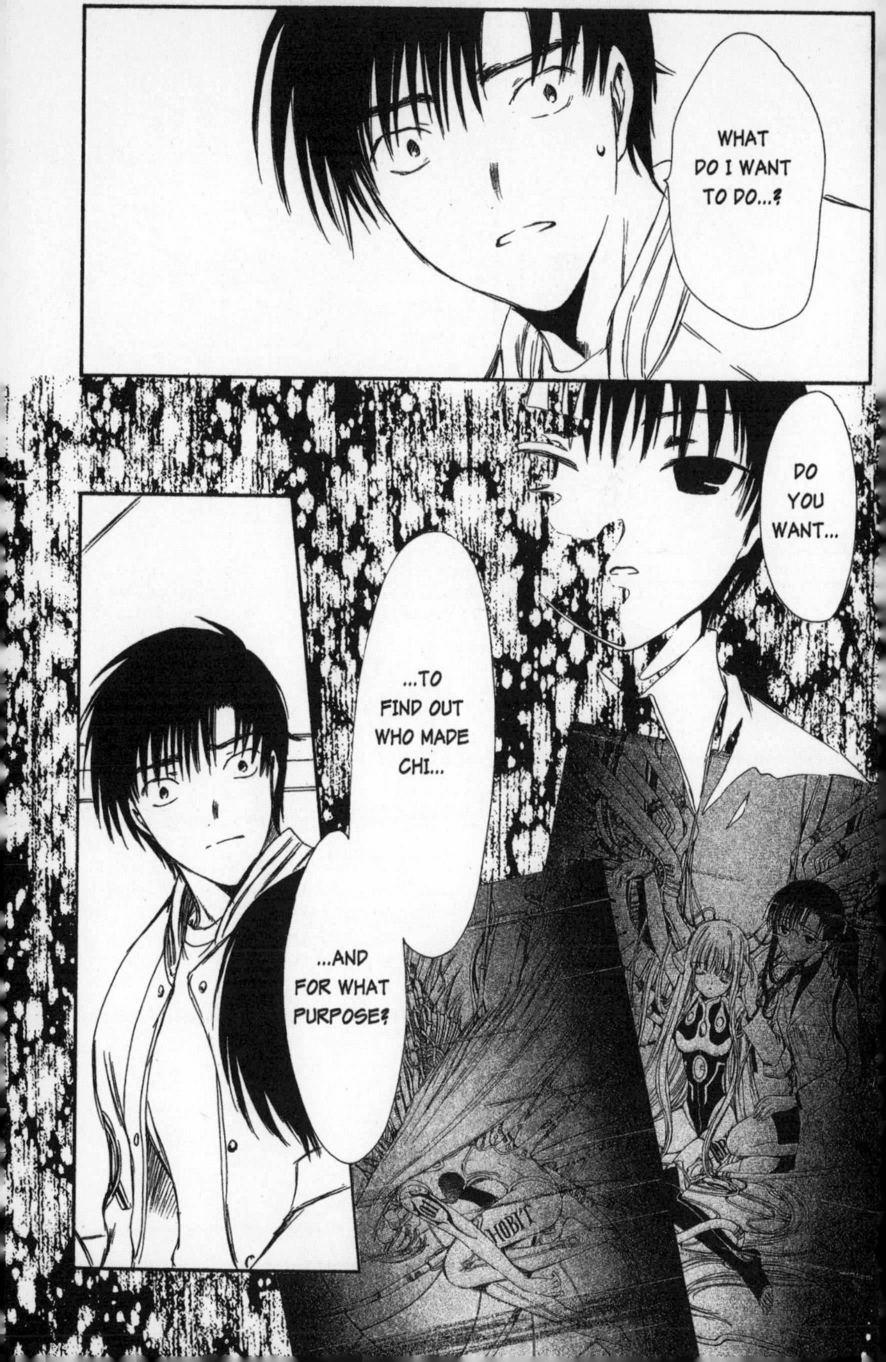
WHAT DO I WANT TO DO...?
DO YOU WANT...
...TO FIND OUT WHO MADE CHI...
...AND FOR WHAT PURPOSE?
HOBIT

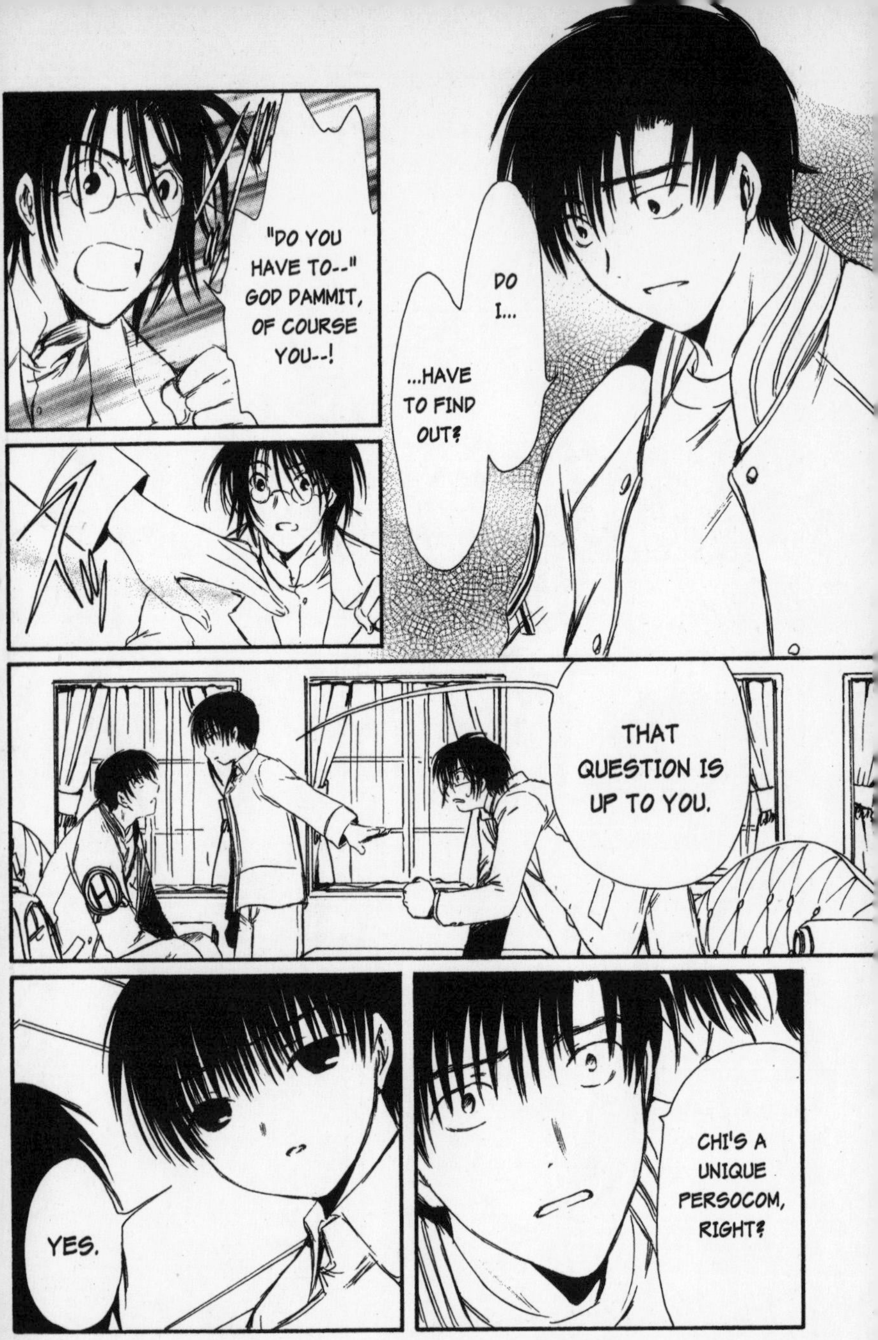
DO I...
...HAVE TO FIND OUT?
"DO YOU HAVE TO--" GOD DAMMIT, OF COURSE YOU--!
THAT QUESTION IS UP TO YOU.
CHI'S A UNIQUE PERSOCOM, RIGHT?
YES.

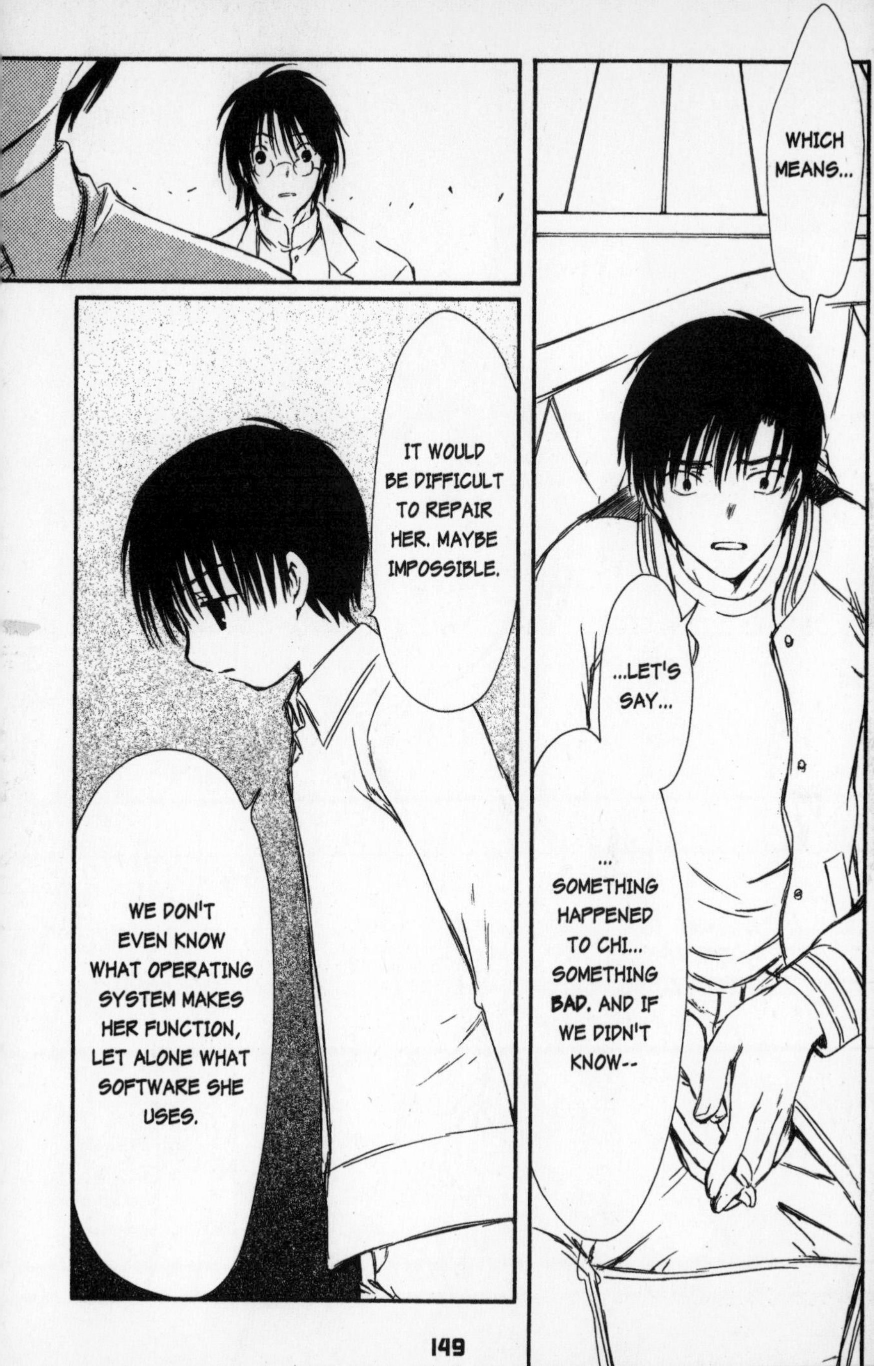
WHICH MEANS...
...LET'S SAY...
... SOMETHING HAPPENED TO CHI... SOMETHING BAD. AND IF WE DIDN'T KNOW--
IT WOULD BE DIFFICULT TO REPAIR HER. MAYBE IMPOSSIBLE.
WE DON'T EVEN KNOW WHAT OPERATING SYSTEM MAKES HER FUNCTION, LET ALONE WHAT SOFTWARE SHE USES.

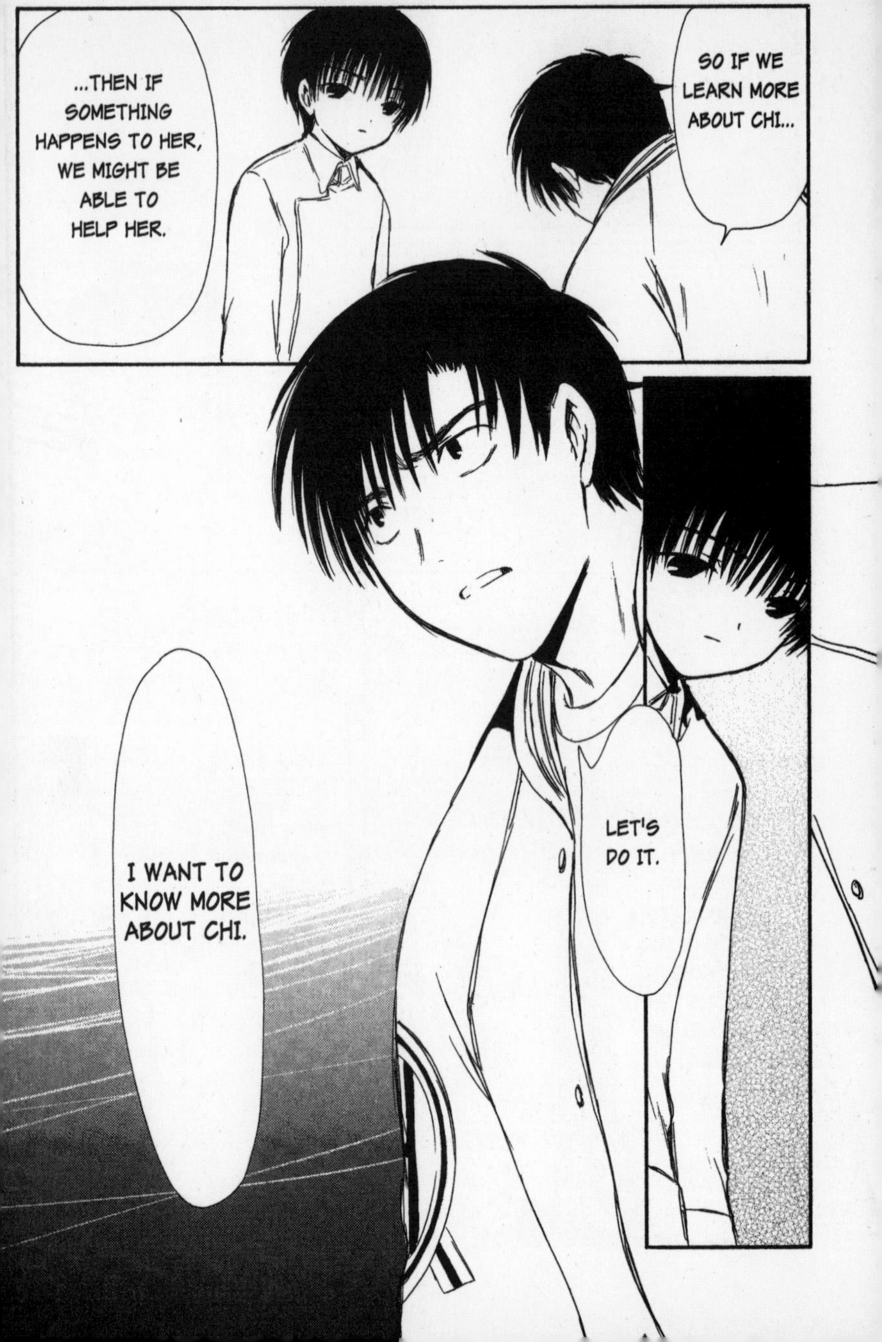
SO IF WE LEARN MORE ABOUT CHI...
...THEN IF SOMETHING HAPPENS TO HER, WE MIGHT BE ABLE TO HELP HER.
I WANT TO KNOW MORE ABOUT CHI.
LET'S DO IT.

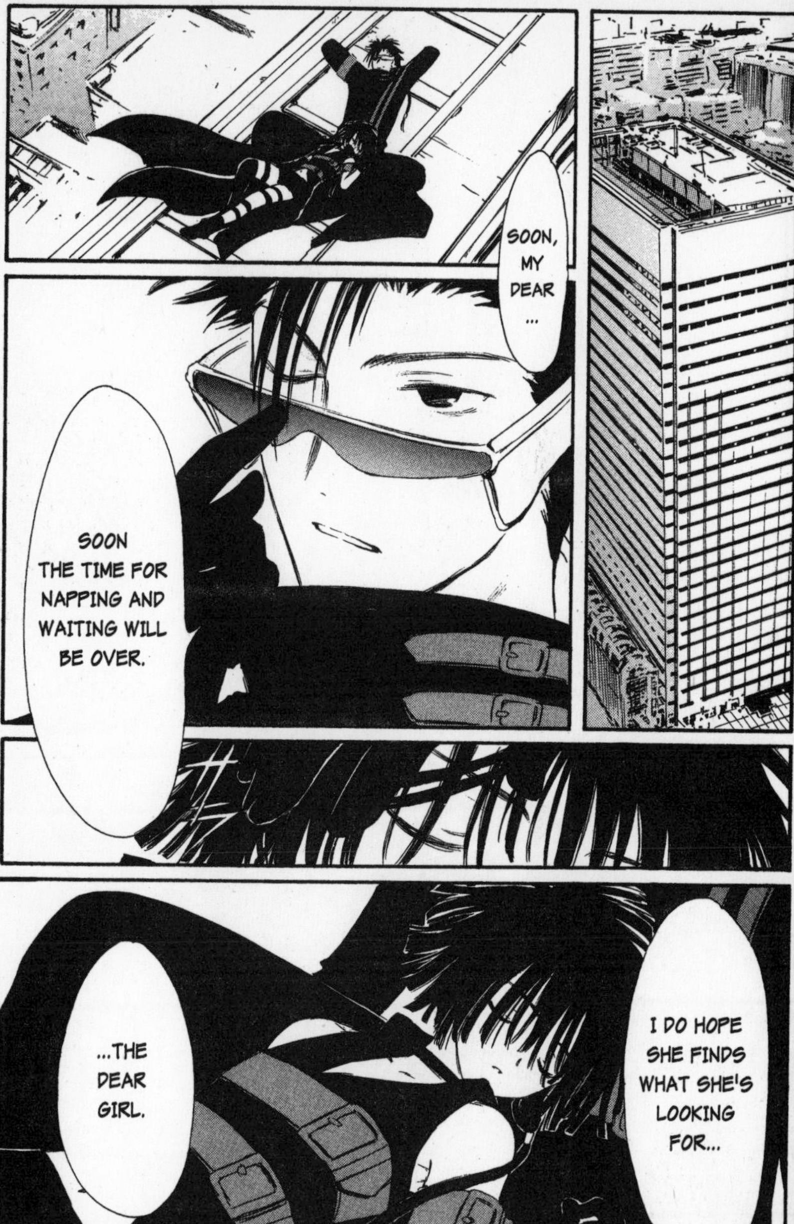
SOON, MY DEAR ...
SOON THE TIME FOR NAPPING AND WAITING WILL BE OVER.
I DO HOPE SHE FINDS WHAT SHE'S LOOKING FOR...
...THE DEAR GIRL.

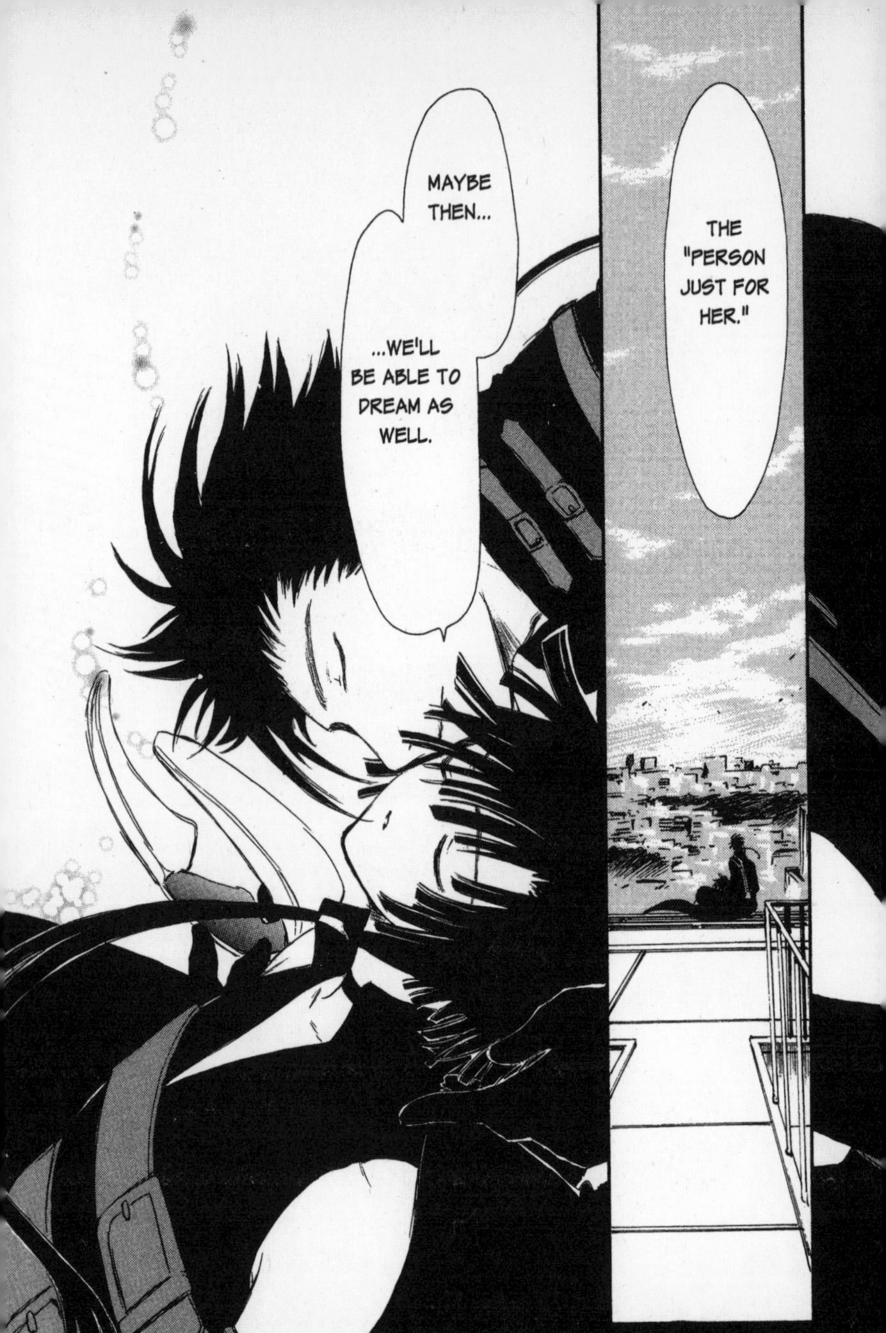
THE "PERSON JUST FOR HER."
MAYBE THEN...
...WE'LL BE ABLE TO DREAM AS WELL.

◀chapter.70▶end

ちょびっツ
Chobits

◀chapter.71▶

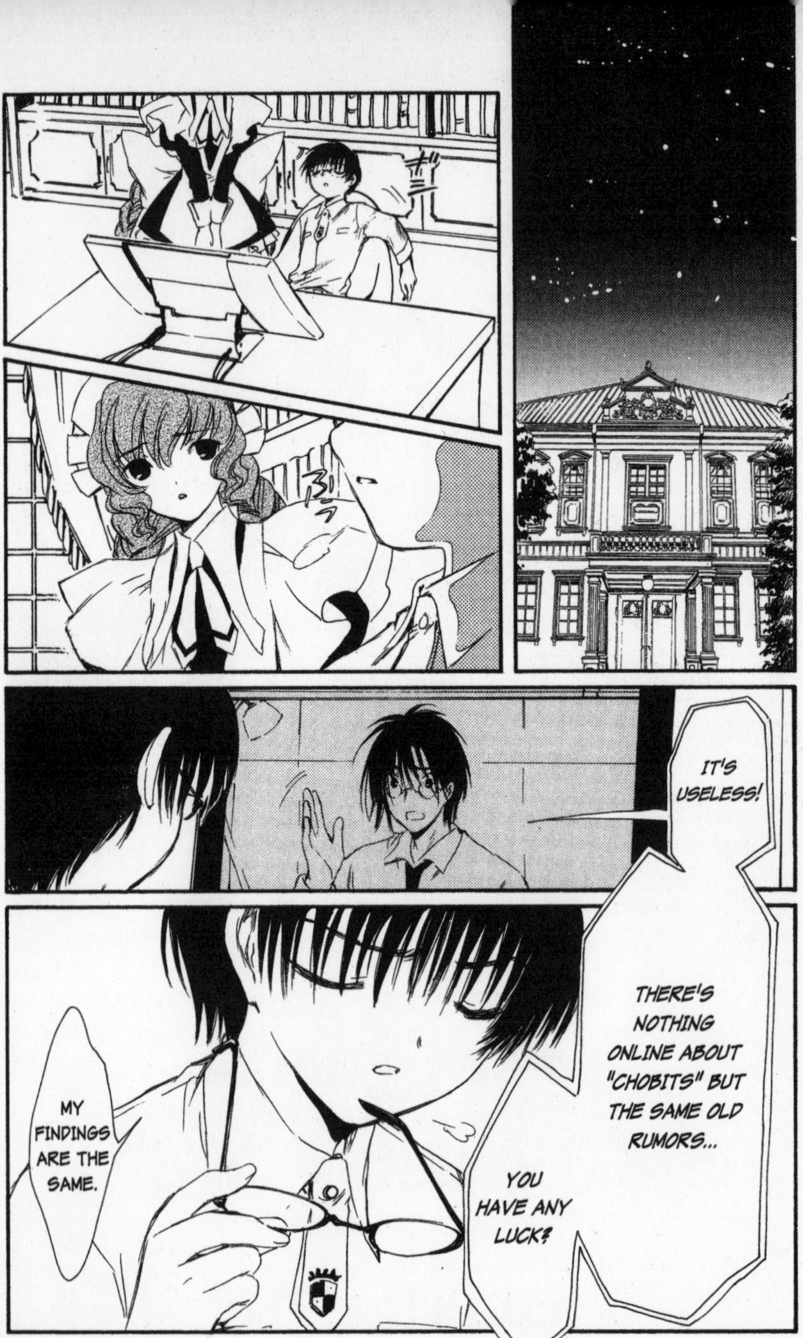
IT'S USELESS!
THERE'S NOTHING ONLINE ABOUT "CHOBITS" BUT THE SAME OLD RUMORS...
YOU HAVE ANY LUCK?
MY FINDINGS ARE THE SAME.

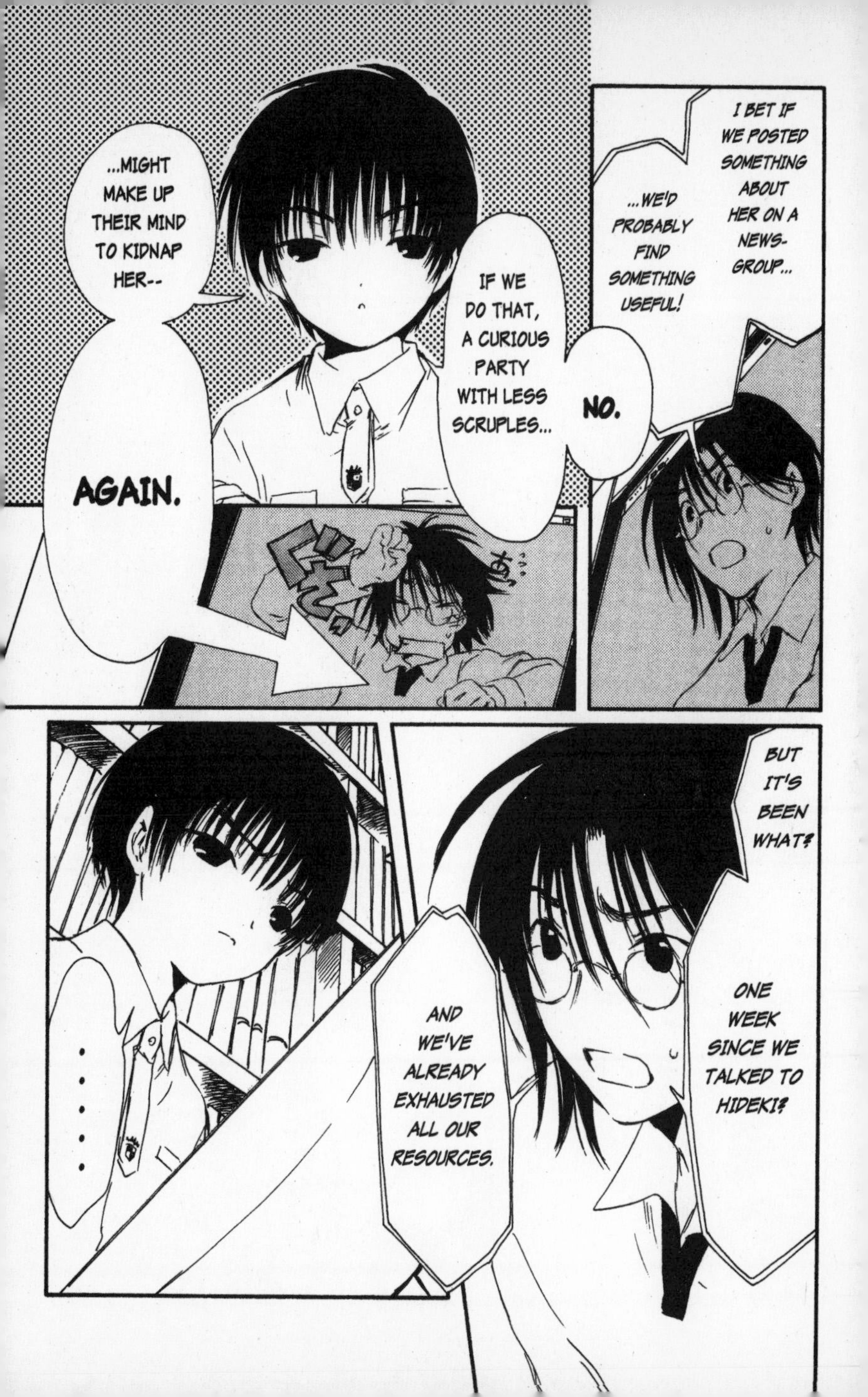
I BET IF WE POSTED SOMETHING ABOUT HER ON A NEWS-GROUP...
...WE'D PROBABLY FIND SOMETHING USEFUL!
NO.
IF WE DO THAT, A CURIOUS PARTY WITH LESS SCRUPLES...
...MIGHT MAKE UP THEIR MIND TO KIDNAP HER--
AGAIN.
BUT IT'S BEEN WHAT?
ONE WEEK SINCE WE TALKED TO HIDEKI?
AND WE'VE ALREADY EXHAUSTED ALL OUR RESOURCES.
......

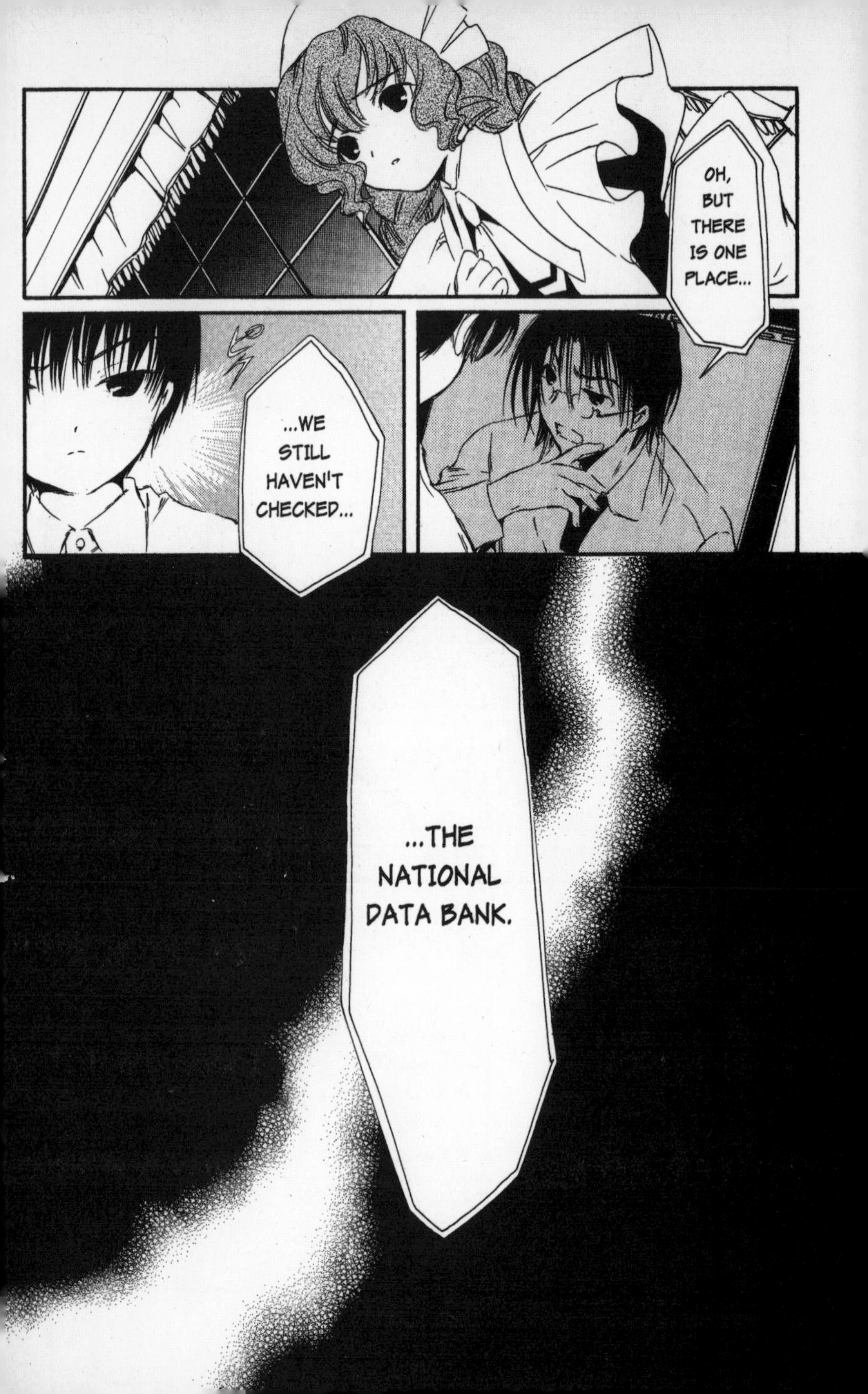
OH, BUT THERE IS ONE PLACE...
...WE STILL HAVEN'T CHECKED...
...THE NATIONAL DATA BANK.

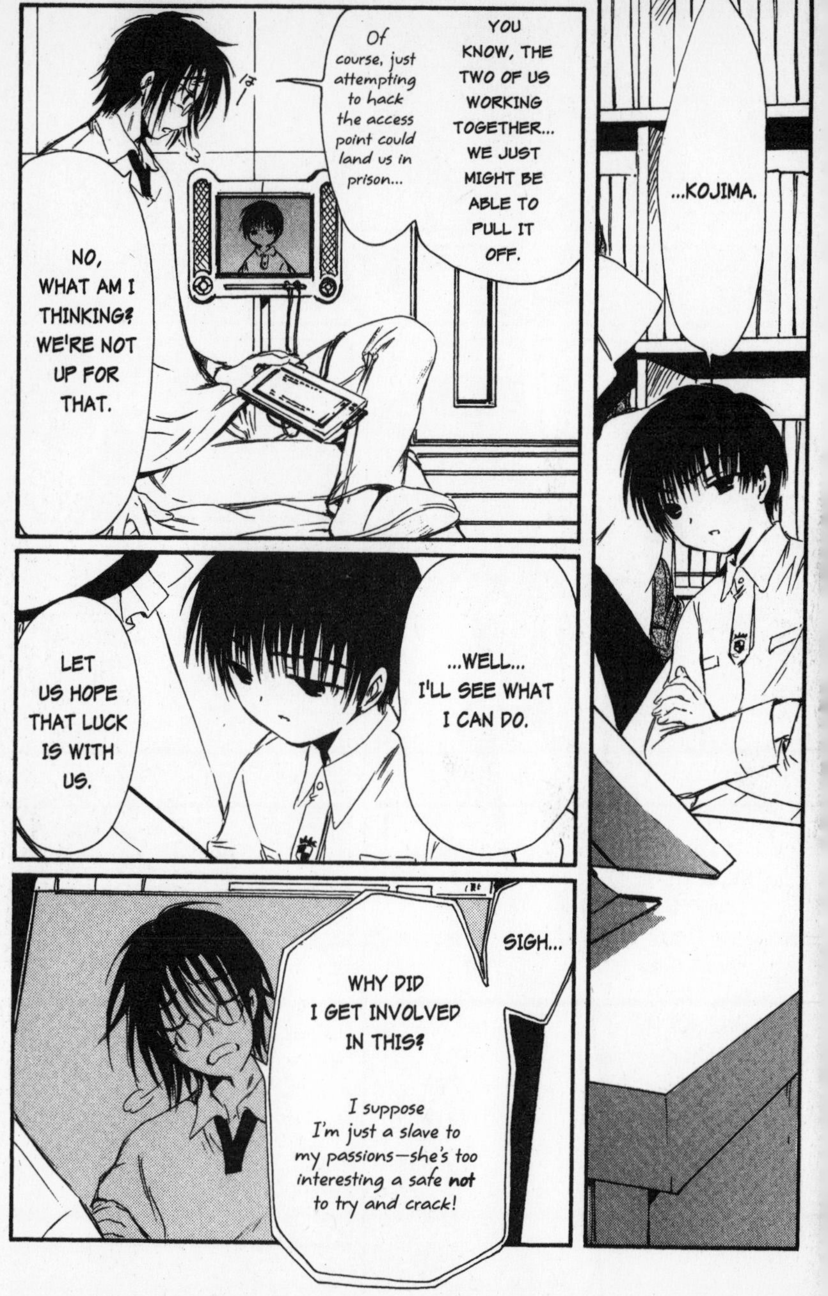
...KOJIMA.
YOU KNOW, THE TWO OF US WORKING TOGETHER... WE JUST MIGHT BE ABLE TO PULL IT OFF.
Of course, just attempting to hack the access point could land us in prison...
NO, WHAT AM I THINKING? WE'RE NOT UP FOR THAT.
...WELL... I'LL SEE WHAT I CAN DO.
LET US HOPE THAT LUCK IS WITH US.
SIGH...
WHY DID I GET INVOLVED IN THIS?
I suppose I'm just a slave to my passions—she's too interesting a safe **not** to try and crack!

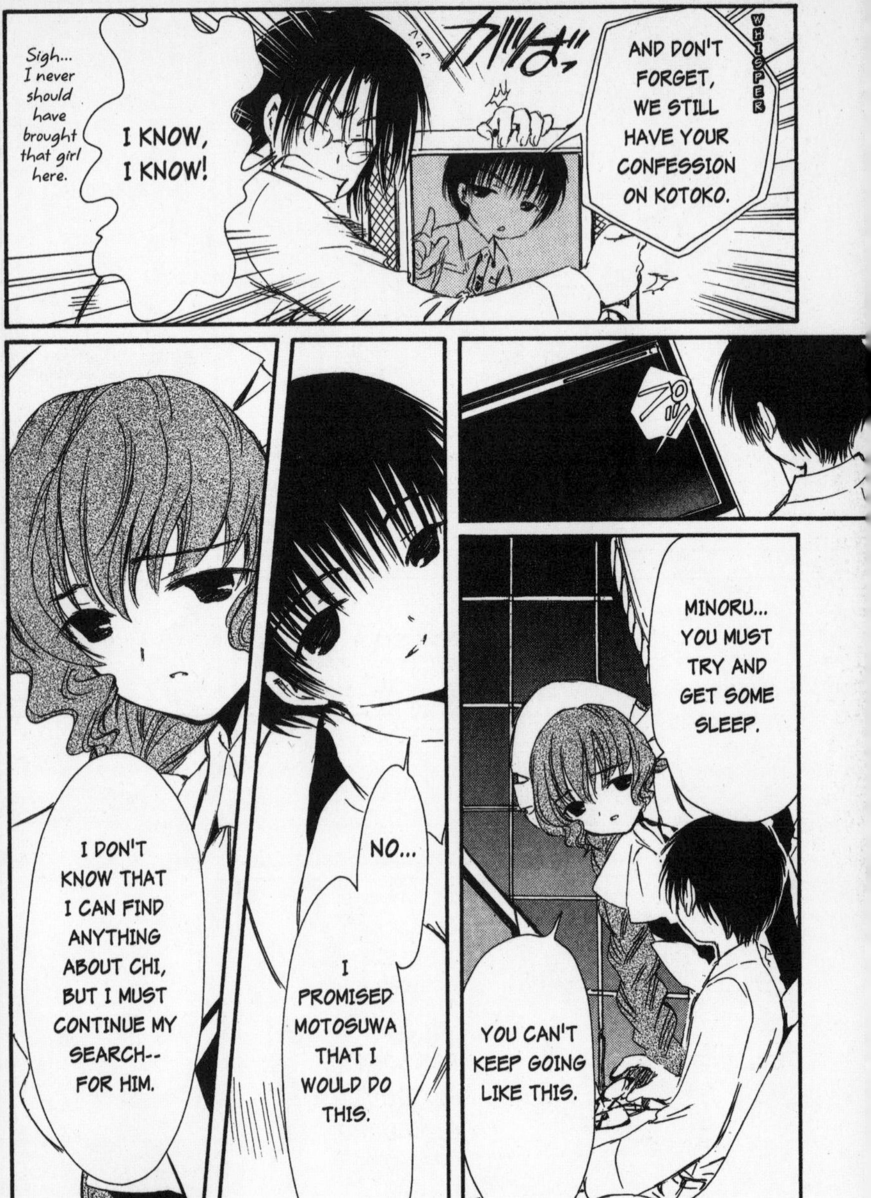
WHISPER
AND DON'T FORGET, WE STILL HAVE YOUR CONFESSION ON KOTOKO.
I KNOW, I KNOW!
Sigh... I never should have brought that girl here.
MINORU... YOU MUST TRY AND GET SOME SLEEP.
YOU CAN'T KEEP GOING LIKE THIS.
NO...
I PROMISED MOTOSUWA THAT I WOULD DO THIS.
I DON'T KNOW THAT I CAN FIND ANYTHING ABOUT CHI, BUT I MUST CONTINUE MY SEARCH--FOR HIM.

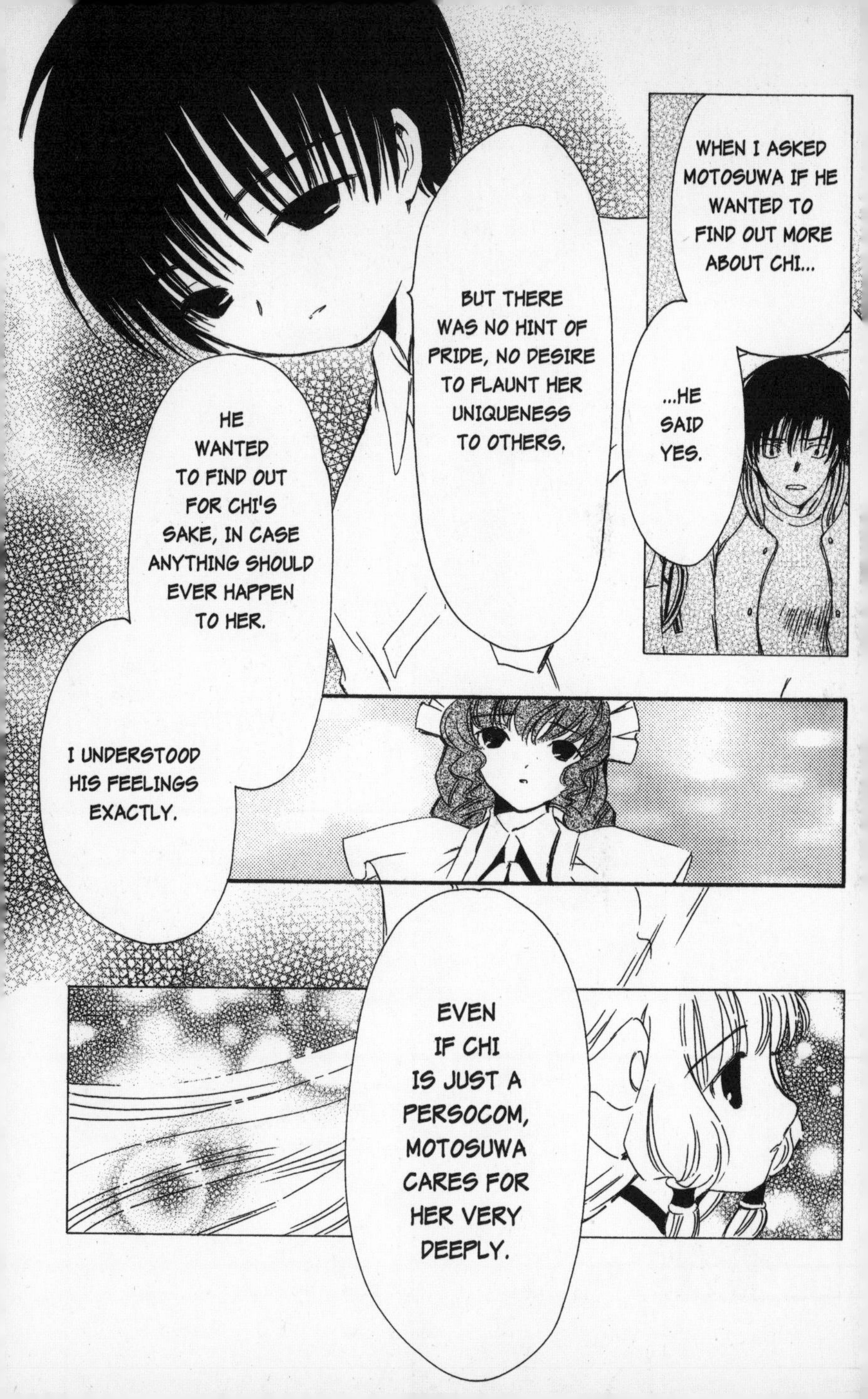
WHEN I ASKED MOTOSUWA IF HE WANTED TO FIND OUT MORE ABOUT CHI...
...HE SAID YES.
BUT THERE WAS NO HINT OF PRIDE, NO DESIRE TO FLAUNT HER UNIQUENESS TO OTHERS.
HE WANTED TO FIND OUT FOR CHI'S SAKE, IN CASE ANYTHING SHOULD EVER HAPPEN TO HER.
I UNDERSTOOD HIS FEELINGS EXACTLY.
EVEN IF CHI IS JUST A PERSOCOM, MOTOSUWA CARES FOR HER VERY DEEPLY.

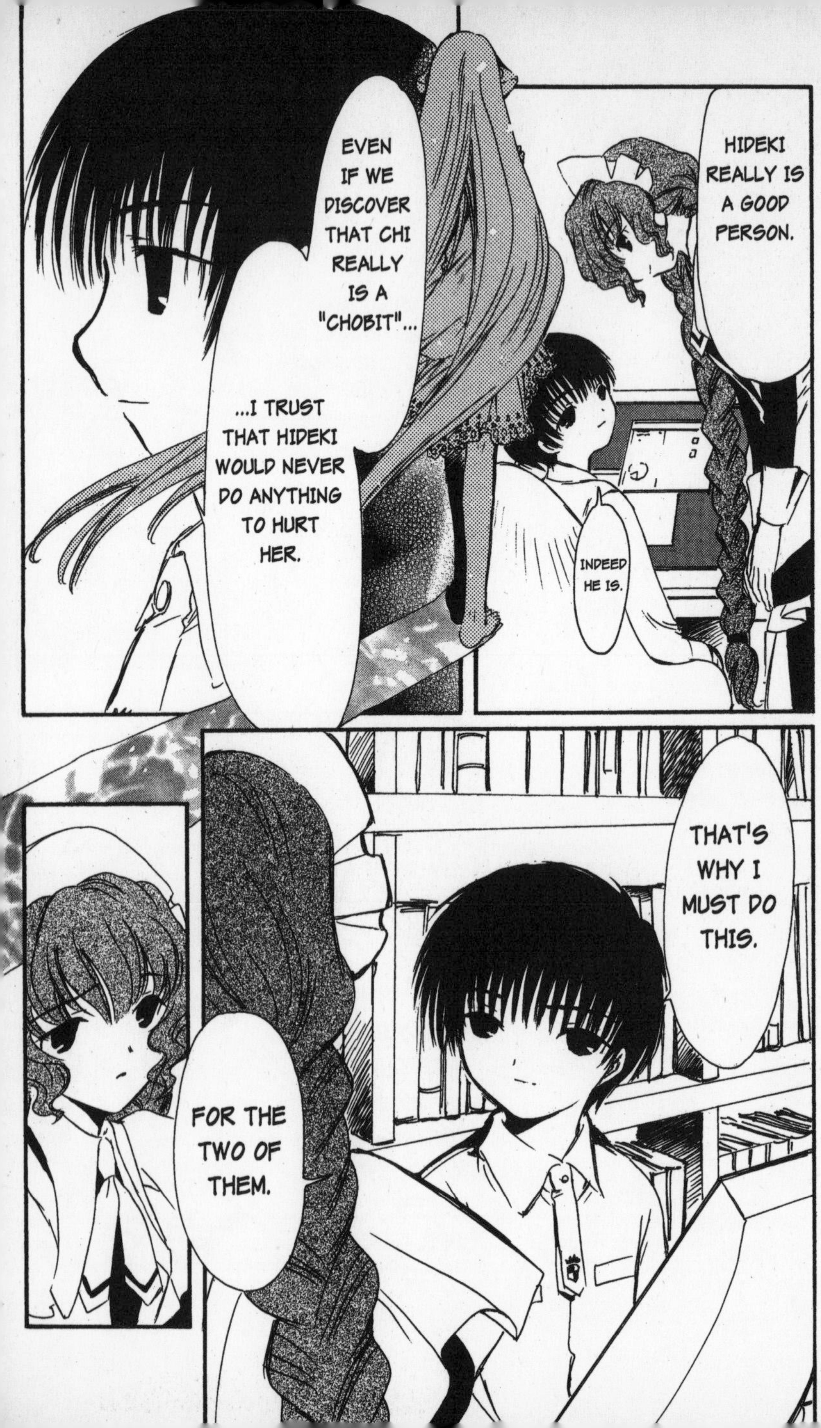
HIDEKI REALLY IS A GOOD PERSON.
INDEED HE IS.
EVEN IF WE DISCOVER THAT CHI REALLY IS A "CHOBIT"...
...I TRUST THAT HIDEKI WOULD NEVER DO ANYTHING TO HURT HER.
THAT'S WHY I MUST DO THIS.
FOR THE TWO OF THEM.

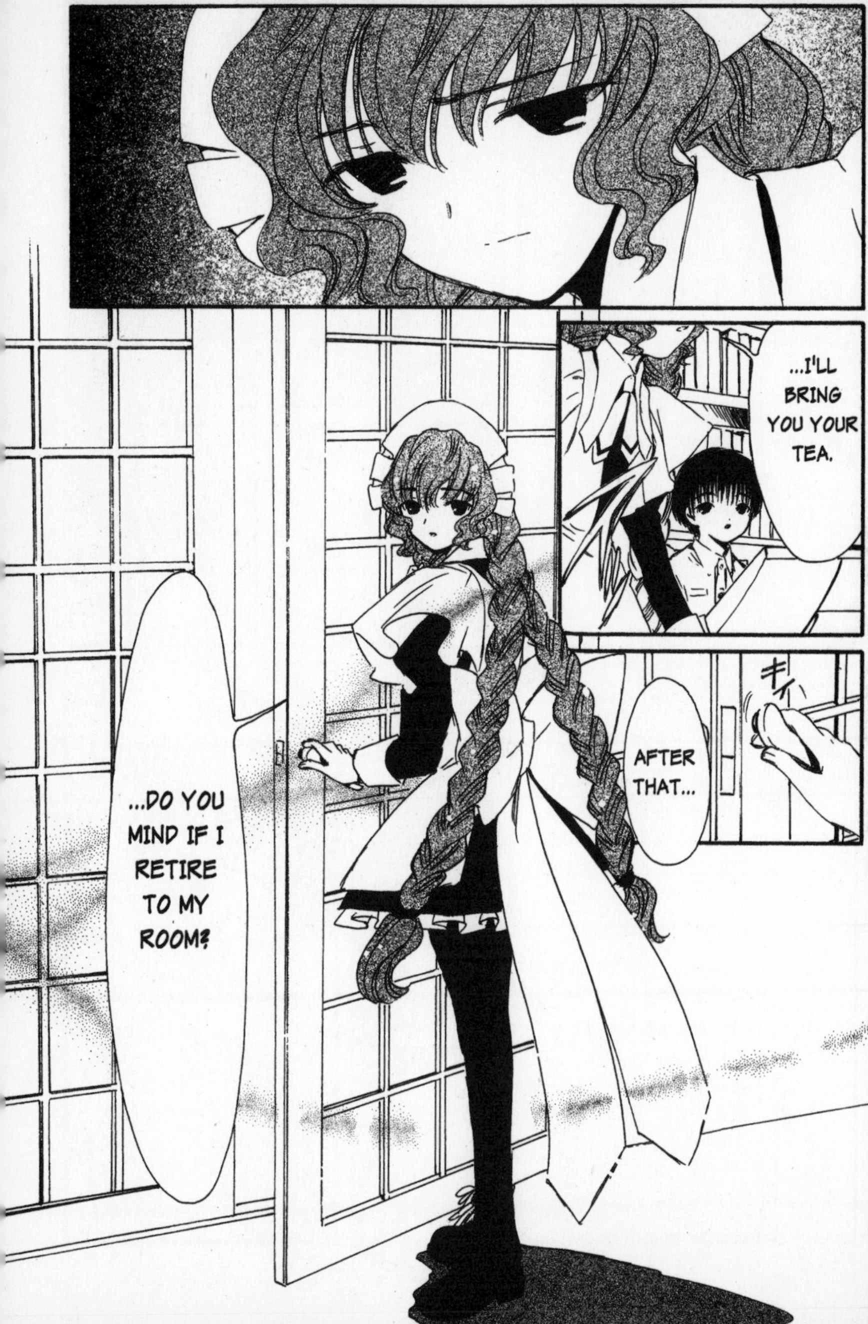
...I'LL BRING YOU YOUR TEA.
キィ
AFTER THAT...
...DO YOU MIND IF I RETIRE TO MY ROOM?

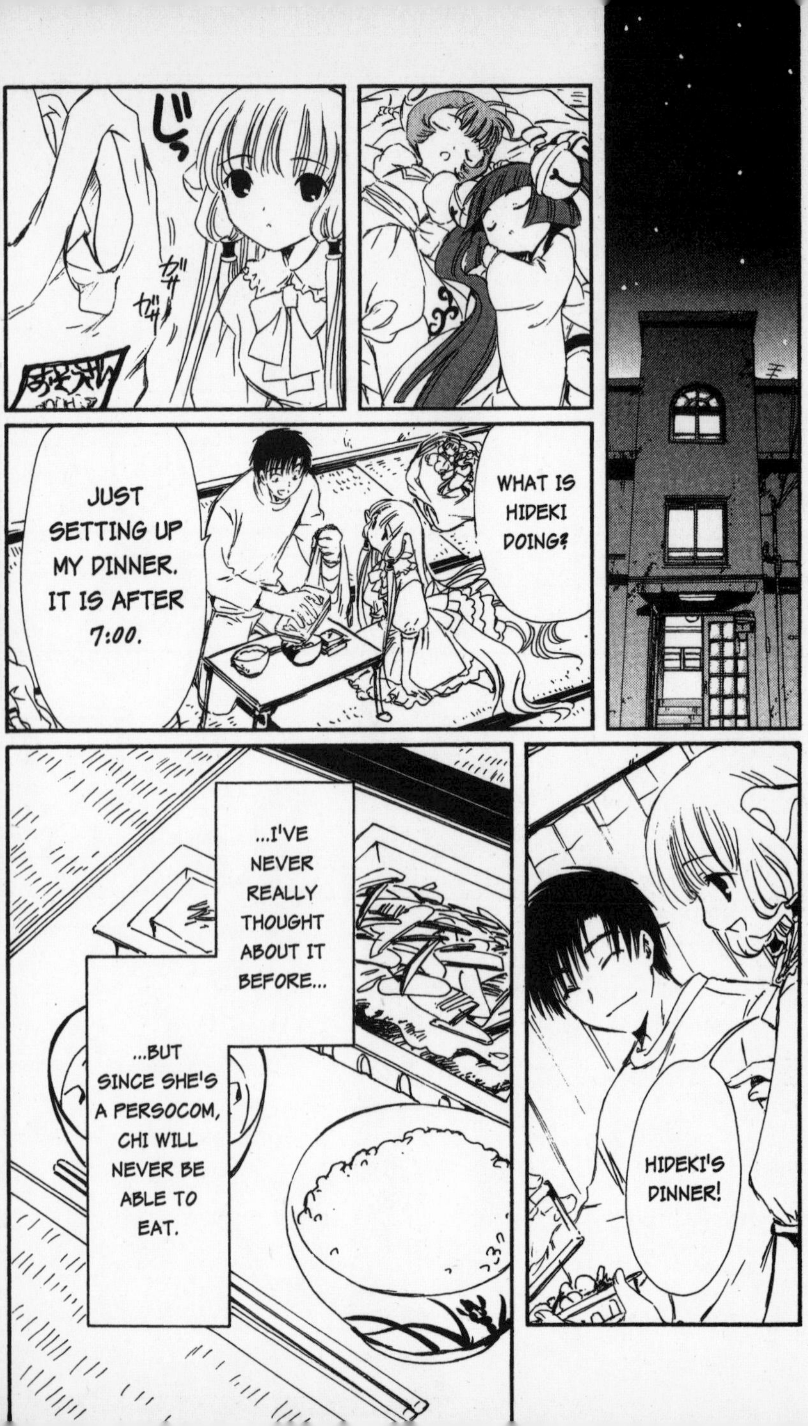
じっ
ガサ ガサ
WHAT IS HIDEKI DOING?
JUST SETTING UP MY DINNER. IT IS AFTER 7:00.
HIDEKI'S DINNER!
...I'VE NEVER REALLY THOUGHT ABOUT IT BEFORE...
...BUT SINCE SHE'S A PERSOCOM, CHI WILL NEVER BE ABLE TO EAT.

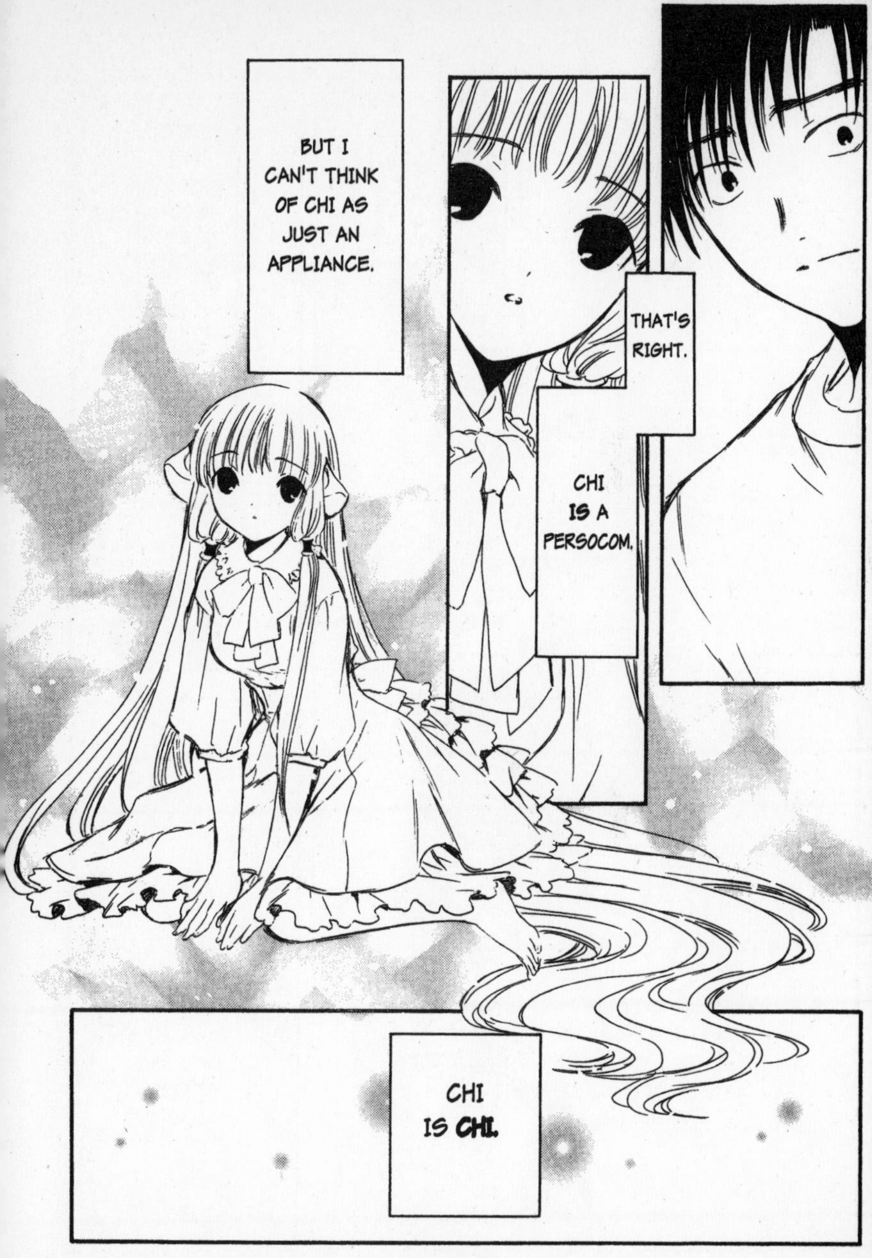
THAT'S RIGHT.
CHI IS A PERSOCOM.
BUT I CAN'T THINK OF CHI AS JUST AN APPLIANCE.
CHI IS **CHI.**

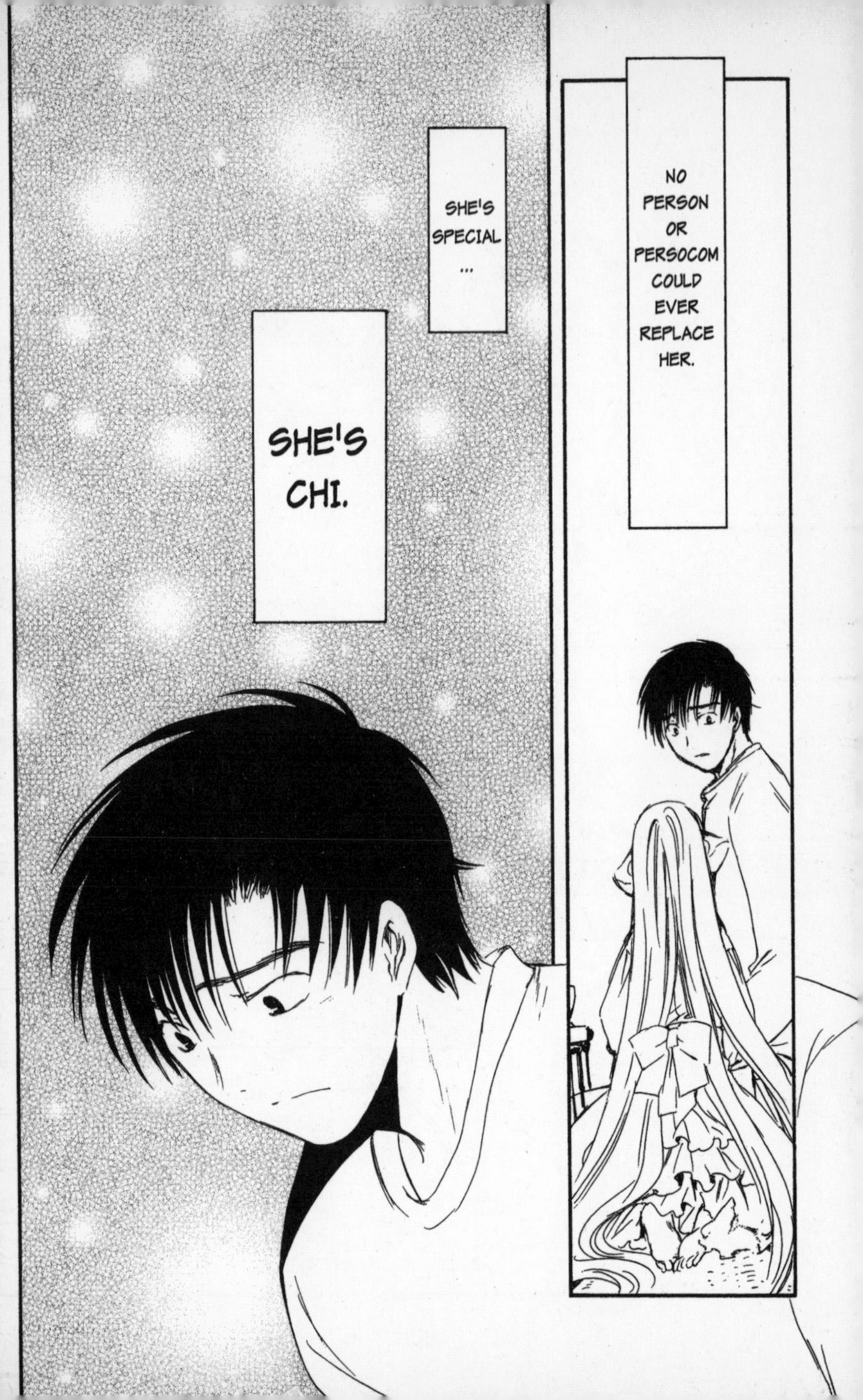
NO PERSON OR PERSOCOM COULD EVER REPLACE HER.
SHE'S SPECIAL ...
SHE'S CHI.

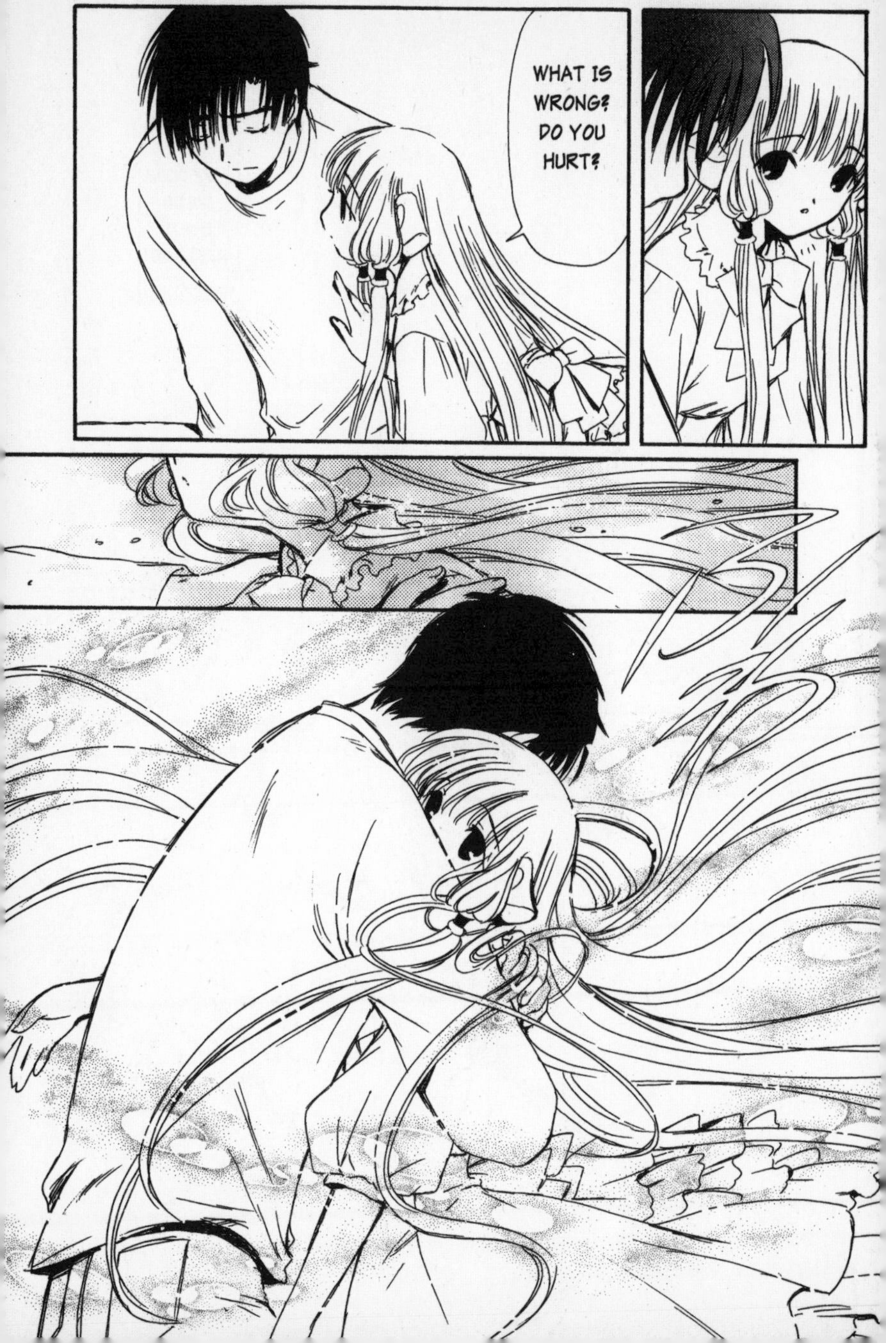
WHAT IS WRONG? DO YOU HURT?

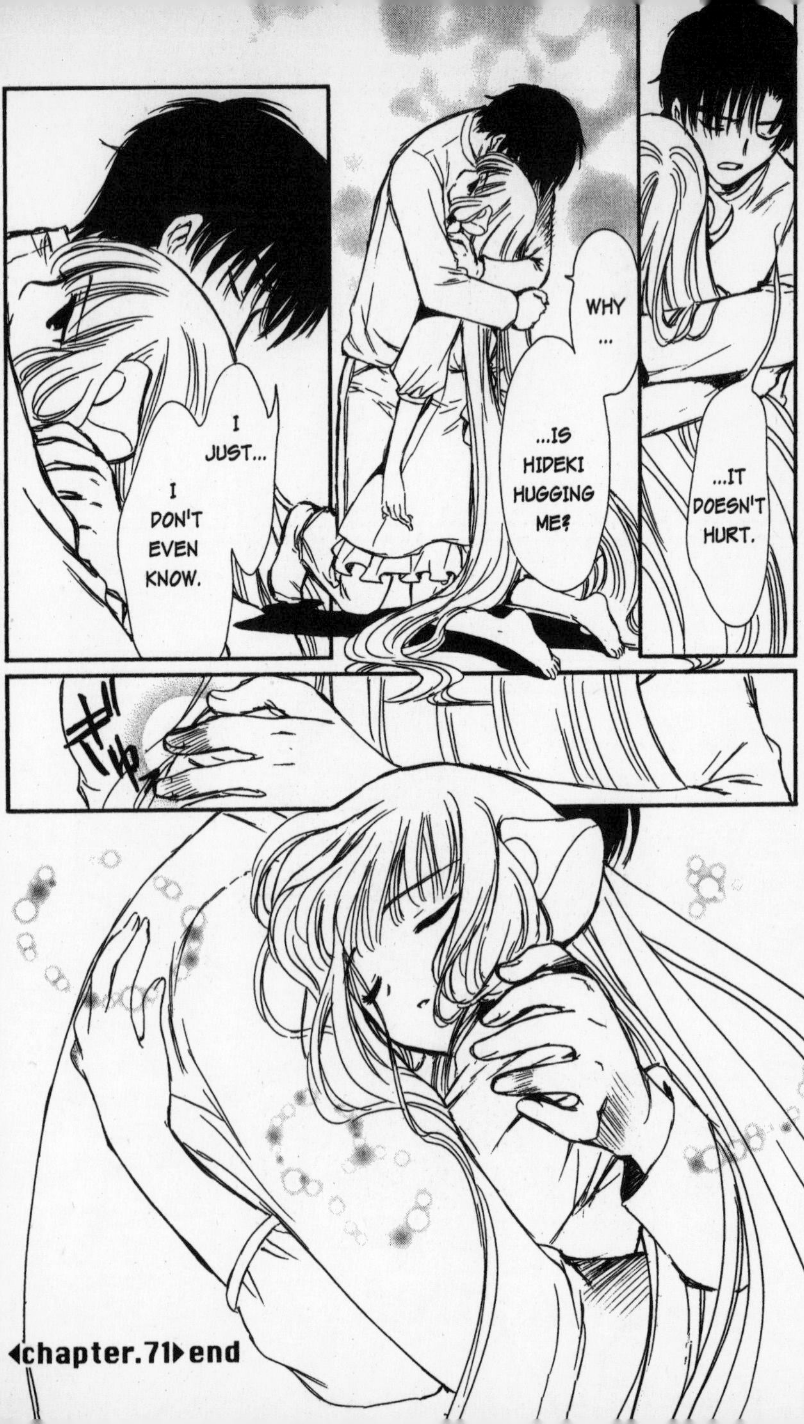
...IT DOESN'T HURT.
WHY ...
...IS HIDEKI HUGGING ME?
I JUST...
I DON'T EVEN KNOW.
ギュ

◀chapter.71▶end

ちょびっツ
Chobits

◀chapter.72▶

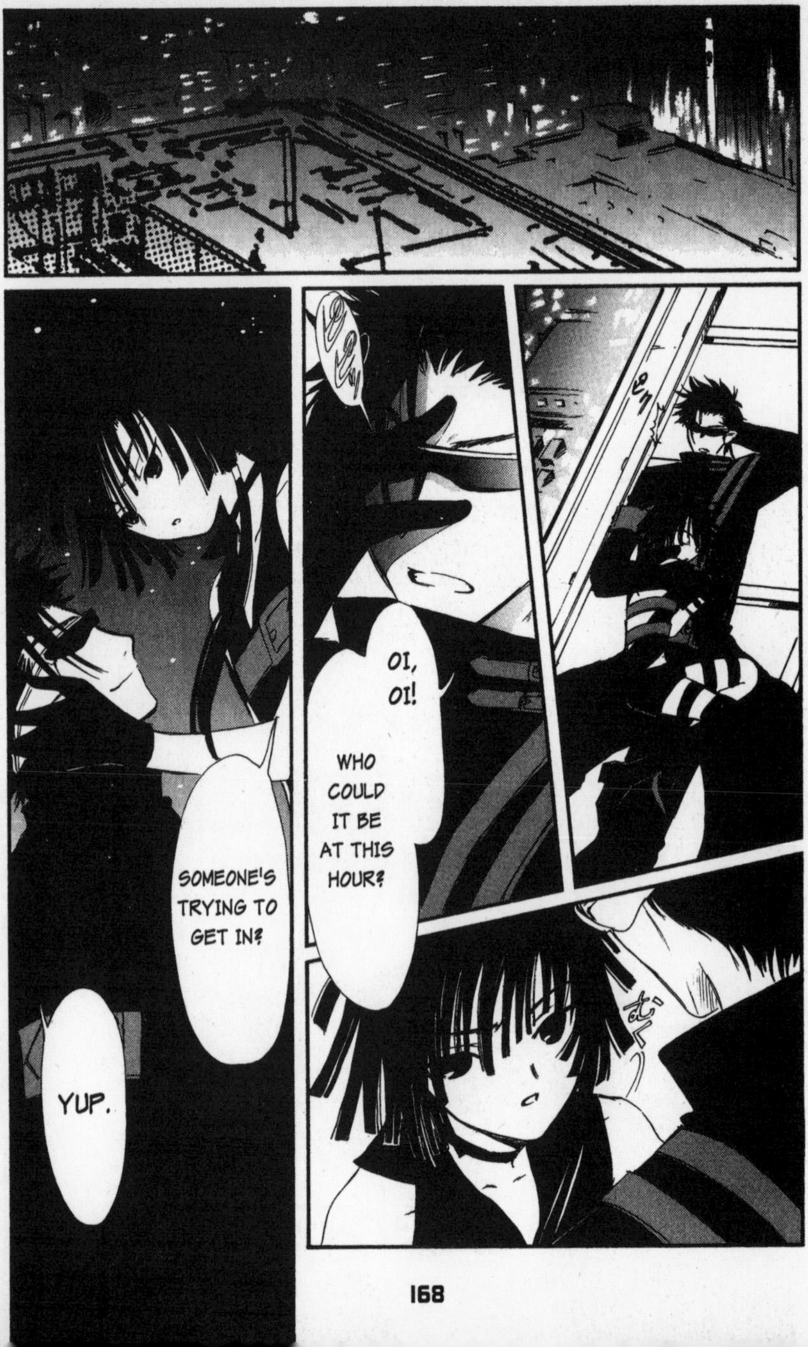

OI, OI!
WHO COULD IT BE AT THIS HOUR?
SOMEONE'S TRYING TO GET IN?
YUP.

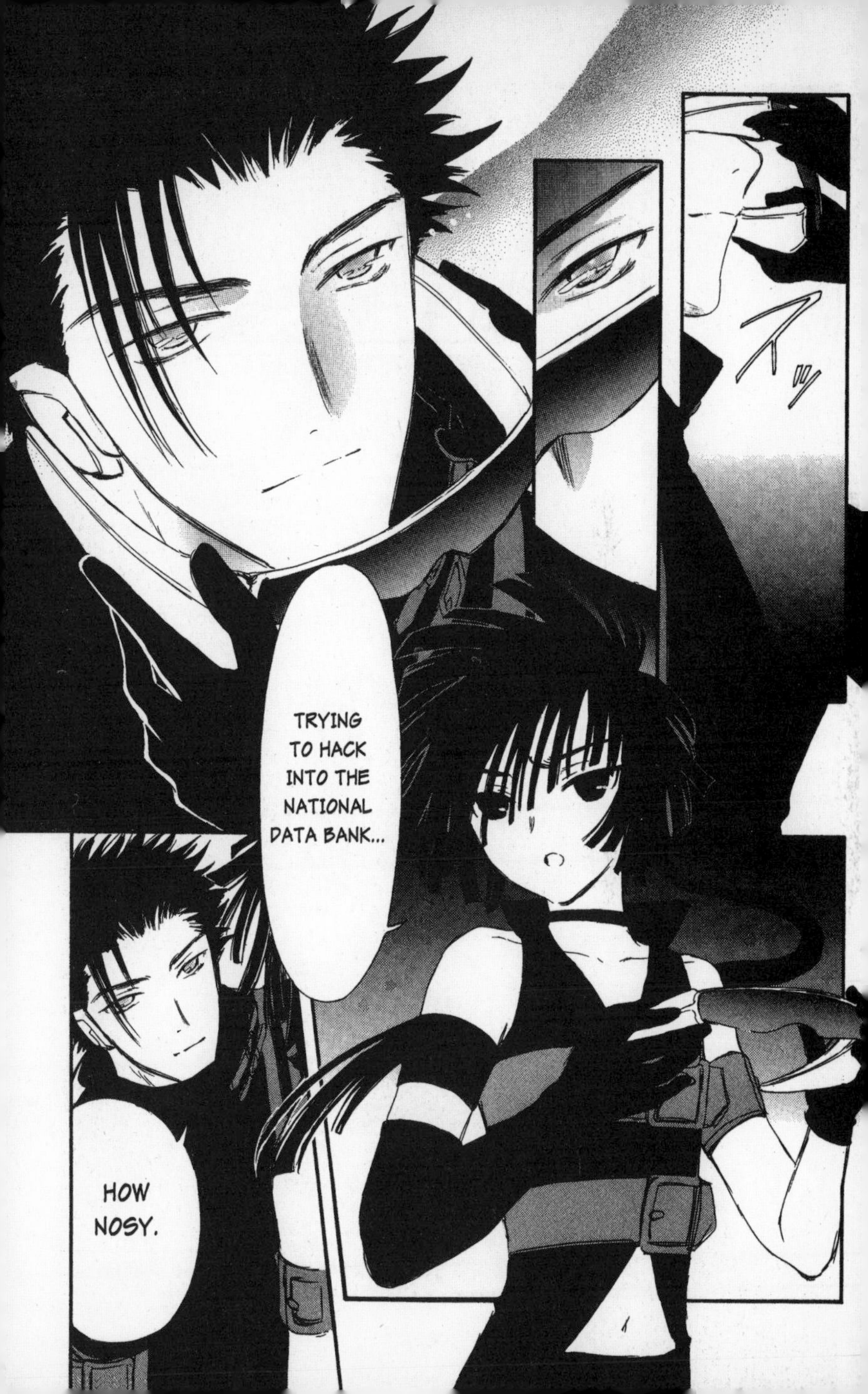
スッ
TRYING TO HACK INTO THE NATIONAL DATA BANK...
HOW NOSY.

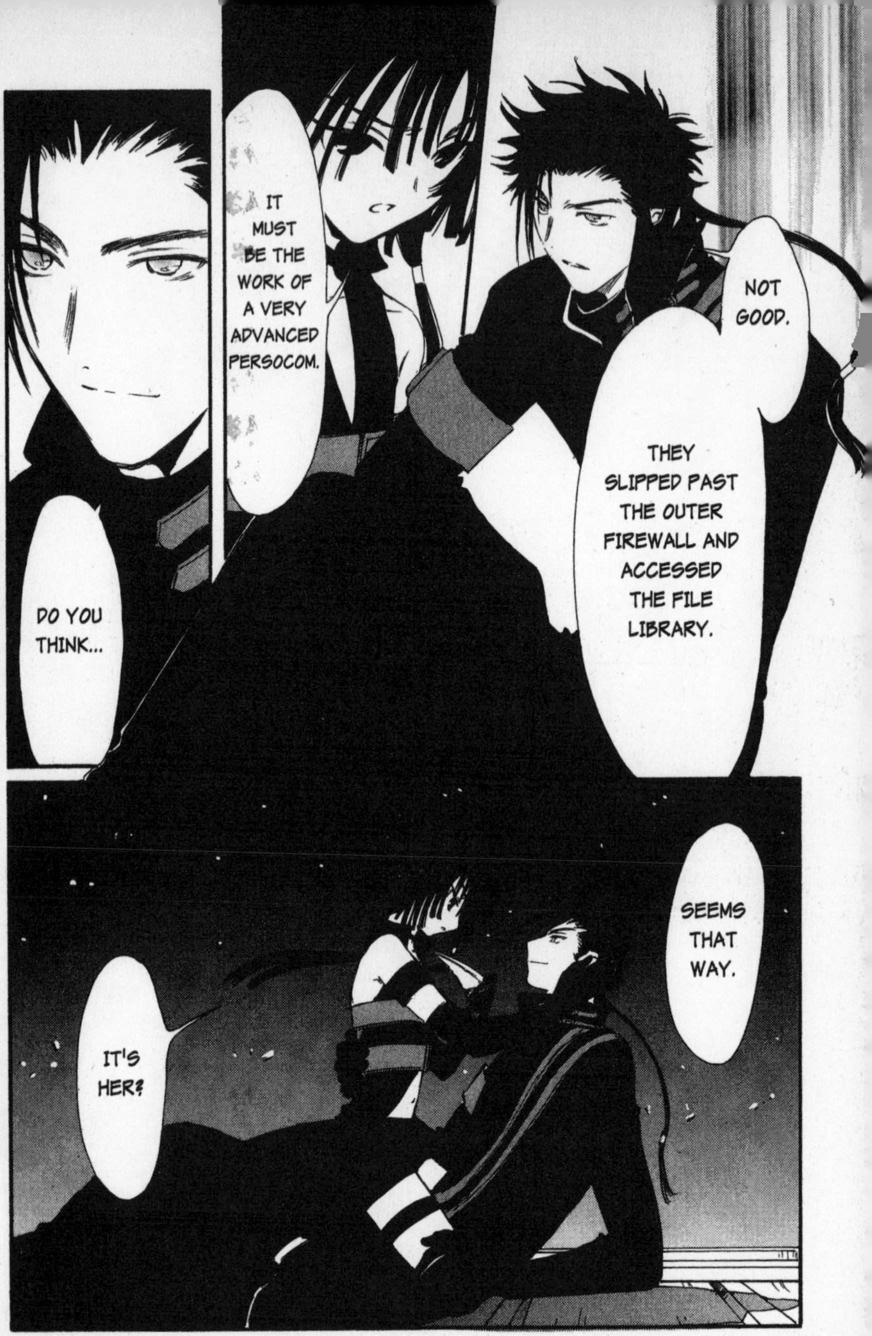
NOT GOOD.
THEY SLIPPED PAST THE OUTER FIREWALL AND ACCESSED THE FILE LIBRARY.
IT MUST BE THE WORK OF A VERY ADVANCED PERSOCOM.
DO YOU THINK...
IT'S HER?
SEEMS THAT WAY.

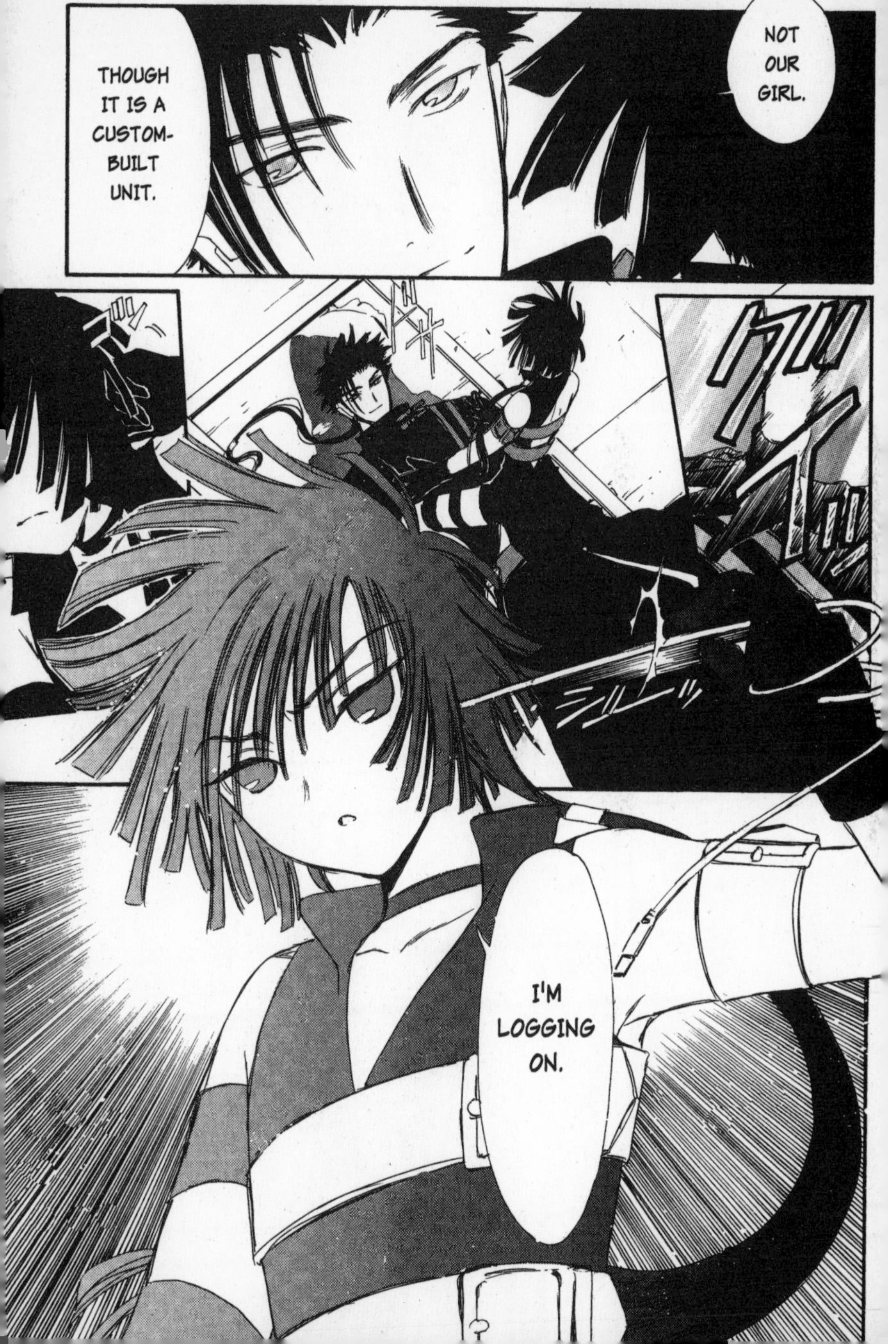
NOT OUR GIRL.
THOUGH IT IS A CUSTOM-BUILT UNIT.
I'M LOGGING ON.

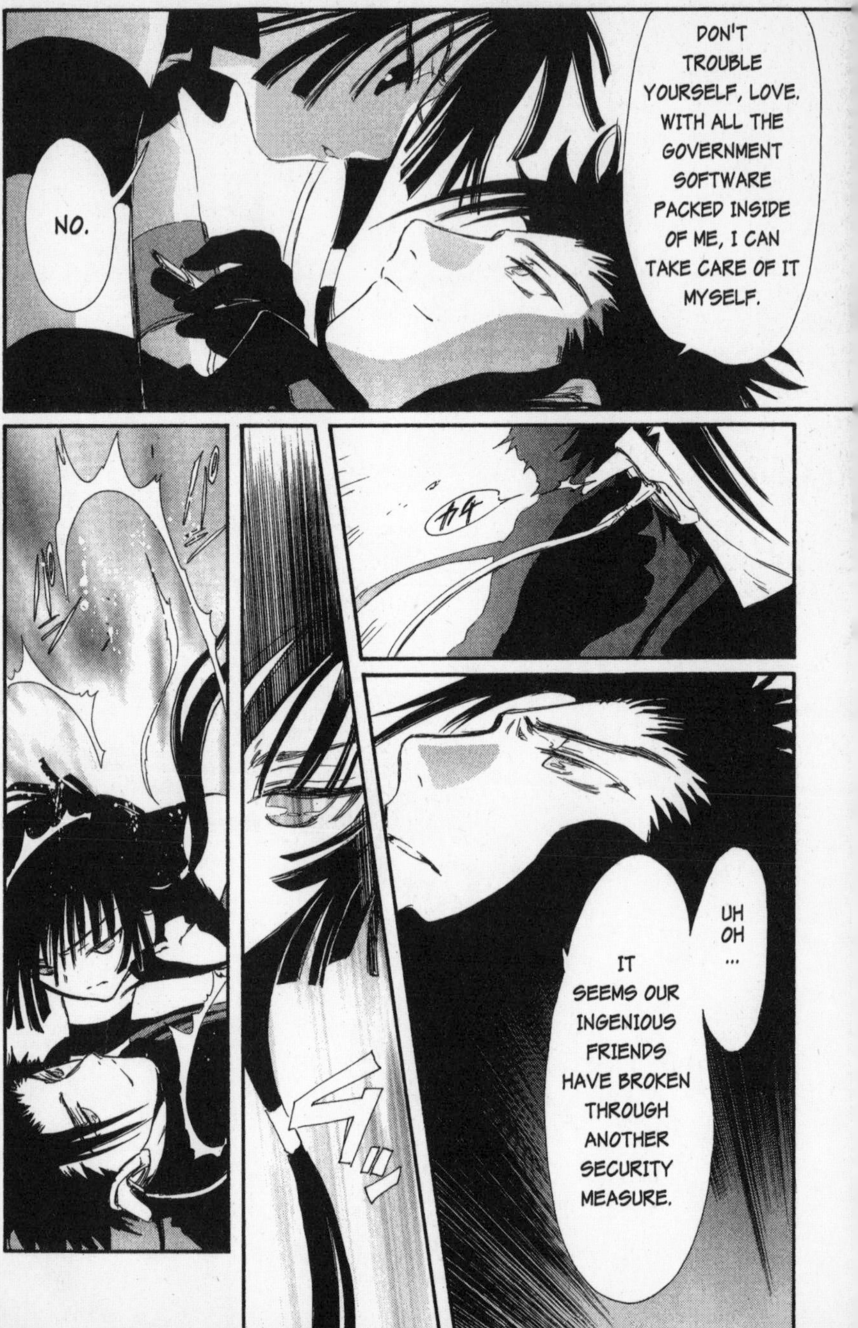
DON'T TROUBLE YOURSELF, LOVE. WITH ALL THE GOVERNMENT SOFTWARE PACKED INSIDE OF ME, I CAN TAKE CARE OF IT MYSELF.
NO.
UH OH ...
IT SEEMS OUR INGENIOUS FRIENDS HAVE BROKEN THROUGH ANOTHER SECURITY MEASURE.

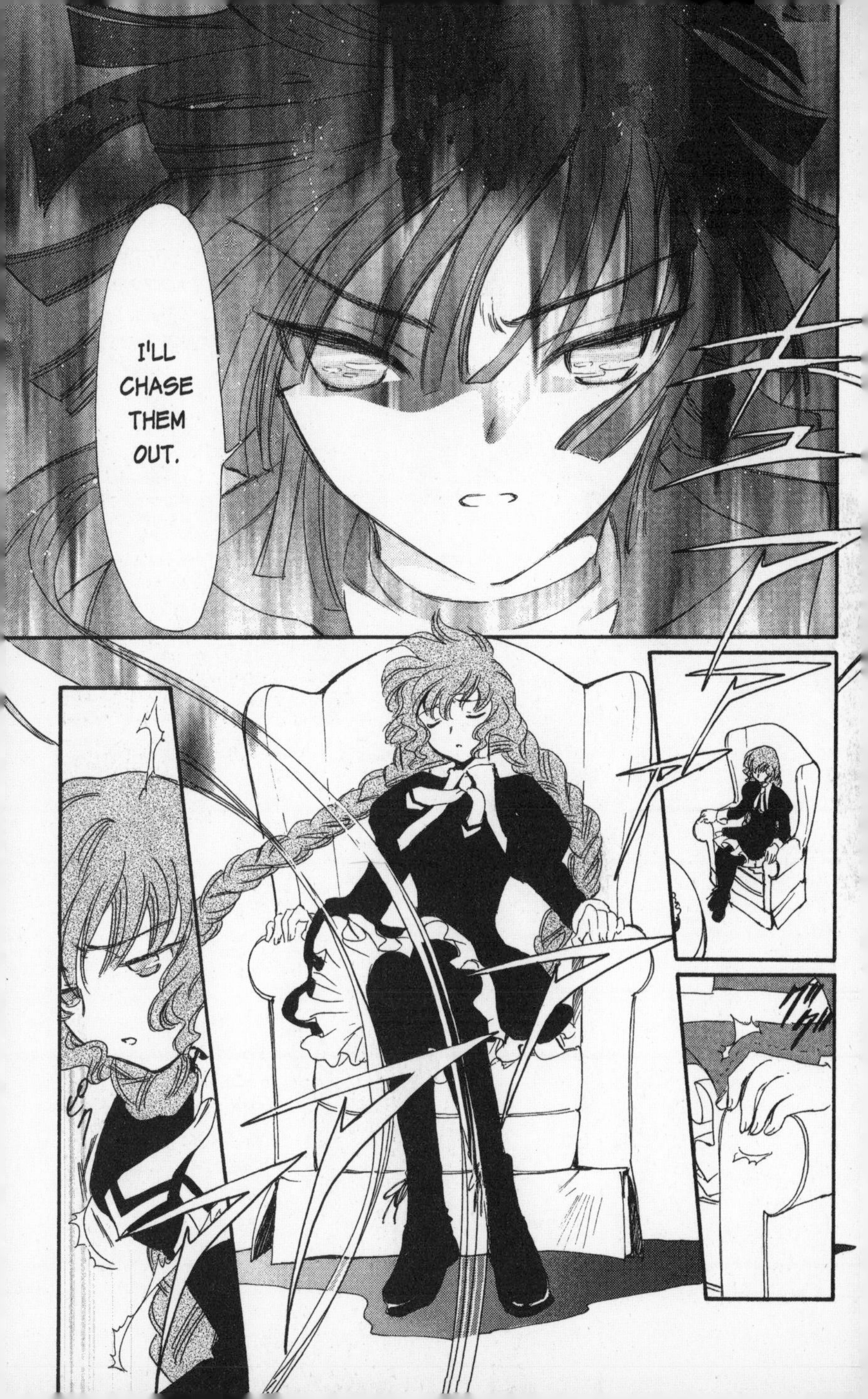
I'LL CHASE THEM OUT.

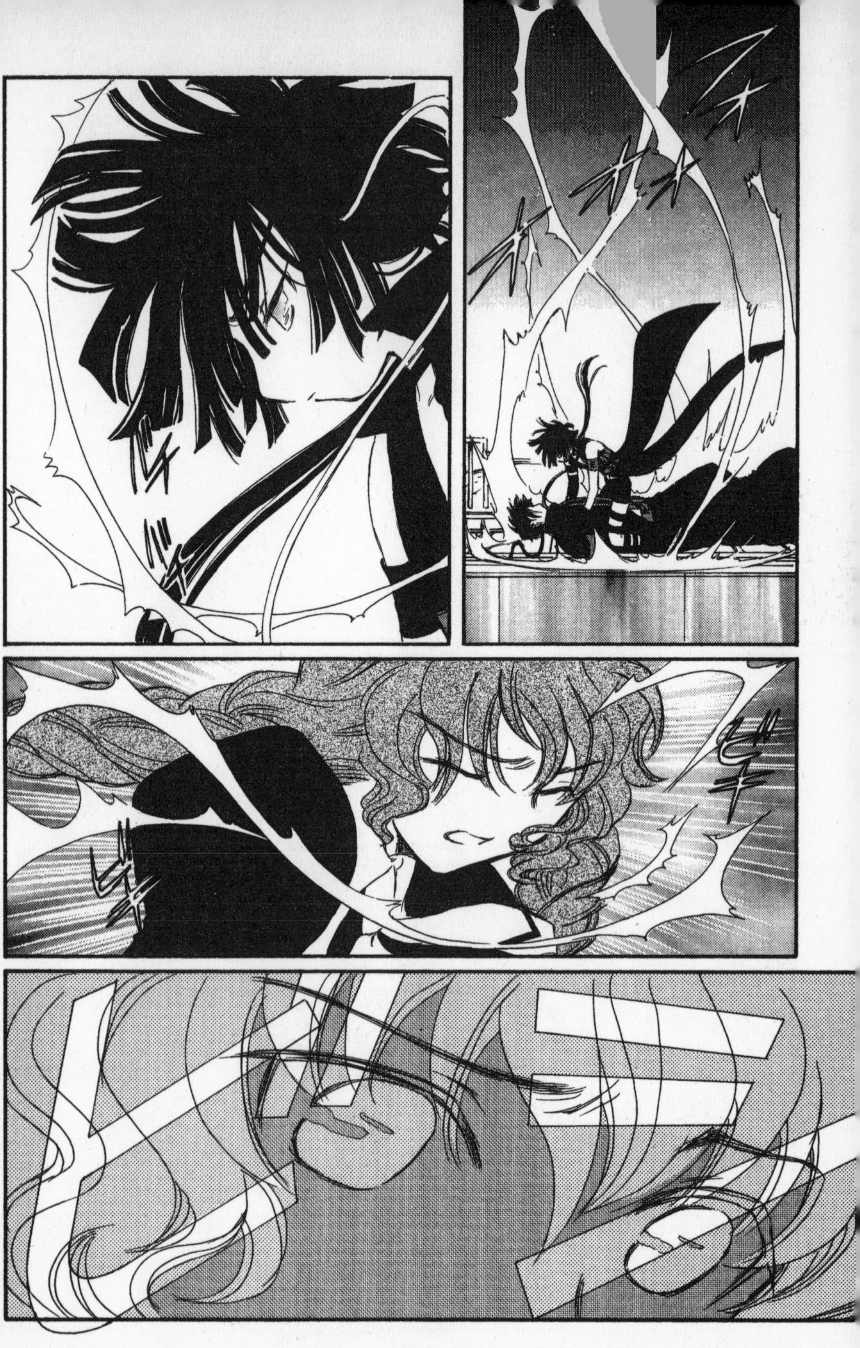

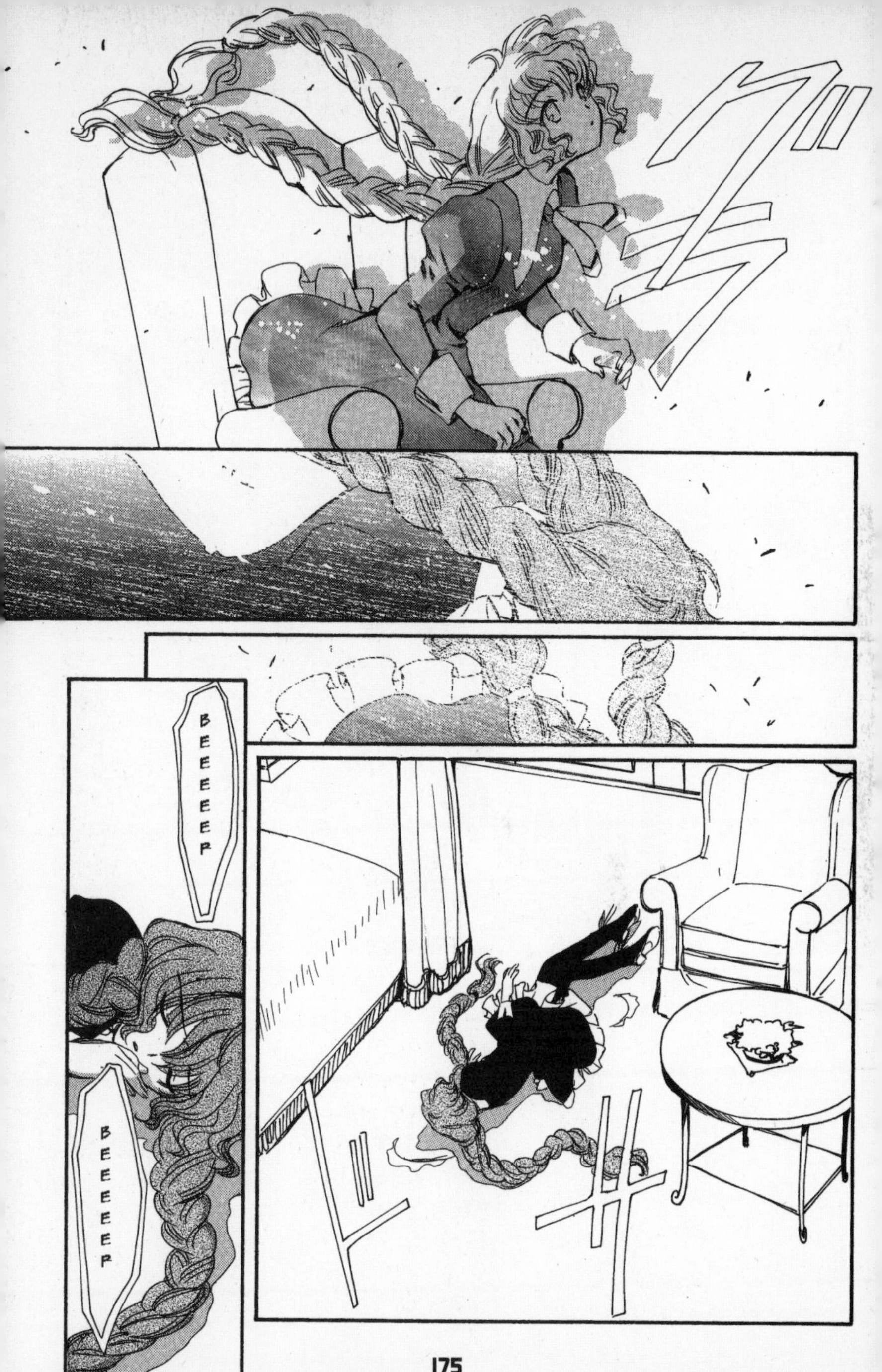
BEEEEEEP
BEEEEEEP

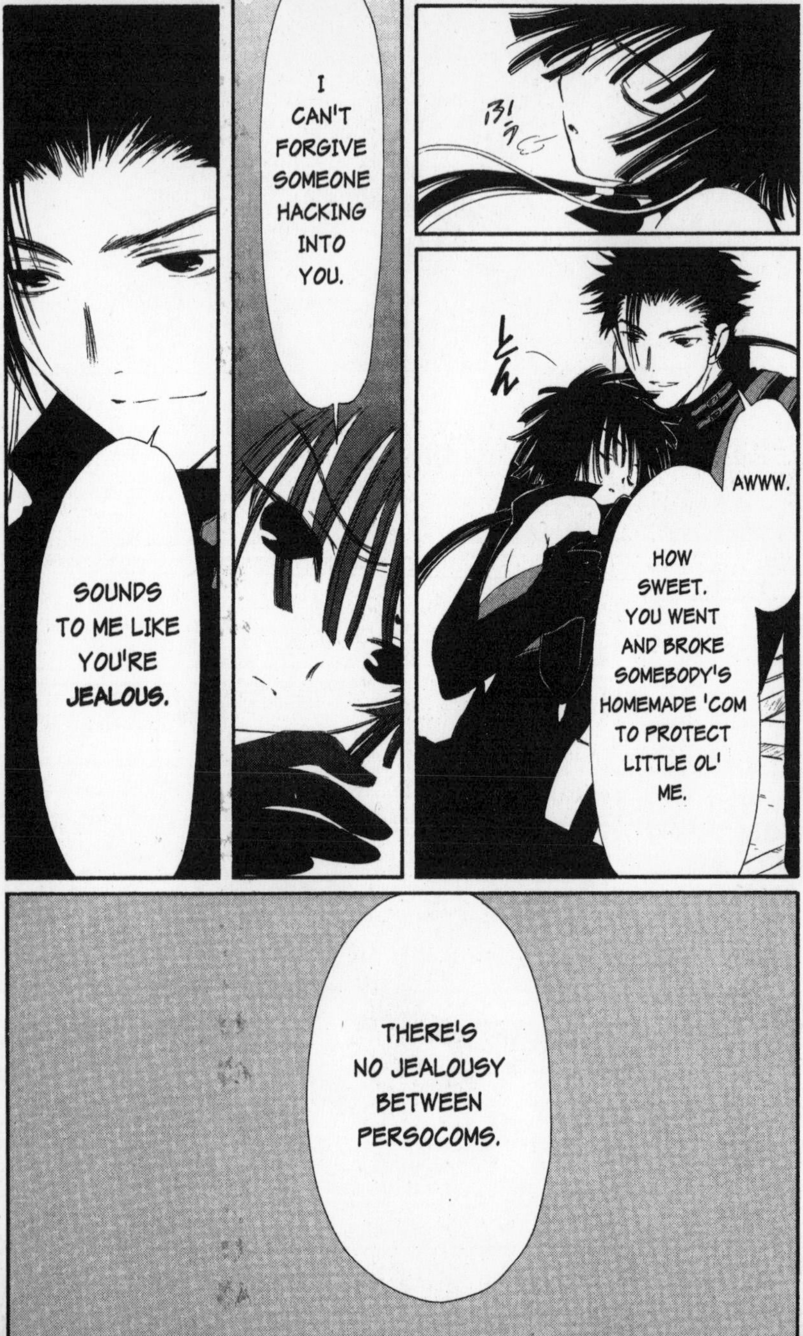

とん
AWWW.
HOW SWEET. YOU WENT AND BROKE SOMEBODY'S HOMEMADE 'COM TO PROTECT LITTLE OL' ME.
I CAN'T FORGIVE SOMEONE HACKING INTO YOU.
SOUNDS TO ME LIKE YOU'RE JEALOUS.
THERE'S NO JEALOUSY BETWEEN PERSOCOMS.

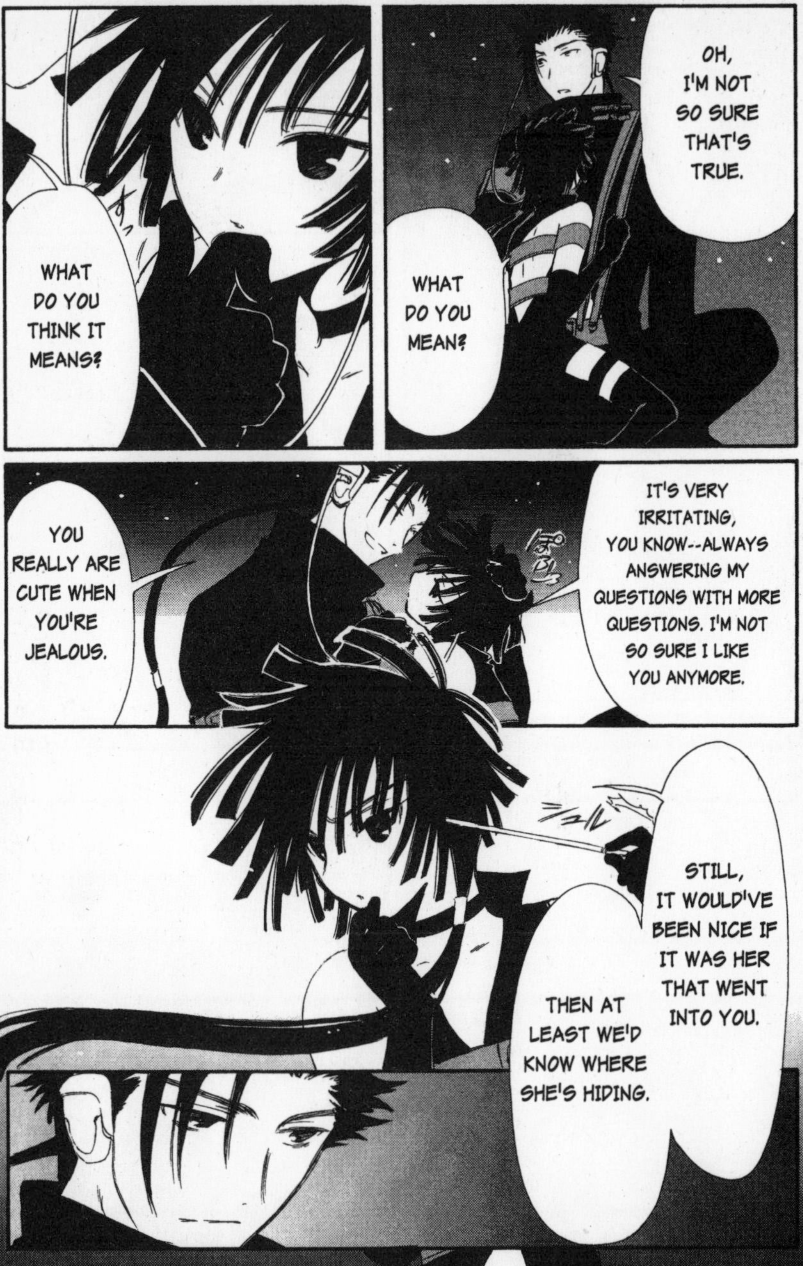
OH, I'M NOT SO SURE THAT'S TRUE.
WHAT DO YOU MEAN?
WHAT DO YOU THINK IT MEANS?
IT'S VERY IRRITATING, YOU KNOW--ALWAYS ANSWERING MY QUESTIONS WITH MORE QUESTIONS. I'M NOT SO SURE I LIKE YOU ANYMORE.
YOU REALLY ARE CUTE WHEN YOU'RE JEALOUS.
STILL, IT WOULD'VE BEEN NICE IF IT WAS HER THAT WENT INTO YOU.
THEN AT LEAST WE'D KNOW WHERE SHE'S HIDING.

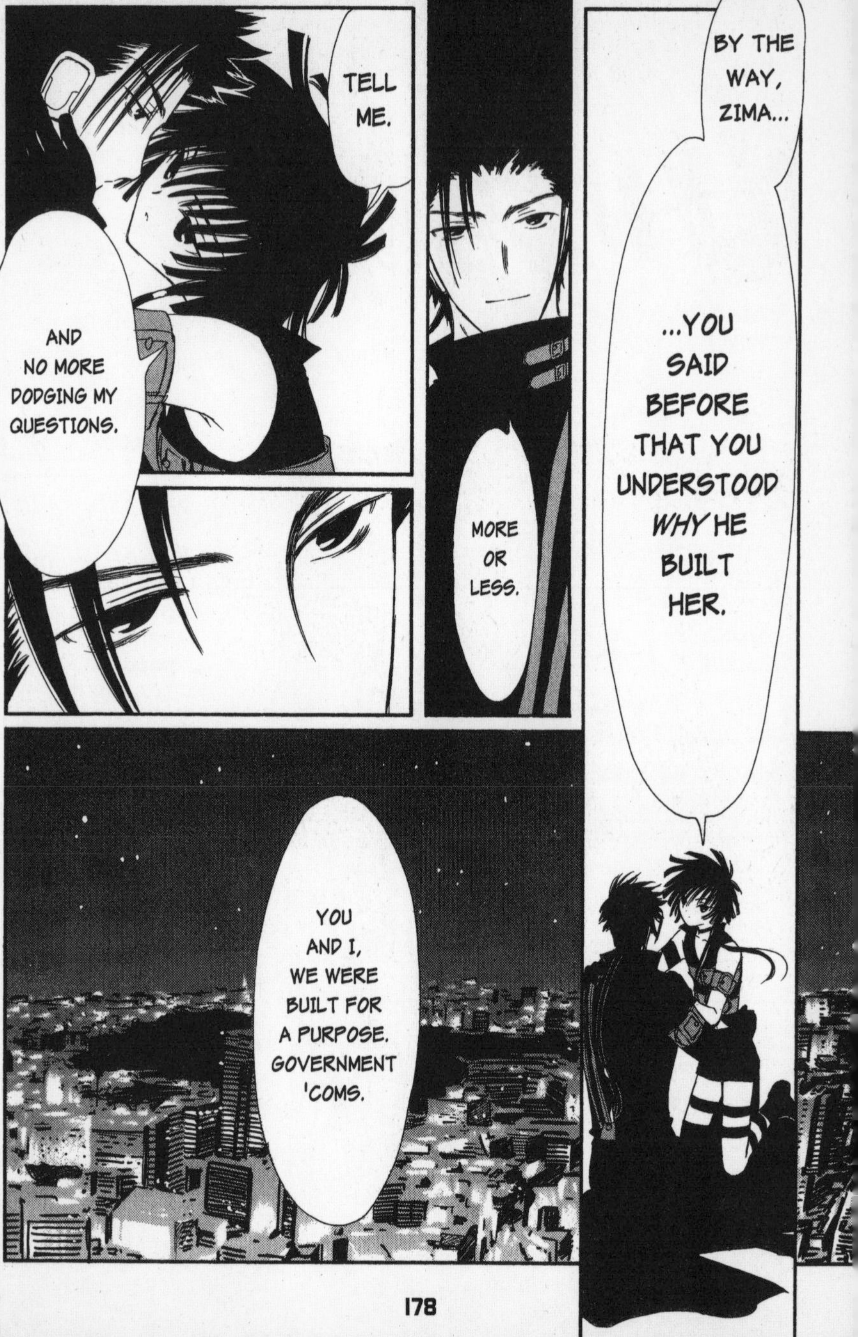
BY THE WAY, ZIMA...
...YOU SAID BEFORE THAT YOU UNDERSTOOD *WHY* HE BUILT HER.
MORE OR LESS.
TELL ME.
AND NO MORE DODGING MY QUESTIONS.
YOU AND I, WE WERE BUILT FOR A PURPOSE. GOVERNMENT 'COMS.

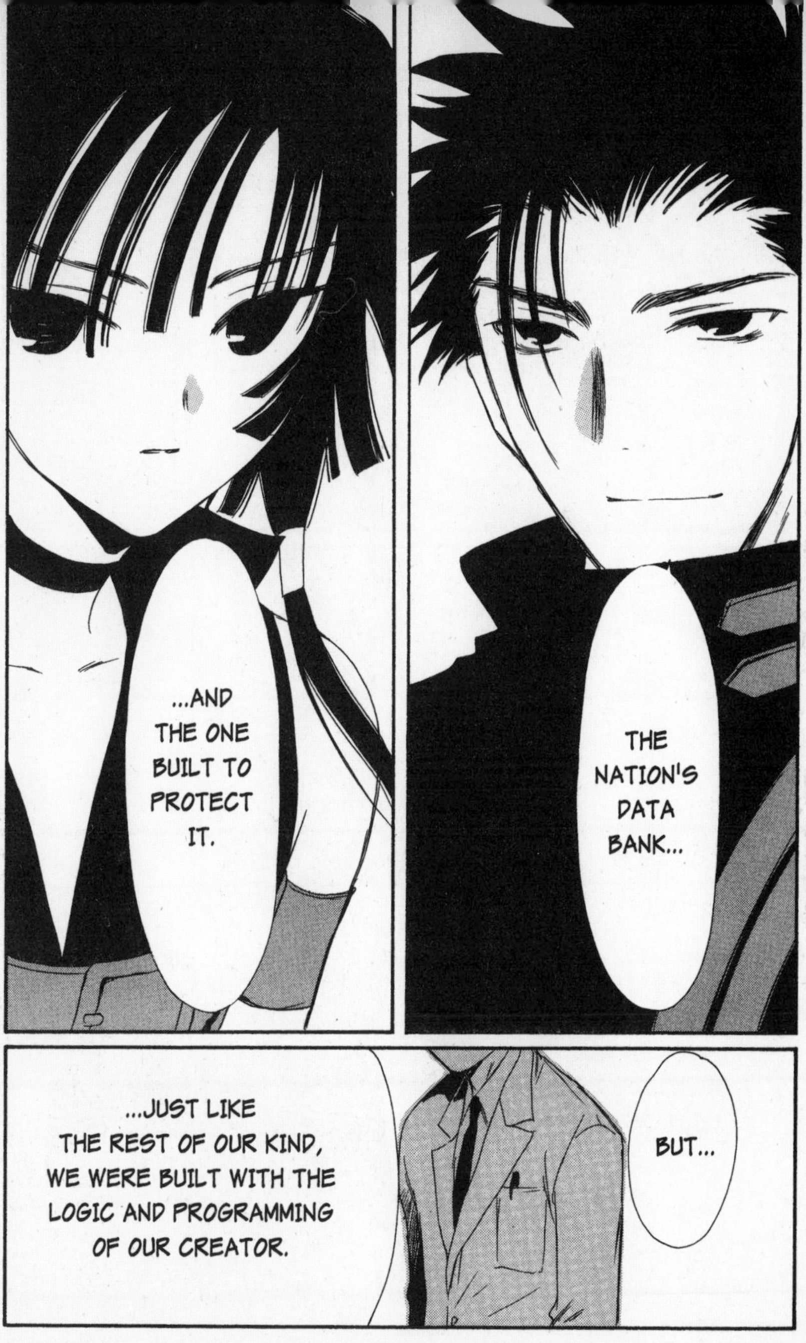
THE NATION'S DATA BANK...
...AND THE ONE BUILT TO PROTECT IT.
BUT...
...JUST LIKE THE REST OF OUR KIND, WE WERE BUILT WITH THE LOGIC AND PROGRAMMING OF OUR CREATOR.

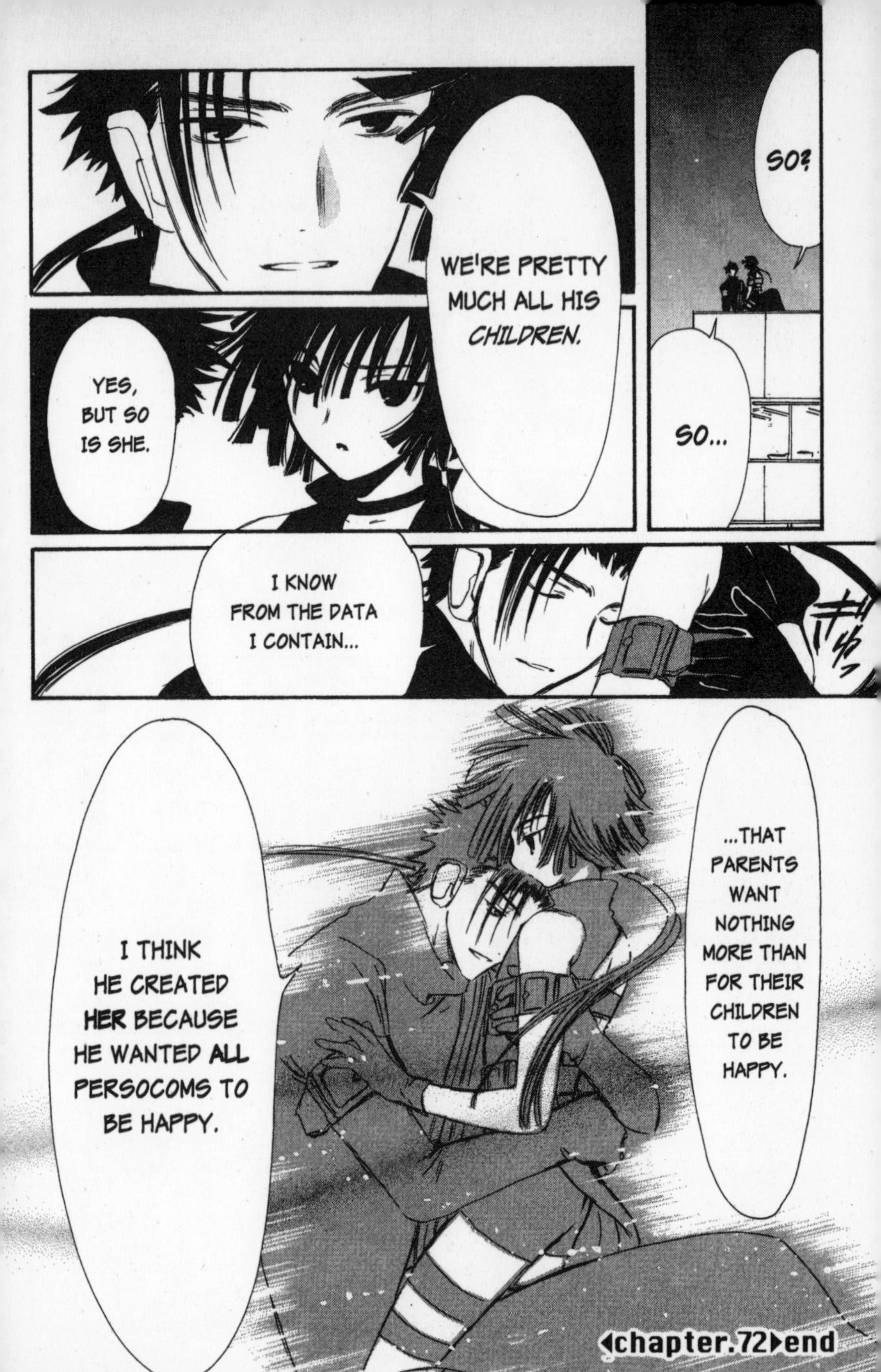
SO?
SO...
WE'RE PRETTY MUCH ALL HIS CHILDREN.
YES, BUT SO IS SHE.
I KNOW FROM THE DATA I CONTAIN...
...THAT PARENTS WANT NOTHING MORE THAN FOR THEIR CHILDREN TO BE HAPPY.
I THINK HE CREATED HER BECAUSE HE WANTED ALL PERSOCOMS TO BE HAPPY.
chapter.72 end

MUST SEE Personcoms

address:

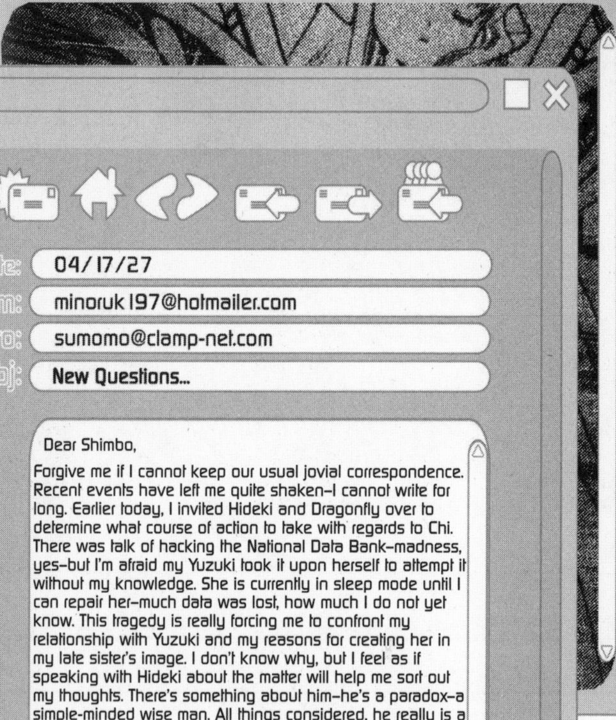

date: 04/17/27

from: minoruk197@hotmailer.com

to: sumomo@clamp-net.com

subj: **New Questions...**

Dear Shimbo,

Forgive me if I cannot keep our usual jovial correspondence. Recent events have left me quite shaken–I cannot write for long. Earlier today, I invited Hideki and Dragonfly over to determine what course of action to take with regards to Chi. There was talk of hacking the National Data Bank–madness, yes–but I'm afraid my Yuzuki took it upon herself to attempt it without my knowledge. She is currently in sleep mode until I can repair her–much data was lost, how much I do not yet know. This tragedy is really forcing me to confront my relationship with Yuzuki and my reasons for creating her in my late sister's image. I don't know why, but I feel as if speaking with Hideki about the matter will help me sort out my thoughts. There's something about him–he's a paradox–a simple-minded wise man. All things considered, he really is a nice guy. In the meantime, it would please me if you could do some research on the National Data Bank. I've heard rumors that it exists in a single persocom. Could this be true? You might also want to do a background check on "Icchan."

Your saddened friend,

Minoru

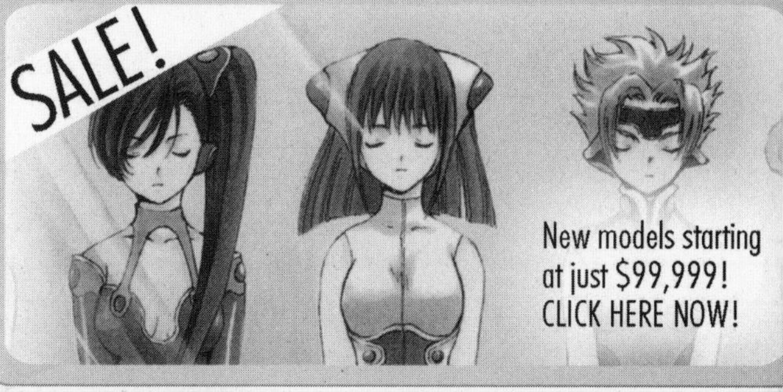
SALE!
New models starting at just $99,999!
CLICK HERE NOW!

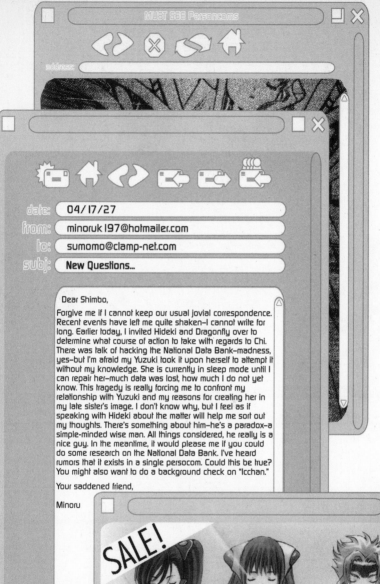

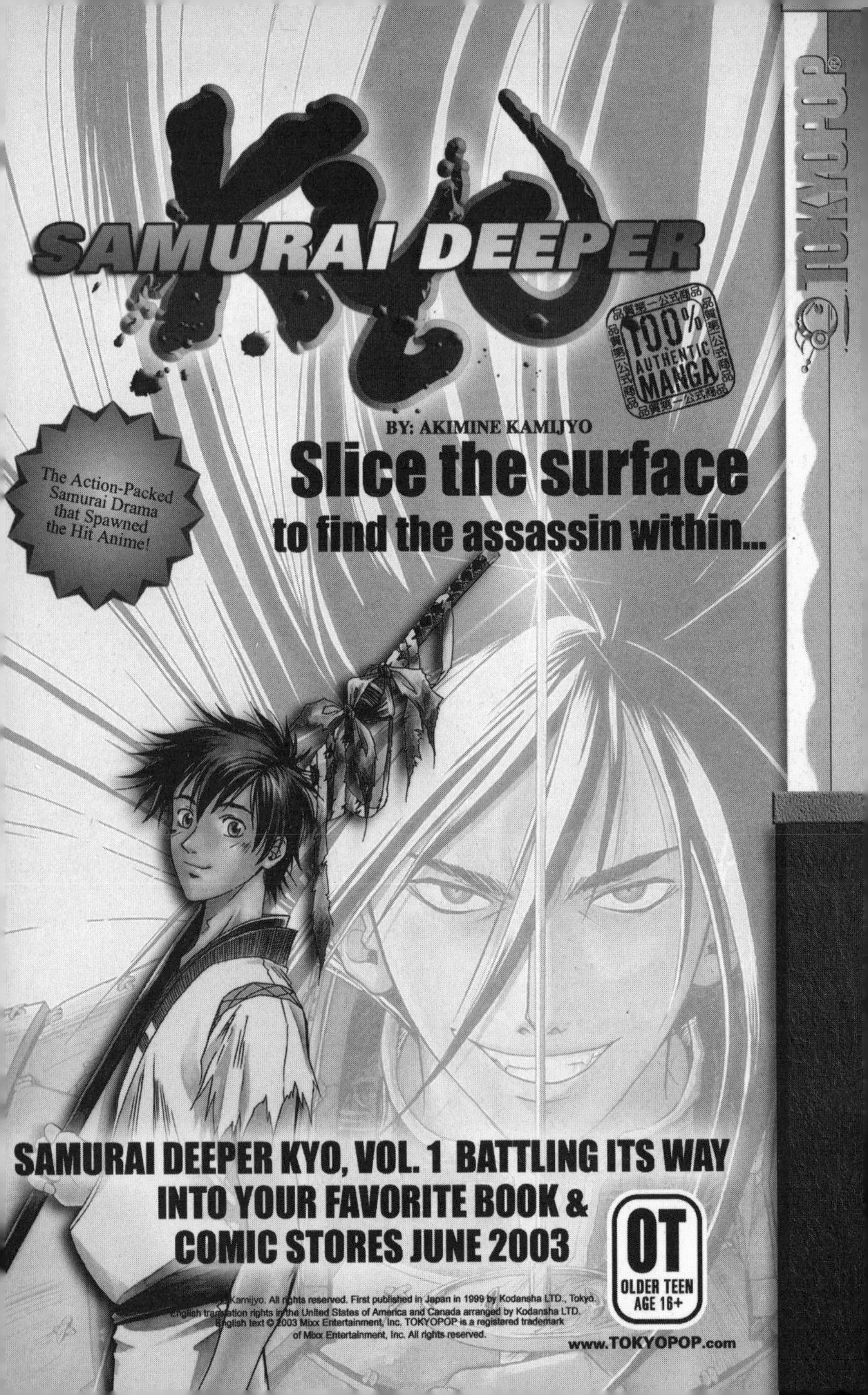

SAMURAI DEEPER
KYO
100% AUTHENTIC MANGA
BY: AKIMINE KAMIJYO
Slice the surface
to find the assassin within...
The Action-Packed Samurai Drama that Spawned the Hit Anime!
TOKYOPOP
SAMURAI DEEPER KYO, VOL. 1 BATTLING ITS WAY
INTO YOUR FAVORITE BOOK &
COMIC STORES JUNE 2003
OT
OLDER TEEN
AGE 16+
Kamijyo. All rights reserved. First published in Japan in 1999 by Kodansha LTD., Tokyo.
English translation rights in the United States of America and Canada arranged by Kodansha LTD.
English text © 2003 Mixx Entertainment, Inc. TOKYOPOP is a registered trademark
of Mixx Entertainment, Inc. All rights reserved.
www.TOKYOPOP.com

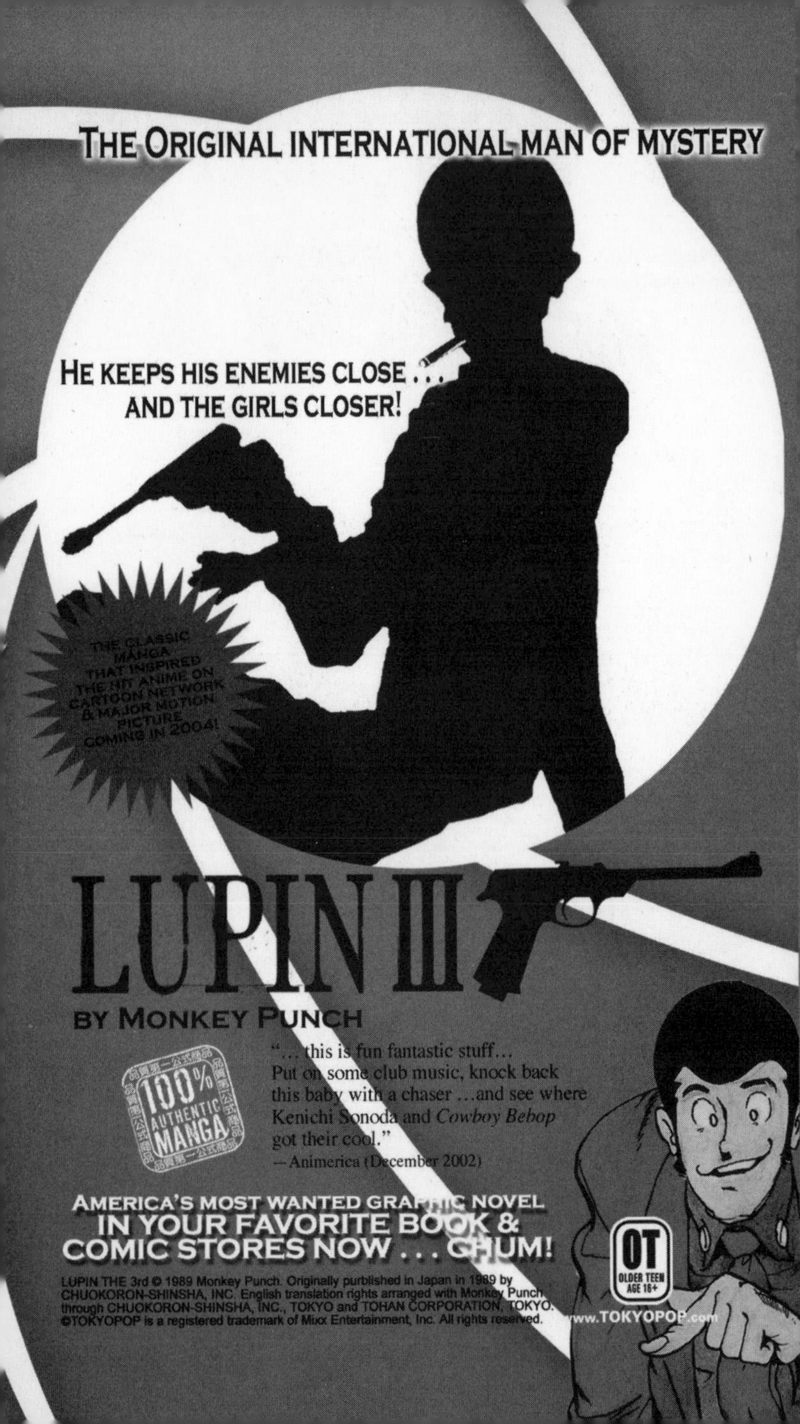

THE ORIGINAL INTERNATIONAL MAN OF MYSTERY
HE KEEPS HIS ENEMIES CLOSE . . .
AND THE GIRLS CLOSER!
THE CLASSIC MANGA THAT INSPIRED THE HIT ANIME ON CARTOON NETWORK & MAJOR MOTION PICTURE COMING IN 2004!
LUPIN III
BY MONKEY PUNCH
100% AUTHENTIC MANGA
"... this is fun fantastic stuff... Put on some club music, knock back this baby with a chaser ...and see where Kenichi Sonoda and *Cowboy Bebop* got their cool."
—Animerica (December 2002)
AMERICA'S MOST WANTED GRAPHIC NOVEL
IN YOUR FAVORITE BOOK & COMIC STORES NOW . . . CHUM!
LUPIN THE 3rd © 1989 Monkey Punch. Originally purblished in Japan in 1989 by CHUOKORON-SHINSHA, INC. English translation rights arranged with Monkey Punch through CHUOKORON-SHINSHA, INC., TOKYO and TOHAN CORPORATION, TOKYO. ©TOKYOPOP is a registered trademark of Mixx Entertainment, Inc. All rights reserved.
OT
OLDER TEEN AGE 16+
www.TOKYOPOP.com

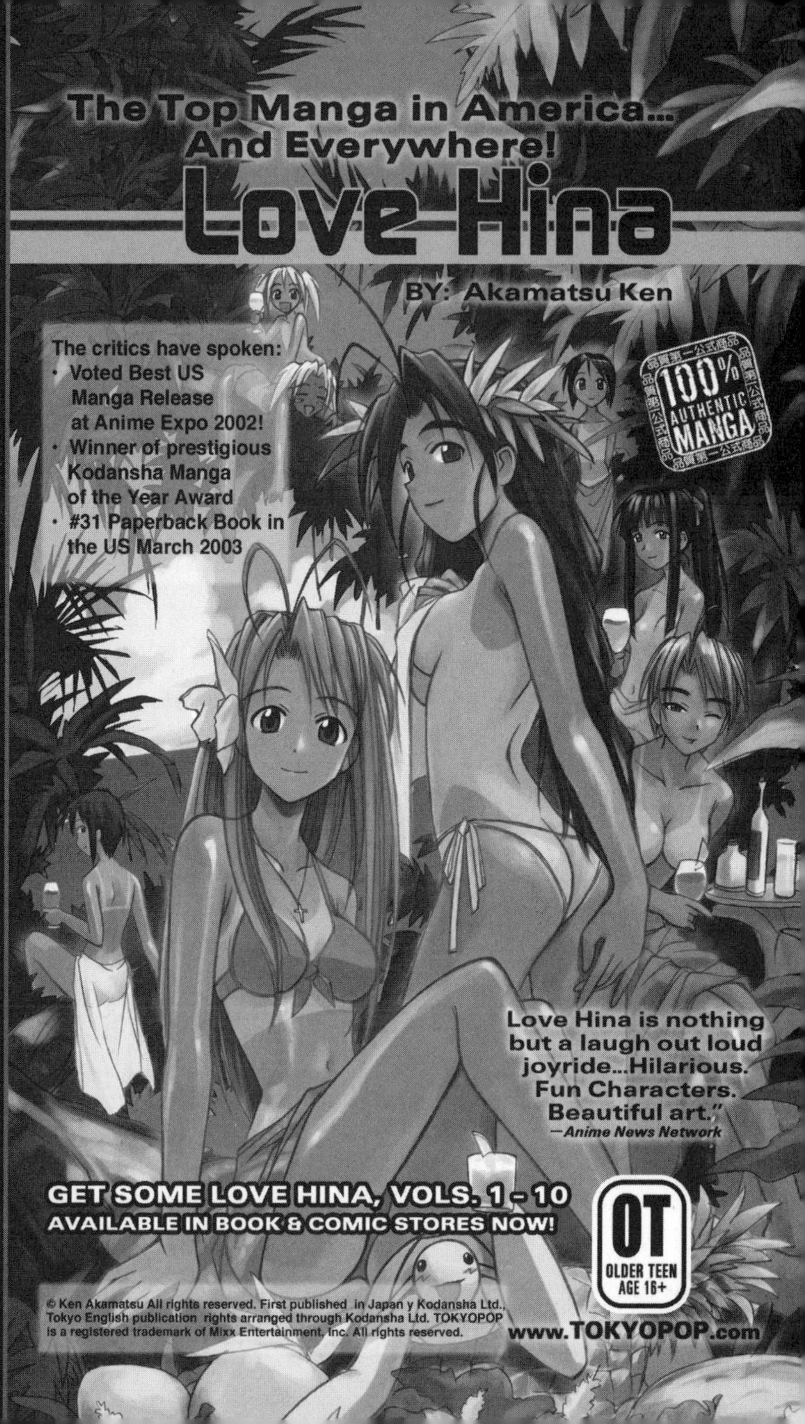
The Top Manga in America...
And Everywhere!
Love Hina
BY: Akamatsu Ken
The critics have spoken:
• Voted Best US Manga Release at Anime Expo 2002!
• Winner of prestigious Kodansha Manga of the Year Award
• #31 Paperback Book in the US March 2003
100% AUTHENTIC MANGA
Love Hina is nothing but a laugh out loud joyride...Hilarious. Fun Characters. Beautiful art."
—Anime News Network
GET SOME LOVE HINA, VOLS. 1 - 10
AVAILABLE IN BOOK & COMIC STORES NOW!
OT
OLDER TEEN
AGE 16+
© Ken Akamatsu All rights reserved. First published in Japan y Kodansha Ltd., Tokyo English publication rights arranged through Kodansha Ltd. TOKYOPOP is a registered trademark of Mixx Entertainment, Inc. All rights reserved.
www.TOKYOPOP.com

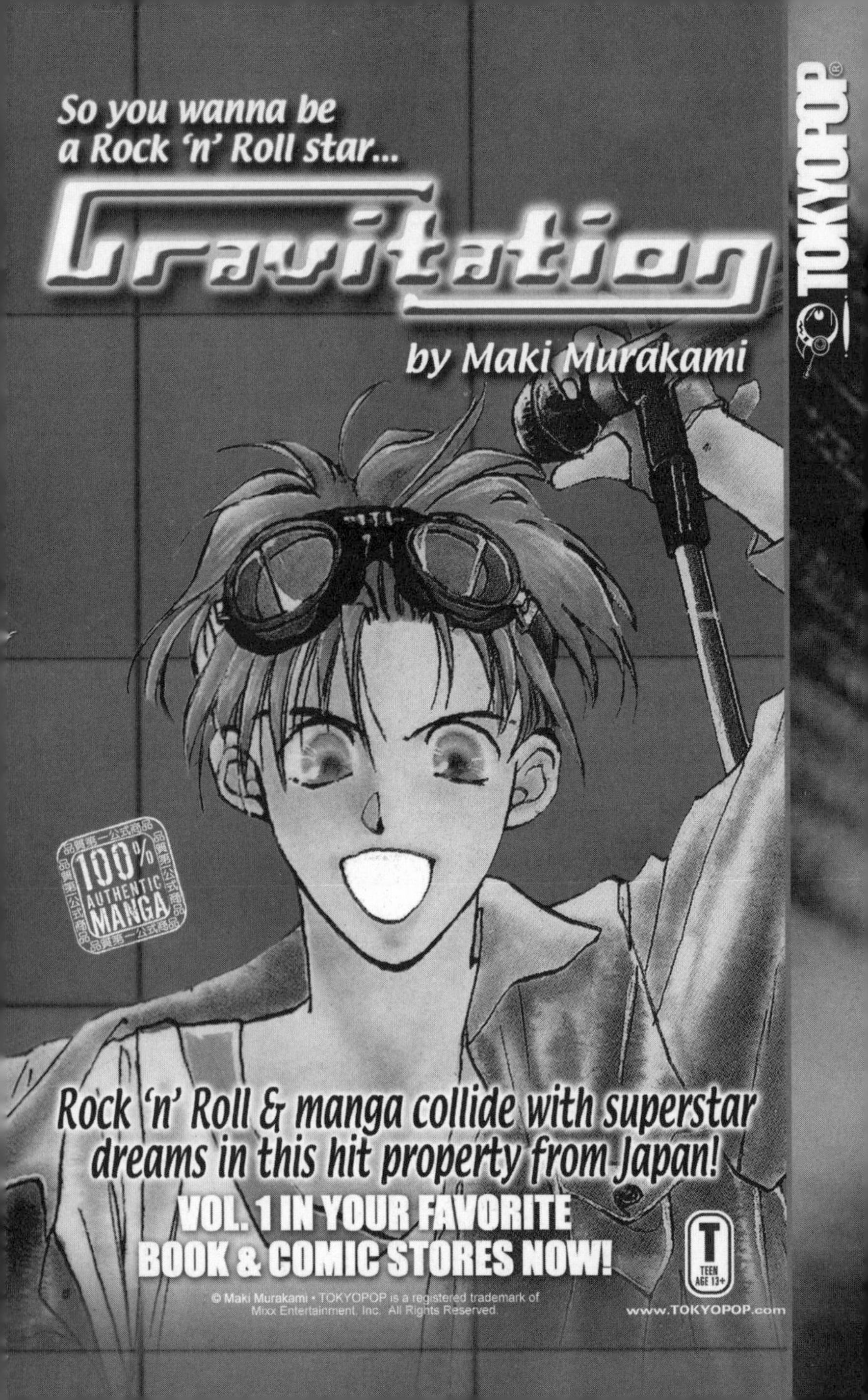
So you wanna be
a Rock 'n' Roll star...
Gravitation
by Maki Murakami
TOKYOPOP
100% AUTHENTIC MANGA
Rock 'n' Roll & manga collide with superstar
dreams in this hit property from Japan!
VOL. 1 IN YOUR FAVORITE
BOOK & COMIC STORES NOW!
T
TEEN AGE 13+
© Maki Murakami • TOKYOPOP is a registered trademark of
Mixx Entertainment, Inc. All Rights Reserved.
www.TOKYOPOP.com

STOP!

This is the back of the book.
You wouldn't want to spoil a great ending!

This book is printed "manga-style," in the authentic Japanese right-to-left format. Since none of the artwork has been flipped or altered, readers get to experience the story just as the creator intended. You've been asking for it, so TOKYOPOP® delivered: authentic, hot-off-the-press, and far more fun!

DIRECTIONS

If this is your first time reading manga-style, here's a quick guide to help you understand how it works.

It's easy... just start in the top right panel and follow the numbers. Have fun, and look for more 100% authentic manga from TOKYOPOP®!